MAHARISHI PATANJALI

195 Yoga Sutras

from ASTÃNGA YOGA

AF560193

S.V. SUBRAMANYAM

PUSTAK MAHAL®

Publishers
Pustak Mahal®

Administrative office and Sales Centre
J-3/16, Daryaganj, New Delhi-110002
☎ 011-23276539, 23272783, 23272784, 23260518
E-mail: info@pustakmahal.com • *Website:* www.pustakmahal.com

Branches
Bengaluru: ☎ 080-22234025, 40912845
E-mail: pustakmahalblr@gmail.com
Mumbai: ☎ 022-22010941, 22053387
E-mail: unicornbooksmumbai@gmail.com

© Author

ISBN 978-81-223-1153-2

Edition : 2024

The Copyright of this book, as well as all matter contained herein (including illustrations) rests with the Publishers. No person shall copy the name of the book, its title design, matter and illustrations in any form and in any language, totally or partially or in any distorted form. Anybody doing so shall face legal action and will be responsible for damages.

Printed at : Sharma Printers, Delhi

Invocation to Sage Patanjali

To the noblest of sages,
Maharishi Patanjali,
Who gave Yoga,
The tool for serenity and unity,
And grammar for clarity and purity.
Let humanity prostrate, until eternity.

Preface

Bertrand Russell in his *Impact of Science on Society* voiced his concern decades back when he said: "*Broadly speaking we are in the midst of a race between human skill as to means and human folly as to ends..... It follows that, unless men increase in wisdom as much as in knowledge, increase of knowledge will be increase of sorrow.*" Today we are witnessing what was foretold by Bertrand Russell: There is increased knowledge, but alas there is also increased sorrow. The violence and hatred that is widespread indicates the increased ignorance, aversion and attachment and its consequences that Sage Patanjali so eloquently explained, when he extolled the seeker to free himself from the bondage. The clinical precision with which the great sage dissects this disease of ignorance is indeed astounding.

If there is one text that is regularly being read, commented upon and whose instructions are sought to be practised and which is yet not a religious text, it is *Patanjali Yoga Sutras*. If there is yet one text that is truly internationally being read in the last few decades and its essence is found to be most appropriate to be understood and adhered to, it is *Patanjali Yoga Sutras*. If there is one text that is found in every library of universities world over and referred to by students of Theology, Philosophy and Psychology it is *Patanjali Yoga Sutras*.

The subject of mind and matter interests the physicist, theologist, psychologist, spiritualist and the philosopher world over, especially today, when modern science is moving ever so closer to a stage of concurring with spiritualists and finding less area of conflicts.

There is a big list of reference materials and commentaries available on the *Yoga Sutras*. One more book on *Patanjali Yoga*? I wasn't sure I should attempt, until I realized that a whole new FAQ generation of youngsters are up there used to richly illustrated manuals and learning through question answer and user friendly format. This generation also has the added advantage of computers at their disposal as also tools that enable pictorial presentation. This book fully utilizes available technology to ensure easy readability.

I realize too that it is a difficult task to raise right questions and provide right answers on a subject like *Yoga Sutras*. Even then I decided to attempt for I am aware that my book will be used as a primer by the seeker. He will then graduate to reading commentaries by learned and noble souls of which there is no dearth, until he reaches a stage when he will neither have questions to ask nor answers to seek.

I have carefully selected quotations from the sayings of the enlightened ones as a testimony for the seeker to refer to. An aphorism is short and terse and leaves it to the reader to infer more. I have attempted a similar English aphorism to enable English speaking readers to benefit by.

There is an old saying in Sanskrit, "Wisdom begins where word ends". Any attempt therefore to describe truth in words is bound to fail. To go a step further and attempt at illustrating spiritual messages in tables, charts and diagrams is nothing short of blasphemy! I have dared to do so in earnestness to be of help to the spiritual seekers seeking clarity in the rather terse verses. My attempt is to lead the seekers to the doorsteps of enlightened souls who are ever ready to guide sincere seekers.

It is my endeavour to

Make Yogic wisdom available to a wider audience.

Enhance understanding of the Eternal Truth.

Improve readability of the admittedly terse verses.

Enable a quicker understanding of seemingly complicated logic.

I do hope that this book will be well received by the spiritual seekers.

Auṁ

Asato mā sad gamaya!
Tamaso mā jyotirgamaya!
Mrityormā amritamgamaya!
Aum shantih! Shantih! Shantih!

O! Almighty,
Lead us
From falsehood to truth,
From darkness to light,
From mortality to immortality.
O Almighty! May there be
Peace, Peace and Peace.

– S. V. Subramanyam

Yoga: The Genesis

To be always happy
And to make merry
Has been the aim of everyone
From days bygone.

Man made many an attempt
To keep himself content
With kith and kin around
To sing joy aloud.

To his utter dismay
He found everyway
He chose to proceed
In an attempt to succeed.
Dejection and despair followed
Never was he allowed
To keep himself at ease
With a single moment of peace.

He soon discovered
The devil is within uncovered
The reason why he is tense
Is his wily sense,
Which forever wandered
Making him surrender
To times of momentary pleasure
Resulting in infinite displeasure;

To understand the reality
Of the tiresome duality
To cut cycle of pleasure-pain
Fought he in vain.

At last appealed he to his creator
To deliver him forever
From this chain of misery and mirth
And of birth and death.
Such appeals to Almighty

From the heart of devotee
Moved Him to action
To provide seeker a prescription,
A sure cure of deliverance
From miserable state of existence;
Yoga was His prescription
An aid to avoid mental modification.

Problem did not end there,
There was confusion everywhere
As to what He said
And how it was expressed.

Now devotees met in prayer again
And invoked Him to explain again.

God realized the problem well
He decided how someone should tell
In a language simple and plain
Lest there be confusion again.

To reveal truth and uncover its mask
Is indeed a tough task
In this task commissioned He
The great exponent PATANJALI.

PATANJALI understood His command
And its implied demand
Revealed He, His words of wisdom
In the form of Aphorism.

Aphorisms are thus the result.
There is no religion or cult
They are addressed to everyone
Who want to know the only One.

Introduction

1. **What is Yoga?**

   The word Yoga is derived from the Sanskrit root "*yuj*" meaning to bind, join, attach and yoke, to direct and concentrate one's attention on, to use and apply. It also means union or communion. It is the true union of our will with the will of God.

2. **Is Yoga a means or an end?**

   It is both. Yoga is the process of taking us back home to our un-obscured true nature. Hence it is a means. Yoga is a state of Union. Hence it is the end.

3. **Is Yoga a Science?**

   Yoga is a science. It is not a vague, dreamy drifting or imagining topic. It is an applied science, a systematized collection of laws applied to bring about a definite end. It takes up the laws of psychology, applicable to the unfolding of the whole consciousness of man on every plane, in every world, and applies those rationally in a particular case. This rational application of the laws of unfolding consciousness acts exactly on the same principles that you see applied around you every day in other departments of science.

4. **Is Yoga a religion? Is Yoga Hinduism?**

   No. Yoga has nothing to do with religion. It is a systematic method of understanding one's true self. Yoga accepts that God as a special person can be used by the seeker in seeking liberation. Yoga is not Hinduism, as it is commonly known as.

5. **Is Yoga a philosophy?**

   No, it is not, in the sense of being a hypothesis. Instead it embodies mostly a practical do it yourself type of instructions.

6. **Is Yoga metaphysical?**

   No. It does not bother about distant questions about past lives, heaven and hell or God or Satan. Yoga is concerned with the present. With the 'Now', with the current problem caused by ignorance, called mind. It gives practical ways to avoid mental modifications so that perception becomes clear, so that one obtains freedom from bonding duality.

7. **What is Patanjali Yoga about?**

   Patanjali's Yoga is essentially related to the mind and its modifications. It deals with the training of the mind to achieve oneness with the Self. Incidental to this objective are the acquisition of *siddhis* or powers

8. **What is the aim of Patanjali Yoga?**

   The aim of Patanjali Yoga is to set man free from the cage of matter, thus removing his ignorance. Mind is the highest form of matter and man freed from this dragnet of *Chitta* or

Ahankāra (mind or ego) becomes a pure being. The mind or *Chitta* is said to operate at two levels; intellectual and emotional. The aim is liberation.

9. Is Patanjali Yoga and Hatha Yoga same?

Some of the eight aspects (*Ashtānga*) like *Āsana* and *Prānāyāma* that Patanjali prescribes as part of the steps towards spiritual progress, constitute a very important part of Patanjali Yoga Sutras. These parts are so important that a whole branch of specialized knowledge has sprung up out of these two important aspects. That is what is now referred to as Hatha Yoga.

10. What do we know about Patanjali?

He lived a few millenniums before Gautam Buddha, and was a great philosopher. His best known work is **Yoga Sutras** or Aphorisms on Yoga. The path outlined is called *Rāja Yoga* or the sovereign path. It is so called because of the regal, noble method by which the self is united with the over self.

11. Is Patanjali the originator of Yoga?

Patanjali was not the author or originator of Yoga. He has only compiled and reformulated what was already orally given down the generations for centuries. He was the first to reduce the teachings to writing for the use of students and rightly so he is regarded as the founder of *Rāja Yoga school.*

12. Is Yoga sutras a sermon?

No. It is no preaching either. It is just a set of principles and dictums which when practised and followed will lead the aspirant to the state of Union.

13. What is "Sutra'?

Sutra means thread. *Sutra* in this context could be interpreted as a terse link or thread of essential points. These "threads" are extremely terse, stating concisely, and often concisely and precisely, essential points or techniques.

Originally these teachings were oral and were explained and interpreted by commentaries from a teacher guiding the student. *Sutra* (aphorism) enshrines, in a few words, vast expanses of meaning, vast depths of fundamental significance.

The following Sanskrit verse defines a sutra:

Alpāksharama samdigdhe saravat vishvato mukham,
Asto Bhamanavadhyam cha sutram sutra vido viduhu.

A sutra should be:

i. Concise, consisting of minimum number of letters.
ii. Clear, without doubt with regard to the meaning.
iii. Convey the essence of an Upanishadic Statement.
iv. Multi-faceted. Reflect all aspects of the subject.

v. Without glorifications

vi. Faultless (There should be no defects in the words and meanings).

14. In which language were the Sutras written?

The *Yoga Sutras* of Patanjali were originally written in Sanskrit which is an Indo-European language. Sankrit is the oldest of the Indo-European languages still in active use.

15. Which are the early commentaries written on Patanjali Yoga?

i. *Rājamārtandavritti* of Bhojadeva

ii. *Yogasutrapradipikā* of Bhavaganesha

iii. *Yogasutravritti* of Nagojibhatta

iv. *Yogasiddhāntacharika* of Narayanathirtha

v. *Yogasudhākara* of Sadāsivabrahmendra

In recent times the commentaries of Swāmi Vivekānanda and Swāmi Lāhari Mahāsaya are from amongst the best.

16. A final question, how should one proceed with the study?

Remember Lord Buddha's "Four Reliances":

i. Rely on the message of the teacher, not on his personality,

ii. Rely on the meaning, not just on the words,

iii. Rely on the real meaning, not on the provisional one,

iv. Rely on your wisdom mind, not on your ordinary judgemental mind.

Patanjali Yoga Sutra

	Chapter I	Chapter II	Chapter III	Chapter IV
Title	*Samādhi Pādah*	*Sādhanā Pādah*	*Vibhuti Pādah*	*Kaivalya Pādah*
	Attainment of Unity	The Means	Powers En-route	Liberation
No of aphorisms	51	55	55	34
Page Ref	1- 107	109-203	205-297	299-364

CONTENTS

Chapter 1

Chapter 2

Chapter 3

Chapter 4

16.	The object's existence is independent of mind	न चैकचित्ततन्त्रं वस्तु तदप्रमाणकं तदा किं स्यात्	Object, on the mind does not subsist on mind's absence it ceases not to exist. 331
17.	The presence of object depends upon mind's expectations	तदुपरागापेक्षत्वाचित्तस्य वस्तु ज्ञाताज्ञातम्	On mind's coloured expectation; depends, objects perception or absence of perception. 332
18.	The unchanging Self is the witness	सदा ज्ञाताश्चित्तवृत्तयस्तत्प्रभोः पुरुषस्यापरिणामित्वात्	The unchanging self always knows mind's moods and where it goes. 334
19.	Mind is not the Self, but a reflection	न तत्स्वाभासं दृश्यत्वात्	Mind, the object of perception is not the light, but a reflection. 336
20.	Mind cannot play a dual role	एकसमये चोभयानवधारणम्	Mind functions not in two different role; to see and to fabricate is an impossible goal. 337
21.	There cannot be two minds	चित्तान्तरदृश्ये बुद्धिबुद्धेरतिप्रसङ्गः स्मृतिसंकरश्च	If first mind were to on a second prevail disorder ensures and memories fail. 338
22.	Mind detached from object reflects Self	चितेरप्रतिसंक्रमायास्तदाकारापत्तौ स्वबुद्धिसंवेदनम्	Mind, delinked from object it sees reflects perceiver as it is. 339
23.	Mind presents objects to perceiver	द्रष्टृदृश्योपरक्तं चित्तं सर्वार्थम्	Mind presents objects to perceiver reflects the perceiver to itself. 341
24.	Mind is not independent of Self	तदसंख्येयवासनाभिश्चित्रमपि परार्थं संहत्यकारित्वात्	Mind, though tainted in many ways serves the cause of the Perceiver always. 342
25.	The desire to know reality ceases with clarity	विशेषदर्शिन आत्मभावभावनाविनिवृत्तिः	The desire to know the reality ceases in one with clarity. 343
26.	The discriminating aspire for realisation	तदा विवेकनिम्नं कैवल्यप्राग्भारं चित्तम्	The discriminating mind gravitates there where freedom is seen in full glare. 344
27.	Regress to the path of realisation	तच्छिद्रषु प्रत्ययान्तराणि संस्कारेभ्यः	Thoughts pour in, where there is regress. Tendencies resurface blocking progress. 346
28.	Means of removal of latent impressions	हानमेषां क्लेशवदुक्तम्	Means of removal of latent impressions are like that of afflictions. 347
29.	Effect of attainment of awareness	प्रसंख्यानेऽप्यकुसीदस्य सर्वथा विवेकख्यातेर्धर्ममेघः समाधिः	On the one who discriminates and desires not even the highest

Chapter 1

Samādhi Pādah

Attainment of Unity

अथ योगानुशासनम् ॥१॥

Atha Yoga_Anushāsanam

Now on Union
Explanation.

Atha : now, hereafter
Yoga : union, integration
Anushāsanam : instruction, dictums, laws, rules

Q. *Now, what are we going to study?*
A. What follows, is an instruction on Yoga union.

In the opening *Sutra* Patanjali refers to '*atha*', meaning 'now'. 'Now' here means when one is ready for further elaborations on Yoga. Who is ready to receive instruction? What are the prerequisites? Who is mentally fit or rather which state of mind can receive instructions that follow? In order to understand the prerequisites we should understand the different states of mind. The great commentator Vyāsa enumerates five states of mind:

Restless state	The butterfly state of mind, which is ever restless and ever wondering, is attached to outside objects. Hence, extremely unsteady.
Forgetful state	Possessed by exessive quality of inertia, the mind is morbid, dull and forgetful.
Unsteady state	Occasionally steady but predominantly unsteady, the unsteady state is either acquired or brought about by the obstacles of disease, disinclination etc.
Focused state	The mind is wholly engrossed in one idea, one pointed and focused. It is a frame of mind devoid of obstacles to practice. Practice, disinclined towards outside objects and prepared for a state of union.
Restrained state	Perfectly controlled and restrained state of mind.

Union is then,
when the seer and the seen are one.

Persons with wandering and forgetful states of mind would find it hard initially to concentrate on practice. They will be the ones who find some excuse to convince themselves that practice is not necessary for them! The unsteady ones will be the ones who will jump from one week-end seminar to another for a few weeks followed by total absence of practice for the next few months. They will again return to practice after a period of time. They get steady gradually as the practice of yoga proceeds. Ādi Shankara enlists requirement of a sincere seeker:

1. Discrimination between the eternal and the transitory.
2. Renunciation of enjoyment of fruit of action, here and hereafter.
3. Six fold wealth, comprising of
    a. *sāma*: Undisturbed concentration on the object of perception.
    b. *dāma*: Control of sense organs.
    c. *uparati*: Condition of state of withdrawal from the object world.
    d. *titikshā*: Endurance of pleasure and pain, without dejection or elation.
    e. *shradhā*: Faith in the scriptures and the teachers.
    f. *samādhāna*: Constant focusing of the mind on the self.
4. Yearning for liberation.

A serious student of yoga, seeking union of the self with the super self should have:

1. Right attitude of mind, open, without prejudice and free of preconceived notions.
2. A spirit of enquiry, and be enthusiastic and possessing kindly disposition.
3. A desire for emancipation from the wheel of birth and death.
4. Lessened liking for the external world of object towards which the senses drag the mind.
5. Appreciation of the fact that the external is transitory and as a consequence reduction or renunciation of the desire to enjoy the fruit of action here or hereafter.
6. Capability for prolonged and undisturbed concentration on a chosen object.
7. Attitude of mind to endure all pain and sorrow without thought of retaliation, without dejection and without lamentation.

"Arise, awake; having reached the great (teacher), learn (realise).
Like the sharp edge of a razor is that path difficult to cross
And hard to read- thus the wise say."

Katha Upanishad

In the seeker, the above enumerated requisites, may be imbibed in a low or moderate degree. As yoga practice is adhered to, the requisite qualities would come to accrue in slow degrees and hence there is no need for the seeker to despair.

The qualifications of a teacher

Ādi Shankara summarizes the qualities needed of a teacher:

(as outlined in the Mundaka and Brihadāranyaka Upanishads)

Shrotriya	• Teacher must be well versed in the scriptures.
Brahmanishtam	• Teacher must be well established in the Brahman (Super Being).
Akāmahata	• Teacher must be unsmitten by desire. • Teacher must be unmotivated by any selfish purpose.
Avrijina	• Teacher shall be stainless. • Teacher shall be simple and guileless.

The student should not be an overflowing cup

A university professor went to visit a famous Zen master. While the master quietly served tea, the professor talked about Zen. The master poured the visitor's cup to the brim, and then kept on pouring. The professor watched the overflowing cup until he could no longer restrain himself. "It is overflowing and full. No more will go in. It can hold no more," the professor blurted.

"You are like this cup," the master replied. "How can I show you Zen unless you first empty your cup?"

In point of virulence, sensuous objects are more fatal than the poison of the black snake; poison kills one who imbibes it, but sensuous objects can kill ((spiritually) even by their outward appearance, by the mere sight of them.

Ādi Shankara, Upadesha Sahashri

Save yourself by saying 'I don't know'

There were four students of philosophy who were quarrelling amongst themselves as to how to determine as to what is right and what is wrong. A sage passed by and the four explained the reason for their quarrel. The sage asked them all to get into a *Pushpak Vimāna*, a celestial helicopter that is fuelled by mind force and can stay in the mid space and yet not fall. The sage however put a condition. He told them, "Come along with me in this helicopter to the forest. You can see an incident in the forest sitting atop this helicopter itself without getting down. Each one of you, in turn, has to give your opinion. If your opinion is wrong, this helicopter will automatically drop you down." The four agreed and the helicopter moved towards the forest.

At a particular spot in space the sage asked the helicopter to stop. He then showed his four students a scene in the forest below. The four students observed that just then a lioness had given birth to two cubs and the lioness was looking for a prey to feed itself and the two cubs.

Just then from a close by bush was coming out a doe. This doe had also just a few minutes back given birth to two small ones. The doe was hungry too and looking around for food. The hungry lioness pounced on the doe and feasted, leaving the new born ones orphaned.

The four and the sage looked at this scene. The sage asked the first, "Was the lioness right in killing the doe?" The first responded, "Certainly. It is the nature of lioness to kill and feed itself and its cubs." Immediately after the reply, the helicopter pushed him down. The others were afraid now. The sage turned to the second for a reply. The second knew the fate of the first and said, "No the lioness should not have killed the doe." He was also thrown down by the helicopter. The third was puzzled. It was his turn. He said, "Yes and No. The lioness could have, but yet the doe was also hungry….." He tried to avoid a direct reply. He knew the fate of the other two. He was also dropped down. Finally came the turn of the last.

He replied, "I don't know."

The helicopter moved on along with him and the sage.

If you don't know what you don't know,
That is a great beginning.
Socrates

योगः चित्तवृत्ति निरोधः ॥२॥

Yogah Chittavritti_Nirodhah.

Union is then
When mental modifications end.

Yoga : union *Chitta* : mind stuff *Vritti* : modifications, fluctuations
Nirodha : cease, stop, avoid, eliminate, suppress, hinder, annihilate

Q. *What is Yoga?*
A. Yoga is avoidance of mental modifications. The cessation of all movements of the mind stuff is called Yoga.

Chitta is the graffiti written on the walls of the mind over several countless births. It is not just written but also scribbled and filled to the brim in the brain. *Chitta* is knowledge stored in the memory.

The mental impression is so firmly impressed in the mind, it calls for centuries of scrubbing. Yoga is the scrubbing. After finally completing the cleaning act, one comes to know that the writing, scribbling, lining and filling are all imagined! And that in the first instance a clean mind is imagined to have been filled and dirtied! The births and the centuries themselves vanish since they are the acts of a magician called *avidyā*!

Vritti: When we see something, hear something or think of something, the mind becomes the thing that is seen, heard or thought of, for the moment. This becoming is called *vritti*. All knowledge we get, either internal through memory and dreams or external through experiences, is *vritti* knowledge.

Vritti can be defined as that modification which results in the knowledge of object. It is of the nature of ignorance. The moment one talks about an object, it *ipso facto* means a subject is born. This birth of a subject is in itself a *vritti*, a modification. When the *'I am'* thinks, *'I am this'* there is a modification that has taken place in the mind stuff. This can be called the very first modification. All other modifications stem out of this first modification.

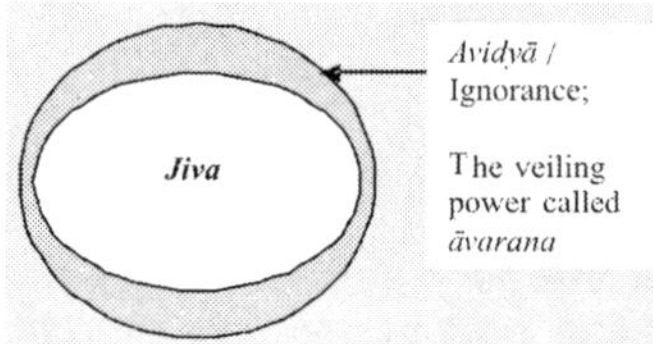

The mind receiving its capacity for gaining knowledge of objects, basks on the reflected glory and yet thinks that it is by itself capable of knowing. Thus deluded, a subject's misidentification takes place and a subject-object relationship follows suit.

The entire gamut of activities that follow this fundamental modification are all mind's modifications. While individualized Consciousness *jiva* is enveloped by *avidyā* or ignorance, the Universal Consciousness is enveloped by *māyā* or illusion. Yoga is when this mistaken perception yields place to knowledge and thus removal of *avidyā* / *māyā* is completed. *Vritti* is thus an *antahkarana parināma* or *agyāna parināma*.

Vrittis can also be classified as *Antahkarana Vritti, Māyā Vritti* and *Avidyā Vritti*

Antahkarana-vritti	• Cognition of knowledge due to mental modification. • Modification of mind or mental state in the form of an object.
Māyā-vritti	• In the case of the divine being it is *māyā-vritti* which enables Him to know everything, plan everything and successfully carry out everything as planned.
Avidyā-vritti	• *Avidyā-vritti* is modification of ignorance at the deep sleep state which gives rise to bliss. Without this modification, bliss cannot be experienced.

These two important components mind stuff and modification need further understanding.

Mind stuff: From the Yogavāshishta we read, "Listen Rama, there is nothing to speak of as mind. Just as ether exists without form, so also the mind exists as the blank insentience. It remains only in name. It has no form. It is not outside, nor is it in the heart. Yet, like ether, the mind though formless, feels all. Wherever thought arises as this and that, mind arises. When thought arises, mind is inferred. In the absence of thought, there is no mind. Mind, though by itself is insentient, appears to be sentient, through the association with consciousness, just as a piece of red hot iron appears to be fire."

Not by drinking the elixir of life and not by the embrace of goddess of wealth, does the mind attain happiness as it does by quietude within?

Yogavāshishta

According to the Upanishads, the entity known as the mind is derived from the subtle essence of the food consumed; which flourishes as love, hatred, lust, anger and so on. Mind is in reality, only consciousness, because it is pure and transparent by nature; in that pure state however, it cannot be called mind. The wrong identification of one with the other is the work of the contaminated mind. That is to say, the pure uncontaminated mind, being absolute consciousness, on becoming oblivious of its primary nature, is overpowered by the quality of darkness and manifests as the physical world and similarly overpowered by the quality of activity, it identifies itself with the body.

Modification: Thoughts are the modifications. Absence of thought is absence of modifications. Thought is only an imagination. Thoughts pertain to things already experienced or not experienced. To think of things not experienced is also a thought. Yoga is the avoidance of all forms of thoughts, experienced or not experienced. Yoga is the cessation of all thoughts and to be in Yoga means to be embedded in a thought-free-state of bliss.

Swāmi Shivānanda says: "Mind is not a gross thing, visible and tangible. Its existence is nowhere seen. Its magnitude cannot be measured. It does not require a space in which to exist. Mind and matter are two aspects as subject and object of one and the same all-full Brahman, who is neither and yet includes both. Mind precedes matter."

"This is Vedāntic theory. But science says matter precedes mind. Mind can be said to be immaterial only in the sense that it has not the characteristics of matter. It is not, however, immaterial in the sense that Brahman (Pure Spirit) as such is. Mind is the subtle form of matter and hence the prompter of the body." *Chitta* is one of the four aspects of mind:

- When the mind is in a state of volition, vacillation or doubt it is called *mānas*, emotion.
- When the mind is involved in the analysis of a situation with the idea of making a determination, discrimination or judgement it is called *buddhi*, intellect.

Q: *How do movement and non movement in the mind, both reach oneness?*

A: Creation (or the world) is only of the nature of the movement of Pure Consciousness. It vanishes on the arrival of right perception or right knowledge. That right perception is born spontaneously when the mind becomes stainless.

Yogavāshishta

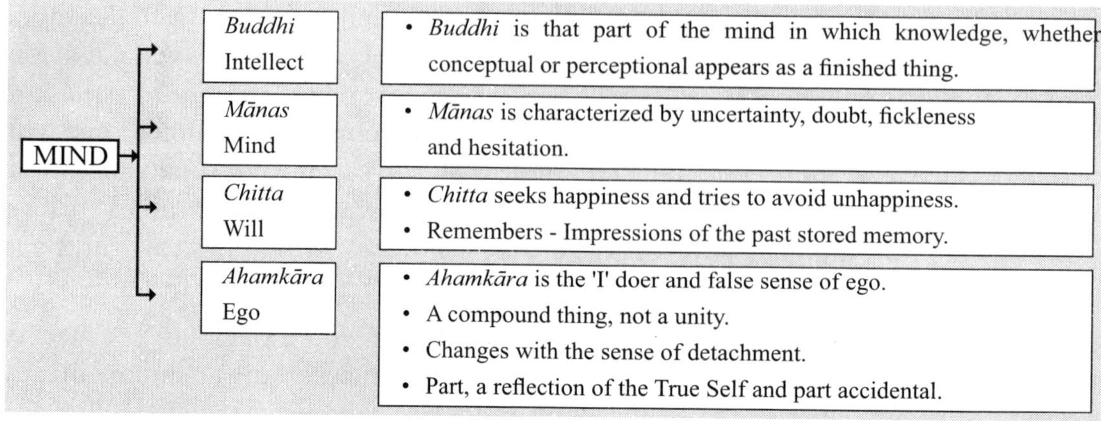

- When the mind considers itself to be the author of action or the enjoyer of pleasure and pain it is called ego, *ahamkāra*.
- The part of the mind that recalls memories and stores subconscious impressions is called *chitta*.

The goddess *Saraswati*: Saraswati literally means 'one who gives the essence *(sāra)* of our own self *(swa)*.' The four hands of *Saraswati* represent the four aspects of the inner personality, namely; *mānas* (mind), *buddhi* (intellect), *ahamkār* (ego) and *chitta* (conditioned consciousness). *Saraswati* is the consort of Brahmā, the creator.

Brahmā: *Brah* means infinite. *Mā* is short form for *man* or *mānas*. *Brahmā* stands literally for endless, infinite mind. The four heads of Brahmā, stand for the four states of consciousness; namely, waking, dreaming, sleeping and *Samādhi*.
Brahmā is not to be mistaken for *Brahman*. *Brahman*, the Absolute Power, has no definition and cannot be deliberated upon.

The mind can be brought under control only by relentless effort like that which is required to empty the ocean drop by drop with the help of the front tip of a *Kusa* grass blade.

Gaudapāda Kārika

Yoga aims at turning the *Vrittis* back to its source.

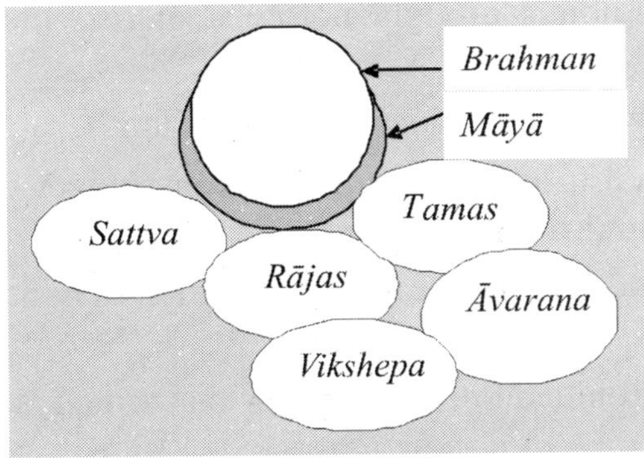

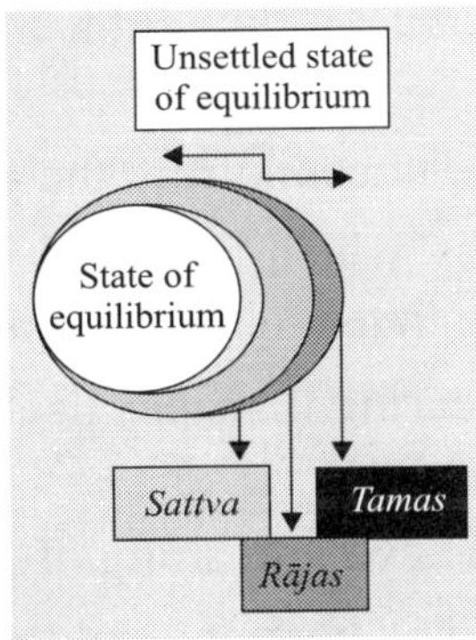

The mind's modifications can also be classified as:

1. *Tāmasic vritti* or turbid modes: Confusion, fear, delusion, dullness etc. are the resulting tendencies while this mode is dominant.
2. *Rājasic vritti* or distracted modes: While this modification is uppermost, it results in attachment, grief, passion, anger, thirst for objects etc.
3. *Sāttvic vritti* or transparent modes: While this modification is predominant there is a feeling of dispassion for objects and there is a generation of series of virtues like forbearance, magnanimity, compassion, kindness etc.

Whatever happiness one experiences is not because of sense gratification, but because of the relief resulting with the cessation of need for sense gratification. Real happiness, that will be everlasting, can be experienced only on the cessation of all modifications. It is only when the mind is turned back of the *vrittis* to their source. There is an unobstructed light of the Brahman constantly shining forth. Brahman, Pure Consciousness, not being an object, cannot be seen or perceived through senses but can be 'known' only when the senses cease their outward orientation.

Ādi Shankara advises that one should, with the help of *rājasic* and *sāttvic* qualities, get rid of the dullness, the *tāmasic* nature. Thereafter by cultivating *sāttvic* temperament or clarity one should get rid of the *rājasic* or activity orientation. The *sāttvic* nature will evaporate everything unwanted, and thus all modifications will cease.

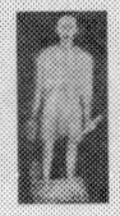

The whole world seems to be but one form of mental modification of a supreme consciousness.

Gaudapāda

How is mind modified?

- Mind is modified by any subject or object brought before it or to which it is directed.
- The modification occurs from the power of reproducing thoughts too.
- The channels by which the mind is led to go out to an object or subject, are the organs of sight, touch, taste, hearing, and so on.
- By means of hearing it shapes itself into the form of the idea which may be given in speech.
- By means of the eye in reading, it is moulded into the form of that which is read.
- Sensations such as heat and cold modify it directly and indirectly by association and by recollection.

What if the mental modifications are avoided?

The seer realizes his true self.

The seer abides in himself.

The seer exists by itself as itself.

Does such a cessation of mental modification occur in one go?

No, except in one in a million. It is a gradual process. As all our sense organs are projecting outwards, our vision is outward-oriented. Men have lagged behind in the practice of developing the inward-look. Only those who can swim counter to the outward-flowing current of sense-organs can succeed in accomplishing the inward vision. Those who have been dwelling in this tree of life should thoroughly understand it and make efforts to know the root which sustains the whole tree in order to achieve real vision.

What is the relationship between modifications and misery?

From the standpoint of the mind, the body, the sense organs and the objects of the world are all "objects". Not only does the mind project all these, but having projected them, it further creates an attachment in man for these "objects". By this attachment he gets bound and becomes limited and sorrowful. From the standpoint of the Being even the mind is an object.

"Apart from the mind there is no ignorance. The mind itself is the ignorance which is the cause for the bondage of rebirth. When the mind is destroyed, everything else is destroyed. When the mind manifests, everything else manifests."

Ādi Shankara

The characteristics that qualify the mind stuff:

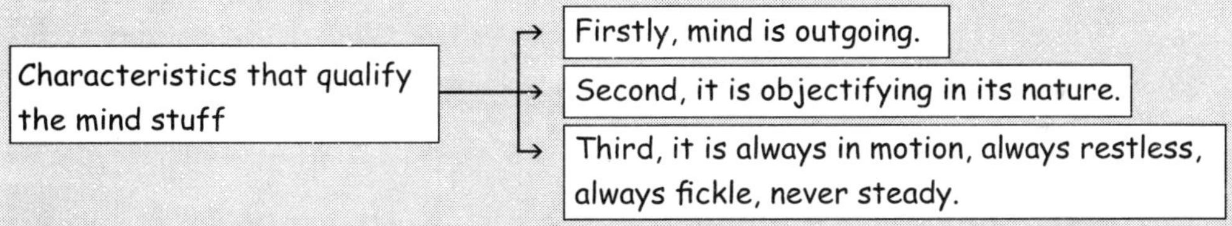

What is mind?

1. Mind is not a gross thing, visible and tangible.
2. Mind's magnitude cannot be measured.
3. Mind does not require a space in which to exist.
4. Mind's existence is nowhere seen.
5. Mind precedes matter.
6. Mind is all electricity.
7. Mind is formed out of the subtlest portion of food.
8. Mind is made up of subtle matter of various grades of density with different states of vibration.
9. Mind is atomic, all pervading.
10. Mind is a bundle of habits, desires and ideas.
11. Mind is ever changing , wavering and unsteady.
12. Mind is intelligent when compared to senses and non-intelligent compared to intellect.
13. Mind is the cause for liberation as well as bondage.
14. Mind is the manifestation of the non-apprehension of reality caused by inertia.
15. Mind is the equipment that orders all types of action that should manifest.

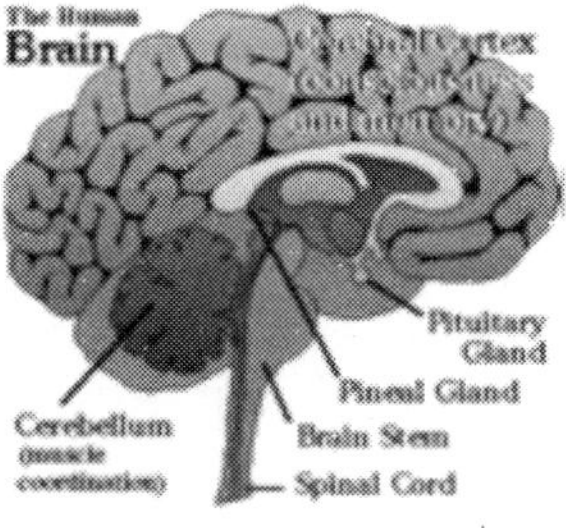

Is brain and mind the same?

The brain is a heap of cells made up of protein and fat molecules. It is formed of nerve cells called neurons. There is no power in this piece of meat to observe the images, to constitute consciousness, or to create the being we call 'myself'.

Dr. Michael Solomon a cardiologist at the Emory University Medical Science in his book, 'Recollection of Death: A medical investigation'- 1982 reports of his extensive research on near death experiences. He concludes that the mind is an entity distinct from the brain and the near death crisis caused the mind and brain to split apart for a brief time. Solomon wrote: 'Could the mind which splits apart from the brain, be in essence, the soul, which continues to exist after the final bodily death, according to some religious doctrines?'

There is no such thing as peace of mind. Mind means disturbance; restless itself in mind. Yoga is not an attribute of mind, nor is it a state of mind.

Nisargadatta Mahārāj

Mind and Intellect

Mind and Intellect: The monkey and the frog

Monkey by its very nature is always restless and jumping from one object to another. It is ever changing and wavering. Imagine such a restless monkey intoxicated with alcohol and bitten by a string of bees, that is the state of mind.

A frog on the river bank can see only what moves. When the wind ruffles water, frog sees the water surface. If wind stops, the water body does not register on the frog's mind. Similarly as long as a minnow is darting around in the pond, the frog's eyes can follow it everywhere. But the moment the minnow stops, it disappears from the mind of the frog. As long as the frog is concerned, the minnow has slipped away- until it flicks its tail again. This is exactly the relationship between the mind and the intellect. As long as there is mental modification, so long will intellect keep following the mind. When mind stops, when its modifications cease, for the intellect, the mind has disappeared, until modifications start again.

When the intellect looks at the Self it does not see anything at all. Right under its nose as it exists in the Self, and yet intellect cannot perceive it until mind stops moving. When mind stops, intellect sees the being. When mind moves, intellect follows the mind.

As long as there is duality, the separateness of the subject and object, there is mental modification. So long as there is mental modification, intellect will keep following what is going on. But when modifications stop, duality ceases. When duality ceases, Self is realized.

Having no attachment in sound and other sense objects and the Self being no object of perception, I have my mind freed of distractions and rendered single pointed. Thus do I, abide in Myself.

Yogavāshishta

तदा द्रष्टुः स्वरूपेऽवस्थानम् ॥३॥

Tadā Drashtuh Svarupe_avasthānam.

The seer then abides
In true self resides.

Tadā : then *Drashtuh* : the seer *Svarupe* : in self
Avasthānam : abides, dwells, resides

Q. *What happens on cessation of mental modifications?*
A. You dwell in your true nature.
In the Samādhi state the individual self is established in the Supreme self.

What is the difference between being and not being established in self?

Individual

Svarupe avasthānam	***Vritti-rupe avasthānam***
Beyond mind Not gripped by thought waves; peaceful, serene and quiet.	Entrapped in mind Gripped by thought waves; restlessness, unease, anxiety, anger, fear, frustration.
Free from bonds of pleasure-pain chain.	Bound by dualities of attachment and aversion.
Established in the Self Being the ocean UNITY I AM.	**Engrossed in thoughts** Becoming the waves DUALITY I AM THIS.

Duality is the result of not being established in oneself. Duality is the cause of bondage and suffering. Duality is the result of ignorance. Unity results in being established in oneself. Unity is the state of liberation and realization. Apart from thoughts, there is no such thing as mind. Therefore, thought is the nature of mind. When the mind comes out of Self, the world appears. Therefore, when the world appears (to be real), the Self does not appear; and when the Self appears (shines), the world does not appear.

Taittariya Upanishad says: "He who establishes himself in his own Self becomes fearless, but he who perceives any difference from the Self is subject to fear."

Q: *What is the true Self?*
Ramana Maharishi: It is that out of which the sense of the personal 'I' arises and into which it will disappear.

वृत्तिसारूप्यमितरत्र ॥४॥

Vritti_Sārupyam_Itaratra.

Otherwise remains
Trapped in mind's domain.

Vritti : mental activity, mental modifications; *Sārupyam* : identification
Itaratra : otherwise, elsewhere, at other times

Q. *What if mental modifications are not avoided?*

A. There is identification of the self with mental modifications. Identification of one with the mind means suffering the mental modifications. The restlessness of the mind stuff becomes the restlessness of the person.

What is the effect of duality on the mind? The ignorant anticipate pleasure and pain before enjoyment, recapitulate after enjoyment and reflect over them so that they leave a strong impression on their minds. Duality means misery.

If one were to be scolded for whatever reason, there are two ways in which he can react. One, he can feel pain, curse the guy who scolded him, plan to scold him on the very next opportune moment etc. All these thoughts are pain causing. All these thoughts mean more and more identification of oneself with the external objects and internal impressions. The more the identification, the more is the reinforcement of duality and consequent pain. On the other hand if his reactions were as if he has not even heard the scolding, there is no identification of the individual with the words of abuse. No ripples are formed in him, no reaction and hence no formation of impression or muddying of the mind.

It is duality that results in mind having the veiling power and the projecting power. It is duality that causes birth and death of an individual.

Pain persists if mental modifications are not avoided. When one dwells on any subject of desire, he gets attracted to it. Attachment gives rise to desire and desire to longing. Frustration of desire leads to anger and anger to delusion and delusion to loss of discrimination. Lack of discrimination results in actions that bind and cause misery.

Neither by the senses nor by human reasoning can we hope to comprehend the nature of Brahman. This is so because the subject, the object and the means are all identical. It is Brahman by which the understanding itself functions. The Supreme Spirit is that by which the mind thinks; it is not one of the concepts that can be conceived by the mind, but it is that by which, indeed, one is able to think through his mind. It is that which enables the eye to see, the ear to hear and the breath to move.

Kenopanishad

वृत्तयः पञ्चतय्य क्लिष्टाक्लिष्टाः ॥५॥

Vrittayah Panchatayyah Klishtā_Aklishtāh.

Modifications of mind are five in kind
That result in pain and gain.

Vrittayah : mental activities, modifications *Panchatyyah* : of five kinds
Klishtā : producing suffering, painful *Aklishtāh* : not producing suffering, not painful

Q. *What are the types of mental modifications?*
A. The mental modifications are fivefold and are painful or pleasant. When associated with the phenomenal world it is painful and when disassociated with the phenomenal world it is without misery.

In the process of meditation all the vrittis, the mental modifications, remain subdued. Vrittis can be grouped into two categories: Painless and painful.

The painless modifications of the mind are *pramāna*, *viparyaya*, *vikalpa*, *nidrā* and *smriti.*

Vrittis : Mental Modifications: Aklishtāh (Painless):	1. *Pramāna* : Right perception without the interference of mind (Aphorism 1.07) 2. *Viparyaya* : Erroneous knowledge born of defects in perceptive organs or confusion in the mind caused by various factors (Aphorism 1.08) 3. *Vikalpa* : Oscillating conditions of mind as to the true nature of things known (Aphorism 1.09) 4. *Nidrā* : Negative condition of the modification where activities of mind are temporarily suspended (Aphorism 1.10) 5. *Smriti* : Memory of previous experience (Aphorism 1.11)

The painful vrittis/modifications are: *Avidyā*, *Asmitā*, *Rāga*, *Dwesha* and *Abhinivesha.* Chapter 2 discusses these modifications in greater detail.

That which is like poison in the beginning, but is like nectar in the end, is declared to be 'good' pleasure born from the serenity of one's own mind. That which is like nectar in the beginning from the connection of the sense-object with the senses, but is as poison in the end, is held to be of 'passion'.

Bhagavadgitā 18:37-38

Whatever may be the thoughts that arise; they either cause pain or do not cause pain. When one looks at a lamp-post in front of him, a non-pain causing mental modification takes place. It is a modification of the mind, because the mind has transformed itself into the form of the lamp-post which he is looking at. But, it does not upset his emotion. To the extent that he is aware that there is some object outside him, the mind has transformed itself; it has ceased to be itself for the time being, though it has not caused him any pain. The lamp-post neither attracts him nor repels.

But if he sees a few dollar currency notes lying, the modification of the mind at that time is painful. His emotion acts at the sight of currency notes, while it did not act in that manner when he looked at the lamp-post. Until he manages to pick up the currency notes, he is anxious. He is afraid someone else may pick it up or watch him pick up. Then sets a new chain of thought that may run on the course of his being arrested when changing the currency and being noticed that the currency notes are counterfeit. These later thoughts are fantasy.

For the purpose of yoga, both these modifications have to be subdued. Both the painful ones and the not painful ones are modifications to be eliminated. A yogi would be as indifferent to the currency notes as he will be towards a lamp-post. There will be no modifications in his mind on seeing either of them. When the mind's modifications cease then arises a state of super consciousness and a vision of reality. Until then one suffers from ignorance. The purpose of yoga is to be in a state of equilibrium, whereby no experience or thought produces painful or gainful reaction. Yogi's actions have no reactions.

The reference to painful and not-painful is a reference to duality. The obstacles to realization are caused by pairs of opposites. A 'painful' thought wave is not really painful in the beginning, but results in pain eventually. A 'not-painful' thought wave might appear painful in the beginning, but results in unlimited joy. What one perceives as an opportunity to make a million eventually turns out to be life threatening activity. A business man perceives an opportunity in expanding his business to make more millions but fails to recognize the hidden threat to his organization in terms of diversion of working capital from existing activities and thus killing today's breadwinners, organizational weaknesses etc.

The fruit of detachment is knowledge
The fruit of knowledge is relaxation.

Adhyātma Upanishad

प्रमाणविपर्ययविकल्पनिद्रास्मृतयः ॥६॥

Pramāna_Viparyaya_Vikalpa_Nidra_Smritayah.

They are misconceptions, proven theory,
Fancy, deep sleep and memory.

Pramāna : right knowledge, correct cognition, proven conviction
Viparyaya : wrong knowledge, misconception, illusion, contrary knowledge
Vikalpa : imagination and fantasy; *Nidrā* : sleep *Smritayah* : Memory

Q. *What are the five modifications of mind?*
A. Cognition, misconception, verbal delusion, sleep and memory.

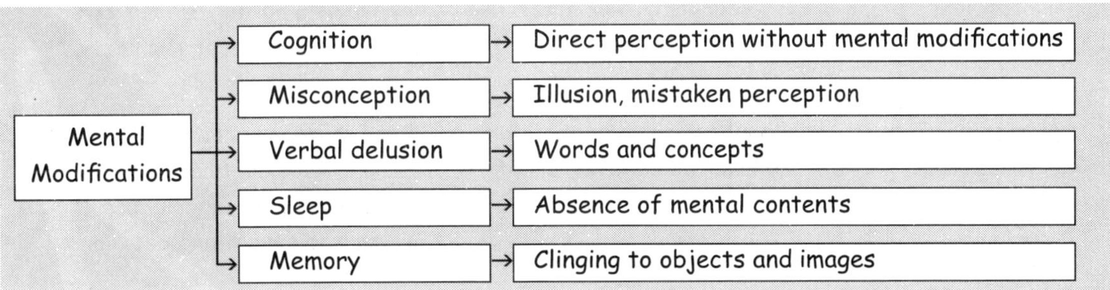

All modifications having the form of conviction can be reduced to one the three conditions: direct perception, inference or accurate evidence. What happens on right Yoga process? The right Yoga process leads to right control of mental modifications. Steadiness is gained so that the real self can use mind as an organ of perception. Once right use of the organ of perception is ensured, right interpretation through intuition and reason is also ensured.

In the waking stage, *Ātmā* enjoys all the experiences; in the dream stage, all the senses of perception and action hold back their activities but, it creates its own forms and names on the basis of experiences and impressions collected from the outer world; in the 'deep sleep' stage, it becomes immanent everywhere and assumes its basic role of pure bliss, unaware of any thing outside or inside.

Aitareya Upanishad

A mental modification is an act of mind. It is not a product so to say to which this activity culminates. Here this activity and its product are intimately and indissolubly bound. For instance the *vritti* '*anumāna*' is the activity by means of which the mind constructs an inference or reasoning which implies a conclusion. This act of mind is a modification of the mind, considering that mind assumes the form of the object which it perceives.

The same incidence can have different modifications in different minds depending upon the nature of the individual. While one anticipates pleasure and pain before enjoyment, another keeps his mind in check even while experiencing.

The ignorant and the knowledgeable

Ignorant Not Aware of Self	Anticipate pleasure and pain before enjoyment. Recollect them after enjoyment. Reflect over them.	Very strong imprint on the mind. A single painful experience like death of a parent can leave very strong imprint for the rest of their life.
More knowledgeable Realises Self On & Off	Recollection and reflection broken up by intervals of realization.	Less strong imprint on the mind. Recover fast from unpleasant experiences. Learn to forget and get along.
Very knowledgeable Never Forgets Self	Keep their mind in check even while experiencing pleasures and pain.	Their response to the world is as indistinct as that of a man in sleep to a gentle breeze playing on him or an ant creeping over his body.
Very Knowledgeable of the highest order Embedded in Self	Totally unconnected with the experiencing. The experiencer is now the witness of the experience.	Always aware of his perfection. Not affected by the seeming pleasures and pains which he regards as a mere illusion like the horns of a hare.

He who lives only to nourish his own body, is like one who wants to cross a river on an alligator thinking it to be a log of wood.

Ādi Shankara - Viveka chudāmani

प्रत्यक्षानुमानागमाः प्रमाणानि ॥७॥

Pratyaksha_Anumāna_Āgamāh Pramānāni.

Right knowledge
Is intuition, deduction and testimony.

Pratyaksha : direct perception
Anumāna : inference, deduction;
Āgamāh : testimony worthy of faith, revelation
Pramāna : correct grasp

Q. *What are the sources of right knowledge?*

A. Sources of right knowledge are direct cognition, inference and testimony. Direct cognition is derived through intuition. Inference is reliable when based on sound reasoning. Testimony is not reliable unless the person has right knowledge to begin with and has the ability to instruct without mistake. This is where the Master (Master of the self) or Preceptor becomes invaluable.

Right Knowledge can be had from three sources: 1. Direct cognition, 2. Inference and 3. Competent evidence / words of the awakened one. Direct knowledge or intuition is independent of the sensory perceptions. That is why the intuitive faculty is referred to as the 'sixth sense'. As Yoga practice advances, this intuitive faculty improves.

Paths to knowledge	Observe Direct perception **See**	Follow the dictum, **seeing is believing**	• Subject to prejudices • Sense perceptions are clouded • Illusory	Truth is beyond the reach of intellect, (thought) and mind.
	Observe Deductive or inductive logic **Think**	Follow the dictum, **thinking is knowing** The so-called scientific scrutiny	• Where there is smoke. there is fire • Subject to wrong application of the principle of logic	
	Trust Scriptural testimony **Hear**	Follow the dictum, **You believe then you see.**	• Such acceptance, at times turns blind and fanatical. • Right interpretation depends upon enlightened teacher	Yoga practice, ensures intuitive knowledge improves perception and thus directs knowledge.

"All Scriptures are God-breathed and are used for teaching, rebuking, correcting and training in righteousness, so that the man of God may be thoroughly equipped for every good work."

Timothy 3:16,17.

Scriptural Inferences *Āgama Pramāna* *Pramāna* means direct knowledge, (not inferential knowledge.) It is confirmed knowledge of the seers, rishis, prophets, saints, sages and messiahs. All of them are accepted as true, by their respective followers.		
	Muslims	Holy Qoran
	Christians	The Old and New Testaments
	Hindus	Vedas, Sutras, Bhagavadgitā, Smriti, Purāns Upanishads etc.
	Jews	The Torah
	Buddhists	Tripitakas and the Dhammapada

Right knowledge can be had only if seer, sight and seen are one, that is when one is absorbed and where there is no duality. Direct cognition is something that is known without the help / hindrance of the senses. The second tool for right knowledge is inference. When one is not centred and one does not have direct knowledge then he can only infer, one deduces from what he sees. But this knowledge can only be termed secondary.

When one can not have right cognition and one cannot infer, then what? One must simply trust some one else, some one who is a man of wisdom, some one who is a Buddha. *Āgamas* are authored scriptures considered as authority only when they do not contradict *Vedas*. The *Āgamas* are found to deal with temple worship, consecration of idols in temples, temple festivals etc. Each *Āgama* consists of four parts. The first part includes the philosophical and spiritual knowledge, the second part covers the yoga and the mental discipline, the third part specifies rules for the construction of temples and for sculpting and carving the figures of deities for worship in the temples and the fourth part of the *Āgamas* includes rules pertaining to the observances of religious rites, rituals, and festivals.

"When oneness of the totality of things is not recognized, then ignorance as well as particularization arises, and all phases of the denied mind are thus developed....all phenomena in the world are nothing but the illusory manifestation of the mind and have no reality on their own"

Ashvaghosha.

Pramāna: "Authority" is known as *Pramāna*

There are three authorities that are accepted. They are:

Shabdam **The heard.** **Verbal testimony**	The Vedās Bible Qoran	*Shruti*. The heard. Vedas are not authored by any one including the God Almighty. Veda Vyāsa only bifurcated the Vedas and compiled them that is why he is called Vyāsa (In Sanskrit, Vyāsa means compiler). Similarly, the Bible and Qoran are revelations.	Given maximum importance
Pratyaksham **Direct observation**	*Pratyaksha* is observed and understood through our sense organs	Direct observation is what is perceived through our sense organs like eyes, ears etc., and understood by us. It is considerable and not to be rejected or accepted without proper and foolproof inquiry.	Direct observation is of certain importance still it is susceptible to error. But, if it is corroborated the Vedic conclusion is acceptable.
Anumāna **The inferred** **Logic and argumentation**	Inference based on observation	*Anumāna* is inference based on observation(s). For example, if one observes smoke coming from behind a mountain, he may infer based on this observation that there is fire behind the mountain. He may be right or wrong. It can be even a mist or cloud passing behind the mountain. So *anumāna* is not foolproof but is accepted if it is substantiated with proper valid logic.	Inference is given least importance because it is susceptible to error. Sometimes it leads one to make downright absurd conclusions.

"...no one can establish his existence experimentally beyond the proof of *shruti*, or Vedic wisdom.....there is no source of understanding the soul except by studying the Vedas. In other words, the soul is inconceivable by human experimental knowledge."

Bhakthivedānta Swāmi Prabhupāda

विपर्ययो मिथ्याज्ञानमतद्रूपप्रतिष्ठम् ॥८॥

Viparyayo Mithyā_Gyānam_Atad Rupa_Pratishtham.

Misconception is erroneous notion
That arises from incorrect cognition.

Viparyayo : error, mistake, misconception, erroneous impression;
Mithyā : incorrect, false; wrong inference, *Gyānam* : knowledge, learning,
Atad Rupa : not on that true form or nature, *Pratishtham*: based, established

Q. *What is misconception?*

A. Misconception is false illusory knowledge which does not correspond to a real object. An example is we see something and take it to be something else; this could be based on wrong knowledge or *Avidyā*. Cognizing the false as truth is misconception.

Incorrect knowledge or illusion (*viparyaya*) is false knowledge formed by perceiving a thing as being other than what it really is. Ādi Shankara introduces *Brahmasutra* through the introduction of misconception / error. Shankara explains the common misconception of every human being. The purpose is to show that the human problem is the result of an error about one's Self. The solution lies in removing this error through knowledge. When a rope is not clearly visible, a person mistakes it for a snake. This is called partial knowledge, *sāmānya jnānam*. The specific aspect (*vishesha amsha*) that it is a rope is covered partially by darkness (ignorance). Darkness makes one mistake a rope to be a snake. When darkness is removed the rope is known and we say, "There is a rope."

Ādi Shankara says:

1. Error can be defined as misapprehension of the rope - *anyathā grahanam*
2. Error is super-imposition of snake - *adhyāsa āropa.*
3. Error is a combination of a real rope and unreal snake - *satya mithyā mithuni karanam.*

The aim of yoga is to remove this error by negating the superimposed misconceptions.

They consider his mind as 'lost' whom states of happiness and misery, misfortune, pride, dullness and jubilation do not lead to difference in nature.

Yogavāshishta

Mind has the capacity of wrong knowledge also. That wrong knowledge is called in Sanskrit *viparyaya* -- false, *mithyā*. *Viparyaya* or misapprehension is equivalent to ignorance (*avidyā*) in Yoga philosophy. And knowledge borne out of misconceptions such as mistaking a rope for a snake and vice versa are false, leading to afflictions of the greatest kind. *Viparyaya* gives rise to the following *kleshas* or obstacles to meditation.

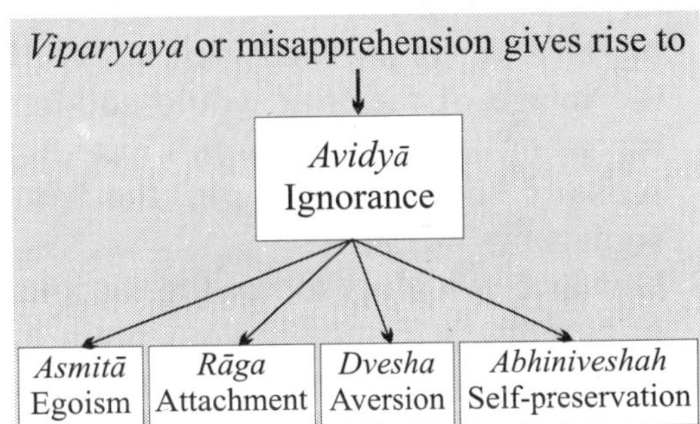

To think of the transient as permanent is misapprehension. Vedic literature gives us a simple formula for differentiating the permanent and the transient.

1. That which has existed in all periods of time; past, present and will exist in future is permanent and true.
2. That which exists only in one or two of the three, past and present but not in future, is transient.
3. That which has not existed at anytime in the past or present is untrue.

World is a mixture of truth and untruth

Sat/Real/Truth	Truth exists in all three periods, present and future. PERMANENT
Mithyā/False	That which is existent in one or two periods, but not at all times in all three, is *mithyā*. Example: all material objects, the physical body and physical relationship. TRANSIENT
Asat/unreal/not true	That which is absent in the three periods of time, Example: The child of a barren woman, the horn of a rabbit. NON-EXISTENT

It is *Mithyā* when there is a mixture of truth and falsehood; neither true nor untrue, but something in between. The world is not untrue, *a-sat* (false, unreal, non-existent, bad) but *mithyā*.

Thinking is dreaming with words,
Dreaming is thinking with images.

What modern science says:

1. Everything we perceive as the 'matter', 'world' or 'universe' is nothing but electrical signals occurring in our brain.
2. Someone eating a fruit in fact confronts not the actual fruit but its perception in the brain. The object considered to be a 'fruit' by the person actually consists of an electrical impression in the brain concerning the shape, taste, smell, and texture of the fruit. If the sight nerve travelling to the brain were to be severed suddenly, the image of the fruit would suddenly disappear. Or a disconnection in the nerve travelling from the sensors in the nose to the brain would completely interrupt the sense of smell. Simply put, the fruit is nothing but the interpretation of electrical signals by the brain.
3. Distance, which is to say the distance between you and this book, is only a feeling of emptiness formed in your brain. Objects that seem to be distant in that person's view also exist in the brain. For instance, someone who watches the stars in the sky assumes that they are millions of light-years away from him. Yet what he 'sees' are really the stars inside himself, in his centre of vision. While one reads these lines, one is, in truth, not inside the room one assumes that he is in; on the contrary, the room is inside him.
4. The 'external world' presented to us by our perceptions is merely a collection of the electrical signals reaching our brain. Throughout our lives, these signals are processed by our brain and we live without recognizing that we are mistaken in assuming that these are the original versions of matter existing in the 'external world'. We are misled because we can never reach the matter itself by means of our senses.
5. The truth of the matter is rather that all the qualities we ascribe to objects are inside us and not in the 'external world'.
6. Since each object is only a collection of perceptions and those perceptions exist only in the mind, it is more accurate to say that the only world that really exists is the world of perceptions. The only world that one knows of is the world that exists in his mind: the one that is designed, recorded, and made vivid there; the one, in short, that is created within one's mind.

What is wrong knowledge?

Wrong knowledge is false conception. Knowing something as IT IS NOT is wrong knowledge. Almost all knowledge that one possesses before achieving Unity can be construed as wrong knowledge. Wrong knowledge results from play of the senses, prejudices, ill conceived notions, unquestioning acceptance of so-called words of wisdom from ill-informed people etc.

It is easy to accept tentatively that the world is not ultimately real, but it is hard to have the conviction that it is unreal.

Ramana Maharshi: Even so is your dream world real while you are dreaming. So long as the dream lasts everything you see and feel is real.

शब्दज्ञानानुपाती वस्तुशून्यो विकल्पः ॥९॥

Shabda_Jnāna_Anupāti Vastu_Shunyo Vikalpah.

Verbal delusion is an instance
Of sound devoid of substance.

Shabda : word, speech, sound;
Anupāti : following upon
Shunya : without any, empty
Jnāna : cognizance, knowledge
Vastu : reality, of an object, of matter
Vikalpah : verbal delusion, fancy, fantasy

Q. *What is only an imagination?*

A. Verbal delusion is fantasy and imagination that captivates and may even entertain the mind for some time, but without the perception of an object.
Fantasy is an image conjured up by words without any meaning.
Deriving meaning from words that are substantial as far as words go, but in actuality nothing; is fancy or fantasy.

On hearing a word, irrespective of the fact whether the word originates from another or from within one's own self, knowledge is produced in the mind and a meaning is grasped. This knowledge is a 'verbal knowledge' since it is produced by word. Likewise on looking at an object, the perception of an object produces knowledge about the object.

Vikalpa Verbal knowledge Verbal delusion	• Created by words • Not necessary to have an object in front • Words occupy the place of objects	**Example: The head of Rāhu** Rāhu is a planet that is symbolized by only a head. To say, 'head of Rāhu' is akin to saying 'head of head' which makes no sense. On the other hand it makes sense to say, 'crown of a king'.

Verbal delusion lacks material correlatives, that is, nothing actually existing corresponds to it in reality. Verbal delusion does not really refer to anything. It is 'empty of thing'.

"As long as there is the assumption of ignorance,
as long as there is the idea that one is not the Brahman,
as long as there is the regard for illusion of the world,
as long as the idea pot reality is the 'seen' and
as long as there is the sense of 'I' in the body,
so long there is the imagination of mind."

Yogavāshishta

अभावप्रत्ययालम्बना वृत्तिर्निद्रा ॥१०॥

Abhāva_Pratyaya_Ālambana Vrittih_Nidrā.

Deep sleep is then
When mind is a dulled one
When mental modifications are none
And subject matters are gone.

Abhāva : non existence, absence
Pratyaya : cognition, experience of wakeful state
Ālambana : being in support of
Vrittih : thought waves, mental modifications
Nidrā : deep sleep

Q. *What is deep sleep?*

A. The state of sleep is when there is an absence of awareness. The cessation of bodily experience can be termed as sleep. In the state of deep sleep, though there is no knowledge of anything, there is still the knowledge of not having known anything.

When a person is in the condition of sleep, in Sanskrit he is referred to as being in '*svapiti*', 'He sleeps'. '*sva*' is the self. What is made out is that one gets absorbed into oneself in the sleep. In other conditions like waking etc, one gets drawn out into the external, unreal world.

Difference between wakeful state and sleeping state:

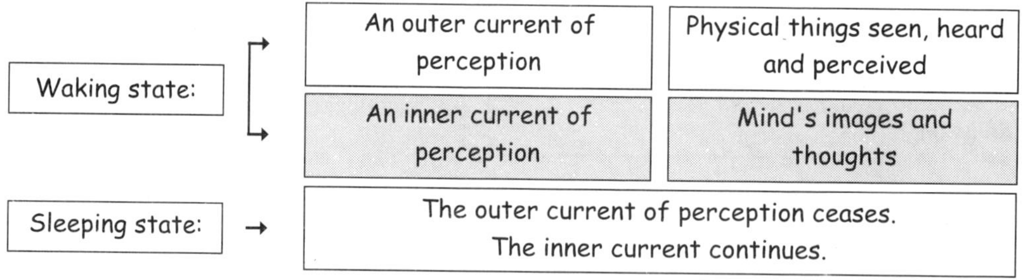

When one who is asleep, feels no desires, sees no dreams- that is deep sleep. All the experiences of the waking and the dream state dissolve in the experience of deep sleep. From the consciousness deep sleep arises the whole phenomenon of waking and dream states.

Māndukya Upanishad

Sleep is a condition of inactivity of mental modifications. The question naturally arises as to whether sleep is then a state of union, as by definition state of union is then when mental modifications cease. The answer is an emphatic no. The essential difference is that in sleep there is no awareness, whilst in a state of absorption there is total awareness.

Deep sleep	*Samādhi* - Absorption
1. After the sleep one gets back to same old ignorant self. The soul hastens back due to working of the *karmas*.	1. After *Samādhi*, there is no more ignorance.
2. On waking up one sees multiplicity where one exists as earlier, as before going to sleep.	2. After Samadhi one sees unity in everything.
3. Consciousness is submerged in the shell of the individual mind, but has not yet been able to emerge out of that shell.	3. Consciousness is fully integrated with the Being.
4. In this introverted inactive condition a slight reflection of bliss is enjoyed and on waking up forgotten. It is a state of forgetfulness of the world.	4. Bliss is directly enjoyed with no forgetting. There is total awareness while enjoying the bliss. There is always wakefulness.
Senses remain temporarily suspended.	**Senses are permanently transcended.**

Like the tired falcon

Like a falcon that is tied with a long rope keeps flying as far as the rope permits, mind keeps wandering within its confines of images, objects and ideation.

Tired and unable to go any farther, being tied to the rope, the falcon gets back to the place where its legs are tied and sleeps.

Mind is also tethered to the root of the Being. But mind does not know about it. It thinks it has freedom. It searches for happiness all over. Unable to satisfy its desires, it gets back to where it is tethered and sleeps.

"O loved One! As birds fly towards their shelter in trees, so all senses proceed towards and are established in the higher Self."

Prashanopanishad IV.6

Different states– a comparison

	Waking	Dreaming	Dreamless Sleep	
Intellect	✓	✓	✗ Remains only in the form of a seed	I did not know anything.
Senses	✓	✗	✗	
Avidyā Ignorance	✓ Patent	✓ Patent	✓ Latent	
Source of Knowledge	✓	✓	Still	

The special character in the dreamless state is that in this state the intellect and the senses are completely absent and do not function. The intellect remains in this state in seed form. So much so, the next morning on waking up one says: "I did not know anything." The dreamless sleep state is distinguished from the waking state by the presence of intellect and senses in the waking state. In the dream state intellect functions, but the senses are dysfunctional. But *avidyā*, the ignorance, is present in all the states-waking, dreaming and deep sleep. Whereas in the waking and dreaming state the ignorance is patent, in the deep sleep state it is latent. Unlike dreamless sleep state, in the dreaming state mind enjoys and suffers what is already enjoyed and suffered during the waking state. The Upanishad states, "The deity (mind) enjoys greatness in dreams. He sees again what he has seen, hears again what he has heard, enjoys again what he has enjoyed in different countries and quarters of the world. Whatever is seen and unseen, heard and unheard, experienced and un-experienced, real and unreal, he being all, experiences it." (*Prashnopanishad 4.5*)

Adi Shankara says: "Sensuous perceptions are to be regarded as the waking state. Those very perceptions revealed in sleep as impressions, constitute the dream state. The absence of perceptions and their impressions is known to be deep sleep. The witness of these three states, one's own Self is to be regarded as the Supreme Being to be realized"

In the dream state, mind experiences greatness. Whatever was seen, it sees again; whatever was heard, it hears again; whatever was perceived at different places, it experiences again and again. It perceives all by becoming all that was seen or not seen, heard or not heard, perceived or not perceived and whatever is real and unreal.

Prashanopanishad V .5

When an impression that is stored in the subconscious as memory becomes powerful, it makes an effort to be recognized by the conscious self. Then it is experienced and also realized in the form of a dream. The dream becomes explicit and vivid, real and actual at the time of dream.

When one is dreaming, he does not recognize the dream as a dream, but experiences it as real. It is only after waking up; one recollects and says that he had a dream. The feelings of fear, anger, frustration, are all real, while one dreams. The dreams affect the body. The experiences of trembling, sweating and jerking reported at one time or another, by most people are proof of the effect of dream on the body. Mind enjoys and suffers during dreams.

Often one wonders why he dreamt of scenes and experienced events which are in no way connected to the impressions he would have formed during his waking state. It should be noted that not only impressions formed during this life that is stored in the subconscious, but also that of earlier incarnations. Even impressions formed in earlier lives as beast or bird, fish or worm are stored in the subconscious. That explains the unconnectedness of the dreams. All the different types of experiences in dreams are the result of impressions and memories of actual experiences obtained at different times, ages and births. They get linked during sleep when logic and will are absent and hence perform no filtering action. Dreams prove to be an exit route for the impressions.

Says Descartes: " When I consider the matter carefully, I do not find a single characteristic by means of which I can certainly determine whether I am awake or whether I am dreaming. The vision of a dream and the experiences of my waking state are so much alike that I am completely puzzled and I do not really know I am not dreaming at this moment."

Adds Pascal: "If a dream comes to us every night, we should be as much occupied with it as by the things we see every day, and if an artisan were certain that he would dream every night for full twelve hours that he was a king, he would just be as happy as a king who dreams every night for full twelve hours that he is an artisan."

When fantasies, fears and feelings have expressed themselves out for that day, the person slips into the state of deep sleep.

He who is awake while in deep sleep, for whom there is no waking and for whom the perception is free from past mental impressions, that is, perception is free from knowledge derived from memory; is said to be liberated while living.

Yogavāshishta

अनुभूतविषयासंप्रमोषः स्मृतिः ॥११॥

Anubhoot_Vishaya_Asampramoshah Smriti.

Memory is mental retention
Of a conscious action.

Anubhoota : experienced *Vishaya* : any object or topic
Asampramoshah : not forgotten, not lost, not eliminated *Smriti* : memory

Q. *What is memory?*
A. Memory is not letting go of a perceived object of a subjective experience. Memory is recollecting and reliving the past as if it is the present.

1. Memory is to keep past experienced sense perceptions and not letting them go. The ability to bring out the sub/unconscious impressions of the mind, memories, *samskārs*, and archetypes and accurately unfold them with the conscious mind is the faculty of *smriti* / memory.
2. Memory influences are any influence by which past experiences cloud current perception.
3. Memory is retention of impressions and information over a period of time
4. Essentially remembering is the activity of attending to present ideas which are determined by past experiences. A past event which we are able to revive as a present experience leaves a physiological change in the brain structure called a memory trace.
5. Memory is the innate power of reproducing past impressions by an association of ideas principally suggested by objective things by some action on our external sensory organs.

Memory is of two kinds: Conscious memory and subconscious memory

Conscious memory	• Involves recollection of things already experienced. • To recall the experiences of the past.
Sub-conscious memory	• Is dream. • One does not consciously remember, but unconsciously recapitulates.

"My I is the Christ,
nor do I recognise any other I than He."

Saint Catherine of Sienna

Subconscious memory in turn can be classified into two categories:

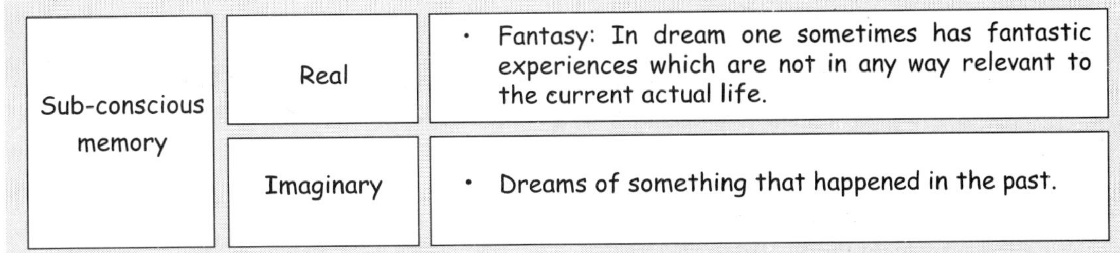

According to Vyāsa, memory is twofold. When the phenomenon to be remembered has BECOME the very nature of mind and when it has not. The two states are the dream and waking states.

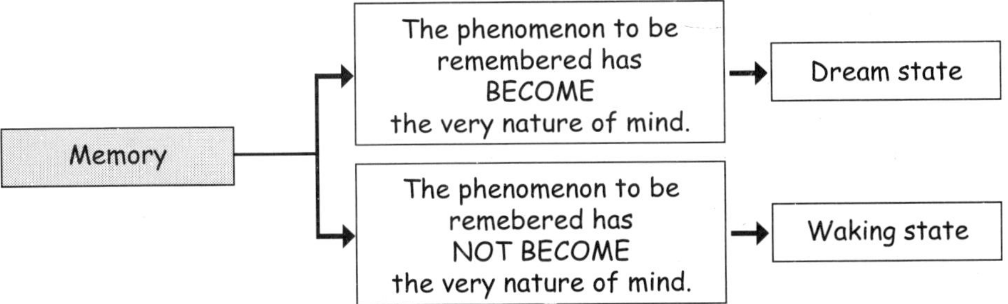

Modern science has established that human memory is nothing but a very complicated electromagnetic system. If there is a way to switch off or alter the memory cells containing information about the mundane pleasures and painful events, it should be possible to guide the individual towards permanent bliss. It is nothing but a state of unawareness about pain and transient pleasures.

One can also categorise memory as: sensory memory, working memory and long-term memory.

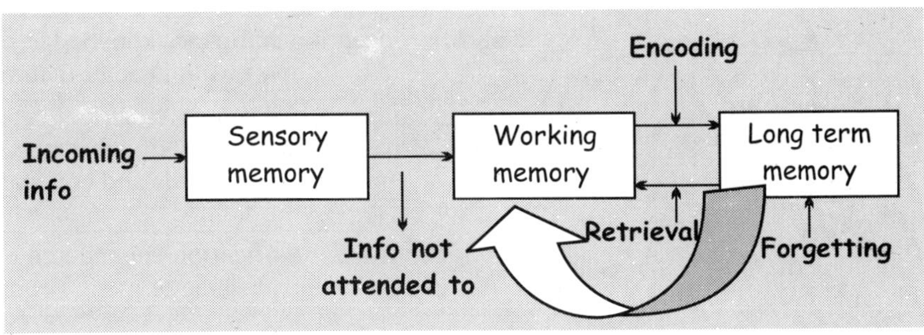

SUMMARY: Aphorism 1.01-1.11

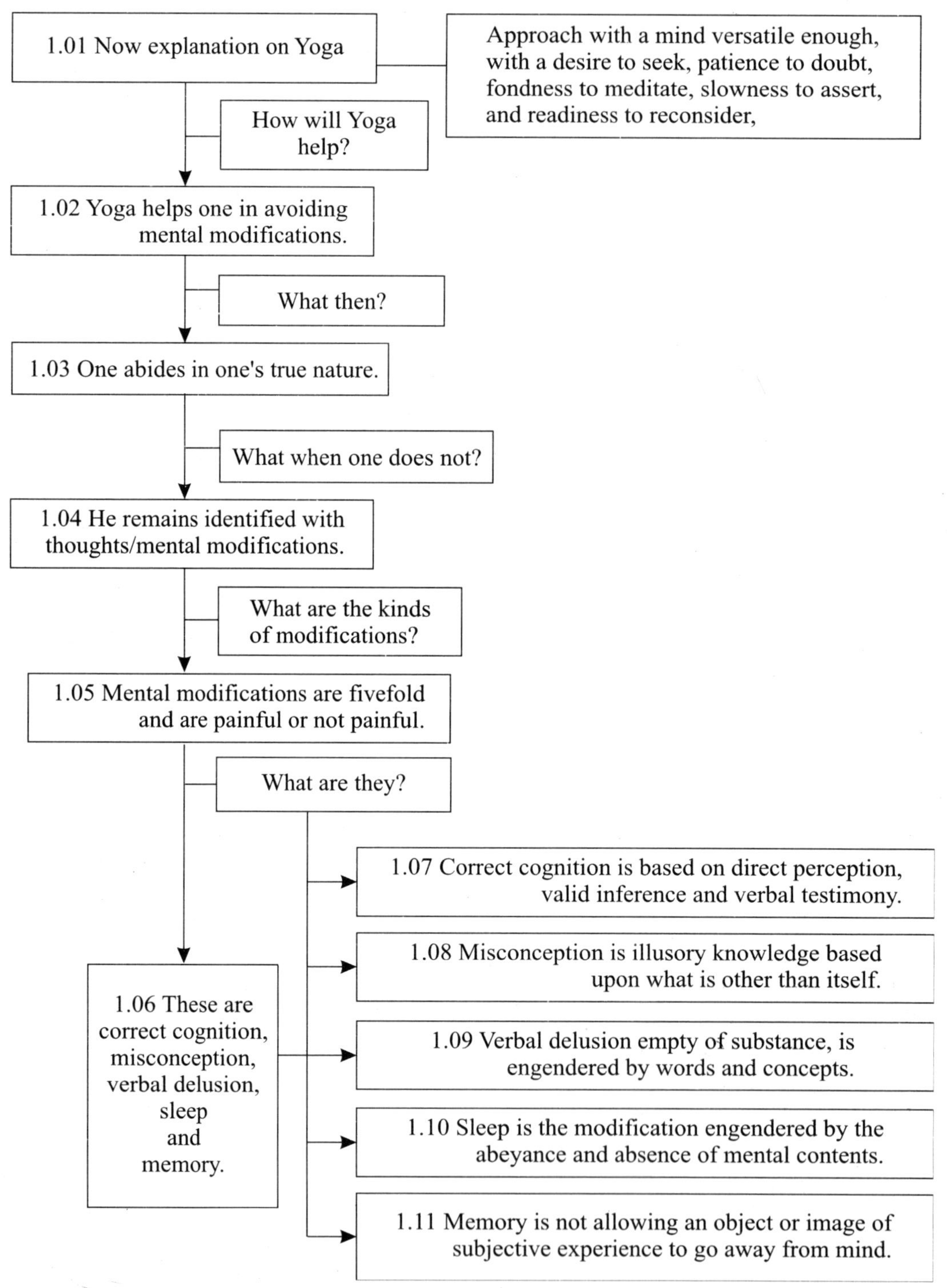

अभ्यासवैराग्याभ्यां तन्निरोधः ॥१२॥

Abhyāsa_Vairāgyābhyām Tannirodhah.

Mental modifications cease
With detachment and practice.

Abhyāsa : repeated practice
Vairāgyābhyām : non attachment, detachment
Tan : that, the referred to obstructions
Nirodhah : controlled, avoided, cease

Q. *How are mental modifications like the above to be avoided?*
A. Through detachment and practice.

Practice makes one perfect. Practice would mean constantly reinforcing the thought that one lives in duality and hence is subject to miscomprehension, delusion etc and that the only way to overcome the limitations imposed by ignorance is to become knowledgeable.

The English word **HABIT** is very interesting. One removes H, **ABIT** remains. With great difficulty if A is also removed, **BIT** remains, with even greater difficulty B is also removed, even then **IT** remains! Habits born out of countless number of births cannot be removed without practice. Practice here would mean going back again and again to the steps of removal of duality. As often as the mind perches itself to the external world of objects, so often it should be reined in to focus internally.

Character is nothing but a bundle of habits. If over centuries of birth wrong habits of object orientation and ideation has been acquired, at least hundreds of times every day the counter habit of inward orientation and concentration needs to be practised. If repeatedly even an iron rod is heated and hit, it is bound to soften up and get pliable. The heating process is the *tapas* referred to elsewhere in the sutras. It is the hitting process that is referred to in repetition of mantras, the *japa*. The *Tapa* and the *Japa* are the tools available to first reverse the habit of sense orientation and build up a fresh habit of concentration on the chosen object of meditation.

Habit is the second nature of man. It is also the first nature, the very nature of un-illumined man. Tendencies are the result of the habits. Habits reinforce tendencies and tendencies in turn build up habits. If one has to get out of this vicious circle of tendencies and actions resulting from tendencies that binds man, repeated practice of focusing attention on the object of meditation and reinforcing in oneself the thought that one is not the body, one is not the vital energy, one is not even his intellect, but one is the eternal Being, is necessary.

Realization is not attained by going far,
but by staying still.

Detachment is a state of mind in which one does not rejoice in inactivity, nor is bound by actions, one who is thoroughly even in his outlook and who gives up the desire for fruit of actions.

There are two kinds of attachments:

1. The barren and useless
2. The commendable

The barren and hence useless	Mental impressions impure Bereft of knowledge of the nature of pure self Caused by objects like the body Greatly attached to worldly life
The commendable	Born of discrimination between truth and the world of elements Mind abides in the delight of the self Free from exultation and dejection Soul arrived at the state devoid of individuality

One can begin by being neutral. On every issue and in every field it is not necessary for one to take a side or a stand. One should cultivate the quality of dispassion. Thereafter one will notice that in due course of time a certain sense of detachment sets in. When detached, one observes more and learns and understands more. But let it be understood that it is by attaching to reality, the goal of Yoga, that one develops detachment to the relativity that are objects.

Practice of detachment is a continuous process. When one repeats a thing it gets ingrained and engraved on the brain cells. The more it becomes one's nature, less is the effort needed.

But this attachment to truth and the desire for liberation also need to be given up eventually. If a thought such 'let there be liberation for me' is caused in the within, mind is raised and becomes operative. On the springing of thinking in the mind intensely, the bonding of worldly existence becomes firm.

Enquiry into the nature of the *Ātman*, or Self and Yogic practices done without intense detachment becomes fruitless.

Objects fall away from the abstinent man, leaving the longing behind. But his longing also ceases, who sees the Supreme." (11-59)

Bhagavadgitā

तत्र स्थितौ यत्नोऽभ्यासः ॥१३॥

Tatra Sthitau Yatno_Abhyāsah.

The effort that steadies
Is practice.

Tatra : That, there, of these
Sthitau : steadied, established
Yatna : effort
Abhyāsah : practice

Q. *What constitutes practice?*

A. The effort, that ensures stillness of mind, is practice. There are no prescriptions on practice. There are no dogmas. It is now left to the individual seeker and his teacher to arrive at a practice that is suitable to the seeker, yet one that ensures that there is steadiness and stilling of mind and no modifications.

What is the aim of practice? The aim of practice is not happiness. The aim is to be in the state of Being. The aim of practice is to be in a state of attributelessness. Spiritual practice needs perseverance. Jumping, from a seminar here to a week end workshop there, does not constitute practice. They are activity-oriented, propelling one to compare, discuss and deliberate. Such an exercise kindles mind activity instead of calming it.

Practice means different things to different people:

The devotional	Practice consists of always being with God, not to separate oneself from his God.
The Duty-bound	Practice consists of devoting every bit of action to God and serving everyone looking at them as representatives of God.
The intellectual	Practice consists of constant pondering over the question, 'Who am I?' and constant reinforcement of the thought that one is not his body.
The Yogi	Practice means concentration and meditation as often as possible.

"Thinking of That alone, speaking of That alone, conversing with one another about That alone and utter dedication to That alone, is considered as constituting practice by the wise."

Yogavāshishta

Ādi Shankara in *Sādhana Panchakam* lists out several dos and don'ts:

1. Study the scriptures every day.
2. After the study, put into good practice, what you study.
3. Dedicate all those actions (*karmas*) as worship unto the Lord.
4. Recognise that the pleasures of sense-objects (*samsāra*) are riddled with pain
5. Seek the Self with consistent endeavour.
6. Cultivate companionship with noble men.
7. Be established in firm devotion to the Lord.
8. Instantly get rid of all binding desires.
9. Worship 'Om' the Immutable.
10. Listen in depth, the *Upanishadic* declarations.
11. Reflect ever upon the meaning of the *Upanishadic* commandments.
12. Avoid perverse interpretation of what the scriptures say, and stay peaceful.
13. Give up the 'I' thought. Pull the ego plug out!

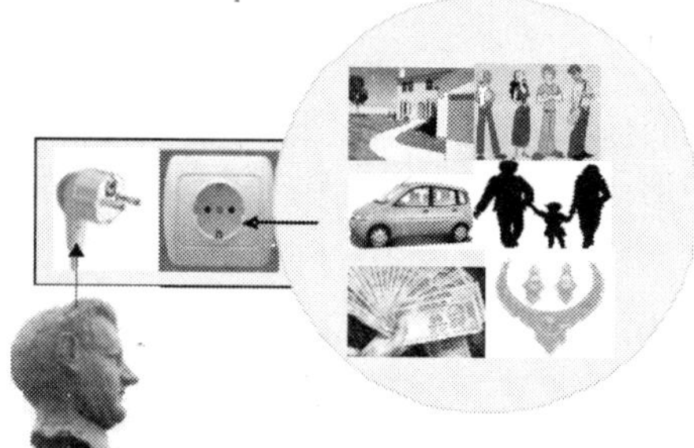

14. Give up the delusory misconception, 'I am the body'.
15. Give up totally the tendency to argue with wise men.
16. Be satisfied with what destiny delivers.
17. Avoid wasteful talk.
18. Detach yourself with the mesh of other people's kindness or curses.
19. In solitude live joyously.
20. Know the seen to be just a projection.

Sādhanā is conscious performance of disciplined actions that are in conformity with the Vedic wisdom. These actions while by themselves do not lead to deliverance from ignorance, undoubtedly help one in preparing the ground, with the help of a *Sadguru*, to perform the journey that leads to enlightenment.

स तु दीर्घकालनैरन्तर्यसत्कारा सेवितो दृढ़भूमिः ॥१४॥

Sa Tu Dirghakāl_Nairantarya_Satkārā Sevito Dridha Bhoomih.

Practice long without break and with devotion
Is firm in foundation.

Sa : that *Tu* : but, indeed *Dirghakāla* : long time, long duration
Nairantaryya : uninterrupted, non-stop, continuously *Satkārā* : earnest, sincere
Sevita : well-attended *Dridha Bhoomih* : Firm foundation

Q. *What is the result of practice?*
A. Practice continued for long without interruption and with devotion gets firmly grounded.

How long is long enough? Spiritual practice cannot and should not be counted in terms of an hour or a day. It should 24x7x365. Even as one attends to day-to-day chores in the initial years, a state of detachment and commitment to duty should prevail. Continuous association with virtuous persons is good and it helps. In the association of wise men even calamity appears like an advantage or a blessing.

Practice has a long history of success in achieving some phenomenal goals and dissolving others. Practice works because it includes not only the usual aspects of chanting, meditation, contemplation, and selfless service, but much more. Practice is as varied as life itself. Practice becomes whatever one does with his goal as his motive.

The nature of mind goes beyond all substantialities. This being so, in the meditation practice it is important neither to invite the future nor recollect the past, but to remain in the state of nowness. The now-ness of the mind is the practice which should be developed by one and all.

Contentment is the key. The contented one approaches the supreme beatitude, which is of the nature of tranquillity and happiness. He is called a contended man who does not feel depression or elation, having abandoned the wish not fulfilled and remaining equable in that acquired. He indeed is contended who is of gentle and has proper conduct and does not long for what has not been acquired and enjoys what has arrived in due order.

The control of mind can be achieved by the untiring practice over a long period, even as the ocean can be dried up by bailing its waters drop by drop with a blade of grass.

Gaudapāda Kārika 3.41

दृष्टानुश्रविकविषयवितृष्णस्य वशीकारसंज्ञा वैराग्यम् ॥१५॥

Drishta_Anushrāvika_Vishaya_Vitrishnasya

Vashikāra Sangyā Vairagyam.

There is dispassion
When, for objects seen or heard, there is no attraction.

Drishta : seen | *Anushrāvika* : heard, imagined
Vishaya : object | *Vitrishnasya* : without craving | *Vashikāra* : attraction
Sangyā : definition | *Vairagyam*: detachment, dispassion

Q. *What is detachment?*

A. That particular state of mind, which manifests in one who does not hanker after objects seen or heard, and in which one is conscious of having controlled or mastered those objects, is non-attachment. The highest detachment is that state where one feels no desire even for the joy of union or heaven.

Four stages in detachment *(Vairāgya)*

1st Stage	*Yātamanya Samjnā*: Effort towards freeing oneself from attachment to things.
2nd Stage	*Vyatieka Samjnā*: Isolation of the things to be avoided from among many things of the world.
3rd Stage	*Ekendriya Samjnā*: Where one discovers that it is after all the mind from which the freedom is to be attained, the one sense which is the cause of all trouble and not from the world as such.
4th Stage	*Vasikarana Samjnā*: Complete mastery over all things, by a total absence of desire for everything, whether seen or only heard of.

In enjoyment there is fear of disease; in social position, the fear of falling off; in wealth, the fear of (hostile) kings; in honour, the fear of humiliation; in power, the fear of foes; in beauty, the fear of old age; in scriptural erudition, the fear of opponents; in virtue, the fear of traducers; in body, the fear of death. All the things of this world pertaining to human beings are attended with fear; renunciation alone stands for fearlessness.

Vairāgya Shatakam of Bhartrihari

I left her there

Tanzan and Ekido were once travelling together down a muddy road. A heavy rain was still falling. Coming around a bend, they met a lovely girl in a silk kimono and sash, unable to cross the intersection. "Come on, girl" said Tanzan at once. Lifting her in his arms, he carried her over the mud. Ekido did not speak again until that night when they reached a lodging temple. Then he no longer could restrain himself. "We monks don't go near females," he told Tanzan, "especially not young and lovely ones. It is dangerous. Why did you do that?"

"I left the girl there," said Tanzan. "Are you still carrying her?"

Karna had no attachment whatever

In the Mahābhārata one reads a lot about the generosity of Karna and his tendency to unhesitatingly give whatever is asked from him. Such was his non attachment to objects. Once Karna was having an 'oil bath', massaging his whole body with oil and after allowing the oil to soak his pores for couple of hours, took bath. As he was applying oil from a diamond studded cup that was with him, Krishna entered his chambers on an errand.

Krishna saw Karna applying oil from the diamond studded cup to his body. Krishna asked Karna whether he will be willing to gift that cup to him. Unhesitatingly, without even waiting for a second, Karna gave away the cup he was holding in the left hand to Krishna.

To test him, Krishna asked him whether it was proper for Karna to hand over the cup to him, with his oil soaked left hand.

Karna responded, "Krishna, if I had gone to the bathroom to wash my hands, *en route* anything could have happened. I could have slipped and fallen. Or, I could have changed my mind and not gifted it to you. I did not want to waste any opportunity to gift. Hence then and there, though I knew that I was using my oil soaked hand to hand over the cup, I did."

ARJUNA: Krishna! you praise renunciation of actions and also the pursuit (of them). Tell me determinately which one of these two is superior.

KRISHNA: Renunciation and pursuit of action are both instruments of happiness. But of the two, pursuit of action is superior to renunciation of action. He should be understood to be always an ascetic who has no aversion and no desire. For, O you of mighty arms! He who is free from the pairs of opposites is easily released from (all) bonds.

तत्परं पुरुषख्यातेर्गुणवैतृष्ण्यम् ॥१६॥

Tat_Param Purushakhyāteh_Guna_Vaitrishnyam.

He is a supreme being
Who has, even for qualities of objects, no craving.

Tat : non-attachment *Param* : beyond *Purushakhyāteh* : supreme among beings
Guna : triple qualities, attributes *Vaitrishnyam* : free from desire, free from craving

Q. *What is the state of supreme detachment?*
A. Indifference to the *gunas* (*sattva*, *rājas* and *tamas*) or the attributes achieved through knowledge of the nature of Self, that comes about, is called supreme detachment.

Renouncing should not involve forcing or negation or effort. Renouncing should be the byproduct of practice. As practice proceeds automatically mind's desire for sensory objects, gets loosened. Thereafter comes a stage of total disinterestedness or disinclination. The anticipation of action, the anticipation of sensory enjoyment, the involvement in action or enjoyment and the subsequent analysis of action and recollection and experiencing the action once again after the completion of action at the mental plane will all give way. The actions, thereafter, do not stop. What follows is disinterested or uninvolved action. Patanjali says, "While detachment in itself is good, better still is detachment from attributes of action. Such a detachment from the attributes of action means non-accumulation of attributes/ qualities that bind mind."

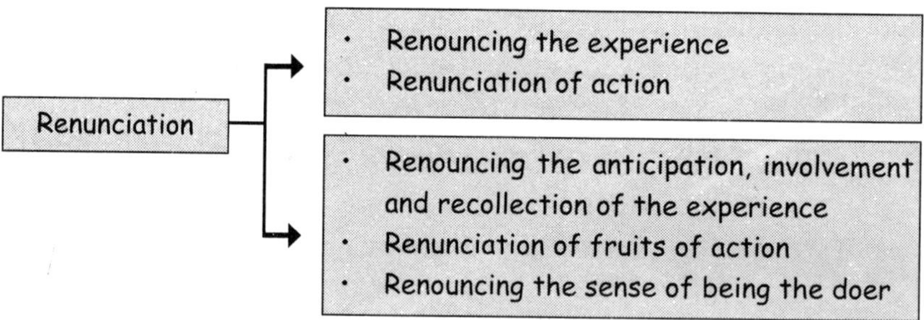

There is a great difference between knowing the physiology of drunkenness and being drunk. Similarly, there is a great difference between knowing the nature of and cause of mystical experience, and being a mystic.

Ghazali: al-munquidh min ad-Dalal

The concept of Guna/quality:

Guna is usually translated as quality or constituent. Strictly '*Guna*' does not refer to quality in the sense of something inherent in a substance. It is also not a constituent, since it is not something separable or separating. *Guna* refers to the characteristic manifestation of reality. *Sattva* is intelligence, *Rājas* is motion or vibration and *Tamas* is matter or inertia.

In the beginning there was equilibrium. The equilibrium was unsettled. This unsettling resulted in the vibration or *chitta vritti*. This *chitta vritti* referred to as mental modifications are basically of three types: The *Sāttvic* or knowledge, *Rājasic* or motion, and *Tāmasic* or matter. Knowledge, motion and matter are the triple constituents of the single state of equilibrium.

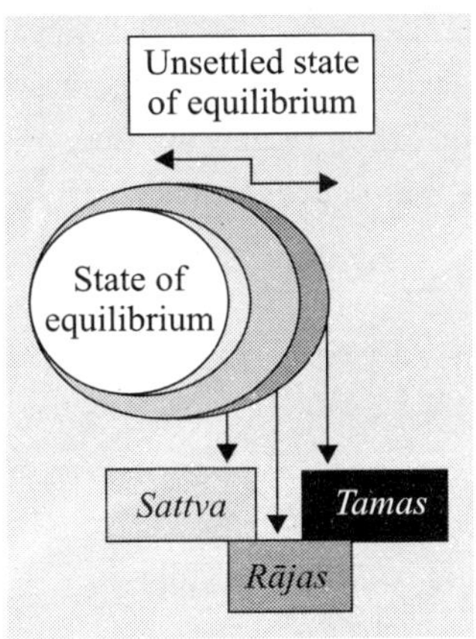

The Hindu trinity of Brahmā, Mahesh and Vishnu represent the triple aspects of the Self same Being. Brahmā represents the knowledge aspect, Mahesh the motion aspect and Vishnu the matter aspect.

Their respective consorts: Sarasvati represents intelligence, Durgā represents energy and Lakshmi represents prosperity.

The triple qualities are so to say the projected (assumed in the state of ignorance) mental modifications of the Being. The *Sāttvic* modification are detachment, fortitude etc. The *Rājasic* modificationss are thirst for and love of objects, attachment, greed and so forth. The *Tāmasic* modifications are delusion, fear and so forth. One should of course, not jump to the conclusion that the respective gods and goddesses of the trinity represent these qualities. All accept them as the ultimate Being, all graceful and all merciful.

Modern science tells us that matter is condensed energy and energy is released matter and the third component that enables such conversion is knowledge. Again electron, neutron and protons can be assumed to be the modern day version of the triple qualities.

"The demerits of *Tamas* is removed by *Rājas* and *Sattva*, *Rājas* by *Sattva* and *Sattva* by purified *Sattva*; therefore remove the erroneous perception that Non-spirit is Spirit"

Viveka Chudāmani, Ādi Shankara

God is not subject to triple qualities, not subject to *Karma* and not in the least affected by actions or inaction. The triple qualities of clarity, activity and inertia is an important aspect of Hindu philosophical thought.

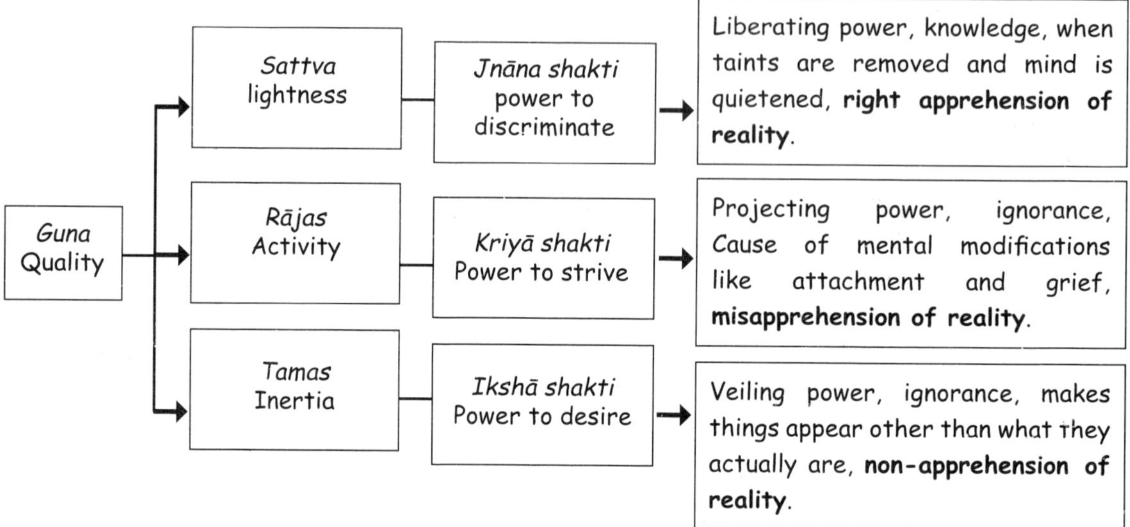

Plato, the ancient philosopher in his *Republic*, speaks of three active principles, which he calls as Epithumia, Thumos and Logistikon.

Plato and the triple qualities

Epithumia	Corresponds to *Tamas*	❖ A multiplicity of blind appetite or desires which dominates the votaries of sensuous enjoyments, ❖ Aim is the gratification of animal appetite.
Thumos	Corresponds to *Rajas*	❖ Dominates the man of action who works with frenzied zeal for worldly position and power ❖ Grasping and greedy, such a man is always unhappy.
Logistikon	Corresponds to *Sattva*	❖ Represents the rational elements, ❖ Characterizes the philosopher and sage, ❖ Endowed with qualities such as detachment, moderation, purity and harmony.

To the unwise, knowledge of scriptures is a burden;
To one who is full of desires, even wisdom is a burden;
To one who is restless, his own mind is a burden
and to one who has no self-knowledge;
the body (life-span) is a burden.

Yogavāshishta

Rāvana in Rāmāyana *symbolizes quality of Rājas*/passion
Inward thirst, fondness, passion, covetousness, unkindness, love, hatred, deceit, jealousy, vanity, fickleness, unstableness, emulation, greed, patronizing friends, family pride, aversion to disagreeable objects, whispering, prodigality, these are the reslts of the quality of *Rājas*/passion.

Maitrāyana-Brahmya-Upanishad

Kumbhakarna in Rāmāyana symbolizes quality of Tamas/darkness
Bewilderment, fear, grief, sleep, sloth, carelessness, decay, sorrow, hunger, thirst, niggardliness, wrath, infidelity, ignorance, envy, cruelty, folly, shamelessness, meanness, pride changeability, these are the qualities of darkness.

Maitrāyana-Brahmya-Upanishad

Vibhishana in Rāmāyana symbolizes quality of Sattva/knowledge
Poise, purity, intelligence, creation, thought force, self-control, reverence, regard, desire for knowledge and abstinence from wrong-doing.

Maitrāyana-Brahmya-Upanishad

THE TRIPLE QUALITIES

Knowledge, poise and purity
are the qualities called clarity

Restlessness, desire and motivity
are known as the quality of activity

Inactivity, delusion and dullness
are the ones that is called heaviness

Gunas and relationships

Sattva	Expansion	Intelligence	Creation	Thought
Rajas	Activity	Energy	Preservation	Will
Tamas	Obsruction	Mass	Destruction	Feeling

What is the power of *Sattva?* Pure *Sattva* is the power to discriminate. *Sattva* is mixed with the other two qualities much like water of different types, when mixed is indistinguishable. The properties of *Sattva* are self-respect, self-control, reverence, regard, desire for knowledge and abstinence from wrong doing. The other properties are purity, perception of the Self within, tranquillity, contentment, cheerfulness, capability to concentrate mind on a chosen object.

What is the power of *Rājas?* The power of *Rājas* is extension, the power of projection, which is the essence of action, a manifestation of inherent tendencies accumulated from earlier actions. The modifications of mind is known through *Rājas*. Attachment and other qualities are produced by *Rājas*. As also, lust, greed, arrogance, malice, aversion, jealousy, envy etc. *Rājas* is the cause for bondage. Absence of right perception, contradictory thinking, thinking of possibilities, and taking unsubstantiated things for substance, belong to *Rājas*. One associated with *Rājas* is perpetually carried away by its expansive power.

What is the power of *Tamas?* The power of *Tamas* is called *āvritta*, the enveloping force by which one appears as another; it is the force that is the ultimate cause of mistaking of the body as the self. *Tamas* is the cause for *Rājas*. The power of *Tamas* is such that even a very intelligent and educated and skillful person may lose sight of the need to exercise discrimination when enveloped by *tamas*. Such a person would on account of ignorance consider the unreal as real. He gets overpowered by the objects of sight and the properties of objects by error. Often one comes across instances of very learned persons committing unbelievably stupid things! Ignorance, laziness, dullness, sleep, delusion, folly and other allied qualities are attributed to power of *Tamas*.

Do these qualities remain eliminated in the state of absorption?

Yes, mostly. As practice proceeds *Tāmasic* inertia gets significantly reduced, so does *Rājas* the projecting quality which propels one to get constantly entangled in all and sundry matters. Discriminating faculty improves reducing the effect of ignorance. In advanced stages of practice the sloth, dullness, anger, jealousy, lust, greed, aversion etc remain totally eliminated; the individual is engulfed with qualities of purity, tranquillity, cheerfulness, contentment with a taste of eternal bliss.

In the case of *Samādhi* with seed, just one impression, the object of meditation, lingers on. Everything else is obliterated. In the state of *Samādhi* without seed, all impressions vanish and so do all *gunas*.

Science explains the realm relativity.
Spiritual science indicates the reality, without which, there is no relativity.
In the reality there is no relativity.
Recognize the reality as thy own self,
Be happy and free from captivity.

Sattva Guna	Rajo Guna	Tamo Guna
Serene	Vigourous	Sullen
Mental	Vital	Material
Balanced	Dynamic	Inert
Normative	Irascible, Ivate	Indolent
Good	Indifferent	Evil
Lucid	Vivid	Blurred
Equable	Active	Passive
Attractive	Distractive	Repulsive
Centripetal	Convoluted	Centrifugal
Cohesive	Volatile	Diffused
Conscious	Cognitive	Unconscious
Integrated	Integrating	Disintegrated
Intelligent	Un-intelligent	Ignorant
Luminous	Vivacious	Obscure
Neutral	Positive	Negative
Orderly	Organizing	Chaotic
Pervasive	Revolving	Contracting
Quiescent	Boisterous	Benumbed
Rarefied	Expanding	Dense
Resolute	Passionate	Dissolute
Transparent	Translucent	Opaque
Lucidity	Passion	Darkness

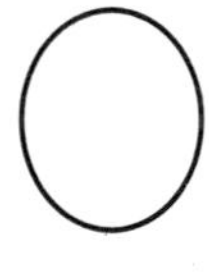

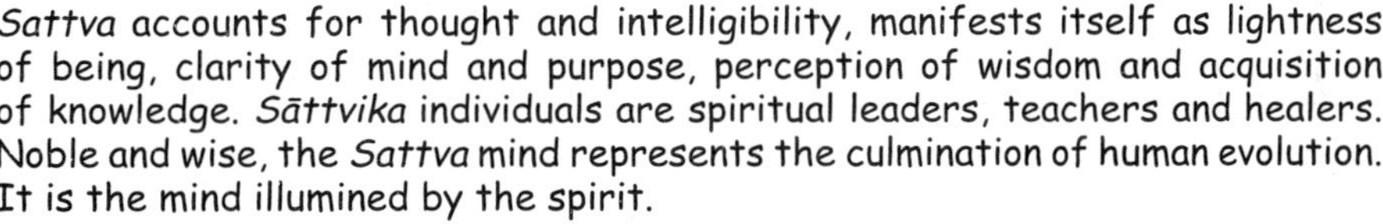

Sattva accounts for thought and intelligibility, manifests itself as lightness of being, clarity of mind and purpose, perception of wisdom and acquisition of knowledge. *Sāttvika* individuals are spiritual leaders, teachers and healers. Noble and wise, the *Sattva* mind represents the culmination of human evolution. It is the mind illumined by the spirit.

Rājas represents motion, energy and activity. Experienced psychologically as suffering, craving and attachment, represents the world of action, movement from the darkness of *Tamas* into the light. But the mind in *Rājas* is easily fooled by illusion, and those suffering from an imbalance of *Rājas* often succumb to ambition, greed, lust, materialism and a desire to control and dominate.

Tamas is the state of mind dominated by density and inertia. An imbalance of *Tamas* causes apathy, lethargy, delusion and drowsiness. In severe instances, these can turn to hate, vindictiveness, addiction, perversion and other forms of self destruction.

"As the *Urnanābhi* (spider) spins out thread out of its own body, even so the whole universe has come out of the Being"

— *Vedas*

In order to be able to understand the triple qualities, it is essential one has a quick look at the Vedāntic idea of creation.

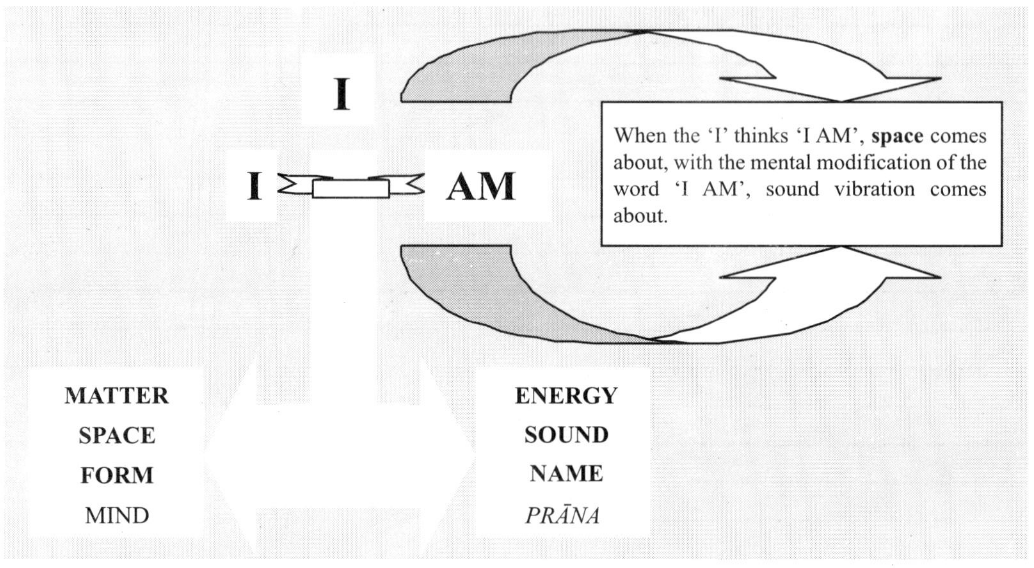

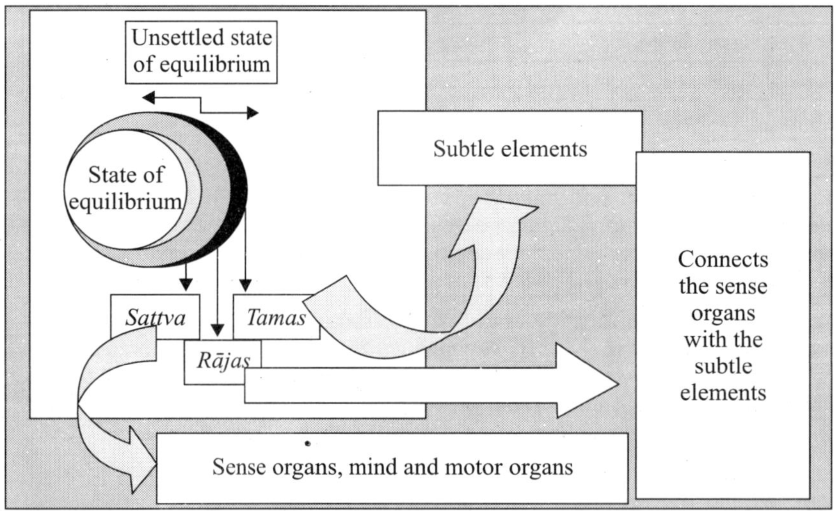

When the 'I' thinks, 'I am', there is disturbance in the state of equilibrium. This disturbance is the cause for 'mind' to spring up. The birth of mind is synonymous with the birth of triple qualities.

The mind can perceive objects only because of the presence of triple qualities in them. If these qualities are withdrawn, there will be no object at all.

Solidity represents the quality of inertia, liquidity represents the quality of activity and gaseousness represents the quality of clarity. The quality of *sattva* is the cause for the mind, sense organs and motor organs; the quality of inertia, the cause for subtle elements (matter) and the quality of activity is the cause for connection between the mind and the matter.

The following diagram illustrates the creation process and the position of triple qualities. *Purusha* represents the latent force of nature, unexpressed and unknowable. Emanating from the Being *(Purusha)* is the Nature *(Prakriti)*. From the desire of the Nature arose *Mahat*, the cosmic intelligence. Arising from *Mahat* is *Ahamkāra*, the force that separates each one into an individualized and incomplete experience of the whole. From *ahamkāra* issues three primordial qualities, the clarity, activity and inertia.

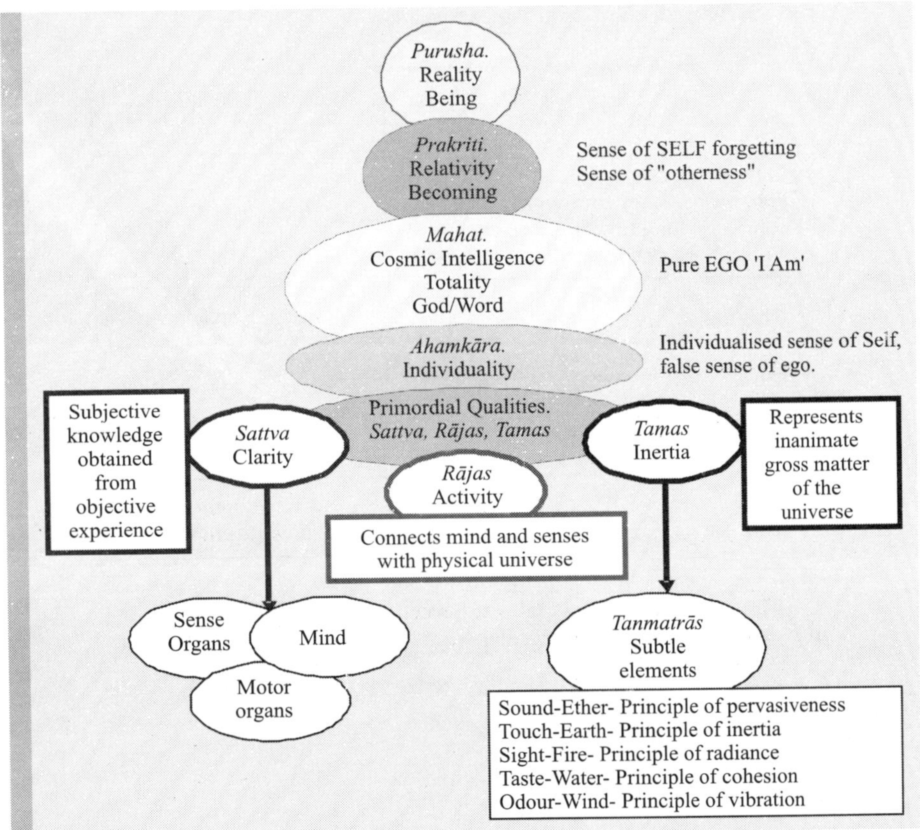

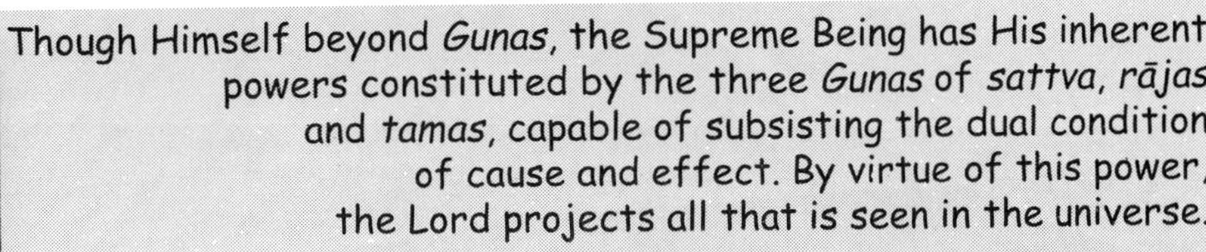

Though Himself beyond *Gunas*, the Supreme Being has His inherent powers constituted by the three *Gunas* of *sattva*, *rājas* and *tamas*, capable of subsisting the dual condition of cause and effect. By virtue of this power, the Lord projects all that is seen in the universe.

Bhāgavata

Aphorism 1.12-1.16

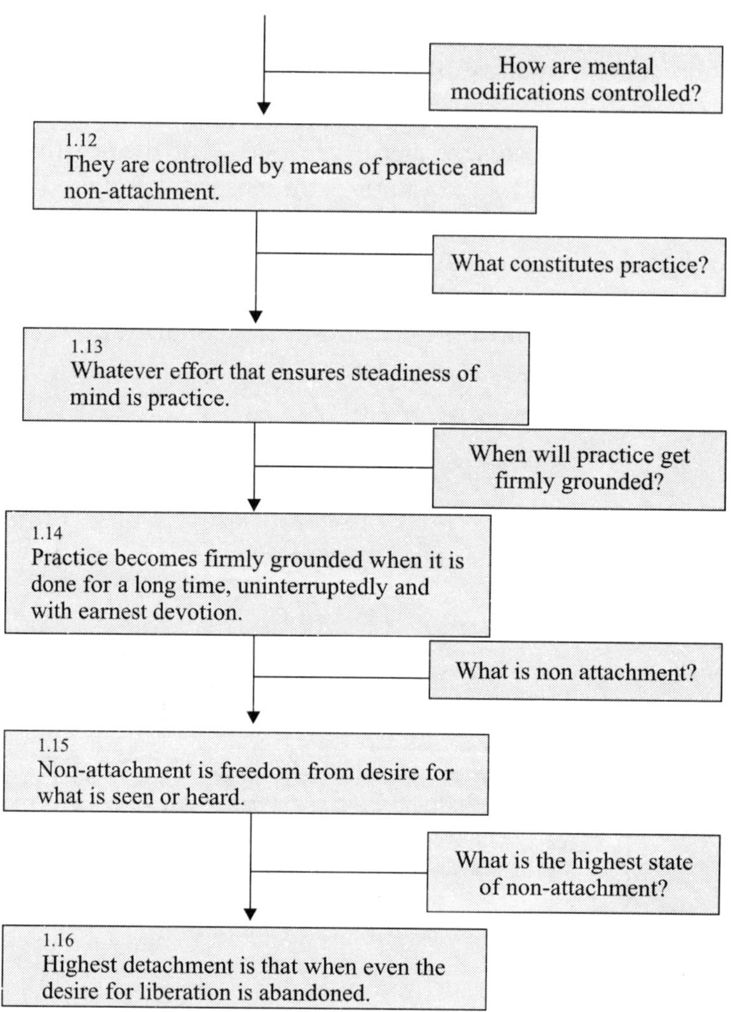

वितर्कविचारानन्दास्मितारूपानुगमात्संप्रज्ञातः ॥१७॥

Vitarka_Vichāra_Ānanda_Asmitā_Rupa_Anugamāt Samprajnātah.

Reasoning, reflection, elation and the ego true
These lead to awareness pure.

Vitarka : analysis, reasoning, inference through questioning
Vichāra : differentiating knowledge, discrimination, reflection, deliberation
Ānanda : bliss, joy *Asmitā* : I-ness, pure ego *Rupa* : form, appearance
Anugamāt : associated with *Sam* : perfect, complete *Prajnātah* : awareness

Q. *What is samprajnāta Samādhi?*
A. *Samprajnāta* is made of sam (derived from *samyak*, meaning, completely or perfectly); *pra* (clearly); and *jña* (to know). Thus the meaning is: knowing clearly and completely. This is liberation with support.

There are four states of awareness that constitute *Samprajnāta Samādhi*:

1. Self-analysis or engrossment in conjecture, inference and analytical study
2. Synthesis, consideration and discrimination
3. Bliss or elation
4. The experience of a state of pure being

Vitarka	• Process of intellectual analysis leading to study of root cause and effect, • Involves the thinking faculty,	Front of the brain ANALYSIS
Vichāra	• Process of investigation, reflection and consideration resulting from calming of the mind, • Involves the thinking faculty,	Back of the brain REASONING
Ànanda	• State of joy caused not by satiation of desires but by absence of desires • Does not involve the thinking faculty,	base of the brain BLISSFUL
Asmitā	• State of dwelling in oneself with the mind and corresponding thinking faculty totally stilled,	Crown of the head THE SELF

If the mind ceases to be, the body ceases to be, too, on account of the cessation of thought-force and mental conditioning, but mind does not cease to be when the body dies. Hence one should strive to kill the mind.

Yogavāshishta

Ego	*Ahamkāra* The Wrong sense of "I"	I am the doer.
	Asmitā The right sense of "I"	I am the witness.

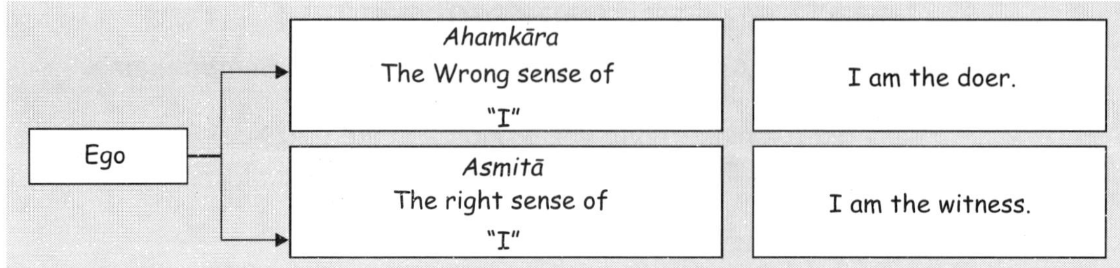

Tarka	*Kutarka* Wrong reasoning	Convoluted logic, perverted mind Fault finding, Negative connotation Counts horns in the rose Ego in action, and Stupidity in full flow
	tarka reasoning	Crowded thoughts Reasoning without a goal, Counts horns sometimes, and petals Sometimes Intelligence in action
	vitarka Right reasoning	Reflection, Focused thinking Thinker is aware of the thought Focused on the total beauty of the rose Intuition in action
Vichāra		Right reasoning leads to *Vichāra* ← Reflection
Ānanda		Reflection leads to an experience of *ānanda*- Bliss, but a temporary one.
Asmitā		Bliss leads to feeling of ONESELF- ONENESS.

The one, who has not thought it out has the thought of it.
The one who has thought it out does not know it.
It is not understood by those who understand it.
It is understood by those who do not understand it.
Kena Upanishad

विरामप्रत्ययाभ्यासपूर्वः संस्कार शेषोऽन्यः ॥१८॥

Virāma_Pratyaya_Abhyāsa_Purvah Sanskāra_Shesho_Anyah.

Practice with no break
Removes all impressions without trace.

Virāma : stoppage, cessation *Pratyaya* : constant *Abhyāsa* : repeated sincere practice
Purvah : previous *Sanskāra* : recollections, impressions
Shesho : remaining, traces, remnants *Anyah* : that which is different from

Q. *What is other form of concentration?*

A. The other form of concentration is that in which the consciousness contains no object. It contains only subconscious impressions, which are like burnt seeds. It is attained by constantly checking the thought waves through the practice of non-attachment.

Sampajnāta Samāhi	❖ Fixing one's thought on an object or an idea ❖ Absorption with support ❖ Is attained with the help of an object or an idea
Asampajnāta Samādhi	❖ This state is independent of the support of concentration ❖ Absorption without support ❖ Beyond all modes of the memory ❖ A state where there is nothing to be known

Samprajnāta samādhi is the result of constant reasoning of discrimination. That which is different from *Samprajnāta Samādhi* namely *A-samprajnāta Samādhi* a state where there is nothing to be known. This state is independent of the support of concentration – beyond all modes of the memory. The state of *asamprajnāta*, the experience of one's own nature – is described as the state of *sat-chit-ānanda*, existence, consciousness and bliss. The consciousness contains no object. It contains only subconscious impressions, which are like burnt seeds. It is attained by constantly checking the thought waves through the practice of non-attachment while the 4 stages of concentration described in the earlier *sutra* is with object, the state described herein is without an object. This state has only been experienced by saints. Since the faculties of logic and reasoning are absent in this state, those who have attained this state have said that this state is indescribable. This state is beyond all modes of memory.

"When the heart is full, tongue is silent;
when the mind is still, intuition functions;
when the passions are quelled, devotion dawns;
when the senses are controlled, soul force is obtained;
when the intellect is silent God speaks;
when the 'I' dies, 'He' shines as Radiant Reality."
Swāmi Shivānanda

भवप्रत्ययो विदेहप्रकृतिलयानाम् ॥१९॥

Bhava_Pratyayo Videha_Prakriti_Layanām.

Becoming aware, the disembodied
In own nature abides.

Bhava : Becoming, arising spontaneously *Layanām* : involved, absorbed
Pratyayo : knowing the cause of ignorance, cognition *Prakriti* : own nature
Videha : one who is free from identity with own physical body, disembodied

Q. *Who experiences liberation?*
A. 1. *Videha*, one who is devoid of body consciousness and
2. *Prakritilaya*, one who has complete self-control and absorbed in own nature.

One who has eliminated one's own identity with the physical body is said to have attained the blissful state of *samprajnāta Samādhi*. They become free from body consciousness. Those who have given up identity with the body and have dissolved their own nature, with the knowledge of the world, enter the state of *samādhi*. In two ways, *asamprajnāta samādhi* might arise:

Bhava- pratyaya

- The state of *asamprajnāta samādhi* or the awareness that arises spontaneously
- Spontaneous knowing of the cause of ignorance

Upaya- pratyaya

- The state of *asamprajnāta samādhi* that is attained as a result of following certain methods or means (practice of *Kriyā Yoga*)
- Systematic and methodic elimination of causes of ignorance

Pratyaya is the secondary condition or conditions pre-existing allowing primary causes to function. In the case of the first, the primary is *Bhava*- spontaneous, and in the second case the primary is means or methods. The following are the generally accepted four-part breakdown of *Pratyayas*:

(1) *Ālambana Pratyaya* relates to the objects, which are the causes of the cognitions in which, in the absence of those objects, is can not come into being.

(2) *Samānatara Pratyaya* is a cognition that enables the succeeding cognition to receive the form of the external objects.

(3) *Sahakāri Pratyaya* refers to light etc. which are responsible in making the cognition distinct with regard to its object. The absence of light disables a person from having a clear apprehension of an object placed in the darkness. Therefore, light is *sahakāri* (assistive).

(4) *Adhipati Pratyaya* refers to the sense organs. It is the sense organs that make the objects present their forms to the cognition in the succeeding moment.

According to Vāchaspati Mishra:

Prakritilaya Purusha	Those who remain in any of the elements like *prakriti, mahat, ahamkāra* and *tanmātrās* after the dissolution of their mortal frames are called *Prakritilaya purusha.*
Videhalaya purusha	Those who attain *samprajnāta* Yoga and remain absorbed in them even after the dissolution of their physical bodies are called *videhalaya purusha.*

These relative states of absorption are not in anyway comparable to the absorption with the Ultimate Being.

The body consciousness in the illumined is totally absent. In the recent past, there lived a Saint in South India named Sadāshiva Brahmendra, who was totally devoid of body consciousness. Regarding his time there is not enough evidence. It has to be some period of time between the middle of the sixteenth century and the middle of the eighteenth century.

There is an interesting incident reported involving the Saint Sadāshiva Brahmendra. Since he was devoid of body consciousness, at times he was not even aware that he is moving around naked. As a realized soul who sees nothing but Brahman everywhere, he would not distinguish between the different human figures who crossed his path nor would he be distracted by the sights or noises that his environment may present to him. It was in this state of trance, once he was walking along. He, the naked *sannyāsi*, walked straight into the harem, entering it at one end and walking out at the other all the while walking through a maze of inmates of the *Nawāb's* harem. The news reached the nawab, he had his men chase him, cut off both his hands as he was walking along, the hands fell off and ... still he was walking along silently as if nothing had happened. The *Nawāb's* men went with this news of the Saint and showed him the severed hands. The *Nawāb* was greatly astonished at this strange condition of the sage. He thought that this Saint must indeed be God. He repented much and followed the sage to apologize. Sadāshiva Brahmendra never knew that his arms were cut off. When the *Nawāb* narrated to the sage what had happened in the camp and handed over both the hands that were severed, the Saint simply touched his maimed arms. He had a fresh arm! Thereafter the Muslim chieftain gave up his violent ways and became a disciple of the Saint.

Mortal in the body, held by death,-----it is the abode of that immortal (unbodied) self. The bodied one is held by pleasure and pain.....but pleasure and pain do not touch the unbodied self.

Chhāndogya Upanishad

श्रद्धावीर्यस्मृतिसमाधिप्रज्ञापूर्वकः इतरेषाम्॥२०॥

Shraddhā_Virya_Smriti_Samādhi Pragyā Purvakah Itreshām.

Faith, Vitality, Memory, Absorption and Illumination
These then are the requisites for self-realisation.

Shraddhā : faith, trust,devotion
Virya : energy, vitality
Smriti: memory, recollectedness
Samādhi : absorption, concentration
Pragyā : illumination, contemplative knowledge, wisdom
Purvakah : prerequisite, preceding
Itareshām : others

Q. *What are the prerequisites for achieving self-realisation?*
A. 1. Faith 2. Vitality 3. Memory 4. Concentration 5. Contemplative knowledge are the prerequisites for achieving self-realisation.

Prerequisites for achieving self-realization are:

1. **Faith:** Having chosen the yogic way, one should cast aside all doubts and be firm in his conviction that the path chosen will lead one to spiritual salvation. The concept of faith is well illustrated by Robert Murray M'cleyne who wrote:

"My hope is built on nothing less
Than Jesus' blood and righteousness
I dare not trust the sweetest frame
But wholly lean on Jesus' name
On Christ the solid rock I stand
All other ground is sinking sand."

- Faith is the head chemist of the mind.
- Faith is the eternal elixir which gives life, power and action to the impulse of the thought.
- Faith is the only known antidote for failure.
- Faith is the element, the 'chemical' when mixed with prayer, gives one direct communication with the 'Infinite Intelligence'.
- Faith is the element which transforms the ordinary vibration of thought created by the finite mind of man to extraordinary equation with cosmic intelligence.
- Faith is the natural inclination of man to turn towards his source.

If you have faith no bigger than a mustard seed, you will say this to the mountain: Move from here to there. And it will move; Nothing will prove impossible by you.

Jesus Christ

What is faith?

A conversation amongst the great Sufi Saints:

Hasan	:	Having faith means being patient when God inflicts suffering.
Rabi'a	:	That stinks of egoism.
Shaqiq	:	Having faith means being grateful to God for the suffering he has inflicted.
Rabi'a	:	We need a better definition.
Malik	:	Having faith means seeking delight in the suffering inflicted by God.
Rabi'a	:	We need some better definition than this.
All	:	Now you speak
Rabi'a	:	Having faith means having such a clear vision of the Master that one is oblivious to the suffering he inflicts.

2. **Vitality:** Vitality is the strength that arises from out of faith and the purity of the senses, control over the mind, elevating outlook, and forbearance of all pain and suffering. Vitality arises out of conviction. Vitality is when one can say "I can".
3. **Memory:** Memory is to have constant remembrance of the goal-elimination of mental modification and attaining *Samādhi*. One should note that memory here is to mean remembering the ultimate goal and constantly reinforcing the will to achieve the goal of overcoming impediments and ignoring other attractions on the way. Memory is not to be mistaken as keeping in memory day-to-day events. For the devotee, memory is that faculty which recalls his true nature as made in the image of God.
4. ***Samādhi*:** Samādhi is the state of mind concentrated and absorbed in an object or objective. The seeker should be all the time absorbed in the goal of achieving oneness with reality. *Samādhi* is the temporary state of avoidance of mental modification.
5. **Contemplative knowledge:** Contemplative knowledge is one's own experience attained through deep meditation, devoid of imagination, hallucination, etc. Contemplative knowledge slowly replaces information gained through teachings and books. Contemplative knowledge becomes the guide. Contemplative knowledge is attained on removal of misconceptions and misapprehension. This knowledge is the result of elimination process, elimination of attachment and aversion. The scriptural and bookish knowledge on the other hand is a result of acquisition process, resulting from memorization.

Even the inhabitants of the highest heaven are subject to the laws of rebirth and reincarnation. He alone is free from birth and rebirth, who transcends all phenomena, who after knowing the absolute truth and after realizing the Supreme Spirit, becomes one with Divinity.

Bhagavadgitā

Spider to the rescue

It was a time of terror and confusion. Persia had been invaded and Zoroastrians were being put to sword. A few important resistant fighters had eluded capture. Weary and half starved they moved from one hiding place to another. Finally they came to the base of a tall mountain. They knew they could not scale it in their weakened state and they prepared to make their last stand there. Suddenly one of them spotted a little cave, way up the face of the mountain.

Summoning the last reserves of their strength they made their way to it, and entering fell exhausted on the floor. Hardly had they recovered their breath, they heard the enemy soldiers riding up the mountains. The men in the cave felt their end was nearer. They were trapped.

All that they could do was to pray, and that is what they began to do, silently but fervently. Their faith in God was strong. And then an amazing thing happened. A spider appeared at the mouth of the cave and began to spin a web. Within seconds it had spun a web so big it covered the entire entrance of the cave.

The enemy soldiers saw the cave and prepared to climb up to it. Their leader saw the spider's web stung across the entrance. He said, "the spider's web is intact. That means no one has entered the cave. Let us not waste time here!" The soldiers rode away, to the great joy of the fugitives. They thanked God, convinced that he had heeded their prayers. They were convinced that God listened to their prayers and sent the spider to help them out.

Desire, deliberation, doubt, faith, want of faith, steadiness, unsteadiness, shame, fame, intelligence, fear – all these are but the mind.

Kena Upanishad

तीव्रसंवेगानामासन्नः॥२१॥

Tivra_Samvegānām_Āsannah.

Those of intense will
Remain still.

Tivra : intense, extreme
Vegānām : quick speed, zeal,
Sam : total, good
Āsannah : about to happen, close to happening

Q. *When is spiritual progress possible?*
A. Spiritual progress is possible for those who are intensely energetic, totally committed and who earnestly aspire for knowledge.

Samvega is derived from *Sam* meaning 'together' and *Vij* meaning 'to move quickly'. The word *Samvega* in this context could be interpreted to mean moving quickly towards liberation. The intense dispassion is not a negative running away from the object world, but a positive passion for the subject-object union. *Samvegam* could also be interpreted to mean good propensities or tendencies. Depending upon the effort put in, in the previous birth, the tendency to work towards spiritual salvation could be strong. Those, like Ramana Maharshi, needed no new inputs like effort or faith and yet could attain *Samādhi* effortlessly. The seeker should note that effort put in by him even if it does not lead him to *Samādhi* now will definitely propel him in this direction in future. It is like a bank account. The balance will be carried forward in the next birth. There is no wasted effort in the spiritual field. The Bhagavadgitā says: "*The Yogi whose mind is perfectly tranquil, whose passions are subdued, who is sinless and has become Brahman, attains supreme bliss.*" How intense should the practice be? The desire must be strong and abiding, in order that it may bear fruit. The efforts are in proportion to the intensity and duration of the desire. Intense will, will bring results. It is difficult to answer this question of how serious is considered a serious enough effort. Intensity will not, cannot and should not be measured in terms of number of hours of meditation or the degree of self inflicted injuries in the name of sacrifices. The intensity should be understood as intensity of desire for realization, a desire to know. Then, the inner light will throw enough light on the tendencies, impulses and propensities hidden in the individual that come in the way of knowing. The very awareness of obstacles will slow the momentum of the obstacles. This slowing down is the beginning of detachment to desires and an attachment to Self.

Just as a man scalded by fire runs immediately to in search of soothing medicines and does not waste time in other pursuits, so also must the aspirant run after emancipation to the exclusion of other pursuits. Such an effort is fruitful and is preceded by indifference to all other attainments."

Dattātreya to Parashurāma

How long is long enough?

There was a great Devarishi, called Nārada. Just as there are sages among mankind and great Yogis, so are there great Yogis among the gods. Nārada was a good Yogi, and very great. He travelled everywhere. One day he was passing through a forest, and saw a man who had been meditating until the white ants had built a huge mound round his body, so long had he been sitting in that position. He said to Nārada, "Where are you going?" Nārada replied, "I am going to heaven."

"Then ask God when He will be merciful to me; when I shall attain freedom." Further on Nārada saw another man. He was jumping about, singing, dancing, and said, "Oh, Nārada, where are you going?" His voice and his gestures were wild.

Nārada said,"I am going to heaven."

"Then, ask when I shall be free." Nārada went on.

In the course of time he came again by the same road, and there was the man who had been meditating with the ant-hill round him. He said, "Oh, Nārada, did you ask the Lord about me?" "Oh, yes." "What did He say?"

"The Lord told me that you would attain freedom in four more births." Then the man began to weep and wail, and said, "I have meditated until an ant-hill has grown around me, and I have four more births yet!"

Nārada went to the other man. "Did you ask my question?"

"Oh, yes. Do you see this tamarind tree? I have to tell you that as many leaves as there are on that tree, so many times, you shall be born, and then you shall attain freedom."

The man began to dance with joy, and said, "I shall have freedom after such a short time!" A voice came, "My child, you will have freedom this minute." That was the reward for his perseverance. He was ready to work through all those births, nothing discouraged him. But the first man felt that even four more births were too long.

Only perseverance, like that of the man who was willing to wait eons brings about the highest result.

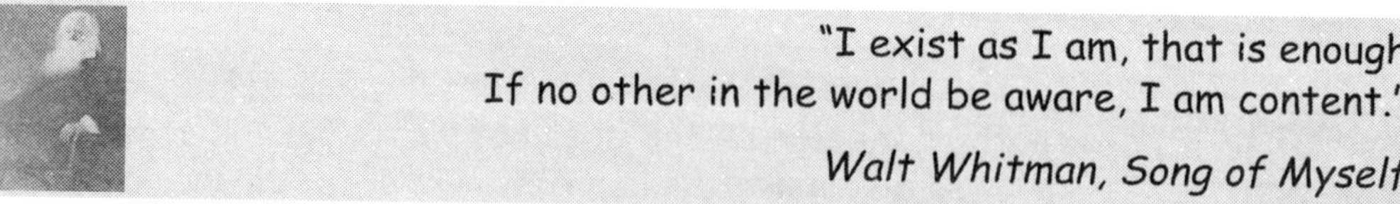

Asanga's aspiration

Asanga is a famous Buddhist who lived in ancient India. He wanted to have a vision of Lord Buddha. He meditated and meditated for six long years undergoing all kinds of hardships on a mountain called Kukkutapāda. Yet he could not have even one auspicious dream. Dispirited, disheartened and dejected, he decided to discontinue meditation. He abandoned his retreat and left his hermitage.

As he got down the hill slopes and hit the plains he saw a man rubbing an enormous iron bar with a silk strip. Curious at the strange sight, Asanga approached him and asked him, "What are you doing?"

He got a response, "I haven't got a needle. I am making one out of this iron bar." Astounded Asanga turned back to his hermitage, wondering whether he has even a small percentage of dedication and faith that the man who wanted to make a needle had.

Disappointed after another three years, he again made ready to leave but one day, while taking a walk outside his cave, Asanga noticed some birds landing on a nearby overhanging rock. Where the birds' wings brushed the rock as they landed, Asanga noticed a deep crevice that had worn in the rock. Asanga reflected on the countless years it must have taken for the soft brushing of birds' wings to make such a deep indentation. He decided to continue meditation. But yet did not succeed in having an auspicious dream. Attempt after attempt, even after twenty long years, he could not succeed.

Heavy-hearted, he made his way towards the city of Achintya, where he saw a dog which had only its front legs in good condition. Dragging its body on the front leg the poor creature was moving around. Asanga saw that the dog was infested with worms. Overcome with compassion, Asanga cut a piece of flesh from his own body and gave it to the dog. Thereafter he wanted to rid the dog of the worms and yet did not want to pluck the worms for that would definitely kill them. He started licking the worms out of the dog's body.

No sooner had he started licking than the dog vanished and in its place stood Maitreya, Lord Buddha, resplendent in a halo of divine grace. Asanga could not contain himself. Overcome with emotion, Asanga spoke to Champa: "For so many years and in so many ways I have tried to see you. Why now - now that my thirst is gone, do you appear before me?" Champa replied: "It is only now, through your great act of compassion, that your mind is pure and therefore able to see me. In truth I have been here all the time."

Then Champa instructed Asanga to carry him on his back into the city so that other people might see him. This Asanga did, but the people, their minds clouded by impure thoughts, could not see Champa, and they thought Asanga was mad when he cried that he had Champa on his back. One old woman who looked and saw a puppy on Asanga's back was immediately endowed with riches. A poor porter caught a glimpse of Champa's toes, and from that moment onwards attained power and tranquillity of mind. Champa then took Asanga to the Tushita heaven, and there he was able to receive the teaching and gain the insight that had eluded him for so many years.

मृदुमध्याधिमात्रत्वात्ततोऽपि विशेषः॥२२॥

Mridu_Madhya_Adhimātra_Tvāt Tato_Api Visheshah.

Success on the means depends
Mild, medium or intense.

Mridu : gentle *Madhya* : medium *Adhi mātra* : extreme, intense
Tvāt : therefore *Tato* : from that *Api* : also *Visheshah* : speciality, distinct

Q. *On what does spiritual success depend?*
A. The success depends on the effort – be they mild, medium or intense.

The practice effort could be classified as mild, medium and intense. The seeker should know that Yoga practice is not a situation of 'Union or None'. It is not as if, the state of absorption, called *Samādhi*, is not attained, all efforts are wasted. There are various levels of realization / emancipation that the seeker can recognize as practice proceeds. Undoubtedly, the more sincere the effort, the more quicker the reward.

As practice proceeds, the seeker can recognize that his perception has improved, judgement is better and he tends to take a more dispassionate view of things. These initial beneficial results could propel him to intensify his efforts. The effort graduates from being mild to medium; and the reward even more significant, with one realizing that there is a greater sense of happiness not externally caused and a greater felling of inner joy. This taste of nectar propels him to increase his effort from medium to intense.

The word 'effort' does not really convey well. In many instances what is observed is a longing not to be separated from truth or not in the least wanting to be away from the state of awareness or supreme consciousness.

More important than the effort to progress is the needed effort not to slide down from progress already achieved. Caution should be exercised to make sure that there is no going back to the old ways.

Among thousands of people, rarely some one tries to attain perfection (*yoga siddhi*). Among uncountable seekers someone might know Me in reality; i. e. attains the state of perfection.

Bhagavadgitā 7:3

ईश्वरप्रणिधानाद्वा॥२३॥

Ishvara_Pranidhānād_Vā.

Or union may be had
By surrender to God.

Ishvara : God	*Pra* : completely	*Ni* : without
Dha : to behold	*Anād* : fulfilment	*Vā* : otherwise, or

Q. *Is there no option but to practise intensely?*
A. There is. In addition to practice, also be devoted to God.

Patanjali introduces the concept of God for the first time in his Yoga Sutras and advises to surrender to God completely; heart and soul. The *Rāja* Yoga path to which Patanjali subscribes to and outlines a step by step method of realisation, can be difficult for many. The Yoga of devotion can be supplementary and complimentary to the Yoga of action. As a path of surrender, *isvara pranidhāna* is a non-practice practice as it is non-wilful: as in "thy will be done on earth as it is in heaven".
"Thy will, in earth, in heaven."
Intense effort, determination, perseverance, tenacity .... The qualities needed seem to be daunting? Don't despair, says Patanjali; just surrender to God. This spirit of devotion is very well expressed in Francis Ridley Havergal's well-known hymn, beginning:

"Take my life and let it be
Consecrated, lord, to Thee."

A mild practice with greater devotion to God could be more helpful, when intense practice is not feasible for whatever reason. But when it comes to devotion, there can be nothing like mild devotion to God. Intense devotion to God means remembering Him all the time and dedicating all actions to Him. Automatically, such a devotee finds less distraction of his senses to the object world. This in turn means less modification of the mind.

"God, I know, you and I are one;
Still I like to keep separate from you;
To enjoy the attraction between You and I."

Nārada Bhakti Sutra

Summary: Aphorism 1.17-1.23

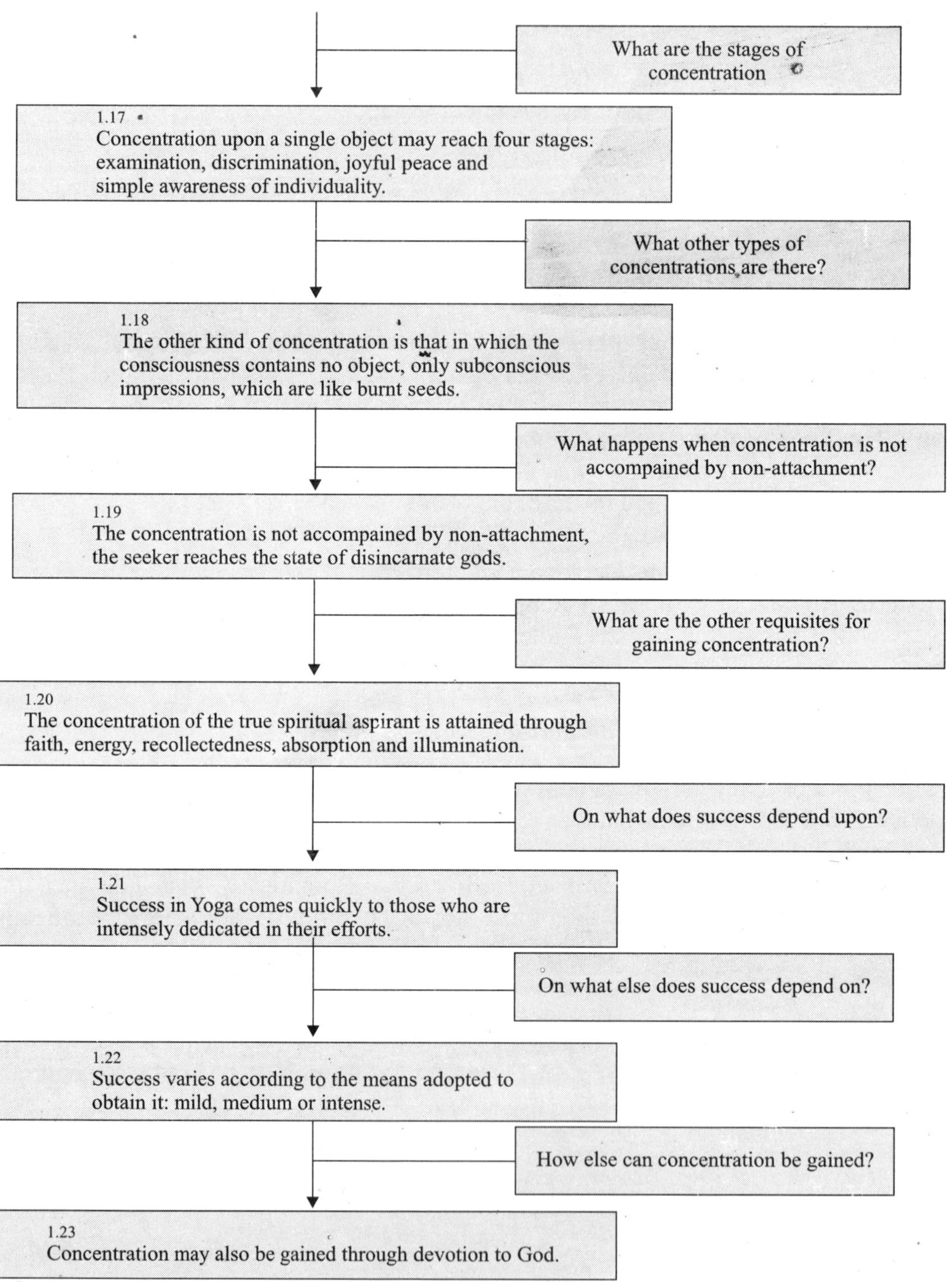

क्लेशकर्मविपाकाशयैरपरामृष्टः पुरुषविशेष ईश्वरः॥२४॥

Klesha_Karma_Vipāka_ Āshayaih Aparāmrishtah

PurushaVishesha Ishvarah.

God is a special person
Beyond affliction or action.

Klesha : afflictions, painful, colored *Karma* : action *Vipāka* : fruit of action
Āshayaih : attachment *Aparāmrishtah* : untouched, untainted, beyond
Purusha : person, *Vishesha* : special, distinct *Ishvarah* : God

Q. *Who is God?*
A. God is a special person beyond afflictions or actions.

The English word God has its roots in the Indo-Germanic term guđan. The earliest written form of the Germanic word god comes from the 6th century Christian Codex Argenteus. Most linguists agree that the reconstructed Proto-Indo-European form *ǵhu-tó-m* was based on the root *ǵhau(∂)-*, which meant either 'to call' or 'to invoke'. So, God is the one who is invoked.

Quantum theory says every particle of the universe has intelligence and each particle of intelligence is indestructible, and has existed from eternity. Intelligence is the same as light and truth. The simplest interpretation is that a basic 'intelligence' is a basic unit of matter/energy – the photon. God or Iswara can thus be surmised as Universal Intelligence pervading each and every photon. There is some support in Quantum Theory for the idea that consciousness is the key to understanding fundamental physics and 'an observer' is needed to 'collapse the wave function' in quantum states. The role of the observer is the basis for almost all modern metaphysics... *Iswara* is the Observer, untouched by afflictions or actions:

God is all knowing. God seeks not, wants not and aims not. God is the causeless cause, the unmoved mover. The *Nyāya* system defines God as the first-efficient cause and not its material cause. While the *Sānkhya* system accepts only the soul and nature as realities and does not accept God. Since Yoga accepts all principles of *Sānkhya* and also accepts God, it is called *Sānkhya* with Iswara (*Sānkhya* with God) The *Uapanishads* say that God cannot be described as the knower, as there is no object outside *It* that *It* can know; God cannot be described as a creator because *It* has no desire; God cannot be described as thinker because *It* has no mind. God is a term applied to what truly Is, the Ultimate Existence.

God defined
Is God defiled.

J. Krishnamurthy

God is the screen

God is like the cinema screen. The screen carries the ocean, but is not drenched by it. It has volcano, but is not burnt by it. It supports rape and murder and loot but is unaffected by them. All characters, the Hero and Heroine, the villain and comedian play their part on the screen and vanish, the screen remaining unaffected. Without the screen there is no play. But the screen has no role to play than being a substratum. So is God. Without God there can be no play, no ocean, no mountain and no mice either. But God has nothing to do with them.

KENA UPANISHAD

That which is not expressed by speech,
but that by which speech is expressed:
know that to be God, not what people here adore.

That which is not thought by the mind,
but that by which the mind thinks:
know that to be God, not what people here adore.

That which is not seen by the eye,
but that by which the eye sees:
know that to be God, not what people here adore.

That which is not heard by the ear,
but that by which the ear hears:
know that to be God, not what people here adore.

That which is not breathed by the breath,
but that by which the breath breathes:
know that to be God, not what people here adore.

It is always difficult to describe God. The disciple asks Guru in the Kena Upanishad: What is it that makes the eyes see, the ears hear, the tongue taste. The teacher first says it is the tongue of the tongue, the eye of the eye etc. At the first sight the answer sounds absurd. After explaining to the student, the teacher says that if the student says he has understood, then he has not understood. If the student says he has not understood, says the teacher, the student has begun to understand. On introspection the student realises that the mind cannot describe that, as that is the very cause for the mind to think, the eye to see etc. Asking mind to describe the Brahman that makes mind function is like asking the bulb to describe electricity.

Concept of Karma: God is untouched by action or inaction. The concept of *karma* as also the concept of *Gunas* / attributes, are very important pillars of Indian spiritual thoughts. *Karma* can be split as *Kar* and *ma*; *Kar* referring to action and *Ma* referring to mind. *Karma* therefore, refers to action involving mind; that is to say actions with expectations. Actions performed surrendering all actions and the result there of, say to God, are not Karmas, they do not bind. They do not result in the formation of impressions and tendencies as there is no anticipation in such actions.

An intelligent mind concludes that God is present;
A sensitive imagination believes that God is present;
A mystical soul sees the presence of God.

Ibn Arabic: Fasal al-hikamb

Any physical or mental action is *Karma*. Thinking is mental *Karma*. *Karma* is the sum total of our acts, both in the present life and in the preceding births. *Karma* means not only action, but also the result of an action. There is a hidden power in *Karma* or action termed '*Adrishta*' which brings in fruits of *Karmas* for the individual. The consequence of an action is really not a separate thing. It is a part of the action and cannot be separated from it.

Karma does not cling to God. The idea implied is that even though a man of knowledge may perform work during his whole life, work does not become a cause of blemish, owing to the presence of his knowledge. Lord Krishna exemplifies this inaction in action.

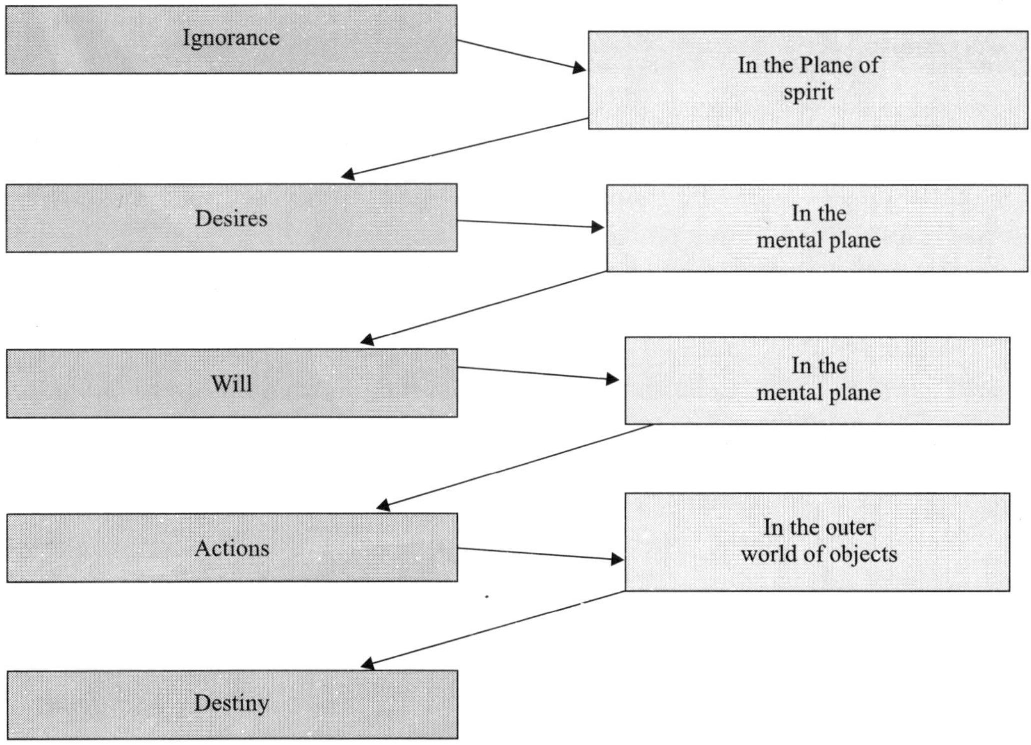

"You are what your deep driving desire is.
As your desire is, so is your will.
As your will is, so is your deed.
As your deed is, so is your destiny"

Brihadāranyaka Upanishad IV 4.5

Karma, past actions bear fruit only when we have a feeling of my-ness in our bodies. It is never desirable to have the feeling of my-self for the body. Thus by giving up the feeling of myself for the body, one gives up the fruits of past actions

Adhyātma Upanishad

तंत्र निरतिशयं सर्वज्ञबीजम् ॥२५॥

Tatra Niratishayam Sarvagya_Bijam.

In God, the germ of all knowledge
Is forever lodged.

Tatra : there, in God
Niratishayam : culmination
Sarvagya : all knowing
Bijam : seed, cause

Q: *What is He like?*
A: In God is the germ of all knowledge for ever lodged. The seed of Omniscience is forever present in God.

God is reality, Man, relativity.

One of the way God could be described as is that He is all knowing, the fountain head of knowledge. God is the source of all knowledge, the very seed of knowledge. Since knowledge flows from Him, He is verily described as the teacher of all teachers. That all knowing God is embedded in every being, hence every one is inherently knowledgeable. One can also put it differently and say "God only knows". He knows all 'That Is' and helps every being know what needs to be known.

Whenever one says 'I know' he should realize that there is an entity in him that makes him say so. That entity is part of the all knowing God. It is God, the Infinite that defines man the Finite. If there is no Infinite, there is no finite.

But that knowledge in beings is covered by layers of ignorance. Hence what is needed is a teacher and a technology that enables one to remove these layers of ignorance. One is therefore, advised to seek the help of a teacher: a God without to know the God within.

Everything that is born is limited to time and space. Being conditioned by time and space, this objective world is finite and perishable, i.e. prone to decay and death. God is one, infinite, formless, absolute, all pervading and the source of immortality. God is beyond the play of nature, the supreme abode of all.

If your lips would keep from slips
Five things observe with care;
Of what you speak, to whom you speak
and how and when and where.

पूर्वेषामपि गुरुः कालेनानवच्छेदात् ॥२६॥

Poorveshām_Api Guruh Kālena_Anavacchedāta.

God is the first teacher in line
Untouched by time.

Poorveshām Api : even of the earliest, those who *Guruh* : preceptor, master, teacher
Kālena : by time *Anavachhedāt* : not limited by, without break

Q: *How can we describe God?*
A: GOD is the first teacher in line (from past till now), untouched by time.

God can variously be defined as:

- God is the proper name of the one Supreme and Infinite Personal Being, the Creator and Ruler of the universe, to whom man owes obedience and worship;
- God is the common or generic name of the several supposed beings to whom, in polytheistic religions, Divine attributes are ascribed and Divine worship rendered;
- God is the name sometimes applied to an idol as the image or dwelling-place of a god.

Patanjali's definition of God is "God is the first teacher in line (from past till now) untouched by time. How did the first person know? How did the Vedic seers know? Who gave them enlightenment? Who revealed? These are natural questions. The logical answer is God. How does it help if one accepts God as the fountainhead of all knowledge? The seeker by accepting Him, surrenders to Him and beseeches Him to merge the seeker back in Him. 'Thine Will, Not Mine' is not a mere attractive phrase. It is pregnant with meaning. The moment one says it is His will, he should understand the futility of seeking to know without His aid and help. The very limitation of body, mind unit with which man identifies himself, will keep him away from Reality. It is only surrender, which is nothing but a process of letting individual ego drop and allowing light from inside and outside glow within and without to illuminate him. That enables one to know the reality. Experience shows. Examples are abundant. God is beyond earthly time, space constraints. Since He is the Knower , the to be Known and the un-afflicted special person who imparts the faculty of the process of knowing. In the process of knowing He can be regarded as the first teacher, teacher of all teachers.; the source of all knowledge.

A passing desire
brings no abiding result.

तस्य वाचकः प्रणवः ॥२७॥
Tasya Vāchakah Pranavah.

His indicator is Pranava.

Tasya : His *Vāchakah* : Verbal indicator *Pranavah* : Sacred symbol AUM

Q: *How can we refer to God?*
A: God can be referred to with the word AUM. It is the sound by which he is distinguished. It is *pranava*.

The first and most effective means which Patanjali prescribed for overcoming the distracted condition of the mind is the *japa* and meditation of the *Pranava*. He calls the *Pranava* the *vāchaka* of Ishwara. A *vāchaka* is a name which has a mystic relationship with the *vāchya*–the entity designated, and has inherent in it the power of revealing the consciousness and releasing the power of the individual for whom it stands. Such a *vāchaka* is Om. It is considered to be the most mystical, sacred and powerful mantra by the Hindus because it is the *vāchaka* of Ishwara, the Greatest Power and the Supreme Consciousness. *Pranava* is a name used for the syllable Om. For example, one might say, "I recited the *pranava* a thousand times," meaning he recited 'Om' a thousand times. *Pranava* means 'pronouncing' or 'humming.' in Sanskrit. The word consists of the prefix *pra* (a cognate of the Latin prefix pro) and the root *nu* meaning 'call out' and 'exult'. *Pranava* is the sound that people hear internally after they practise yoga for a while. *Pranava* is 'that by which God is effectively praised'.

Ādi Shankara states: "How should one perform devotion to the Lord, and what is the means of that devotion? To explain the form in which the devotee contemplates on Him, the sutra says: 'His designator [*vāchaka*] is the *Pranava* [AUM].' Of the Lord Who has been described, the designating word is *Pranava*. ...The word *Pranava* is explained in the following way etymologically: *pra* stands for *prakarshena*: 'perfectly;' *nu* (from *nava*) means *nuyate*: 'He is praised.' Thus *Pranava*, the word Om, praises (*pranauti*) the Lord. That is, the Lord is devoutly worshipped (*pranidhiyate*) through it by His devotees. They bow down (*pranām*) to Him through it. Through it they worship (*pranidhān*) the Lord mentally; here the extra *dha* stands for the final [syllable] *va* of *Pranava*. ...From the termination *ava* is understood *avati*: 'He favours.' He brings out His devotees from *samsāra*, He leads those in *samsāra* to *nirvāna*, He brings to a devotee unsurpassed joy, He grants him *samādhi* to lead him to the highest truth. But all these meanings are associated with the most intense love of the Lord. ...When the Lord is continuously worshipped in the mind by means of this syllable, Om, He gives His grace. ...Through Om the Lord is met face to face." (Commentary on the Yoga Sutras)

"There are two ways of contemplation on Brahman: in sound and in silence. By sound we go to silence. The sound of Brahman is Om.

Maitri Upanishad 6: 23

There are several traditional and allegorical interpretations of this *pranava mantra* AUM. The best explanation of AUM is found within the ancient Vedic and Sanskrit traditions. One can read about AUM in the marvellous *Manduka Upanishad*, which explains the elements of AUM as an allegory of the planes of consciousness.

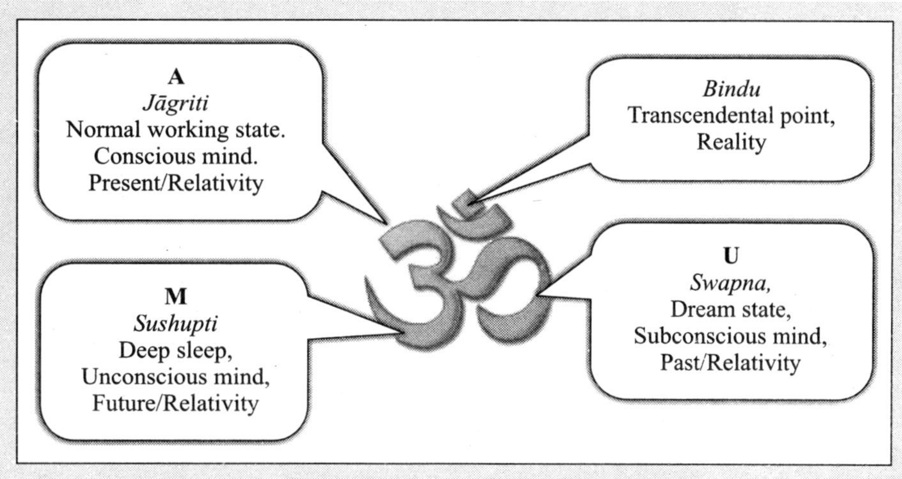

In Sanskrit, this sound is called '*Anāhata Nāda*,' the '**Un-struck Sound**.' Literally, this means '*the sound that is not made by two things striking together*.' When one really "listens" to this silent sound, this un-struck vibration, one comes inevitably to stillness, to pure and open existence.

In simple language, the four states can be categorised thus:

WAKING	:	Consciousness plus Thinking
DREAMING	:	Unconsciousness plus Thinking
SLEEPING	:	Unconsciousness minus Thinking
TURIYA	:	Consciousness minus Thinking

> The mere physical man is like the ant crawling on the paper, who observes black lettering and attributes its production to the pen and nothing more.
>
> *El Ghazali, Alchemy of Happiness*

A	U	M
chanted by feeling the resonance of 'A' in the abdomen, at ravel	allowing the 'U' to resonate in the chest	feeling the 'M' vibration in the head
Jagrit (waking state)	*swapna* (dreaming state)	*shushupti* (deep sleep state)
conscious	subconscious	unconscious
Tamas / ignorance	*Rājas* / Passion	*Sattva* / Clarity
Brahma / Creator	Vishnu / Preservation	*Mahesh* / Dissolution
Present	Past	Future
Viswanārā or *Virāt*	*Taijasa*	*Prajnā*
Physical Condition	Mental condition	Intellectual condition
Conscious of body and mind; one is falsely identified with them.	Aware of mind and its projections, but not conscious of body	Not conscious of body or mind.
Gross / Solid Relativity	Subtle/ Liquid Relativity	Causal/Vaporous Relativity

Benefits of AUM Meditation

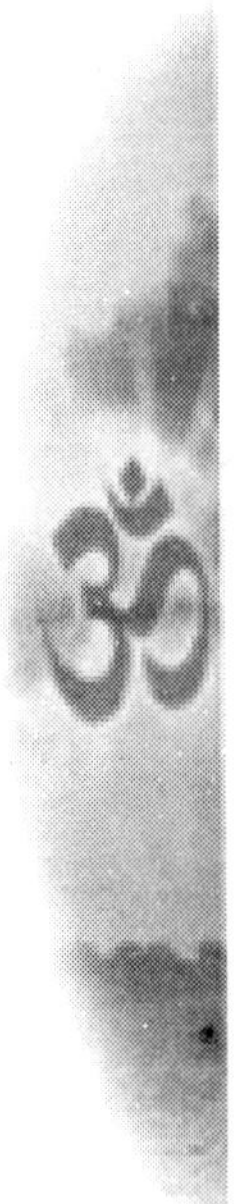

- Assists in controlling the emotions.
- Helps in cleansing the mind.
- Improves the concentration, memory and understanding capacity.
- Relaxes Physically, Mentally, Emotionally.
- Charges the surrounding atmosphere.
- The vibration due to ॐ *AUM kār* meditation increases the efficiency of cells and the organs.
- Regular ॐ *AUM kār* at night gives sound sleep, and requires no sleeping pills.
- ॐ *AUM kār* improves blood circulation and keeps the blood pressure normal.
- Stomach pain and acidity gets eliminated.
- Regular chanting of ॐ *AUM kār* increases the mental strength and helps one gain confidence and concentration.

तज्जपस्तदर्थभावनम् ॥२८॥

Tat_Japah Tadartha_Bhāvanam.

Repeat Word and reflect
Realise content.

Tat : that AUM
Japah : repetition
Tadartha : its meaning, import, significance
Bhāvanam : contemplation

Q: *How should the Word be repeated?*
A: The word must be repeated while meditating upon its meaning.

Japa is the practice of repeating a specific, carefully chosen word, a verse, a phrase or a prayer. Almost all followers of different faiths could be observed to have a rosary or a *Japamālā* or some threaded beads going by a different name in their hands and subconsciously repeating the name of a saint or a *mantra*. The benefits of such a repetition and the salutary effect it has on the mind is well recognized.

When one learns typewriting, he can note that initially he concentrates on the location of each letter in the keyboard. As he continues practice, i.e. as he repeats typing, he notices that slowly the need to focus attention on the location of letters has given way to an automatic, subconscious movement of his fingers to the right location in the keyboard takes place. He types faster and effortlessly. What was initially a directed mental effort has, due to repetition, become an automatic effortless movement of fingers. Intuition has taken over from intelligence. That is the purpose of repetition. Repetition is done focusing attention to the six centres of consciousness, from the lowest centre of the back of the spine to the highest centre in the head, through the intermediate centres located between these two. The purpose is to raise the level of consciousness higher and higher until one merges his consciousness with the Super Consciousness. There are number of rules and regulations with regard to the repetition. These concern the selection of appropriate sound or mantra, place to sit and repeat, number of times of repetition, centres to focus etc. It is a whole science that is related to the Word and vibration produced by the repetition. The objective is to synchronise the individual vibration with the universal vibration.

Among sacrifices, I am the sacrifice of silent repetition.

Bhagavadgitā, 10:25

By repeating an idea, one creates a mental habit. The repetition of any sacred name or a mantra helps in mental concentration. Mere repetition is not enough. Reflection should follow. Reflection enables confused reverie to give way to concentrated thought. When contemplation is 'True', there is no discrimination into 'right' and 'wrong', 'good' and 'bad'. Meditative contemplation is not *merely* a matter of thinking, rather it's what is referred to as 'contemplation in silence'. Whilst going about one's daily routine, one should mindfully consider the real nature of existence through comparisons. This is a coarse kind of investigation but it leads to the real thing.

There are three types of Japa:

Repetition of any *Mantra* or Name of the Lord is known as *Japa. Mantra* can be verbally repeated for sometime, in a whisper for sometime, and mentally for sometime. The mental repetition is very powerful. It is termed *Mānasika Japa*. The verbal or loud repetition is called *Vaikhari Japa*. The loud Japa shuts out all worldly sounds. Repetition in a whisper or humming is termed *Upānshu Japa*. Even mechanical repetition of *Japa* without any feeling has a great purifying effect on the mind. The feeling will come later on when the process of mental purification goes on.

Mental repetition *Mānasika Japa.*	Silent repetition is the most effective one. It can be done anywhere and everywhere, when time permits.
Verbal or loud repetition. *Vaikhari Japa.*	The loud verbal repetition shuts out worldly sounds. The sound reverberates and creates positive vibration in mind.
Repetition in whisper. *Upānshu Japa.*	There is neither silence nor sound in whispering. Starting from sound, before ending in silence, is the whisper state.

Shri Ramana Maharishi says:

- *Japa* must be done until it becomes natural. It starts with effort and is continued until it becomes natural and automatic.
- *Japa* may be done even while engaged in other work.
- *Japa* done repeatedly means effort ripening and sooner or later it leads one to the right path.
- The objective of *japa* is the exclusion of several thoughts and confining oneself to one single thought.
- By repetition of mantras, the mind gets controlled. Then the mantra becomes one with the mind and also with the *prāna*
- The oral *japa* becomes mental and the mental *japa* finally reveals itself as being eternal.

> Our presence to God is in proportion
> to our absence from world.
>
> *Qushayri : Risalah 3*

ॐ The modes of *AUMkār* Chanting

Vaikhari	❖ Loud incantation. ❖ ॐ AUM is repeated audibly to reinforce the vibration mentally.	❖ *Vaikhari* is suited for the early stages till the mind is habituated to the chanting. ❖ Sound proceeds from the mouth.
Madhyama	❖ The sound of incantation is not heard. ❖ It is a stage between sound and soundlessness. ❖ ॐ AUM is recited mentally while lips move silently.	❖ The lips move while repeating the Mantra. ❖ It stems from the larynx but is hardly emitted from the lips.
Pashyanti	❖ There is no utterance of the word; overt or covert. ❖ But chanting continues in the mind without effort. ❖ ॐ AUM is chanted silently without moving the lips.	❖ *Japa* becomes a part and parcel of one's being and one perceives and experiences the Mantra involuntarily. ❖ The state when all is Soundless. ❖ The whole process is from the conscious to the unconscious, from the gross to subtle.
Parā	❖ The Mantra itself is forgotten and only its impact remains within the consciousness. ❖ ॐ AUM is crystallized in the cellular memory and naturally vibrates in the body without conscious effort.	❖ The consciousness reaches its transcendence. ❖ This is the *Turiya* state where there is nothing but bliss.

Vaikhari: Meaning 'opposed to'. In this context 'opposed to efforts' towards attainment. This state describes the situation wherein the seeker remains object oriented. His senses are easily drawn towards the objects; detachment is far from his thoughts. AUM is repeated audibly by him to reinforce the vibration. This situation is described as akin to being like a fruit, far drawn away from the seed (which gave rise to the fruit), but yet containing the seed well within the fruit; the seeker not being aware of the same, looks forward to 'fruits' outside.

- ❖ Most peripheral
- ❖ Absolutely manifested
- ❖ There is clear cut duality
- ❖ Solidity in everything
- ❖ Characterized by sound
- ❖ Attached to objects

Madhyama: Meaning the 'middle'. There is some progress in the direction of attainment, but yet drawn towards objects. Senses are not in total command.

It is compared with a tree, having sprouted from the seed and grown into a big tree with flowers and fruits; attached to what it holds and yet partially aware of it having been part of the seed once. In him the sound of AUM incantation is not heard. He recites mentally while mouthing it silently. This is a stage between sound and silence.

- ❖ Less peripheral
- ❖ Neither manifested nor un-manifested
- ❖ There is clear ambiguity
- ❖ State of liquidity
- ❖ Stage between sound and silence
- ❖ Attached to body

Pashyati: Literally means 'looking back'. The seeker looks back as to how he was drawn to external objects, while he himself was the object he was seeking.

The stage is compared to that of a seed, containing in it the potential to sprout, flower and fruit. But yet it is un-manifested. ॐAUM incantation becomes a part and parcel of one's being and one perceives and experiences the Mantra involuntarily. The whole process is from the conscious to the unconscious, from the gross to subtle.

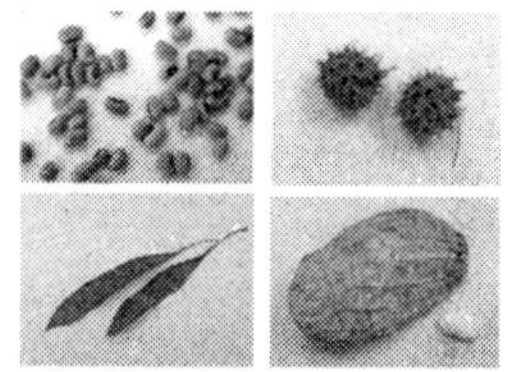

- ❖ Unmanifested
- ❖ There is clarity
- ❖ Vaporous state
- ❖ Stage of silence
- ❖ Attached to mind

"I am the seed of all existence. There is no being, moving or still, that exists without Me."

Lord Krishna in the Bhagavadgitā.

Parā: The Mantra itself is forgotten and only its impact remains within the consciousness. ॐAUM is crystallized in the cellular memory and naturally vibrates in the body without conscious effort. The consciousness reaches its transcendence

- ❖ Beyond the un-manifested
- ❖ Transcendental
- ❖ Devoid of all distinctive marks

ततः प्रत्यक्चेतनाधिगमोऽप्यन्तरायाभावश्च ॥२९॥

Tatah Pratyak_Chetanā_Adhigamah_Api_Antarāyā_Bhāvah_Cha.

Then there is knowledge gain
Obstacles do not remain.

Tatah : thence, arising from supplication to God. *Pratyok* : different
Chetanā : sentient *Adhigamah* : real knowledge *Api* : also *Antarāyā* : obstacles
Bhāvah : absence of obstacles *Cha* : and

Q: *What when such a reflection and repetition is done?*
A: Hence comes knowledge of the Real Self and destruction of the obstacles to that knowledge.

When repetition of AUM is made with an understanding of its meaning, introspection is gained and obstacles disappear.

There are immense spiritual gains from reflection on and repetition of the Word AUM.

1. This practice takes one on a direct route inward, systematically piercing the levels of consciousness, if done with sincerity and dedication
2. It leads inward to a deep awareness that is the root of the sound.
3. It allows the attention to more purely go inward, past body and sensory awareness.
4. Chanting mantra aloud can be a very enjoyable and useful process, whether alone or done with a group of people.
5. AUM chanting has a centering or balancing effect.
6. Repetition of AUM leads to concentration, which in turn leads to contemplation and Samādhi.

AUM represents that Power;

which is omniscient
which rules over the entire universe
which protects one from the evils of life
which fulfills the cherished desires of its devotees,
which destroys ignorance and gives enlightenment.

This syllable OM is indeed Brahman. This syllable is the highest. Whosoever knows this syllable obtains all that he desires. This is the best support. This is the highest support. Whosoever knows this support is adored in the world of Brahma.

Kathopanishad. I. ii. 16-17.

SUMMARY: Aphorism 1.24-1.29

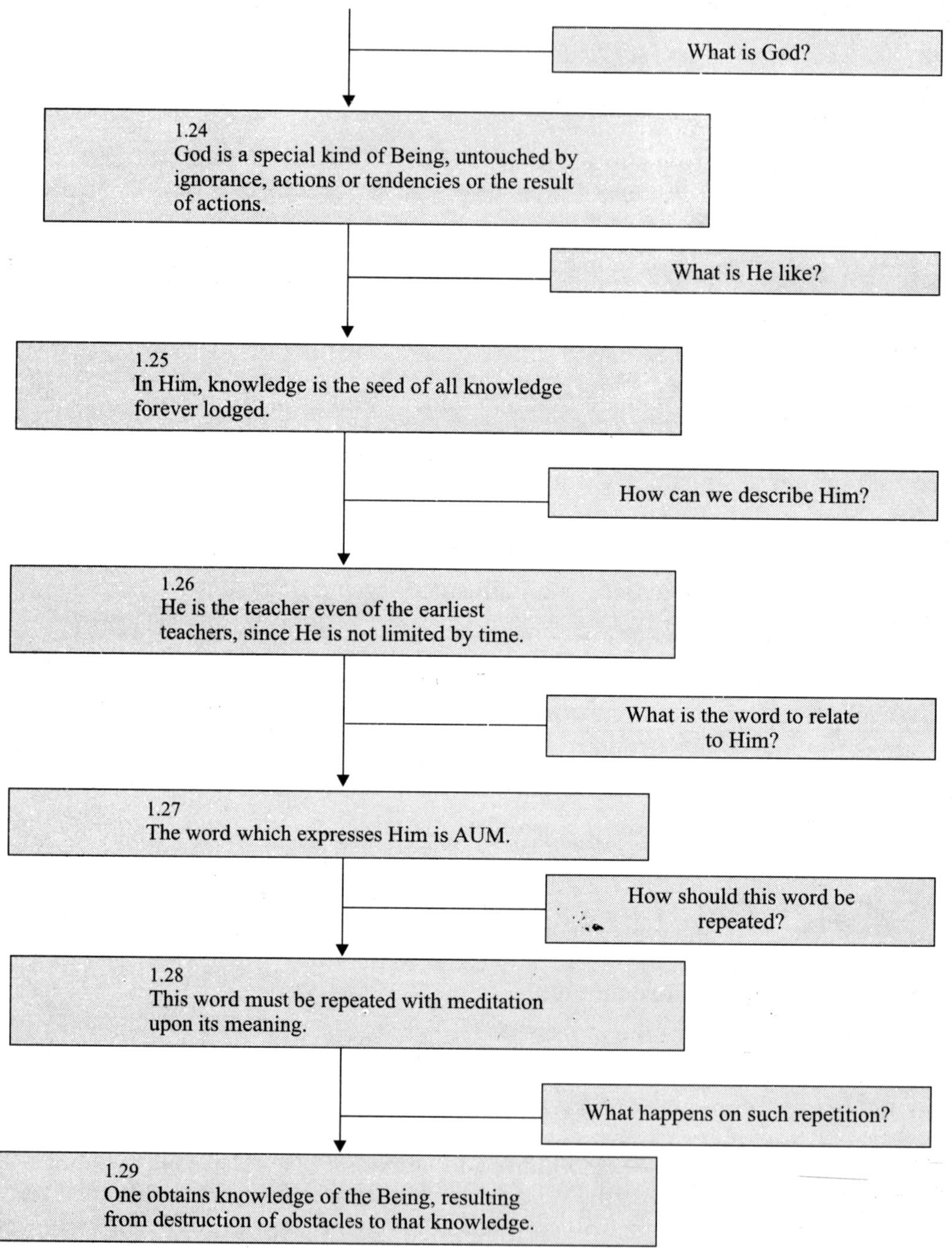

व्याधिस्त्यानसंशयप्रमादालस्याविरतिभ्रान्तिदर्शनालब्ध-
भूमिकत्वानवस्थितत्वानि चित्त विक्षेपास्तेऽन्तरायाः ॥३०॥

Vyādhi_Styāna_Sanshaya_Pramāda_Ālasya_Avirati_Bhrāntidarshan_ Alabdha Bhumikatvā_Anavasthita_Tvāni Chitta_Vikshepāste_Antarāyāh.

Disease, dullness and doubt, laziness and sloth
Confusion and lack of concentration,
False perception and unsteady mind
Are obstacles of different kind.

Vyādhi : disease, sickness
Styāna : incompetence, mental laziness
Anavasthikatva : unsteady yogic states
Sanshaya : doubt, lack of trust in scriptures
Pramāda : delusion, heedlessness
Vikshepah : projecting power, distraction
Ālasya : sloth
Antarāyāh : impediments, obstacles to Yoga
Avirati : dissipation, craving for sensory pleasures
Bhrãntidarshan : false vision, false perception
Alabdhabhumikatva : Failure to concentrate

Q: *What are the obstacles to practice?*
A: Disease, dullness, doubt, laziness, sloth, confusion, lack of concentration, false perception and unsteady mind are obstacles of different kinds.

There are several obstacles to the practice of Yoga. They are:

1. Disease in the body.
2. Doubt as to the efficacy of Yoga practice
3. Carelessness or a state of confusion.
4. Indifference or laziness.
5. Sleep during day time and excessive sleep.
6. Not leaving the objects of senses;
7. Erroneous perception or delusion.
8. Concern with worldly affairs
9. Want of faith.
10. Lack of aptitude

Gross Body	Composed of wind, fire and water is subject to scores of diseases as also many other troubles like bad odour, deformity, inflammation and fracture.
Subtle Body	Affected by desire, anger, greed, delusion, pride and jealousy.
Casual Body	In deep sleep, the state of causal body, the soul knows neither himself nor others and appears as if dead. This causal body is the seed of future births and their miseries.

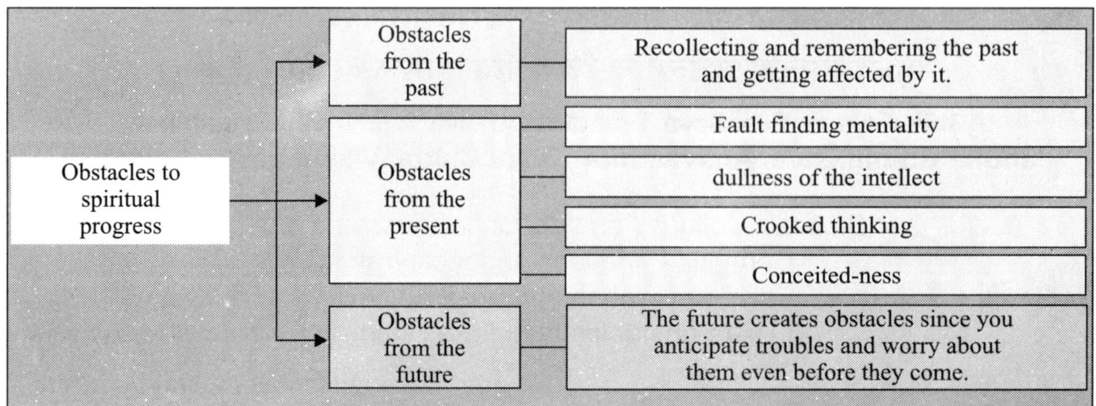

Obstacle from	*Nature of obstacle*	*Palliative*
Body	Sick: A sickly dilapidated body stands in the way of practice.	Regular exercise, *āsana*, *prāṇāyama*, moderation in diet, walking, running in the open air and by regularity in the work, food and sleep
Drowsiness and sleep	Laziness, half sleepy state, sleep	Meditation, if the body is light, if the mind is clear and if there is cheerfulness, know that you are meditating.
Day dreaming	Mind has a tendency to build castles in the air.	Closely watch the mind and be thoughtful, careful and vigilant.
Dreams in meditation.	Various sorts of fantastic dreams.	Ignore and continue to meditate.

Vedānta teaches about 4 types of obstacles

Laya Torpidity	❖ Lapsing into a state of sleep ❖ Kind of stagnation ❖ Kind of mental sleep generated by inertia
Vikshepa Troubled memory	❖ Mind troubled by old thoughts, memories and impressions ❖ Recurrence of old tendencies
Kashāya Seized of violent attachment	❖ Mind under the spell of long forgotten sensual pleasures ❖ Seeker agitated from subconscious depths like a gust of wind
Rasawāda Spiritual emotions	❖ Enjoyment of inferior bliss ❖ Tendency to hold on to temporary joy in preference to movement towards further glory

दुःखदौर्मनस्याङ्गमेजयत्वश्वासा विक्षेपसहभुवः ॥३१॥

Duhkha_Daurmanasya_Angamejayatva_Shvāsa_Prashvāsā. Vikshepasahabhuvah.

Distress, despair and trembling of body
And improper breathing accompany.

Duhkha : distress, grief, sorrow
Daurmanasya : Despair
Angamejayatva : trembling of the body
Shvāsa : improper inhalation
Prashvāsā : improper exhalation
Vikshepa : mental distraction, projecting power
Sahabhuvah: accompaniments

Q: *What is the result of obstructions to practice?*
A: Obstructions to practice can be recognized through symptoms like sorrowfulness, dejection, trembling of body and irregular inhalation and exhalation.

How do we recognize that there are obstacles to practice? Patanjali gives some guidelines to observe.

When we notice a sense of sorrow and dejection after we commence practice, it could be a sign of obstacles in the way. Similarly, irregular inhalation and exhalation and trembling of the body are to be recognised as obstacles.

The antidote to the obstacles is one pointed-ness, a focused attention. Not to be distracted by these obstacles. Not to bother about them and to know that they will disappear in due course. If the mind is focused, then it is far less likely to get entangled and lost in the mire of delusion that can come from these obstacles. The one pointed focus could be a mantra, short prayer, or affirmation. Here the principle of one-pointed-ness is introduced as the antidote for the many obstacles mentioned in the previous sutras. While there is great breadth of choice in objects, a sincere aspirant will choose wisely the object for this practice, with the guidance of someone familiar with these practices. Focusing on the positive is one of the practical applications of the principle of one-pointed-ness.

Sādhanā (spiritual practice) helps one in gradually realizing the reality to the human mind enabling it to slowly and gradually rise above the physical to the subtle and then transcend itself to become Self luminous.

तत्प्रतिषेधार्थमेकतत्त्वाभ्यासः ॥३२॥

Tat_Pratishedhārtham_Eka_Tattva_Abhyāsah

Obstacles to eliminate,
On a single object concentrate.

Tat : Their, that of the obstacles *Pratishedha* : prevention, avoidance, blocking
Ārtham : for *Eka* : single *Tattva* : subject, entity *Abhyāsah* : practice

Q: *How can the obstacles to practice be removed?*
A: By concentrating on a single object the obstacles can be removed.

One should put all his faith in one practice. It is all right to think of safeguarding one's money by putting it in different kitty. But when it comes to practice for making one's mind stable, one should first forget the kitty and then focus on any one of the several methods that is enumerated in the next few *Sutras*. Trying different methods for different periods of time or for that matter, different teachers for different durations does not help. It indicates a fragmented mind.

One should remember that practice is defined by Patanjali as that which is done for long durations, uninterrupted and with devotion. Once, one chooses a particular practice, he should continue long; have faith and be devoted to his teacher. He should quell all doubts. Half hearted attempts for short durations is a waste of time.

To find water, there is no point in digging in hundred different places, a metre deep each. It should be in the same chosen place, using the same drilling tools; all the expected hundred metres depth. If a rock is encountered, one can use dynamite, but not shy away and try another place or practice.

Each mind is different. What appeals to one as correct practice, need not appear so to another. There is no point in allowing oneself to be persuaded to change his practice. All methods are good. What is important is not the method of practice but the perseverance in practice. The goal is important. Not the road. Finally, when one is ready to commit to practice and has acknowledged his ignorance, he should ask himself the most important question of all: "Do I truly want to know who I am?"

"If the wrong man uses the right means,
the right means work in the wrong way."

Chinese Proverb

Concentrating on a single object:

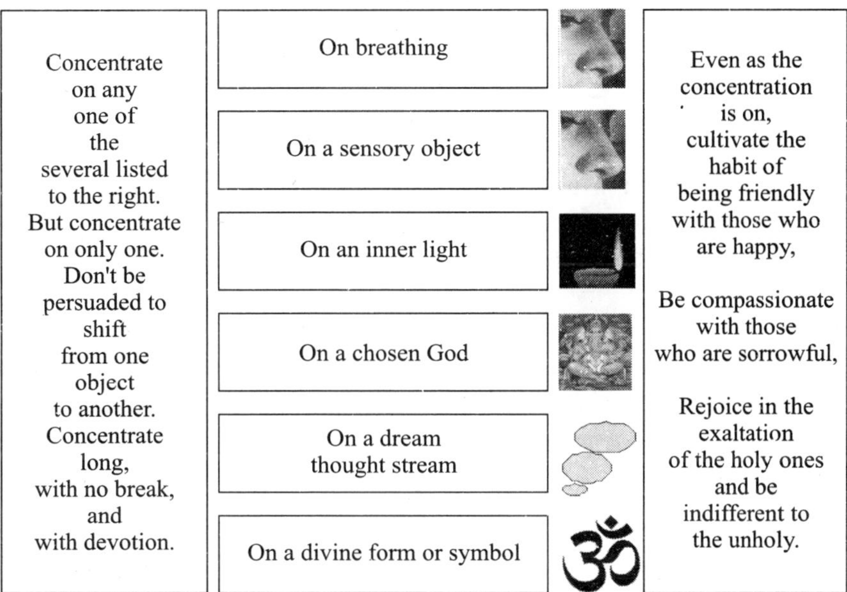

The symbols are only a means of holding on to one image or thought to the exclusion of all else. Ultimately, this one image also disappears. There remains nothing to be meditated upon. Some opine that the meditator alone remains and the other two disappear. Some others think that the meditation remains with the meditator and the meditated disappearing. It is worthwhile noting that all are true. The fourth state of *turiya* is a state beyond mind and hence there can be no memory of what has remained and what has disappeared.

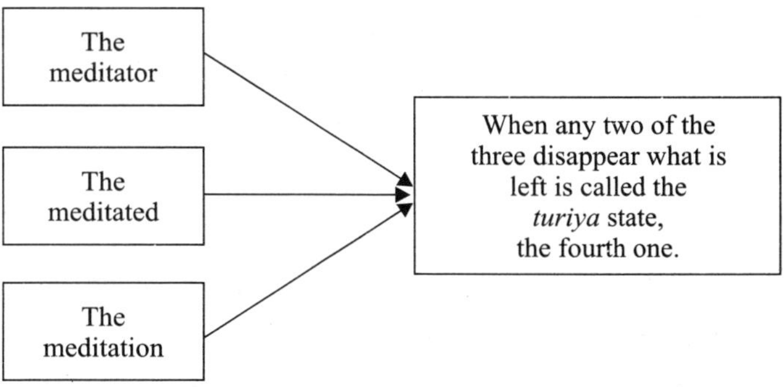

Dropping the meditator and the meditation respectively, when the meditated upon, the goal, remains the only objective and the mind becomes still like the flame of a lamp in a windless place - this is called *Samādhi.*

Adhyātma Upanishad

मैत्रीकरुणामुदितोपेक्षाणां सुखदुःखपुण्यापुण्यविषयाणां
भावनातश्चित्तप्रसादनम् ॥३३॥

Maitri_Karunā_Mudita_Upekshānām Sukha_Duhkha_Punya_Apunya_ Vishayānām_Bhāvanātah Chitta_Prasādanam.

Towards the happy friendship and compassion
Indifference to happiness or unhappiness, elevation or depression
Is the quality that brings tranquillity.

Maitri : friendship, companionship *Karunā* : compassion *Mudita* : Joy
Chitta : mind *Upekshānām* : indifference *Sukha* : happiness
Duhkha : unhappiness, suffering *Punya* : elevating, meritorious
Apunya : depressing, degrading, non meritorious *Vishayānām* : objects
Bhāvanāt : thinking about *Prasādanam* : clarity

Q: *How can calmness of mind be ensured?*
A: Undisturbed calmness of mind is attained by,
a) cultivating friendliness towards the happy,
b) being compassionate with the unhappy,
c) delighting in the virtuous, and
d) being indifferent towards the wicked.

One of the most important aspects of ensuring calmness of mind is outlined in this *sutra*. Even if no other practice is done adhering to these methods of approach to those around can immensely increase the scope of ensuring calmness of mind.

Even while practising one or the other methods of concentration outlined in the next few *sutras*, if the approach to those around during the practice and later is not guided by the principles listed; the practice is bound to flounder, with the seeker mentally agitated because of his wrong approach to those around. For instance, if one is jealous of his teacher (instead of delighting in his virtues) and all the time concentrating on finding some fault or other in the teacher; his practice suffers. The negative impact of the negative thoughts of finding fault harboured by the seeker far outweighs the positive impact of the practice. Alternately, it could be that a student comes across a wicked teacher who is jealous of his progress and consequent popularity amongst his colleagues in the group. If the student chooses to cross swords with the teacher (instead of being indifferent) his thoughts are distracted. It is better he moves out, if he finds it difficult to be indifferent. The aim is stillness of mind. Not correcting people around.

प्रच्छर्दनविधारणाभ्यां वा प्राणस्य ॥३४॥

Prachchhardana_Vidhāranābhyām Vā Prānasya.

Mind may be calmed
By a breath exhalation and retention norm.

Prachchhardana : exhalation	*Vidhāranābhyām* : retention
Vā : or	*Prāna* : life force, breath

Q: *How else can calmness be ensured?*
A: By regulating inhalation and exhalation and retention of breath.

If there is one method that is extensively discussed and tried out to control mind, it is breath, *prāna* regulation. The concept of *prāna* and its manifestations is fundamental to yoga practice. Respiration is considered a direct function of *prāna.* Control of *Prāna* is regarded as the most effective way of control of vital energy, leading to the cessation of thoughts and attainment of *Samādhi*. *Prāna* is not only the hub of the wheel of life, but also of Yoga. Each and every thing, or being, including man, takes shelter under it. *Prāna* is the fundamental energy and the source of all knowledge. It is said about *prānāyāma*, "A more useful science than the science of respiration, a more beneficial science than the science of respiration, a greater friend than the science of respiration has never been seen nor heard." Thought distractions can also be controlled by proper breathing exercise, aided by an experienced teacher. When the mind is agitated, angry or in any way emotionally involved one can notice breath becoming irregular and hard. Conversely, when one is asleep or deeply engrossed in a spiritual text the breath can be observed to be smooth and deep. If a deliberate attempt is made to concentrate mind on the breath or if regular practice is done to control the breathing pattern, mind can be stilled. After a few days of such practice, if the seeker comes across a situation that could disturb him, he will notice that his reaction to the disturbing situation now is more calm and that he is not agitated.

Prānāyāma can be mastered only gradually. It may take months or even years before the practitioner's mind becomes receptive to the regulated flow of breath and he experiences the full benefits of *prānāyāma*. Proper practice of *prānāyāma* can control almost any disease but improper practice may give rise to all sorts of respiratory ailments. So one should take care to acquire control over his breath gradually and none should attempt *prānāyāma* without the guidance of a right teacher.

Prāna (or vital air) and the mind of beings are inseparably connected.
They are associated like flower and its fragrance and
they exist like sesame seed and its oil.

Yogavāshishta

SUMMARY: Aphorism 1.30-1.34

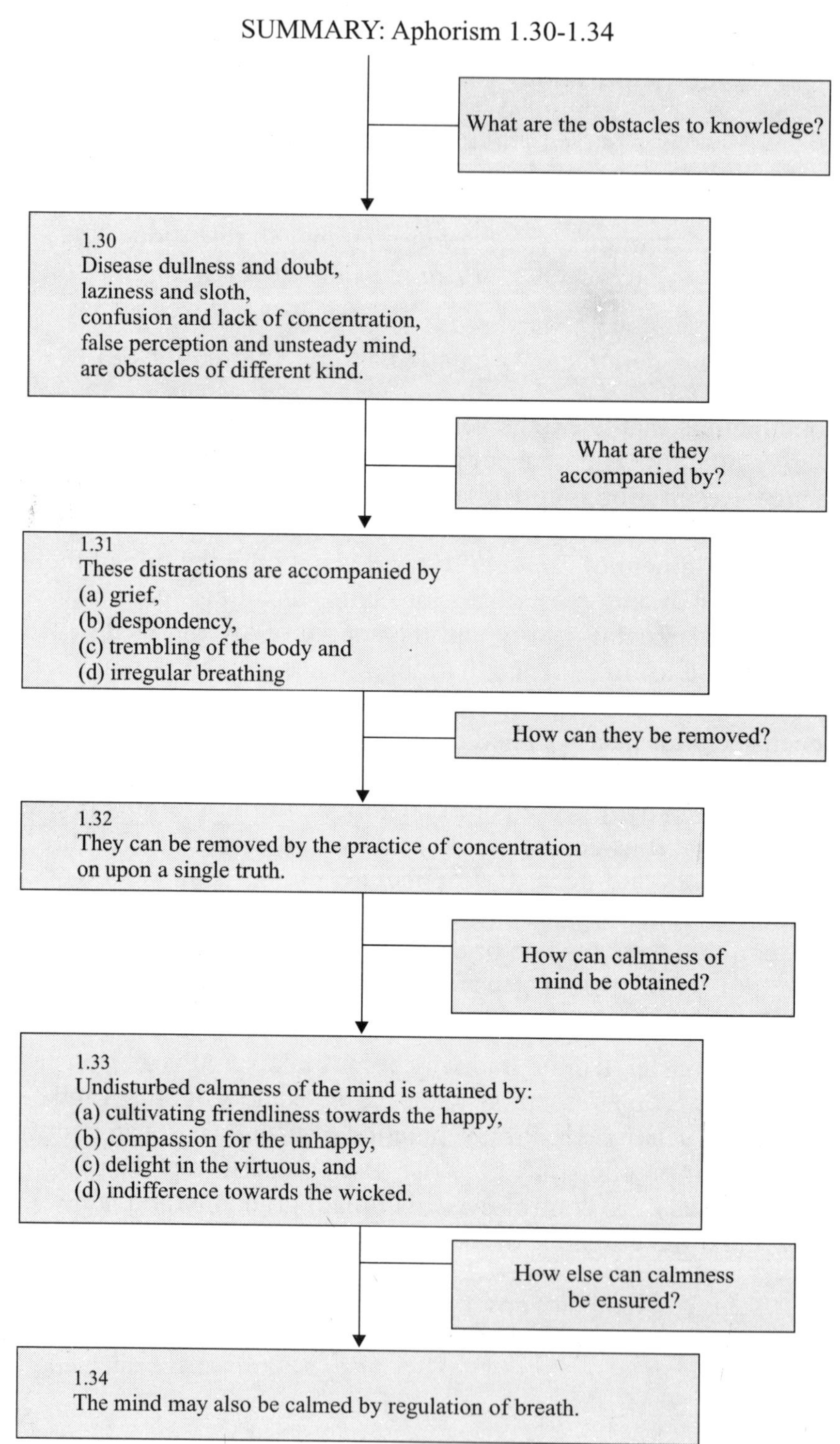

विषयवती वा प्रवृत्तिरुत्पन्ना मनसः स्थितिनिबन्धनी ॥३५॥

Vishayavati wā Pravittih_Utpannā Manasah Sthiti_Ṇibandhini.

Concentrate on a sense perception of any kind
To attain state of stillness of mind.

Vishayavati : sense perception *wā* : or *Utpannā* : brought about, arising
Pravittih : experienced by senses, occupation, activity *Manasah* : mind
Sthiti : steadiness, state of stillness *Nibandhini* : cause, condition.

Q: *How else can steadiness be attained?*
A: By concentrating on a sense organ.

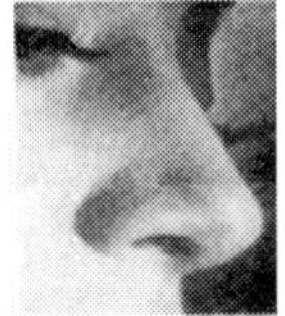

In order to control thought waves one can also concentrate on a sensory object, say tip of the nose or middle of the tongue. One can focus on the tip of the nose and remain focused for a definite duration of time, both in the morning and evening. The focusing should not cause pain or strain the eyes. Yoga practice should always result in pleasant experiences. On regular focusing on the tip of the nose one may experience a pleasant smell.

It would be natural for the seeker to look around to see if there is a scented stick or a flower around. The smell is self caused, not dependent on the scented stick or flower. Much the same way focusing on the tongue can result in "tasting" of good food. These concentrations on a chosen sensory object, effectively withdrawing thoughts from every thing else, results in the stilling of mind.

It should be noted that concentration on sense organ should not be misunderstood to mean pursuing objects attracted by the senses.

There is difference of opinion about the exact location suggested. Some opine that it is not the tip of the nose that is to be concentrated upon, but the centre between eyebrows at the top of the nose. The choice is that of the seeker, whichever is easy to concentrate on, and comfortable with no adverse reactions, is the best centre.

Meditation is a movement in and of the unknown ... it is that energy that thought-matter cannot touch. Thought is perversion for it is the product of yesterday ... Everything put together by thought is within the area of noise, and thought can in no way make itself still ... thought itself must be still for silence to be. Silence is always now, even as thought is not. Thought, always being old, cannot possibly enter into that silence which is always new. The new becomes the old when thought touches it.

J.Krishnamurti

विशोका वा ज्योतिष्मती ॥३६॥
Vishokā wā Jyotishmati.

Focus the mind
On an inner resplendent light.

Vishokā : blissful, without unhappiness, serene, devoid of suffering
wā : or *Jyotishmati* : luminous, resplendent

Q: *How else can concentration be attained?*
A: Concentration may also be attained by fixing mind on an inner light.

The inner light of effulgence is to be conceived as sorrow-less and ever bright and as being located at the centre of heart. Or one can visualize bright light at the centre of the forehead, at the heart region and concentrate on that light.

Imagine a bright light in the heart region.

On continuous and uninterrupted practice the visualized light could be observed to be an actualized light! With mind on the light there will be light in the heart. If it be difficult to imagine an inner light, one can sit in front of a candle and focus on the flame. Visions of inner light include the visions of forms of object of meditation. The object initially is subtle. The seeker will be initially finding it difficult to 'grasp' the object. But the visualized object becomes more and more concrete as practice proceeds.

The imaginary object becomes concretized as practice develops. St John's Gospel says: "By penetrating to the light in one's heart, man can reach the light that lights the hearts of all, the TRUE LIGHT which lighteth every man that cometh into the world."

There are certain characteristics of God-vision. One feels light, feels joy and experiences the upsurge of great current in one's chest, like the bursting of rockets............ I saw the vision described in the scriptures. Sometimes I saw the universe filled with sparks of fire. Sometimes I saw all the quarters glittering with light, as if the world were a lake of mercury............ You see, my experiences tally with those described in the scriptures.

Shri Rāmakrishna Paramahamsa.

वीतरागविषयं वा चित्तम् ॥३७॥
Viitarāga_Vishayam wā Chittam

Focus on a seer
Free from desire.

Viitarāga : without craving, free from attachment
wā : or
Vishayam : sense object
Chittam : mind stuff

Q: *How else?*
A: By meditating on an illumined soul, a saint, a holy person.

For those accustomed to idols and images Patanjali suggests that they concentrate their mind on an illumined one- a Jesus, or a Buddha or a Rāma or a Krishna.

Perhaps focusing on a Person, a form is the most common of all types of meditation. One looks for a perfect soul in his inner self. One wishes to follow this perfect soul. Concentration on an illumined one will draw away all thoughts from elsewhere and enable one to focus on the purity of the holy person.

Devotion to and concentration on the chosen Deity enables one to gain confidence in His guidance, confidence that the Supreme Being is ever present in his heart and at every step He will guide the seeker in his efforts to attain a state of absorption.

The seeker should make sure that having chosen a Saint to focus on; he should desist from discussing this personality, the supposed strengths and weaknesses. Such discussion would loosen the bond of conviction. One should neither countenance any derogative talk about the chosen one. To the seeker, He is pure, the Whole. That is it, and that alone matters. On focusing, the seeker would become pure and whole. That is important. When one reflects on the noble qualities, one becomes noble, then truthful, knowledgeable and blissful.

Know meditation to be hundred times superior to listening, assimilation to be a hundred time superior to meditation and *nirvikalpa Samādhi* (seedless state of *Samādhi*) to be a hundred times superior to assimilation.

Ādi Shankara- Vivekachudāmani

स्वप्ननिद्राज्ञानालम्बनं वा ॥३८॥
Svapna_Nidrā_Gyāna_Ālambanam Wā.

Or, Focus thought stream
On dream.

Svapna : dream *Nidrā* : deep sleep, slumber *Gyāna* : knowledge
Ālambanam: to hold attention, object of meditation *Wā* : or

Q: *How else?*
A: By fixing mind on a dream stream.

Concentration on a dream object is not to be mistaken as dream analysis. The focus of attention has to be on the process of dreaming or a specific dream vision of a known saint. It is the thought stream that matters. As one watches, so it slows down. Mind wanders when one does not watch and slows down on watching. Patanjali suggests several objects for focusing attention on and also suggests the space to focus on. Broadly, these can be categorized as:

Object of meditation	❖ Object of meditation can be one of many gross or subtle objects; ❖ Examples: Feeling of breath at the nostrils, a mantra, a religious symbol, a point of light etc. ❖ It is essential that the seeker does not keep shifting from one object of meditation to another at frequent interval.
'Space' for meditation	❖ Holding mind in one space is important. ❖ The place of meditation may be the whole body, one point such as heart-centre, between the eyes etc.

Says Jung (Modern man in search of a soul): "The view that dreams are merely imaginary fulfilments of suppressed wishes have long ago been superceded. It is certainly true that there are dreams which embody suppressed wishes and fears, but what is there which a dream cannot on occasions embody? Dreams may give expression to ineluctable truths, to philosophical pronouncements, illusions, wild fantasies, memories, plans, anticipations, irrational experiences, even telepathic visions, and heaven knows what besides. One thing we ought never to forget, almost the half of our lives is passed in more or less unconscious state. The dream is specially the utterance of the unconscious."

Just as a single dream ego enjoys a variety of dream objects through the different dream figures projected by itself, so He, the one and only Lord, enjoys all objects of the world through mental modifications.

Bhāgavata

यथाभिमतध्यानाद्वा ॥३९॥

Yathā_Abhimata_Dhyānād_Wā.

Concentrate well
On a chosen symbol.

Yathā : as, in that way
Abhimata : per choice, desired, that which is liked
Dhyānād : through meditation
Wā : or

Q: *How else?*
A: By meditating on a divine form or symbol that one holds in esteem and reverence.

In selecting the symbol one has absolute freedom of choice. Patanjali has no fixed prescriptions on the object of meditation. He has already emphasized that faith is a must for spiritual progress. Depending upon the society one lives in and the socio-religious value systems, different communities have reverence to different symbols. One is free to choose any symbol for concentration in which the seeker has faith.

What is important is that one meditates. There is no need for quibbling on the objects and their supposed relative merits. You can choose a symbol, a physical object, a mental image, a god or a guru or a sound (mantra). What is important is that practice be; uninterrupted, of long duration and with devotion.

Some symbols of reverence:

"All religions, arts and sciences are branches of the same tree. All these aspirations are directed toward ennobling man's life, lifting it from the sphere of mere physical existence and leading the individual towards freedom."

Albert Einstein

परमाणुपरममहत्त्वान्तोऽस्य वशीकारः ॥४०॥

Paramānu_Parama_Mahatva_Anto Asya Vashikārah.

Self becomes one with and knows right
Objects atomic or infinite.

Paramānu : sub-atomic, smallest of the small, infinitely small
Parama Mahatva : Biggest of the big, infinitely big *Antah* : culminating in, ending in
Vashikārah : with no obstruction, having no obstacle *Asya* : of this mind

Q: *How can one recognize that the concentration is culminating in one pointed-ness?*
A: One can recognize by observing that he is totally in control of all, the subtlest or the grossest. He starts knowing without recourse to the normal methods of recollecting from memory, reading, listening to etc.

On continuing practice of concentration on the chosen object, one can start recognizing that he becomes more aware and more conscious and without the use of reasoning and logical faculties, he is getting to know more and more. Knowledge now is the result of the development of intuitive faculties rather than the logic of mind. The stored information and experience which earlier was used to know is now not necessary. Acquisition of spiritual knowledge is not an addition process, but an elimination process. It is the elimination of ignorance caused by misapprehension that blocks vision and understanding. As practice proceeds, the cloud of ignorance enveloping the Self starts slowly disappearing. Such a disappearance automatically results in greater awareness.

It does not matter whether the object is micro or macro. Anything and everything can be understood by the seeker when he makes sufficient progress.

Mind, devoid of its ideation, and weaning away of the strong impressions stored in memory can sharply focus on a chosen object and like a sponge absorb everything knowable about the chosen object in a jiffy. However, it should be understood that this ability to know all things micro or macro is not the end or goal of meditation.

Quantum physicians say: "As we penetrate in to matter nature, nature does not show us any 'isolated building blocks', but rather appears as a complicated web of relations between the various parts of the whole. This relationship always includes the observer in an essential way. The human observer constitutes the final link in the chain of observational processes, and the properties of any atomic object can only be understood in terms of the objects interaction with the observer. This means that the classical ideal of an objective description of nature is no longer valid. The Cartesian partition between the 'I' and the world, between the observer and the observed cannot be made when dealing with atomic matter."

SUMMARY: Aphorism 1.35-1.40

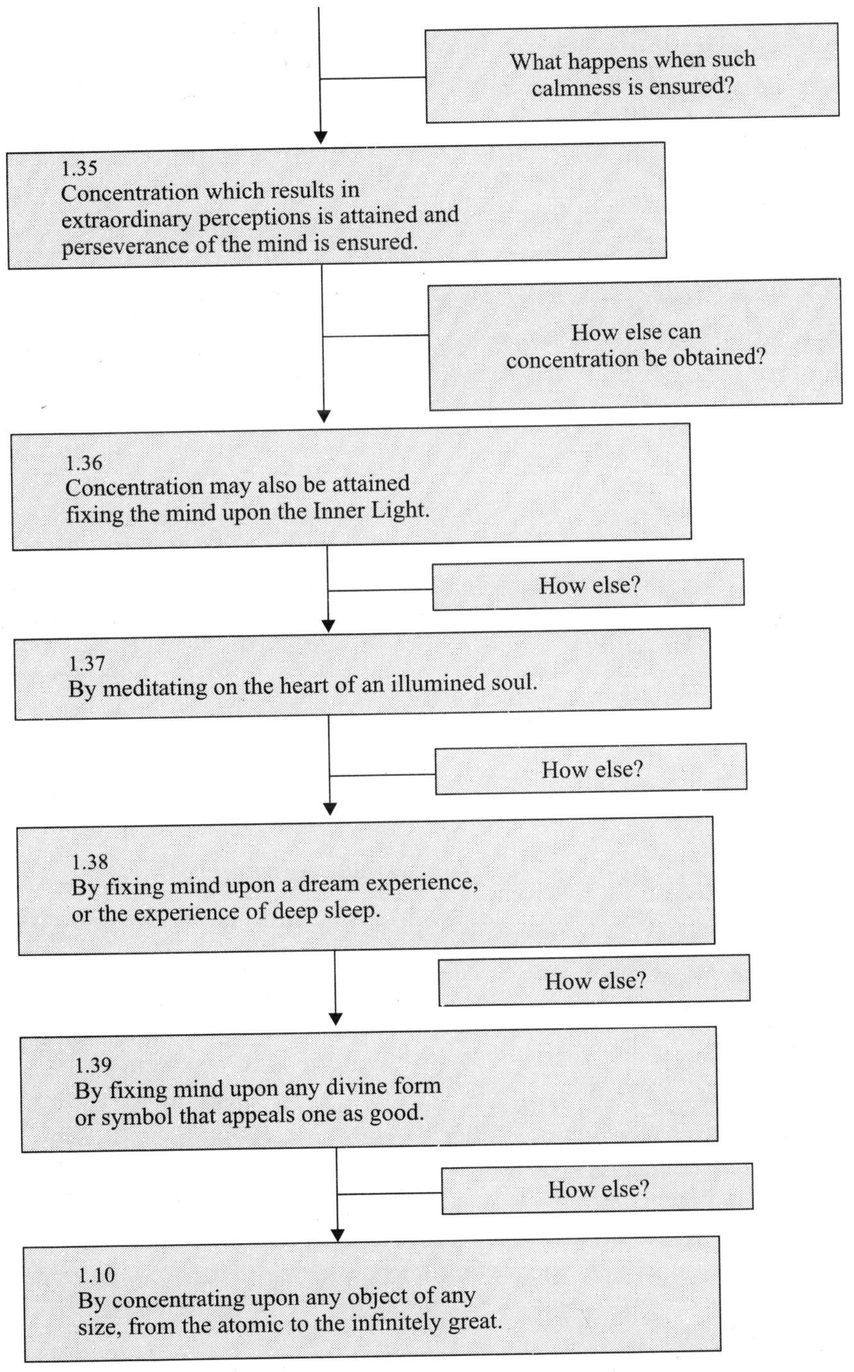

क्षीणवृत्तेरभिजातस्येव मणेर्ग्रहीतृग्रहणग्राह्येषु
तत्स्थतदञ्जनता समापत्तिः ॥४१॥

Kshina_Vritteh_Abhijātasyeva_Maner_Graheetri_Grahana_Grāhyeshu_ Tatstha_Tadanjanatā Samāpattih.

Stilled thoughts result
In oneness with object
Reflects like a crystal
Its name, form and content.

Kshina : weakened, worn out *Vritteh* : modification of the mind
Abhijātasyeva : pristine purity *Maner* : of the flawless crystal *Graheetri* : knower
Grahana : captured by senses *Grāhyeshu* : of the objects
Tatstha : that object of focus *Samāpattih* : transformation
Aanjanatā : similar to the object *Tad* : that

Q: *What happens when such a concentration is attained?*
A: When concentration is attained mind is cleared of thought waves and achieves sameness or identity with the object of its concentration. Just as jewels made of materials such as crystal take on the shine of rays that fall on them, one basks in the glory of knowledge of the Supreme Being.

When the modifications of mind have become weakened, the mind becomes like a crystal, and thus can easily take on the qualities of whatever object observed, whether that object be the observer, the means of observing, or an object observed.

States of *Samādhi* / Absorption
SAVITARKA
NIRVITARKA
SAVICHĀRA
NIRVICHĀRA

When the mind is like a crystal, it has no colouring of its own. It means that when one places his attention on some inner object, such as a thought pattern, his mind is able to fill with awareness of that object.

"He who allows his mind to wander with the senses is an ignoramus, though he is learned. See as a witness, without the burden of seeing. See the world just as you see a drama. See without attachment, look within. Look at the inner light unshaken by mental impressions. Then, floods of conscious bliss shall come pouring in and around you from all directions. This is the supreme Knowledge; realise! Aum Aum! "

South Indian Saint Thāyamānavar (Translation: Pete Brown)

तत्र शब्दार्थज्ञानविकल्पैः संकीर्णा सवितर्का समापत्तिः ॥४२॥

Tatra Shabda_Artha_Gyāna_Vikalpaih Sankirnā Savitarkā Samāpattih.

Oneness with object,
Its name form and content;
Is absorption
With deliberation.

Tatra : there (referred to types of trances) *Shabda* : spoken words
Artha : meaning, import *Gyāna* : knowledge *Vikalpaih* : options
Sankirnā : confused *Savitarkā* : right inference, right analysis
Samāpattih : transformation

Q: *What is the state of samādhi when the concentration is on a gross object?*
A: When the mind achieves identity with a gross object of concentration, mixed with awareness of name, quality and knowledge, this is called *savitarka samādhi.*

The ultimate reality can never be an object of reasoning or of demonstrable knowledge. It can never be adequately described by words, because it lies beyond the realm of senses and of the intellect from which our words and concepts are derived.

Difference between *Savitarka* and *Savichāra Samādhi*

Concentration on → GROSS OBJECT → SAVITARKA SAMĀDHI

Concentration on → SUBTLE OBJECT → SAVICHĀRA SAMĀDHI

There are four types of Wisdom as enunciated by the Buddha:
1. The first is seclusion in which one must free his mind from sensuality.
2. The second is the tranquillity of mind full of joy and gladness.
3. The third is taking delight in things spiritual.
4. The fourth is a state of perfect purity and peace in which the mind is above all gladness and grief.

स्मृतिपरिशुद्धौ स्वरुपशून्येवार्थमात्रनिर्भासा निर्वितर्का ॥४३॥

Smriti_Parishuddhau Svarupa Shunye_wā_Artha_Mātra_Nirbhāsā Nirvitarkā.

Oneness with object with no memory of name, form and content;
Is absorption, without deliberation.

Smriti : memory, recollection *Svarupa* : own nature *Parishuddha* : purification
Shunye : without *Artha* : object *Mātra* : alone
Nirbhāsa : perceivable *Nir* : without *Vitarkā* : question, analysis, inference

Q: *There is a qualifying clause, 'when mixed with quality', What is the state when it is not mixed with quality/ attributes?*

A: When the mind achieves identity with a gross object of concentration, unmixed with awareness of name, quality and knowledge, so that the object alone remains, this is called *nirvitarka samādhi*

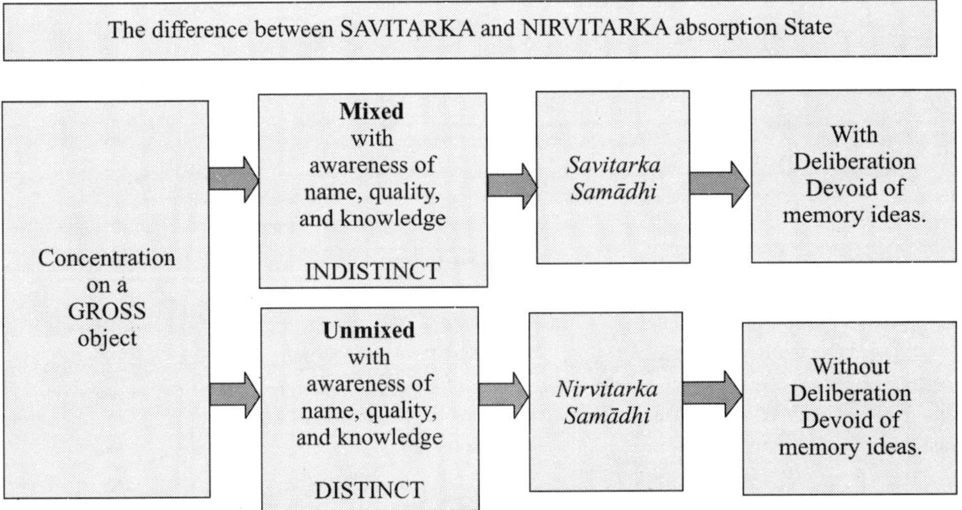

"Like two golden birds perched on the self same tree, intimate friends, the ego and the Self dwell in the same body. The former eats the sweet and sour fruits of the tree of life, while the later looks on in detachment."

Mundaka Upanishad

एतयैव सविचारा निर्विचारा च सूक्ष्मविषया व्याख्याता ॥४४॥

Etayaiva Savichārā Nirvichārā Cha Sukshma_Vishayā Vyākhātā.

Subtle object concentration
Is absorption with reflection.

Etayaiva : only through this analysis
Savichārā : right reflection
Nirvichārā : without reflection
Cha : and
Sukshma : subtle
Vishayā : objects
Vyākhātā : explained

Q: *What is the state of samādhi when the concentration is on a subtle object?*
A: When the rational mind is silenced the intuitive mode produces an extraordinary awareness. The environment is experienced in its own way without the filter of conceptual thinking. When the object of concentration is a subtle object, two kinds of *samādhi*, called *Savichāra. Nirvichāra* may be distinguished in the same manner.

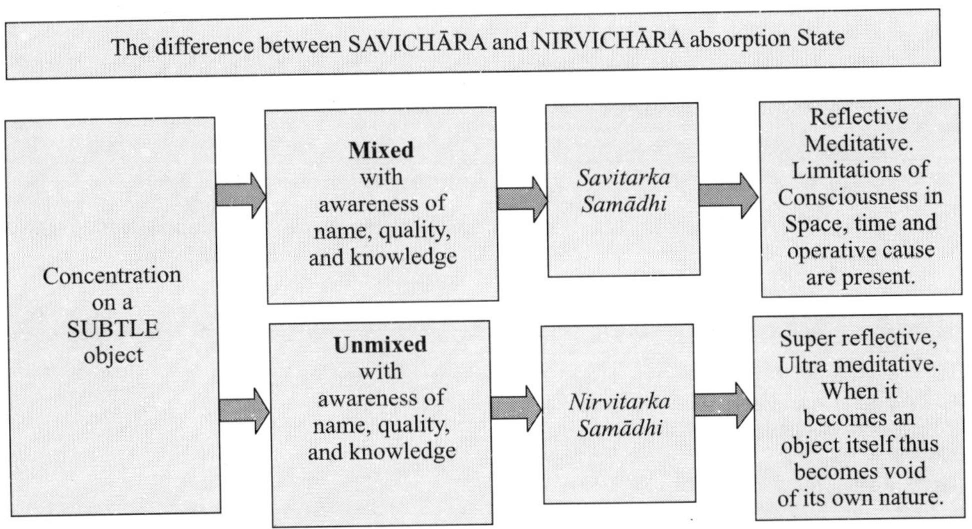

"As far as the laws of mathematics refer to reality,
they are not certain.
And as far as they are certain,
they do not refer to reality."

Albert Einstein.

SUMMARY: Aphorism 1.41-1.44

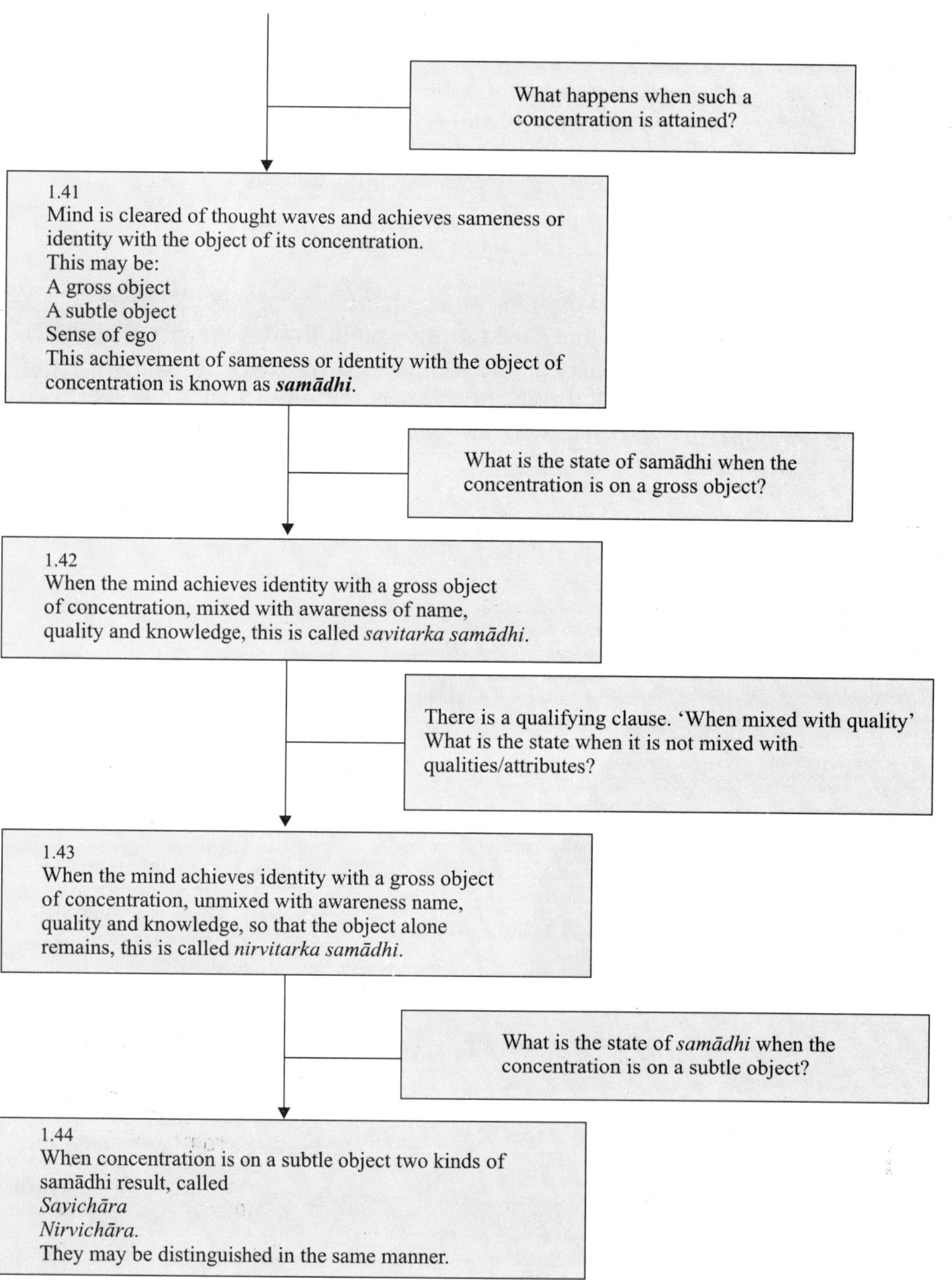

सूक्ष्मविषयत्वं चालिंगपर्यवसानम् ।।४५।।

Sukshma_Vishayatvam Cha_Alinga_Paryavasānam.

Behind objects subtle
Is cause primal.

Sukshma : subtle *Vishaya* : Object *Alinga* : indication
Paryavasānam : extending up to, ending at

Q: *What is behind all subtle objects?*
A: Behind all subtle objects is *Prakriti*, the primal cause.

The apparent creation process

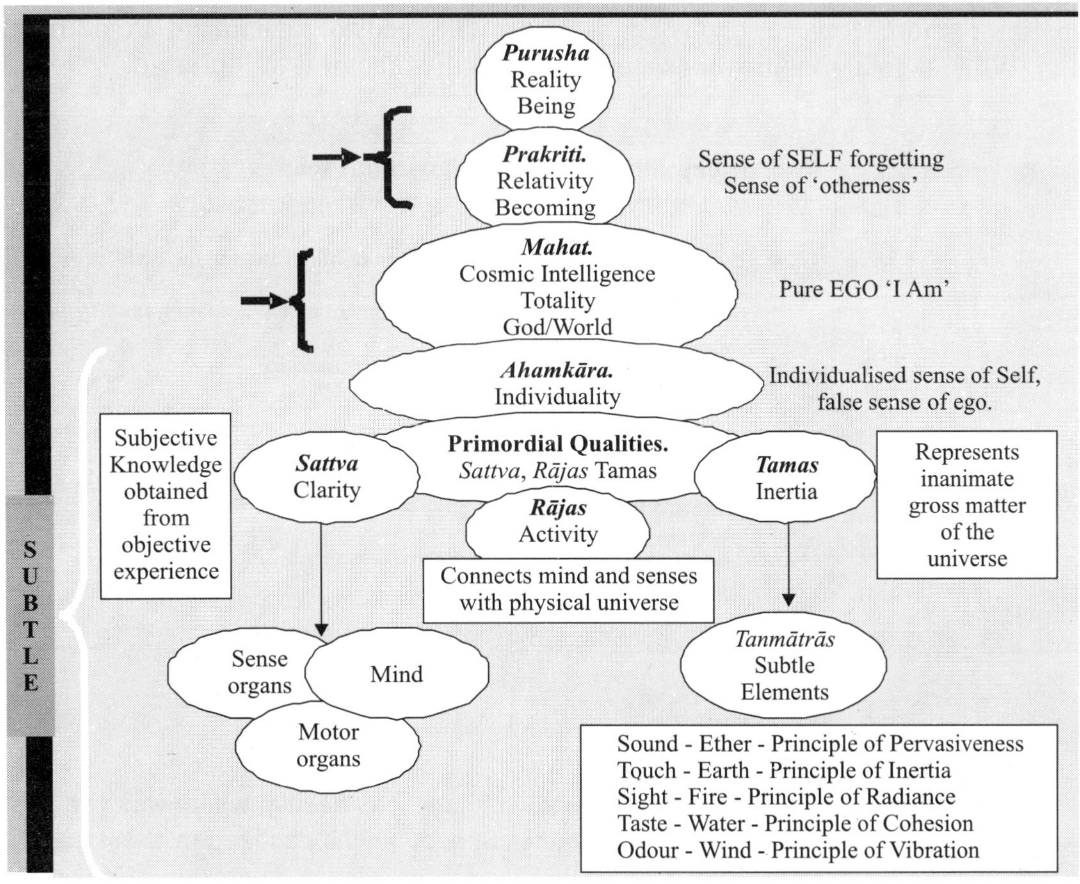

The universe begins to look more like a great thought than like a great machine.

Sir James Jeans, *'The Mysterious Universe'*

ता एव सबीजः समाधिः ॥४६॥
Tā Eva Sabijah Samādhih.

These absorption states indeed
Are but, with seed.

Tā : they, hither to explained
Eva : alone
Sabiijah : with cause, with seed
Samādhih : trance

Q: *How are the above states of absorption referred to?*
A: They are referred to as state of absorption 'with seed.'

The seed referred to is the impression formed in the mind. These absorbed states do not remove impressions of past actions. One cannot be said to be fully liberated, devoid of any impression. However one is almost there. The seeds of attachment are dormant in him. While mental modifications are gone, causative factor is still present.

Absorption with seed and without seed	
A state of absorption with seed is one in which	❖ A distinct object to be meditated upon is still present in the mind. ❖ Seeds of desire and attachment still linger on in a dormant form. ❖ Causative factor of mental modifications remains.
A state of absorption without seed is one in which	❖ The object selected for meditation has disappeared from the mental plane and there is no longer any recognition of it. ❖ There is a progressive absorption on a higher level of consciousness.

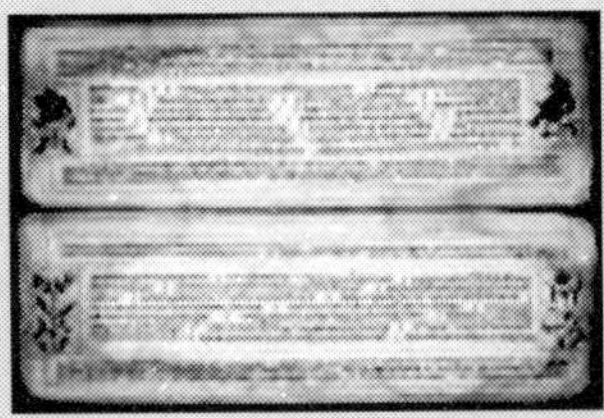

"In the beginning there was desire, which was the first seed of mind; Sages, having realized in their hearts, have discovered by their wisdom the connection of the Existent with the non existent."

- The Hymn of Creation, Rigveda

निर्विचारवैशारद्येऽध्यात्मप्रसादः ॥४७॥
Nirvichār_Vaishāradye_Adhyātma_Prasādah.

On absorption with super reflection
Mind remains with no deflection.

Nir : without, devoid of *Vichār* : reflection *Vaishāradye* : when predominant
Adhyātma : in the mind *Prasādah* : clarity

Q: *What is the state of mind on attaining Nirvichāra Samādhi?*
A: On attaining *Nirvichāra Samādhi*, mind is still, devoid of fluctuations.

By becoming brighter and brighter, a burning lamp reveals itself and its surroundings in an increasing measure. It also begins to throw increasing light on the object brought to its presence. Assume the light is placed in a glass case. Initially the soot dims the light glow. As and when they get removed, the brightness increases. The flame itself produces initially the smoke which causes the soot. This smoke and corresponding soot is because of improper burning. Concentration makes the burning smokeless and brighter. So, two simultaneous actions take place, the existing soot (impressions of past actions) get cleared and no new soot is allowed to accumulate, the burning being proper (new impressions do not form since all actions henceforth become desireless action). What is now left is just bright light reflecting and radiating, shining and showing the way to others. When the mind stuff no longer wavers and is firmly established, the 'concentration without discrimination' is purified. To such a one is everyone like an open book. He can read them well.

A single glance suffices to reveal to Him his contents

F H Humphreys, India 1911, in the British police service in Vellore, a south Indian town, who visited Shri Ramana Maharshi, a well known sage for the first time. In his words: "I went by a motor cycle and climbed up the cave. The sage smiled when he saw me but was not in the least surprised. We went in and before we sat down he asked me a question private to myself, of which he knew. Evidently he recognized me the moment he had seen me. Every one who comes to him is an open book"

"An integral being knows without going, sees without looking, and accomplishes without doing."

Lao Tzu

ऋतम्भरा तत्र प्रज्ञा ॥४८॥
Ritambharā Tatra Pragyā.

Thence perception is pure
And knowledge unfailingly true.

Ritambharā : full of truth *Tatra* : there, in that state of consciousness
Pragyā : knowledge

Q: *What kind / type of knowledge does one have in that state of absorption?*
A: In that state of absorption the knowledge is said to be 'filled with truth'.

Any knowledge derived from reasoning, logic or analysis suffers from the limitation of name-form syndrome. They cannot be totally true.

Aphorism of Einstein says:

> "As far as the laws of mathematics refer to reality, they are not certain.
> And as far as they are certain they do not refer to reality."

It is not possible to grasp reality from the state of relativity. Whatever may be the subject matter so grasped, it is bound to suffer from limitation in representation. Knowledge attained from the state of absorption is always irrevocably and unfailingly true and filled with truth.

The knowledge is unfailingly true because there is no superimposition in this state. The natural human judgement based on the false identification that leads one to say 'I', 'me' and 'mine', are absent in this state of mind. Without the veil of ignorance obstructing the vision, one can know. When a person rises above the limitations of 'I' and 'mine', that is, above the body consciousness, there is serenity of experience. It is like getting out of the effect of alcohol or drug. The sense organs and the mind are the drug in the body. The drug effect is external object orientation of the mind. Once the drug effect is removed, vision is clear. Everything is known as it is.

I asked a child, walking with a candle,
"From where comes that light?"
Instantly he blew it out.
"Tell me where it is gone -
then I will tell you where it came from."

Hasan of Basrā

श्रुतानुमानप्रज्ञाभ्यामन्यविषया विशेषार्थत्वात् ।।४९।।

Shruta_Anumāna_Pragyābhyām Anya_Vishayā Vishesha_Arthatvāt.

Inferential knowledge is of limited kind.
No match to knowledge through absorption gained.

Shruta : heard *Anumāna* : deduced *Pragyābhyām* : cognitive
Anya : different *Vishayā* : object *Vishesha* : details
Arthatvāt : having reference to

Q: *How does knowledge of the state of absorption differ from knowledge gained through study and inference?*

A: The knowledge which is gained from inference and the study of scriptures is as mind perceives. But the knowledge which is gained from *samādhi* is of a much higher order. It is knowing as it is.

Most of the knowledge, one has, in the unabsorbed state of existence, is based on inference and memory. Whatever knowledge one has, is based on whatever knowledge one had. The inductive or deductive logic or reasoning that one adopts to arrive at conclusions are all based on what he had known, what others have said as true, what parents have said as real or what one seemed to have observed. Every time he looked; memory, misapprehension, and delusion presented itself as the distracting spectacles in between him and the object. The distraction in the form of thought waves was in built, in born, and automatic.

To the one who has attained the state of one pointed-ness and absorption, the filtering, prejudicial distractions do not present themselves. Without the influencing factors he looks at things as they are. His is direct perception. That of others' is indirect inference. His observation is correct, but that of other's faulty. His is truth. He is truth.

He who transcends sense perception, has transcended even his intellect, dawns real wisdom. Such a one realizes that all knowledge is within and he is knowledge. There is nothing outside him that can present him with knowledge.

"Not by speech, not by mind, not by sight,
can this be apprehended.
How can this be comprehended
except by the one who says, 'It is'?

Katha Upanishad

SUMMARY: Aphorism 1.45-1.49

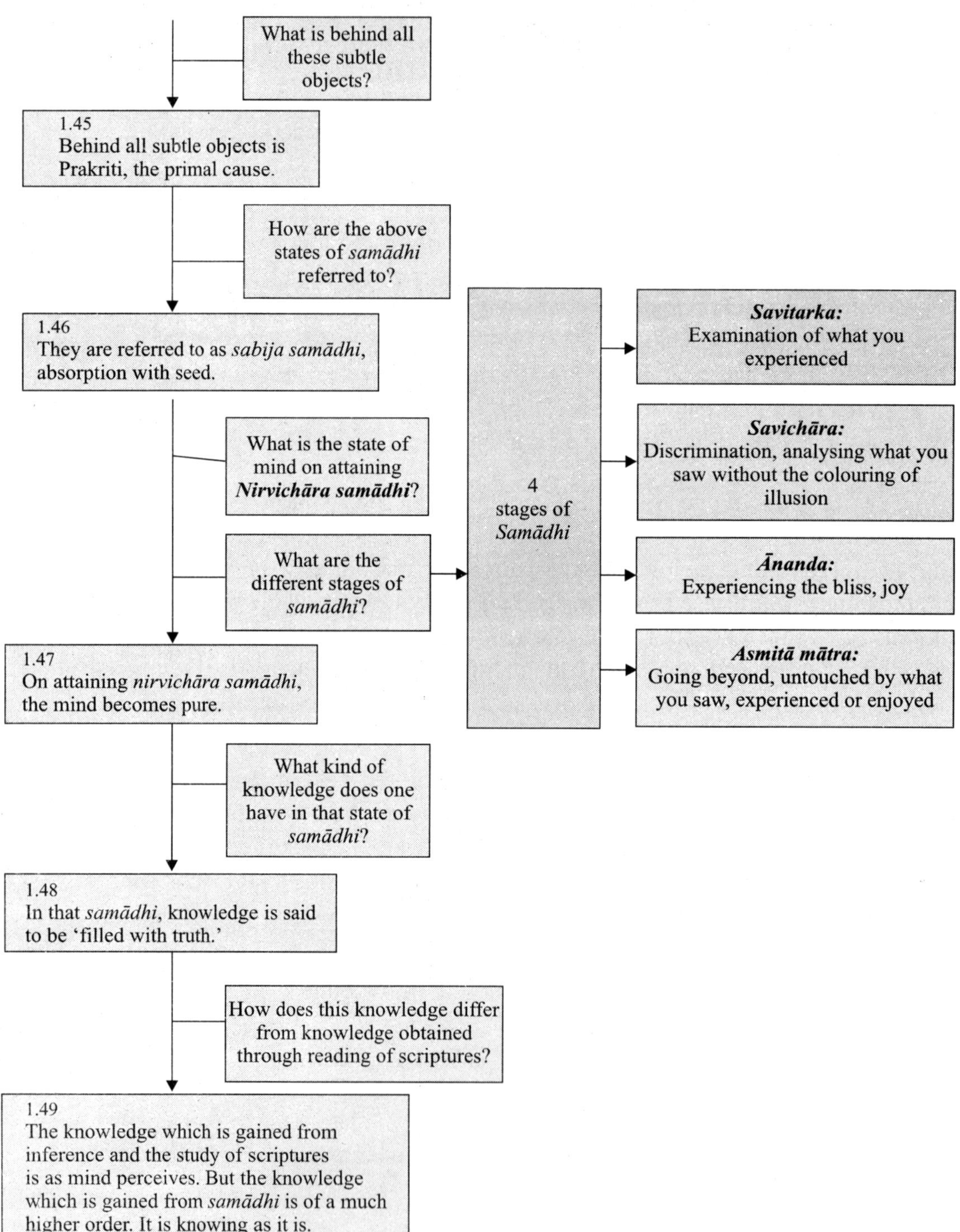

तज्जः संस्कारोऽन्यसंस्कारप्रतिबन्धी ॥५०॥

Tat_Jah Sanskāro_Anya_Sanskāra_Pratibandhi.

This new impression on mind
Wipes out all other kind.

Tat_Jah : Born out of that *Sanskāro* : recollection *Anya* : different, other
Sanskāra : recollection *Pratibandhi* : obstruction

Q: *What happens to the earlier impressions and propensities?*
A: The experience of the state of absorption wipes out all earlier impressions and propensities.

He is truly a 'Born again *dwij*.' The old memories are gone. All tendencies, impressions and propensities and the so-called in born qualities disappear. He becomes a wholly new self, with an engulfing new awareness. He can hardly recollect his past difficulties and misapprehensions and explain them in any detail. The activities of mind referred to earlier (Aphorism 1.6) have a different break up all together.

Mental modifications

Right Knowledge
~~Misapprehension~~
~~Delusion~~
~~Deep Sleep~~
Memory

Cognition and Memory present.
It is a state referred to as *Nirvikalpa Samādhi*.

Not devoid of memory or ideas.

Much the same way as an ace archer sees nothing other than the bird on top of the tree and is devoid of Vision of the obstructing leaves, the attractive fruit or flower on the tree; the seeker is now not aware of anything other than the object of concentration. The mental modifications like misapprehension, illusion, and deep sleep has left him.

He is totally cognitive, apprehends everything right, is devoid of delusion and memory is dim. Deep sleep is of a very short duration. He is no more emotionally involved in anything. There is nothing in Him other than the reality. Thought vibrations are neutralized. Sensory organs do not distract or disturb him. Opposites do not bother him. He is at once sympathetic to all and yet totally detached from all. He goes about his routine activities, but with no motive. The cause is not there. The effect is not felt. He is free. In him the seed of desire is roasted and hence cannot sprout.

All cravings and desires come to an end in the awakened person.
Therefore, liberation arises in him without his seeking.........
like a lamp in whose light all activities take place in which the
lamp is not interested, he lives and acts, but is free from volition.

तस्यापि निरोधे सर्वनिरोधान्निर्बीजः समाधिः ॥५१॥
Tasyāpi Nirodhe Sarva_Nirodhāt Nirbijah Samādhih.

With the last impression also gone
Absorption is now a seedless one.

Tasyāpi : That also *Nirodhe* : cessation, stopped, blocked *Sarva* : all
Nirodhāt : blocking *Samādhih* : state of absorption *Nirbijah* : without seed

Q: *Is it then a different state than the one described as 'absorption with seed'?*
A: Yes. This state can be described as 'seedless' *Samādhi*.
Now, all mental modifications remain stilled.
The seed here refers to a single object of attachment

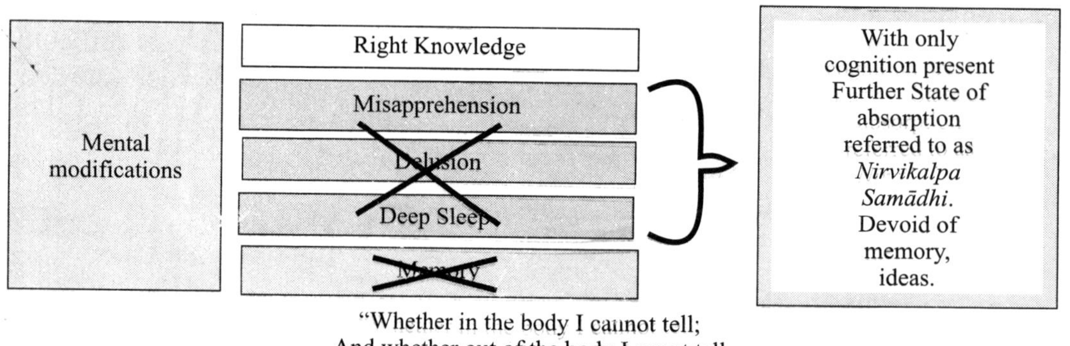

"Whether in the body I cannot tell;
And whether out of the body I cannt tell
God knoweth".
(St. Paul)

The state in which awareness is firm and one pointed, even when objects are sensed, is also called *sahaja sthiti*. The state in which objects are absent is called *nirvikalpa samādhi*.

I do not think I know It well.
Nor do I think I do not know It.
I know too.
He amongst us knows It,
who knows It as other than the known and unknown.
Kena Upanishad

Q: On an enlightened one, what is the effect of *Karmas*?

A: The *Prārabdha Karma* is very powerful, in the absorbed one. The effects continue and is exhausted by Him. Until then He endures cheerfully. The *Prārabda Karma* are like dream objects to one who is absorbed. *Sanchita Karma*, incurred during the present life, are destroyed by the fire of perfect knowledge. So also that of *Āgāmi Karma.*

Q: Is the one in *Samādhi* state not subject to illusion?

A: The absorbed one does not make such distinctions as 'I', 'mine' 'this' with respect to this illusory body and the world to which it belongs, but remains wakeful and conscious of higher self. In him there are no desire strengthening illusory objects, nor does he perceive any advantage in this world. Eating, sleeping, etc are to a wise man but as a recollection of objects seen in a dream. In him mental activity has vanished. He knows neither 'this' nor 'that', nor what this bliss is, its extent, nor its limit.

Some quotations from the scriptures about the state of the one who has attained illumination:

"As water does not stick to the lotus, so after realization future actions cannot stick to the knower."

Chhāndogya Upanishad 4.14.3

"Just as the cotton like flowers of the *Isika* seed are burnt by fire in a moment, so are the accumulated past actions of the knower: burnt up because of realization"

Chhāndogya Upanishad 5.24.3

Just as a blazing fire reduces the fuel to ashes, so, Arjuna, the fire of knowledge burns up all actions"

Krishna, Bhagavadgitā 4.37

"When a man has known the effulgent Self, all his bonds are cut asunder, his afflictions cease. There is no further birth for him"

Shvetāsvatara Upanishad

> The first and foremost of all thoughts, the primeval thought in the mind of every man, is the thought 'I'.
> It is only after the birth of this thought that any other thoughts can arise at all.
>
> *Sri Ramana Maharshi*

SUMMARY: Aphorism 1.50-1.51

What happens to the earlier impressions / attributes / *vāsanās*?

1.50
The impression which is made upon the mind by that *samādhi* wipes out all other past impression.

Is it then a different state than the one referred to earlier as *Sabija* / 'with seed' *samādhi*?

1.51
Yes, This state is different. It is referred to as *Nirbija samādhi*. In this state the impression made by that 'with seed' *samādhi* is also wiped out, so that there are no more thought-waves in the mind.
All mental modifications are erased.

इति श्री पतंजलि योगशास्त्रे समाधि निर्देशो नाम प्रथम पादः।

Thus ends Sree Patanjali Yoga Sutras Chapter 1

Chapter 2

Sādhana Pādah

The Means

तपः स्वाध्यायेश्वरप्रणिधानानि क्रियायोगः ॥१॥

Tapah_Svādhyāya_Ishvara_Pranidhānāni Kriyāyogah.

Austerity, study and to God dedication
Is Yoga in action.

Tapah: Austerity/ refinement, accepting pain as purification
Svādhyāya: Self study/ reflection, asceticism *Ishvara*: God, Supreme Being
Pranidhānāni: Dedication to God / resignation, surrendering all actions to God
Kriyāyogah: Yoga practice

Q: *What are the preliminaries to Yoga?*
A: The preliminaries to Yoga practice are: 1. Austerity - Reflection 2. Study of scriptures – Refinement 3. Dedication of actions to God, Resignation

The steps towards Yoga are detailed in this *sutra*. Where does an aspirant start and what are the requirements? Patanjali Yoga is a step by step approach. The first set of steps is referred to as *Kriyā* Yoga, Yoga of action. It has a triple component.

Preliminaries to Yoga Practice		
***Kriyā* Yoga** **Yoga Practice**	***'tapah'*** **Austerity**	Self control, penance, Process of removal of impurities
	'Swādhyāya' **Study** Reflection	Placing oneself closer to ONE SELF Study of scriptures Repetition of mantra
	'Isvara Pranidhān' Dedication	Dedication of all actions to God Letting ego go ! Resignation is opening up to Let God enter you !

"Unsteady are the boats of 18 forms of sacrifice, which are part of inferior *karma*. The deluded who take delight in them thinking that they would lead them to good, fall again into old age and death... These deluded men regarding sacrifices and works of merit as most important do not know any other good. Having enjoyed in the high place of heaven won by good deeds, they enter again this world or still the lower ones."

Māndukya Upanishad

Kriyā Yoga is defined as purification, reflection and acceptance of the universal order. One performs certain acts of purification, reflects on those acts and accepts the outcome with an attitude of non-attachment. *Kriyā* has come from the root word, '*Kr*' meaning 'to do'. This *Kriyā* or action refers to all practices that enable one to detach from sense objects and attach one to the Being, by Being.

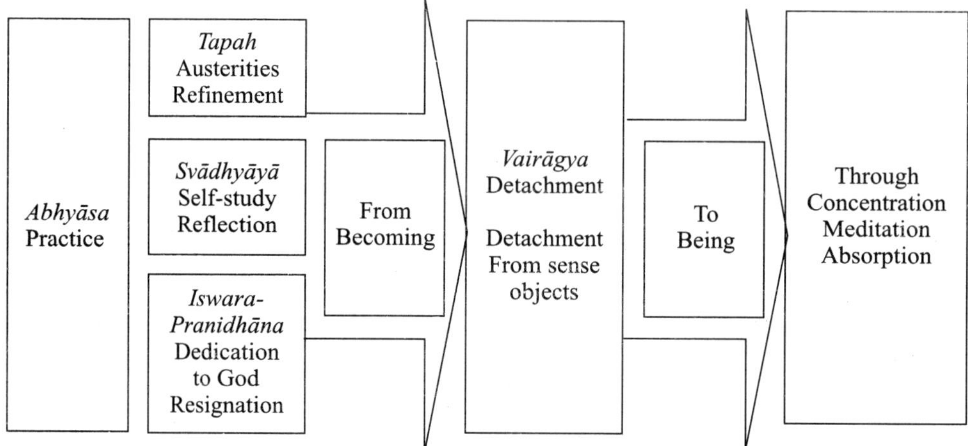

Tapah (austerity): '*tap*' literally means to 'to cook' or "to burn". *Tap* can also mean burning all desires by means of discipline, purification, and penance. fasting, and observing silence. *Tapah* indicates effort and endeavour. It involves the voluntary and cheerful experiencing of a privation, with a view to attain a higher goal. Any form of giving up desires is *tapah*. *Tapah* means the end of the activities of the senses; one must be the master of all of them. There should be no trace of craving or appetite. It involves effort to attain *Brahman*, incessant yearning for that end; it must be expressed through moderate food and sleep: it means agony to realise the principle. Such a *tapah* is called *Sāttvic*. *Tapah* does not mean senseless mortification.

An ascetic is a person who renounces material comforts and leads a life of austere self-discipline, as an act of religious devotion. He leads a life of self-discipline and self-denial, for spiritual improvement. The ascetic practices in the past sometimes turned even bizarre with ascetics indulging in self inflicted bodily torture.

Tapah is a way of asserting one's will and breaking the sensual nature which craves for comfort and indulgence.

The objective of the ascetic practices according to Buddhism is to make improper motive into proper intent, whereby:

1. Greed becomes generosity.
2. Anger becomes patience and endurance, and
3. Stupidity becomes wisdom.
4. Conceit becomes embracing of the precepts with humility and

5. Doubt and distraction becomes mental (meditative) concentration.

Svādhyāya (Self study or study by self): Reflection and introspection, the study of scriptures, repetition of mantra form part of the study of self. Self-inquiry is done by reflecting deeply on the question, 'Who am I?' Associating with enlightened people is also helpful in study.

Ishvarapranidhāna (surrender to God): Opening oneself to the cosmic flow of energy and uniting the individual mind with the universal one requires surrendering the ego self and beseeching the universal self to help. One who sees the Self in all beings and who has surrendered the ego of being the "doer" is the true practitioner of *Ishvarapranidhāna*. Actions without expectation mean surrendering to God. The seeker insures that his actions do not result in forming tendencies.

Tapah **austerity**	'Heating' oneself up sufficiently to let the 'matter' in him be converted to energy, in the process the effluent of impurities is got rid of.
Swādhyāyā **Study/ Reflection**	Understanding that one is not just a 'matter,' subject to death and decay but part of a force, field of knowledge that passes through all: from the place beyond time and space, the very origin of universe through the transition zone where energy turns into mater to the field of energy and matter, perceived as the world of objects and events
Isvara pranidhāna	Opening oneself up to the field of knowledge to flow through by removing forces that block the flow. Understanding that resistance to flow hurts, not the flow but the recipient.

Q: *What is austerity?* *Answer by Sri Nisargadatta Mahārāj:*
"Once you have gone through an experience, not to go through again is austerity.
To eschew the unnecessary is austerity.
Not to anticipate in pleasure or pain is austerity.
Having things under control all the time is austerity.
Both indulgence and austerity have the same purpose in view –
to make you happy. Indulgence is the stupid way, austerity is the wise way."

Powers like levitation and so on are gained by mantra, drugs and so on, even by the ignorant people. He who is prepared to make necessary efforts can gain these, whether he is enlightened or not. It is the ego that makes effort and gains these powers. These powers intensify the tendencies and mental conditioning.

समाधिभावनार्थः क्लेशतनूकरणार्थश्च ॥२॥

Samādhi_bhā vanārthah Klesha_Tanu_Karanārthah Cha.

Such practices remove afflictions
That are obstacles to the state of absorption.

Samādhi: State of absorption
Bhavanā: To make it appear, to establish
Arthah: Intent, goal
Klesha: Afflictions
Tanu: Tenuous
Karana: Production
Arthah: Goal
Cha: And
Karanārthah: In order to do

Q: *What is the result of observation of these practices?*
A: 1. Increased ability to concentrate and consequent removal of obstacles to realization.
2. Reduction in impurities, physical as well as mental.
3. Heightened awareness and capacity for self examination.

The afflictions that trouble one are generally of three types. They are:

Ādhyātmika within ourselves	That which is caused within ourselves; in the body by illness and in the mind by evil desires, anger, greed, folly, pride, envy, etc.
Ādhibhautika Others	That which is caused by other living beings such as beasts, thieves, and evil-mined persons.
Ādhidaivika Natural phenomena	The misery brought about by natural phenomena such as extreme temperature, floods and storms, earthquakes, etc. These may act as hindrances to spiritual life.

How can afflictions be removed?

Refinement, reflection and resignation are the methods through which the miseries related to mind can be removed.

Do not do what you want,
then you may do what you like.

Sadāshiva Brahmendra

अविद्यास्मितारागद्वेषाभिनिवेशाः क्लेशाः ॥३॥

Avidyā_Asmitā_Rāga_Dvesha_Abhiniveshāh Kleshāh.

Ignorance, egoism, attachment, aversion and desire
Are the afflictions.

Avidyā: ignorance *Asmitā*: egoism *Rāga*: craving, attachment, attraction
Dvesha: hatred, aversion, repulsion *Kleshāh*: afflictions
Abhiniveshāh: desire to cling to life, fear of death

Q: *What are the obstacles to realisation?*
A: Obstacles to realization are the afflictions: ignorance, egoism, attachment, aversion and desire.

Vidyā stands for higher knowledge. *A-vidyā* is the absence of higher knowledge. The higher knowledge that one lacks is the knowledge that while his body decays and withers off, one is eternal. The concept 'I am the body' is the primal ignorance. It is known as the '*hridayagranthi*', the firm knot of the heart. It gives rise to attachment, aversion, fear etc.

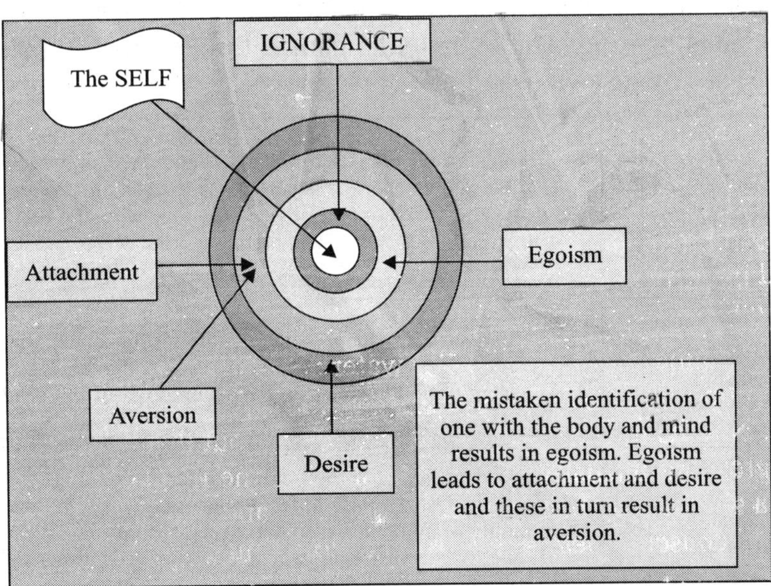

Attachment is the cause of objects.
Attachment is the cause of worldly existence.
Attachment is the cause of hopes.
Attachment is the cause of calamities.

Yogavāshishta

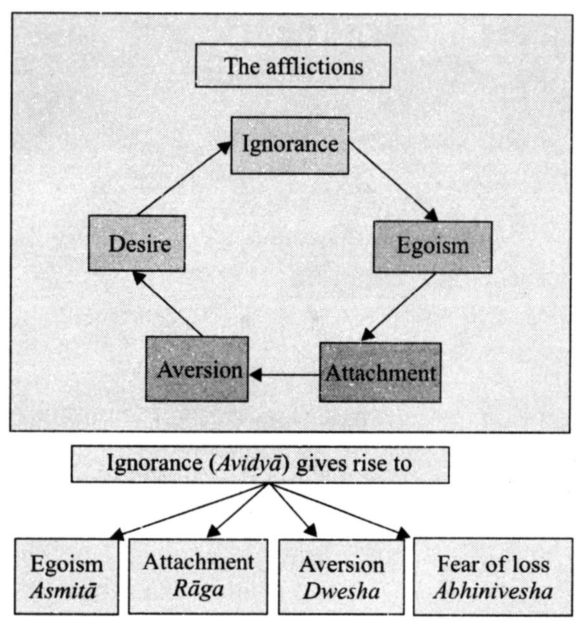

A distinction between knowledge and ignorance can be understood from the story of the ten disciples who crossed a river. One of them, after crossing the river, asks others to line up and counts. He counts only nine, leaving himself out. He tells others that one has perhaps drowned in the river. Each one in turn does the same. All of them are worried that one of them is missing. They weep and wail over the loss of their tenth colleague. The state of not finding the one though he is among them is *Agyāna*, ignorance of truth. The consequent feeling that the tenth one is not there is *Āvarana*, the veil over one's consciousness. The grief over the missing tenth, is *Vikshepa*, the distraction that arose

Faith arises when the eleventh man, their teacher passes by and tells them all ten are there and no one is missing. The knowledge gained through their teacher is the direct knowledge. All sorrow has vanished once this direct knowledge is gained.

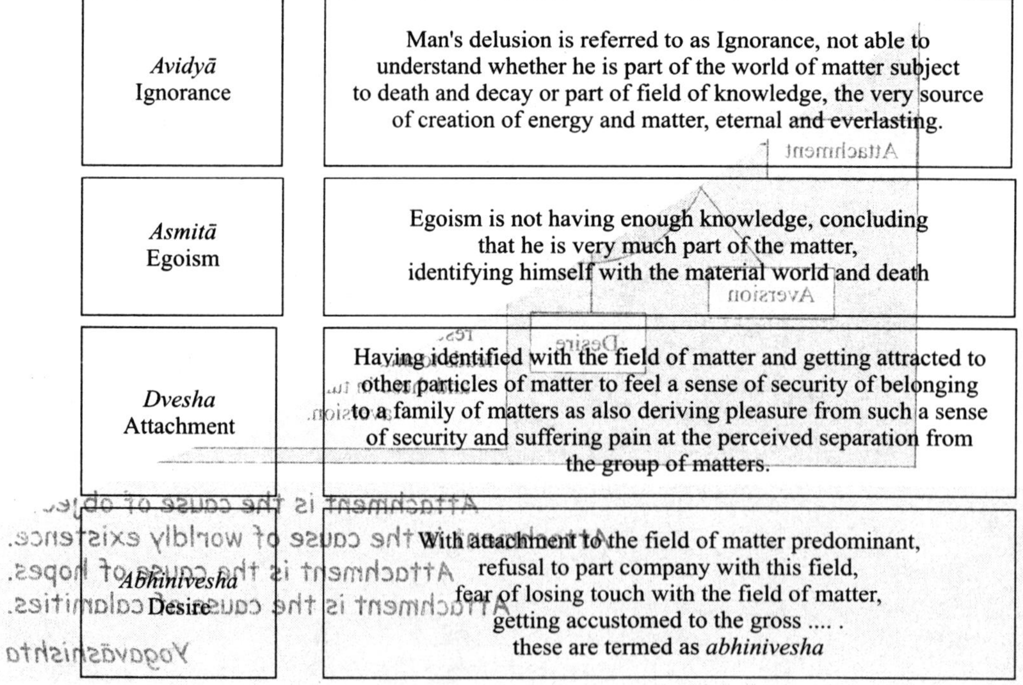

Avidyā Ignorance	Man's delusion is referred to as Ignorance, not able to understand whether he is part of the world of matter subject to death and decay or part of field of knowledge, the very source of creation of energy and matter, eternal and everlasting.
Asmitā Egoism	Egoism is not having enough knowledge, concluding that he is very much part of the matter, identifying himself with the material world and death
Dvesha Attachment	Having identified with the field of matter and getting attracted to other particles of matter to feel a sense of security of belonging to a family of matters as also deriving pleasure from such a sense of security and suffering pain at the perceived separation from the group of matters.
Abhinivesha Desire	With attachment to the field of matter predominant, refusal to part company with this field, fear of losing touch with the field of matter, getting accustomed to the gross .... . these are termed as *abhinivesha*

Avidyā performs a dual function. It veils the real and consequently projects the unreal. These two aspects of *avidyā* are called respectively *āvarana* and *vikshepa*. It is the projected world we come to know through our ordinary avenues of knowledge, such as perception, inference etc. This knowledge, called lower by the Upanishads is rooted in *avidyā*. Hence it can be said that all that the humanity knows is nothing but ignorance. All that is called science can be called ignorance stemming out of the veiling and projecting powers. Even the Upanishads are termed lower by the Upanishadic seers themselves. Ādi Shankara in his commentary on Taittariya Upanishad says, "Knowledge and ignorance belong to the realm of name and form; they are not the attributes of the Self...... and the name and form are imagined, even as day and night are with reference to the sun." From the standpoint of view of sun there is no day and night. Similarly from the standpoint of view of the Self, there is no knowledge or ignorance.

Afflictions (*Klesha*) are usually listed as the following ten:

1. Greed or sensual desire
2. Anger
3. Ignorance
4. Conceit, pride
5. Doubt
6. Lack of belief in cause and effect
7. Clinging to views
8. Belief in ego, egocentric.
9. Belief in extremes, seeing things only in terms of the two extremes
10. Belief that rituals or asceticism will somehow lead to salvation or enlightenment.

There are two ways of elimination of emotional distress:

1. Most of the kinds of emotional distress are conceptual errors (false views or opinions - *darshana-heya klesha*) and can be eliminated by the path of insight, which is proper knowledge of the truth. This is completely true of doubt and the five false views, and partially true of the first four.
2. The most intractable kinds of emotional distress (*bhāvanā-heya klesha*) must be eliminated through the cultivation of meditation practice because they are habitual and ingrained compulsions. This applies to the first four, the emotional troubles of improper intent.

Free from desire, you realize the mystery.
Caught in desire, you see only the manifestations.
Chase after money and security
and your heart will never open the clench.
Care about people's approval,
and you will be their prisoner.

Zen Buddhism: Stephen Mitchell's translation

अविद्या क्षेत्रमुत्तरेषां प्रसुप्ततनुविच्छिन्नोदाराणाम् ॥४॥

Avidyā_Kshetram_Uttareshām Prasupta_Tanu_Vichchhinna_Udārānām.

Ignorance, for other obstacles, the source
Dormant, visible, intercepted or exposed.

Avidyā: Ignorance *Kshetram*: Source, root cause, field
Uttareshām: Of the remaining, following next *Prasupta*: Latent, asleep, dormant
Tanu: Obscure, feeble *Vichchhinna*: Interrupted, broken
Udārānām: Pronounced, active, sustained

Q: *What is the key obstacle to realisation?*
A: The obstacle is Ignorance, in a potential or vestigial form; dormant or developed.

Ignorance is the field on which the other afflictions (klesha) grow. They can be: 1. sleeping (inactive), 2. thin (imperceptible but active), fluctuating between active and inactive or full blown.

	Asmitā Egoism	*Rāga* Attachment	*Dwesha* Aversion	*Abhinivesha* Desire
Latent *Prasupta*				
Feeble *Tanu*				
Broken *Vichchhinna*				
Pronounced *Udāra*				

Deep rooted impressions lie dormant, but could rise any time when the conditions are appropriate and trigger an impulsive action. That reason is enough for cultivating right habit of thinking. If one cherishes deep inside him hatred for another, such hatred will burst open and cause a murderous attempt with all attendant consequences.

- Right, helpful, cheerful, thoughts stored up would mean impulsive helpful actions. Negative, wrong, hurtful, angry, gloomy, vengeful thoughts would equally well trigger impulsive unhelpful actions.

Desire and delusion warp the mind and cloud the understanding obstructing the power to discriminate between the good and the bad, between the lofty and the low. Delusion is the name given to the state where one is unable to distinguish between the true and the false. Desire and attachment are the cause of this delusion.

Bhaja Govindam

Ignorance, the mistaking of the relative to be real is the first of all afflictions and the very source of all afflictions. All these afflictions do not appear simultaneously. At times they are dormant and other time pronounced. When they are pronounced, the actions that follow as a result of such afflictions on the part of individual are there for every one to see. The individual himself after the action based on the affliction, in retrospection starts regretting and feels surprised as to why he did what he did. At the time of action, he is totally blind; in a fit of rage (*dwesha*) one may kill another. In a bout of lust (attachment) (*Rāga*) one may misbehave with a member of the opposite sex; when gripped with egoism (*asmitā*), one may heap unwarranted abuses on another and with a sense of despair resulting from fear of loss of religious identity, one may destroy others' place of worship.

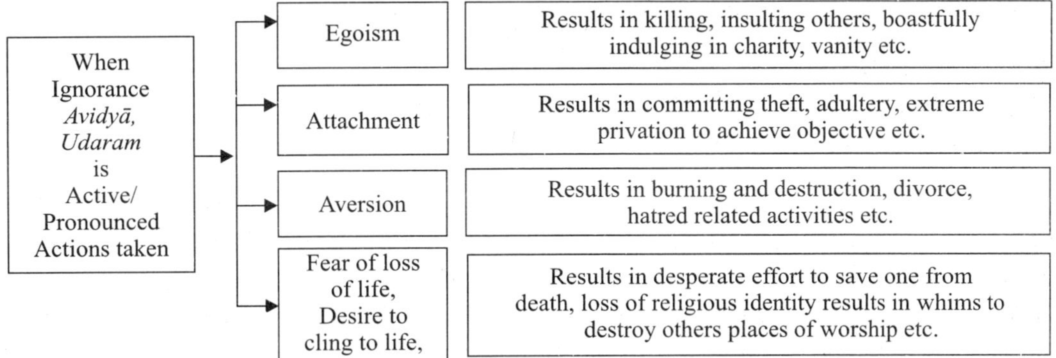

The Upanishad captures the duality caused by Ignorance, in a parable concerning two birds:

There were two birds in a tree
Or, so did it seem,
The one above sitting serene,
The other below, as restless as can be
While the top one in the tree
Is immersed in its glory,
The other one below remains buried,
In mirth and misery
The second one looks a little higher,
On every bite of fruit bitter,
Hops a little more nearer,
To the one above looking holier
Jumping up branches higher,
Eating fruits sweet or bitter,
Joins the second, the first one higher,
Only to find, there was no another.

How little does the common herd
know of the nature of right and truth.

Socrates

अनित्याशुचिदुःखानात्मसु नित्याशुचिसुखात्मख्यातिरविद्या ॥५॥

Anitya_Ashuchi_Duhkha_Anātmasu
Nitya_Ashuchi_Sukha_Ātma-Khyātih-Avidyā.

Ignorance is the mistaking of non-eternal, impure and painful
As eternal, pure and gainful.

Anitya: impermanent *Ashuchi*: impure, dirty *Duhkha*: sorrow
Anātmasu: non-self *Nitya*: permanent, everlasting
Sukha: joy, happiness, pleasure *Ātma*: Inner Self
Khyātih: error, mistake, identifying
Avidyā: ignorance, misapprehension, wrong understanding

Q: *What is ignorance?*
A: Ignorance is taking the 1. Non-eternal as eternal.
2. Impure as pure. 3. Painful as pleasant. 4. Non-self as Self.

The word comes from the root vid, "to know", the prefix a, and the suffix ya. The original meaning of the *vidyā* is, therefore, "the state of a thing as it is", or expressed in terms of the mental plane in one word, "knowledge". *Avidyā* (ignorance) is therefore, not a negative conception; it is just as positive as *vidyā* itself. The state of avidyā is that state in which the mental vibration is disturbed by that of space (*ākāsha*), and some other elements, which thus result in the production of false appearances. Mistaking of one for another is ignorance.

Q: "I suffer from pain. I feel pain in the state of waking and also in the state of dream; again and again after intervals of deep sleep experience. Is it my own nature? If it my own nature, I can have no hope of liberation as one's own nature cannot be got rid of. But if it is causal, liberation from it may be possible by removing the cause."

Teacher: "It is not your nature, but causal."

Q: "What is the cause? What will bring it to an end?"

Teacher: "Ignorance is the cause. Knowledge brings it to an end."

Q: "What is ignorance? What is its effect?"

Teacher: "The contrary knowledge is ignorance, the assumption of non-self as the real self.

"Ignorance not being destroyed, the destruction of desire and aversion is not possible. Actions caused by impurities are sure to follow in case desire and aversion are not removed."

Upadesha Sahashri, Ādi Shankara

Sāmkhya, one of the six schools of Indian philosophy, interprets *avidyā*, the ignorance, as the lack of ability to have the perception of the true reality that is seen as *Purusha*, the pure consciousness. *Avidyā* is seen basically as a state of confusion in which a recipient takes Self (*Purusha*) as a doer thus mistakenly believing that *Purusha* manifested in the world. The same confusion applies to Nature (*Prakriti*) that is also mistakenly seen to possess consciousness. This confusion is experienced at different levels of perception subject to the interplay of elements and characteristics. Ignorance (*avidyā*) becoming prevalent at those levels according to their specific characteristics.

It is obvious that the world with its contents is transient, and yet it is hugged as a real entity. Even the so-called solidity or substantiality of things is challenged today by the discoveries of modern science. The Theory of Relativity has put an end to such a thing as stable matter or body and even a stable law or rule to work upon. Still the world is loved as reality. This is one of the functions of *avidyā*. From today's scientific point of view we may illustrate Ignorance as:

What is Ignorance?

Ignorance is mistaking this finite field of matter as real and unconnected with the field of quantum.

Ignorance is not understanding that in this field of matter time is linear and space is fixed.

Ignorance is the mistaken belief that somehow the individual is in himself complete and is in no way connected to all other beings.

Ignorance is the mistaken notion that each individual mind is a separate entity and is not connected to an universal mind that runs through all minds.

The relationship between *jiva* and *avidyā* is comparable to the one between the fire and smoke, mirror and dust, and foetus and womb. Just as smoke envelopes fire, *avidyā* clouds the *jiva*. Though carefully protected and cleaned constantly, a sheet of glass becomes dusty in no time. Even so, with the best efforts, a person may not succeed in getting rid of *avidyā*, which has a tendency to attach itself to *jiva* again and again. It is only with the grace of God, that the foetus gets separated from the mother's uterus, to which it remained attached for months, and is delivered into earth. Similarly, the *jiva*, which has intimately attached itself to *avidyā*, requires the grace of God to free itself from it.

Shrimad Bhāgavatam

As long as the mind is not dissolved, so long there is no destruction of mental impressions. As long as mental impressions are not destroyed, so long the mind is not extinguished.

Yogavāshishta

Reality does not appeal.

There was an expert who could grunt like a pig. When he grunts, if there are pigs around, they would all look around to see if a new member has come. Such was his expertise; the town folk admired him and were even willing to pay to hear him grunt. His fame spread around to the neighbouring towns too. He could make an easy living, grunting his way around. He would even conduct special shows, in an enclosed arena and collect good sum from the visitors.

Once, a sage was visiting the town, where the grunter's show was on. The sage was moving along with his disciples. For long the sage could not give a satisfactory explanation as to how and why though a seeker understands that the world is unreal and yet is totally attracted by the unreality. The sage saw lots of people flocking to the grunter's show and enquired as to what was on. On being told about the man and his expertise, the sage hit upon an idea to teach his disciples about reality and appearance and as to how even the learned are attracted by the appearance rather than the reality.

The sage purchased a live pig, erected a stage close to the place where the grunter's show was on. His disciples were looking curiously at this funny act of the sage. The sage started squeezing the pig and pig out of pain started grunting loudly. Everyone going to the show now had a live demonstration of a pig grunting and had the choice of not paying for the grunter's show. Yet all were only amused at the sage's action and laughed at the sage and asked him what is so great about a pig grunting. "So what, pigs will grunt", they said and walked away not finding any interest in the sage or his pig.

The sage now turned his attention to his disciples and told them, "Look at the reaction of people. For seeing the reality of a live pig, actually grunting, no one is interested. On the other hand every one is even willing to pay and hear a man grunt like a pig. Appearance is more attractive than reality. Men seldom care for reality, but are always attracted by imitation. That is why this world exists. The attraction of *māyā* keeps this illusory world alive. You give free guidance and teach how to know reality, ye no one comes to you. People would rather suffer as a result of ignorance, than get benefited by sagacious advice to set oneself free of illusion."

Watchfulness is the path of immortality:
un-watchfulness is the path of death.
Those who are watchful never die:
those who do not watch are already as good as dead.

At a glance: Aphorism 1-5

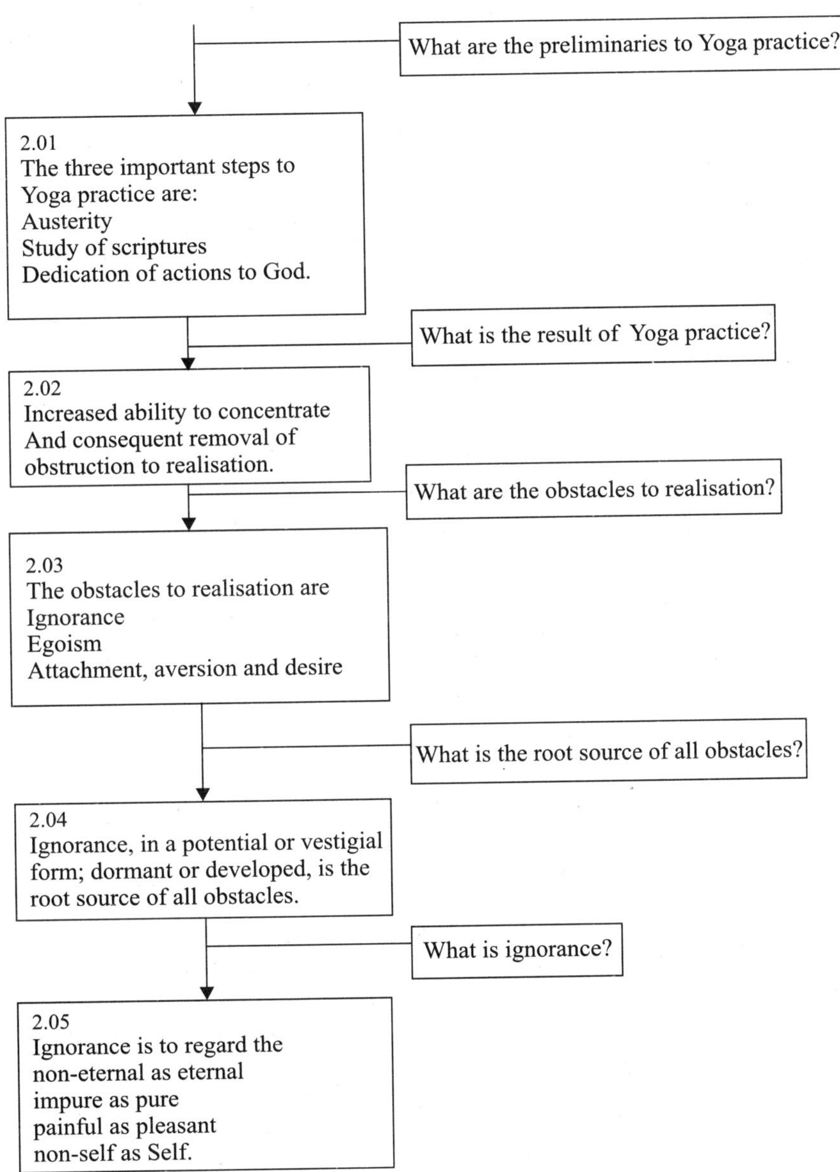

दृग्दर्शनशक्त्योरेकात्मतेवास्मिता ॥६॥

Driga_Darshan_Shaktyoh_Ekātmata_Yeva Asmitā.

Egoism is false identity
With the power to see.

Driga: seer, with foresight, one who sees or observes
Darshan: faculty of seeing, perceiving
Ekātmata: identity, essence, nature
Shaktyoh: capacity, power
Yeva: as if, as it were, only
Asmitā: false identity, egoism

Q: *What is Asmitā/egoism?*
A: Egoism is the false identify, the entity that results when we regard the mental activity as the very source of perception.

There are three types of identification of the Self with ego: *Sahaja*, *Karmaja* and *Brahmaja*.

Sahaja	❖ Identification of the true Self with ego. ❖ It is born along with it. ❖ Its birth and death correspond with the birth and death of the reflection of consciousness in intellect.
Karmaja	❖ Identification of ego with the material body. ❖ It is due ti fructifying karma. ❖ With death this identification vanishes.
Brahmaja	❖ Identification of ego with the intelligence. ❖ Result of the delusion produced by intelligence. ❖ When ignorance disappears, this also disappears.

That which spontaneously follows from Ignorance is Egoism or the sense of being. Egoism is identification of the seer with the instrument of seeing. The seer is the real self. The instruments are the intellect, mind and the sense organs. The 'I' 'Me' 'Mine' syndrome is the result of the false identity. Forgetfulness of universality ends in an assertion of individuality. The wrong notion that the individual is organically separated from the universe and the consequent self-assertion is the root cause of ignorance. The bifurcating attitude of likes and dislikes in regard to things (*Rāga-Dvesha*) and a longing to preserve one's body by all means (*Abhinivesha*) are the graduated effects of ignorance.

How blest in solitude, is he who hears the truth, the call!
How blest to be both kind and good, to practice self restraint to all!
How blest from passion to be free, all sensuous joys to let pass by!
Yet highest bliss enjoyeth he, who quits the pride, 'I am I'.

Lord Buddha

सुखानुशयी रागः ॥७॥
Sukhānushayi Rāgah.

Attachment
Dwells on pleasure.

Sukha: pleasure, happiness *Anushayi*: that which follows
Rāgah: passionate desire, attachment.

Q: *What is attachment?*
A: Attachment is the craving that results from wanting to have a repetition of events, incidences, associations, possessions that had once given a sense of pleasure.

Desire is attachment to objects of pleasure. The next two afflictions are related. The first is "*rāga*" which is strong desire and the second is "*dvesha*," which is strong aversion. Both are actually a form of attachment; one is a positive attachment and the other is a negative attachment. Attachment is based on pleasurable experiences. Because we remember pleasurable experiences, we hanker after them causing ourselves much frustration and dissatisfaction. When an object, repeatedly produces, in our mind, a feeling of satisfaction, our mind engenders the habit of falling again and again into the same state of vibration. The feeling of satisfaction and the picture of the object that seemed to cause that satisfaction tend to appear together, and this is a hankering after the object, a desire not to let it escape us. Wanting something is attachment, arising out of the feeling that one is not complete without some object or the other. The Self longs to be merged with itself. But due to ignorance, one mistakes this longing for objects of the external world and struggles to satisfy this longing. Ultimately, one finds that the more he attempts to get closer to the objective world, the farther away it travels. Mind, tired of such efforts and desirous of getting closer, now looks inward. This saga of human effort in the wrong direction first, and the tendency to reverse the direction and start the search inward is indeed the summum bonum of human history.

Rādhā: Short form of the combination of *Rāga* and *Dvesha*. Strange it may appear that Krishna's consort is a combination of *Rāga* and *Dvesha*! It has to be understood that Krishna (*Krishi* + *mānas*) stands for the tiller/ purifier of mind. Mind is constantly plagued by *Rāga* and *Dvesha*, (attraction and repulsion). Rādhā, the seeker of the purification should be constantly in the company of Krishna the purifier. Hindu mythology is full of symbolisms. Right understanding is needed to ensure that the seeker fully benefits from it.

"Not seeking what is other than the Self is detachment."

Ramana Maharishi

दुःखानुशयी द्वेषः ॥८॥
Dukhānushayi Dveshah.

Aversion
Dwells on pain.

Dukhānushayi: sorrow dwells on *Dveshah*: hatred, aversion, dislike

Q: *What is aversion?*
A: Aversion is a dislike for all such tastes, incidents, associations or events that had once given a sense of pain. Hate follows after experiencing pain.

Memory causes attachment and aversion. One first has an experience and finds it pleasurable. This experience and the feeling of happiness associated with that experience is stored in memory. Now, memory starts telling the individual to search for similar experience that once gave him happiness. When the attempt to repeat the experience is thwarted there is pain. This pain leads to aversion towards the person or the incident that thwarted the attempt to repeat the pleasure. Repetitive craving for enjoyment is attachment (*rāga*). The result of failure is aversion (*dvesha*).The experience of pain is also stirred in the memory. One therefore experiences pain even by recollecting an experience that has gone by. Pleasure and pain can be from the same source. Absence of pleasure is pain and absence of pain is pleasure.

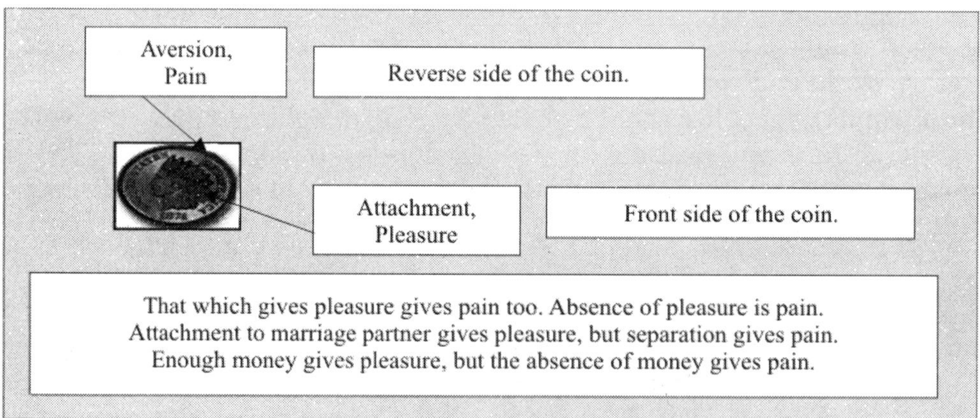

If you take effort in renunciation of mental impressions, then, all your mental anguish and physical illness are severed instantly.

Yogavāshishta

Rāga and *Dvesha* Attachment and Aversion	*Udāra* Fully manifest	Full and un-hiddered play of forces of attachment and aversion
	Vichchhinna Hidden	State where forces of attachment and aversion are hidden, suppressed
	Tanu Thinned out	State of thinning out in persons practising Yoga
	Prasupta Dormant	A dormant state waiting to spring back, in persons giving the practice of Yoga.
	Dagdha Burnt	A burnt out state, devoid of attachment and aversion. This is in a person who is in Union.

In worldly-minded people who are sunk in worldliness, *Rāga* and *Dvesha* assume an expanded state i.e., they have a full and unhampered play. *Vichchhinna Avasthā* is that state in which *Rāga* and *Dvesha* are hidden. The husband and wife sometimes quarrel; then love is temporarily hidden. Later on she smiles; then love comes back. This is *Vichchhinna Avasthā*. Some people do a little bit of *Prānayāma*, *Kirtan* and *Japa*. In them *Rāga* and *Dvesha* become thinned out (*Tanu Avasthā*). Sometimes, on account of unsuitable conditions, they lie dormant (*Prasupta Avasthā*). In *Samādhi* they are burnt - *Dagdha*. *Rāga* and *Dvesha* constitute this *Samsāra*. They constitute the mind.

When man realises God, there is pleasure.
When man perceives world, there is pain.

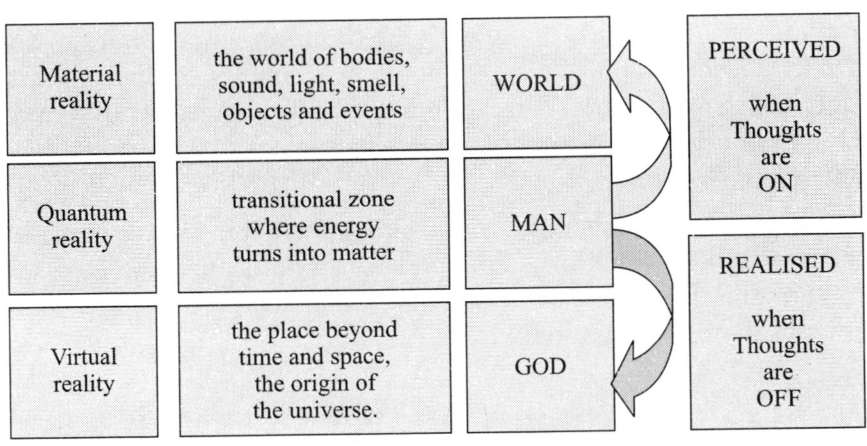

What blocks your vision is attachment and aversion.

स्वरसंवाही विदुषोऽपि तथारूढोऽभिनिवेशः ॥९॥

Svarasamvāhi Vidusho_Api Tathārudho_Abhiniveshah.

Desire for life arises
Even in the wise.

Svarasamvāhi: that carries own essence *Vidusho*: the wise *Api*: even
Tathārudho: strongly rooted in past life experience
Abhiniveshah: desire to cling to life

Q: *What is desire most common for all living beings?*
A: Desire to live forever and wanting not to get separated from the body is common in all living beings.

Lord of Death Yama: "What is the greatest wonder in the world?"

Yudhishthira: "Every day we see people entering the world of death. Yet we see the remaining wanting to live forever and behaving as if they are here to live till eternity."

Fear of death and the converse love of life is common to all living beings; the ignoramus, the intellectual, the bird and the beast, and the fool and the wise. What causes such a fear of death? It is said to be the instinct. But instinct is nothing but solidified intelligence of past experiences.

How good it would be if each one can say unto himself: "Never mind, let this body go. I have several more bodies to follow." Fear of death is due to mistaken identification of one with his gross body. One thinks that end of his gross body is end of his life. One should realize that on the death of the gross body, one continues to live, full of thoughts moving out of the body along with the life force Prāna after the dissolution of the body. On the dissolution of the subtle body, he re-enters another gross body. It is a constant roller coaster drive, and corresponding misery experienced. Real immortality is attained only after the realization that one is eternal and free and one has nothing to do with either his gross or subtle body.

Desire is the root cause of transmigration. Being attached to the desires, the individual soul attains that result to which his subtle body or mind is attached. Says the Mundaka Upanishad, "For the one who has completely attained the objects of his desire and realized the self, all desires dissolve in this very life."

Thought of death needs cause no pain.
The soul can neither slay nor be slain.

Bhagavadgitā

Socrates feared not death

Jacques-Louis David, 'The Death of Socrates'

An Athenian jury charged Socrates of corrupting the youth and interfering with the religion of the city—upon which to convict Socrates, and they sentenced him to death in 399 B.C.E. Just before death, Socrates remembers that he owes a cock and tells Onito: "Onito, I owe a cock to Asciepius, will you remember to pay the debt?". Crito agrees to do so. But he asks Socrates," Master, you are dying, are you not afraid of death?" Socrates replied, "Afraid of what? I have lived my life. It was beautiful. I would like to see what death is now."

In facing death Xenophon describes Socrates as "blithe in glance, in manner, in gait". In fact he consoled those who were weeping in anticipation of his loss. The devoted Apollodorus cried out, "But, Socrates, what I find hardest to bear is that I see you being put to death unjustly!" Socrates, stroking his head, replied, "My beloved Apollodorus, would you rather see me put to death justly?" and he smiled. Xenophon relates that Socrates did not weaken in the presence of death, but was cheerful not only in the expectation but in meeting death as well. Accepting this outcome with remarkable grace, Socrates drank hemlock and died in the company of his friends and disciples.

When he was about to die, the chief of prison guards who was himself a follower of Socrates asks him, "Socrates, I forgot to ask you one thing. How should we bury you?" Socrates responds, "Bury me if you can catch me," and then dies.

The difficulty is not to avoid death,
but to avoid unrighteousness
for that runs faster than death.

Socrates

ते प्रतिप्रसवहेयाः सूक्ष्माः ॥१०॥
Te Prati_Prasavaheyāh Sukshmāh.

Subtle afflictions be erased,
Lest they resurface.

Te: they *Heyah*: destroyed/capable of being reduced or avoided or abolished
Sukshmah: subtle *Pratiprasavah*: resolving back into their cause/re-absorption

Q: *After once being removed through Yoga practice, do these afflictions remain removed?*
A: Yes. But there is every possibility of the afflictions resurfacing again, unless one is vigilant and makes effort to root out egoism.

The afflictions that lie dormant as a result of Yoga practice, can resurface again unless one is vigilant and one goes to the very source of the afflictions and roots them out. The afflictions are the result of impressions. Unless one wipes out impressions, afflictions remain un-removed. The dormant afflictions present in a very subtle form resurface again when conditions needed present themselves. When the sources of afflictions are weeded out, there remains no seed of impressions. Once seeds are burnt, there will be no more sprouting of desires, fear, attachment, or aversion.

It will be erroneous to confuse a temporary state of clarity to a permanent state of detachment. The initial success in subjugating passions should motivate one to persevere with greater effort and determination. One should note that when a stone is thrown on a turbulent whirlpool of water no effect is seen, but the same stone thrown on a pond of still water sets up circles of waves. How disturbed Shri Rāmakrishna felt when a rupee coin was kept under his pillow when he was asleep by Vivekānanda to test his master. Until the veiling power ceases completely, conquest of the ideation and object orientation of the mind is impossible. Says, Ādi Shakara in the Crest Jewel of Wisdom, "Those alone are freed from the bondage of conditioned being, who having transcended all externals, mind, self and egoism, are absorbed in it, not those who simply speak about the mystery."

"From desire I stumble to possession
and in possession I languish in desire."
Goethe in his Faust

At a glance: aphorism 6-10

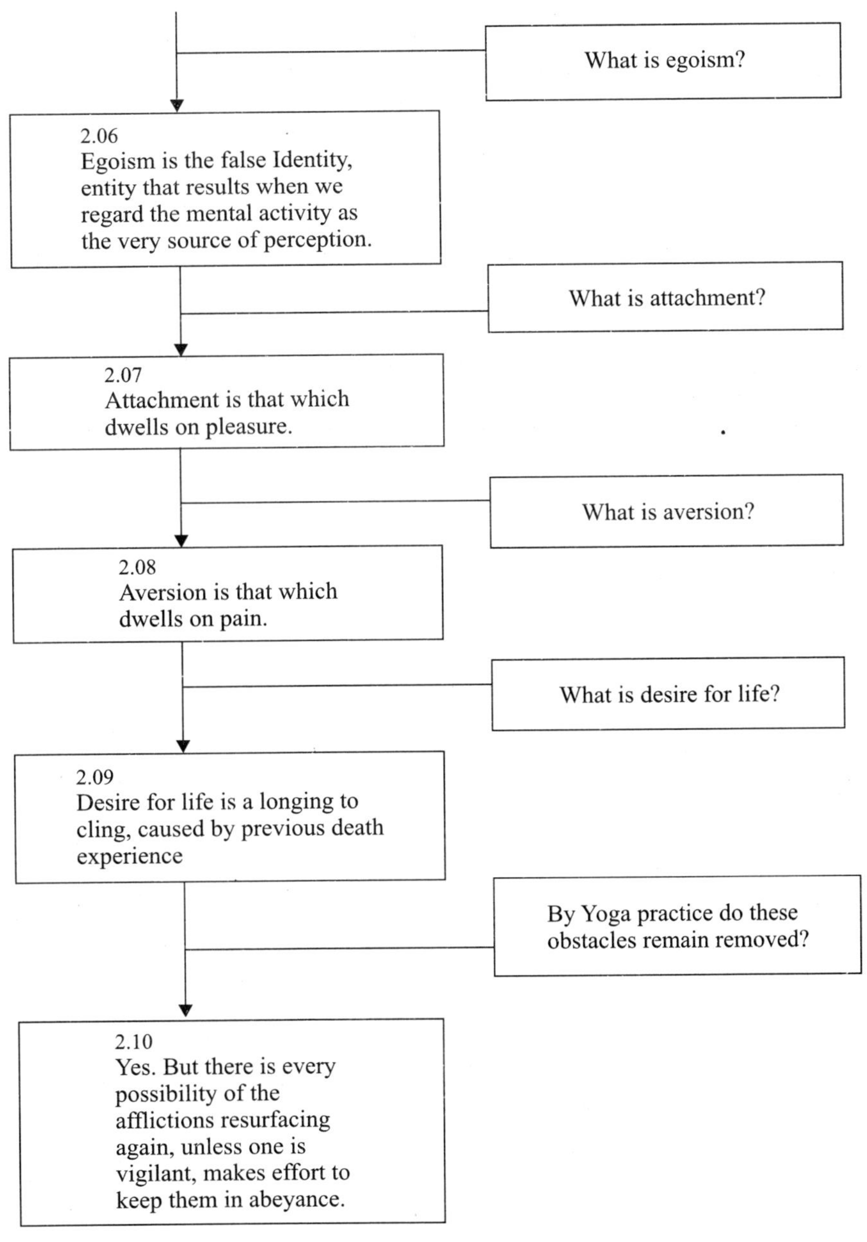

ध्यानहेयास्तद वृत्तयः ॥११॥
Dhyān_Heyāh Tad_Vrittayah.

Such modifications,
Be avoided through meditation.

Dhyāna: contemplation *Heyāh*: destroyable *Tad*: that *Vrittayah*: mental modifications

Q: *How to ensure that afflictions do not resurface?*
A: By meditation and through constant reflection and introspection, one can ensure that afflictions do not resurface.

The yoga of action, consisting of triple components of refinement (austerity), reflection (self-study) and resignation (surrender to God) should culminate in meditation in order to ensure that mental modifications remain subdued. Austerity, detachment and dedication in them are good practices. But that alone will not suffice, if one were to ensure that impressions are eliminated. Meditation is the best of all the means to contain thought waves. Meditation will ensure effortless refinement, reflection and resignation and make them a habit, a second nature as it were, overtaking and overpowering the 'in born' tendencies.

Gautama Buddha prescribes five meditations.

1 Meditation of Love	The first meditation is the meditation of love, in which thou must so adjust thy heart that thou longest for the welfare of all beings, including the happiness of thine enemies.
2 Meditation of Pity	The second meditation is the meditation of pity, in which thou thinkest of all beings in distress, vividly representing in thou imagination their sorrows and anxieties, so as to arouse a deep compassion for them in their soul.
3 Meditation of Joy	The third meditation is the meditation of joy in which thou thinkest of the property of others and rejoicest with their rejoicings.
4 Meditation on Impurity	The fourth meditation is the meditation on impurity, in which thou considerest the evil consequences of corruption, the effects of wrongs and evils, how trivial is often the pleasure of the moment and how fatal are its consequences.
5 Meditation on Serenity	The fifth meditation is the meditation on serenity, in which thou raisest above love and hate, tyranny and thraldom, and wealth and want and regardest thy own fate with impartial calmness and perfect tranquillity.

क्लेशमूलः कर्माशयो दृष्टादृष्टजन्मवेदनीयः ॥१२॥

Kleshamulah Karmāshayo Drishtā_Adrishta_Janma_Vedaniyah.

Past, present or future actions and their fruits
Have in afflictions, their roots.

Kleshamulah: cause of afflictions
Karmāshayo: based on past actions
Drishtā: seen, perceived, in this birth
Adrishta: unseen, not perceived, in future
Janma: birth
Vedaniyah: to be experienced

Q: *What makes afflictions resurface again?*
A: The latent tendencies created by past thoughts and actions make afflictions resurface again.

Gauthama Buddha says, "This rebirth, this renunciation, this appearance of the conformation is continuous and depends on the law of cause and effect. Just as a seal is impressed upon a wax reproducing the configurations of its device, so the thoughts of men, their characters, and their aspirations are impressed upon the others in continuous transference and continue their *Karma*, and good deeds will continue in blessings while bad deeds will continue in curses."

As you so, so you reap. In this cause-effect chain, often the effect is not clearly perceived to be the reaction of a particular cause. The time interval between the cause and the effect can be many births. Thus, the cause of a particular effect is not clearly seen. When one gets what he desires, one says it is because of *adrishta*, unseen, unperceived cause. Again when one encounters difficulties and trouble he says it is because of his *Karma*. But one stops at that. Seldom does he take the understanding further forward and says, "Alright let me now do good deeds and let me now purify my mind so that in future I go beyond experiencing the pain as well as the pleasure." This is because of the colouring effect of past actions. Hence, it requires an extraordinary effort and guidance of a good teacher to overcome the colouring effect.

There are three kinds of *Karmas*:

1. *Sanchita* (Accumulated)
2. *Prārabdha* (Fructifying)
3. *Āgāmi* (Current)

The quality of *Tamas* is eliminated by the other two qualities,
Sattva and *Rājas*,
Rājas by *Sattva* and *Sattva* by pure *Sattva*.
Remove the erroneous impression that non spirit is spirit.

Ādi Shankara-Viveka Chudāmani.

In the Vedāntic literature there is a beautiful analogy:

The bundle of arrows in the quiver on the hunter's back is the *sanchita karma*, the bagful, stared up.	The arrow, the hunter is about to shoot from his bow is the *āgāmi karma*, the oncoming.	The arrows the hunter has already shot are the *prārabdha karma*, the fructifying.

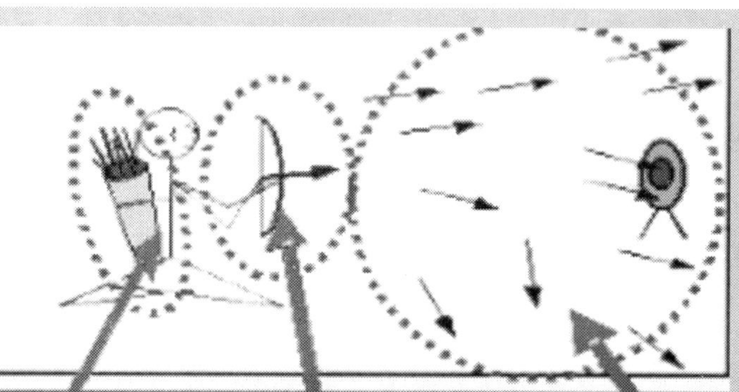

Sanchita karma, the stored up,

Sanchita karma, the stored up are predispositions of earlier actions and consequent impressions formed in mind. Part of it is seen as characteristics of man, in his tendencies, aptitudes, capacities, inclinations and desires. Yoga practice enables one to empty the quiver full of *sanchita karma*.

Āgāmi karma, the oncoming,

Āgāmi karma, the oncoming, is the karma now being performed. One has partial control over it. Through Yoga practice one can ensure that actions are done without expectations and make sure that future effect of current practice is non-binding.

Prārabdha karma, the fructifying.

Prārabdha karma, is that part of karma which is responsible for the present body-mind unit. It cannot be changed. It needs to be endured. It is like paying past debts. Effect of suffering can be mitigated by Yoga practice.

So long as the notion continues that the body is the Self,
Prārabdha exists.
When the notion is no longer cherished,
Prārabdha is abandoned.
Even the notion that the *Prārabdha* belongs to the body
is a delusive one.

Ādi Shankara-Viveka Chudāmani.

सति मूले तद्विपाको जात्यायुर्भोगाः ॥१३॥
Sati Moole Tadvipāko Jāti_Āyuh_Bhogāh

As long as afflictions and their roots remain
So long will rebirth be expressed as class, life span, pleasure and pain.

Sati: associated *Moola*: the cause *Tadvipāko*: the outcome thereof
Jāti: birth *Āyuh*: life *Bhogāh*: experiences, pleasant or painful

Q: *What happens when afflictions remain un-erased?*
A: When afflictions are not erased they bear fruits. They manifest again and again and cause life forms and experiences, the duration and nature depending upon the nature of afflictions. The root cause of misery remains un-erased. As long as afflictions remain they affect all actions.

The action-reaction syndrome, the cause effect cycle is further elaborated. *Karma* means action along with the implied consequence. The consequence is not a separate thing caused by the action, but a part of action which has built in consequence. The consequence is that part of action which fructifies at a future date and is as much part of it as the part done at present. The suffering is not the consequence of a wrong act but very much part of the act.

The actions of the past lead to three consequences:

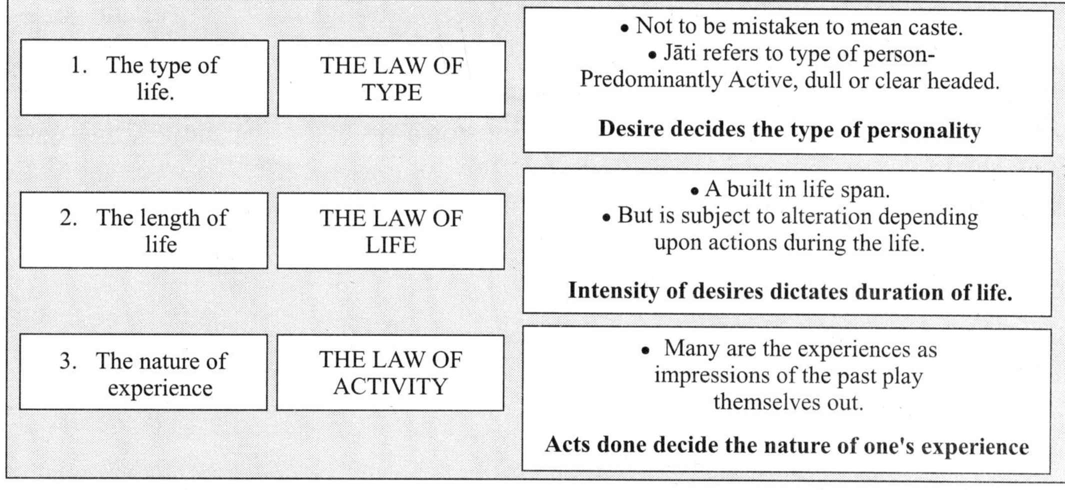

1. The type of life.	THE LAW OF TYPE	• Not to be mistaken to mean caste. • Jāti refers to type of person- Predominantly Active, dull or clear headed. **Desire decides the type of personality**
2. The length of life	THE LAW OF LIFE	• A built in life span. • But is subject to alteration depending upon actions during the life. **Intensity of desires dictates duration of life.**
3. The nature of experience	THE LAW OF ACTIVITY	• Many are the experiences as impressions of the past play themselves out. **Acts done decide the nature of one's experience**

Man verily is desire formed; as is his desire so is his thought; as thought is, so does he act; as he acts, so he attains.

Brihadāranyaka Upanishad

ते ह्लादपरितापफलाः पुण्यापुण्यहेतुत्वात् ॥१४॥
Te Hlād_Paritāp_Phalāh Punya_Apunya_Hetu_Tvāt.

Actions with virtue or vice as its root
Result in pain or pleasure as the fruit.

Te: they *Paritāp*: unhappiness *Phalāh*: outcome *Punya*: meritorious deeds *Hlād*: happiness *Apunya*: non–meritorious deeds *Hetutvāt*: being the cause

Q: *Will every action have a reaction?*
A: Yes. Actions undertaken with full clarity and with the afflictions subdued, results in pleasure. Those carried out under the effect of full force of afflictions result in pain.

The law of cause and effect is unalterable in every respect. Every act has its appointed effect, whether the act be thought, word or deed. The effect lies inherently in the cause as the tree lies encased in the seed. Water exposed to sun cannot avoid getting dried up. The effect automatically follows. The cause holds the effect, so to say in the womb.

Whether one attempts to free himself from his past actions or further binds himself with further actions with attendant benefits is up to him. While one cannot escape the stored up effects as a result of past actions, one does have the freedom to understand the whole process of cause and effect and strive to overcome the same through attempts at purifying his mind. But if he chooses to allow the interplay of his urges, anger and lust to influence his decisions, he should be ready to reap a windfall of sorrow and misery in this life as well as the ones ensuing.

On the other hand if one chooses the path prescribed by Patanjali and strives to avoid mental modification, he sure lays the foundation for a severance of the binding cause - effect chain. One's attempt must therefore be to understand, observe, meditate, concentrate, focus and liberate by negating ignorance, attachment, aversion, egoism and desire.

It is best to remember the laws:

1. The capacity of the mind and senses are governed by the law of *Karma*.
2. The extent to which one is in tune with the Ultimate Reality, to that extent one is loosened from the bondage of *Karma*.

Arjuna: O Krishna, prompted by what does a man sin against his will, as if some force compels him to do so?
Krishna: It is desire and anger, born of quality of *Rājas*. It is insatiable, the great source of all sins. O Arjuna, it is your own *karma*, produced by your own nature, that compels you to do things, even though you may not want to do them.

परिणामतापसंस्कारदुःखैर्गुणवृत्तिविरोधात्च्च
दुःखमेव सर्वं विवेकिनः ॥१५॥

Parinām_Tāpa_Sanskār Duhkhaih Guna_Vritti_Virodhāt_Cha Dukkhameva Sarvam Vivekinah.

The discriminating know involved actions lead to pain
Or change, anxiety or memory and hence give no gain.

Parinām: result *Tāpa*: austerity *Sanskāra*: memory
Duhkha: due to suffering, misery *Guna*: the triple qualities
Vritti: mind *Virodhāt*: conflict *Cha*: and
Dukkham: suffering *Sarvam*: all *Viveka*: discriminating

Q: *Is every action a bondage? Can there be no permanent pleasure from actions?*

A: Yes, it is bondage, if the fruits of actions are not surrendered. Absence of pleasure is pain. Past pleasure induces craving. In an atmosphere of constant change there can be no permanent pleasure.
Hence, the wise consider all experience as painful.

Pleasure can arise only from actions without expectation and permanent pleasure from linking with the permanent entity-God. The perception of 'other' is the cause for action with anticipation from the 'other', and hence, as long as there is duality there can be no pleasure. All actions lead to pain. Actions that initially give pleasure, lead to expectation of a repetition of the action and experience of pleasure. But the disappointment that results from the lack of expected pleasure, leads to pain. Pain is the product of activities arising from the play of triple qualities. Pain is the result of the inherent difference between the pairs of opposites, spirit and matter. Patanjali says that pain is comprehensive, covering past, present and future. The past impressions stored in memory propel one to undertake activities in expectation. The individual is seemingly helpless in resisting the temptation to act and the paying of the price of error. The triple qualities influence the person alternatively in engaging himself in activities that bind.

In renunciation there is pleasure.
Never can one hold on to an object and yet derive happiness from the object.

All bondage is due to either total lack of thinking,
incomplete thinking or wrong thinking.
It can be removed by right and complete thinking.

Tatva Bodham.

At a glance: Aphorisms 11-15

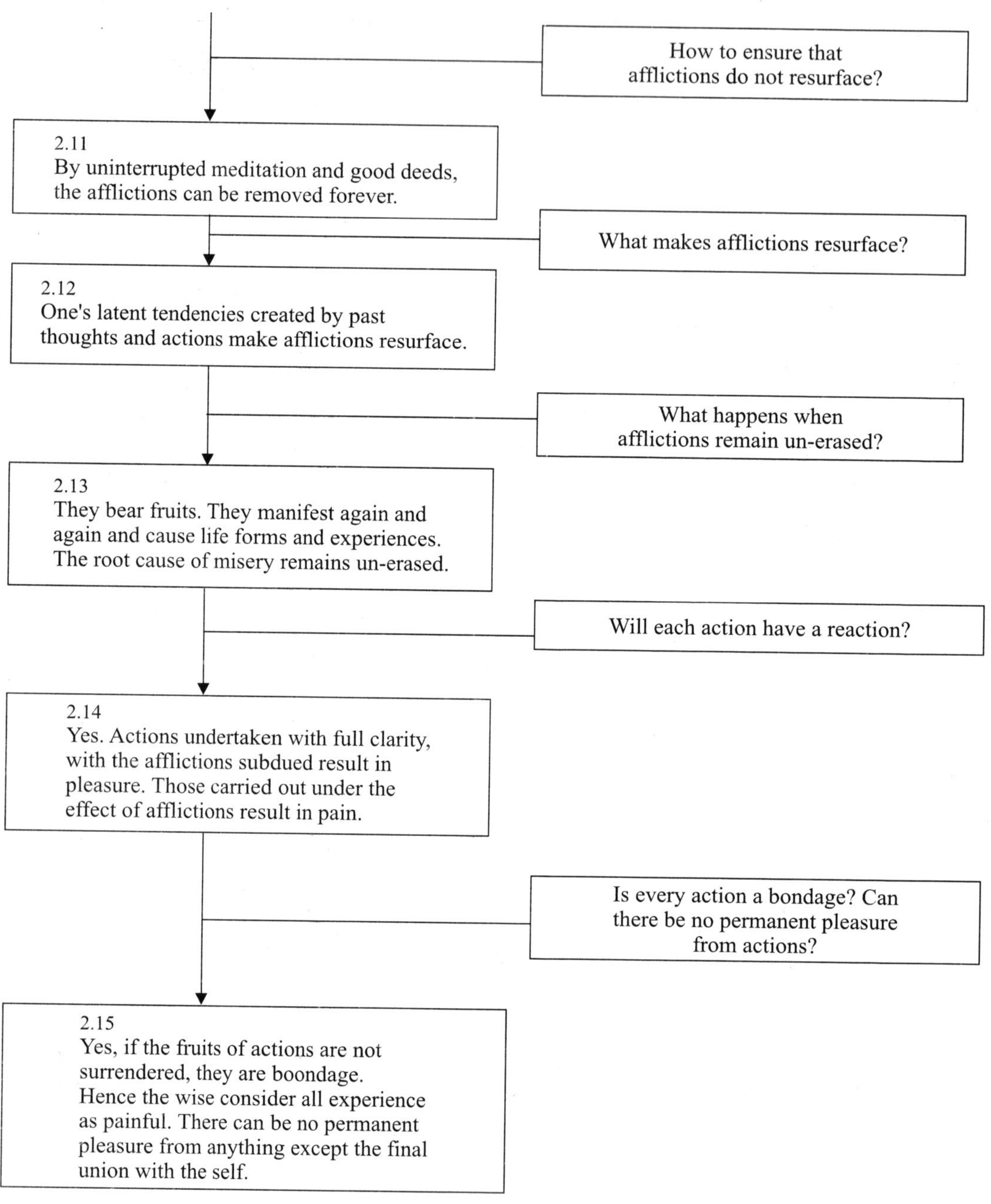

हेयं दुःखमनागतम् ॥१६॥

Heyam Duhkham_Anāgatam.

Sorrow yet to be
Avoided it should be.

Heyam: to be avoided, to be discarded *Duhkham*: pain, suffering, sorrow
Anāgatam: possible occurrences/which has not yet come, may come in the future

Q: *What is a good step towards freedom from binding actions?*
A: Avoiding sorrow that are yet to come is a good step, to be free from binding actions.

There are three types of action reaction units, called *Karma*.

How to avoid sorrow Yet to be

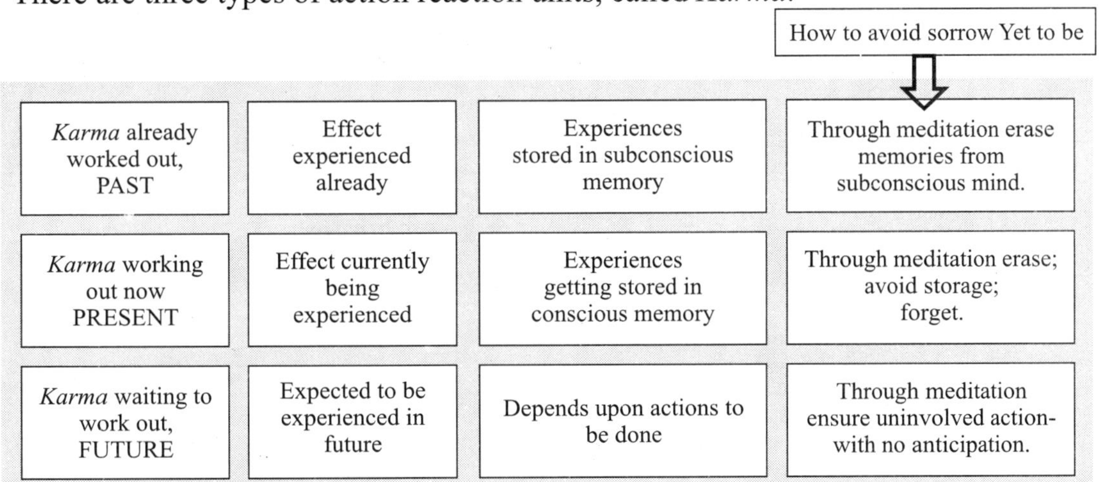

Karma already worked out, PAST	Effect experienced already	Experiences stored in subconscious memory	Through meditation erase memories from subconscious mind.
Karma working out now PRESENT	Effect currently being experienced	Experiences getting stored in conscious memory	Through meditation erase; avoid storage; forget.
Karma waiting to work out, FUTURE	Expected to be experienced in future	Depends upon actions to be done	Through meditation ensure uninvolved action-with no anticipation.

One can avoid sorrow that follows bad actions by avoiding them. It is past impressions that propel one into unconsidered action. One should be constantly aware of this. By meditation, the awareness improves.

With improved awareness one can ensure that:

- every action is a well considered action;
- action is done without anticipation;
- impressions of action is not allowed to be stored in memory; and
- the result of action is dedicated to God.

Outwardly performing all actions but inwardly renouncing their fruits, the wise man, purified by the fire of transcendental knowledge, attains peace, detachment, forbearance, spiritual vision and bliss.

Bhagavadgitā

Lord Krishna says: "People are mad after sense gratification, and they do not know that this present body, which is full of miseries, is a result of one's activities in the past. Although this body is temporary, it is always giving one trouble in many ways. Therefore, to act for sense gratification is not good."

Yoga helps in achieving complete mastery over this action, inbuilt reaction syndrome. It should be noted again that every thought is also an action. A new binding force is created with every thought, word and deed. Each cause that one sets into motion has consequences for him-self. Yoga enables one to get:

the power to forgive and forget;
the power to perform without expectation;
the power to withhold actions that might bind;
the power to read and foresee possible reactions; and
the power to assist others in ensuring actions that will not bind them.

Buddha puts it beautifully and logically while tracing the genesis and growth of the problem of suffering and explains how due to ignorance (not being aware that one is not his body) birth after birth one tends to wallow in misery and pain.

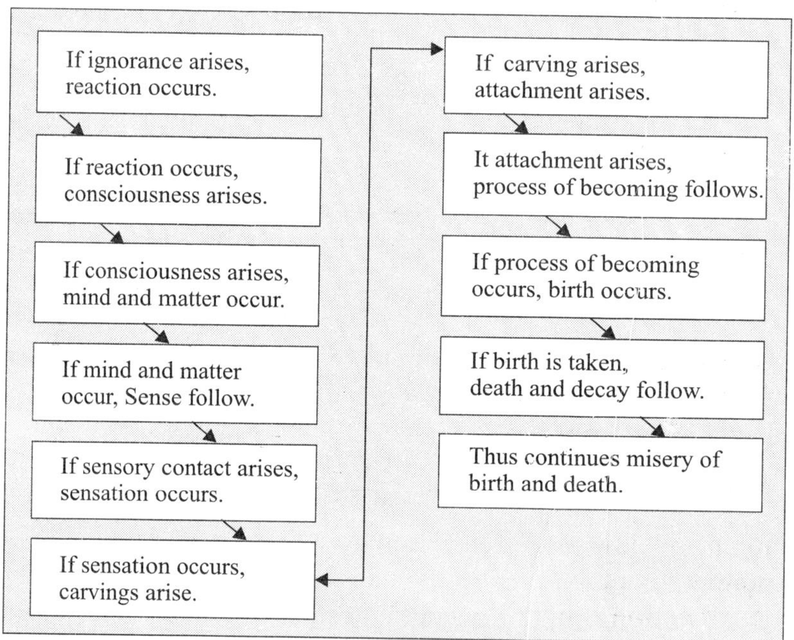

No *karma* can permanently efface the joys and sufferings resulting from *karma*. For the original *karma* and its counteracting *karma* are both products of *avidyā* (ignorance) like a dream that occurs in the midst of another dream.

Bhāgavata

दृष्टदृश्ययोः संयोगो हेयहेतुः ॥१७॥

Drishta_Drishyayoh Samyogo Heya_Hetuh.

The cause to be erased,
Mix up of the seer with the seen.

Drishta: the seer, knower, apprehender
Drishya: the scene, knowable
Samyoga: coming together, union, conjunction
Heya: avoidable, preventable
Hetuh: cause, reason

Q: *How to avoid the sorrow yet to be?*
A: One can avoid sorrow by recognizing the fact that all cause of misery is the mixing up of the seer with the seen. Hence it is essential to constantly keep reinforcing the fact that one is not his body or his thoughts.

There are three types of action-reaction units:

Past Karma: Past *karma* is that which has already worked out, effect already experienced, formed as impressions and stored in subconscious self. Tendencies and attitudes are the result of the stored *karma*.

Present Karma: Present *karma* is that which is currently being experienced, to be endured. One should be able to discriminate and understand that whatever is being experienced now, is the result of whatever was sown earlier.

Future Karma: Future *karma* is that would which will accrue in future because of actions now being done. The sorrow yet to be can be avoided by taking up actions without expectation. Making sure of 'desire-less actions', so that impression formation is avoided. If one sows hatred, anger, injury and pain now, one has to be ready to reap a harvest of misery later. It is up to an individual to understand this simple rule of action being sown will return to reward or punish depending upon whether one has initiated good actions or bad. The foundation for a future life is now being laid. It is therefore essential to discriminate and ensure that right foundation of peace and tranquillity is laid right now, so that progress towards ultimate freedom from actions and its binding nature is attained at least at a later date, in a future birth.

What is perceived as fate now is the result of free will exercised earlier. If the free will of ensuing good actions are carried out now, the fate of good life can be ensured later.

Into blinding darkness enter those who worship ignorance and into greater darkness those who worship knowledge alone.

Isha Upanishad

प्रकाशक्रियास्थितिशीलं भूतेन्द्रियात्मकं भोगापवर्गार्थं दृश्यम् ॥१८॥

Prakāsh_Kriyā_Sthiti_Shilam Bhutendriya_Ātmakam Bhoga_Apavarga_Artham Drishyam.

The knowable consists of elements
And the power of senses;
They exist for experience
And for deliverance.

Prakāsh: visible, illumination, light *Kriyā*: action *Sthiti*: stoppage of the two
Shilam: nature *Ātmakam*: mind *Bhutendriya*: sense organs
Bhoga: enjoyment *Apavarga*: liberation *Artham*: effect
Drishyam: seen, the knowable

Q: *What is the seen? How does it come into being?*
A: Seen is the object that one sees and that which one's senses bring before him. It comes into being because of conjunction of seer with the seen.

The relationship between the subject and object is severed in *Samādhi*. When all three are realized in Brahman, the Self becomes infinite, universal and free from relationship. The subject, the self is the goal of realization in Yoga, to know 'Who am I?' The object which the senses bring before us, comes into effect because of triple qualities. The objects include the mind and the senses. They share the three qualities of clarity, activity and heaviness.

There are three elements of thought

1. The subject 2. The object 3. The relationship between the two.

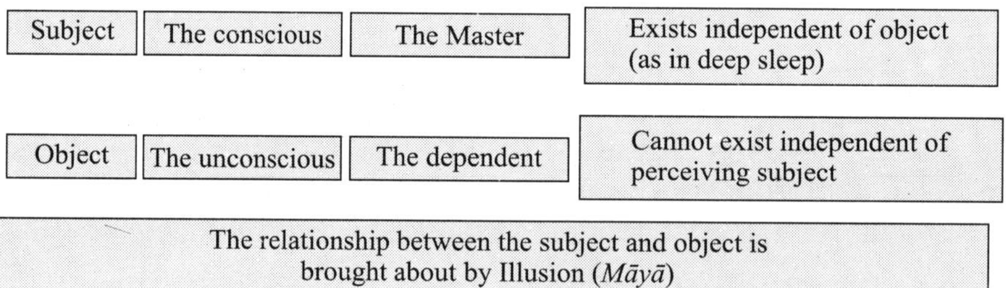

As often as the wavering and unsteady mind runs away,
so often reining it in, it should be brought back under control.

Bhagavadgitā

Student: Can you elaborate the difference between the perceiver and the perceived?
Teacher: The perceiver is the changeless, all knowing effulgence.
The perceived change, they include mind and senses.

S: You mean to say that the mind is not a perceiver, but a perceived?
T: Exactly. Mind is also a perceived. You use your mind to perceive. But the real YOU is the changeless entity. The problem arises because you identify yourself with your mind. The real YOU, the experiencer, is utilizing the mind as an instrument of perception. You will be wrong if you think you are the mind and the objects are perceived by your mind.

S: That is really revealing. But I really do not seem to be convinced. Can you explain further?
T: You say you see an object. Can you give me an example?

Object

S: A tree
T: Who is seeing the tree?

Senses → Object

S: Me. Let me say my eye:
T: Your eye is helping your mind identify an object as a tree. Right? The senses are gathering information about qualities of things outside, known as object. But how do senses gather information?

S: By direct contact.
T: By direct physical contact?

S: No.
T: So you agree that there is another factor involved which enable senses to perceive without necessarily coming into physical contact. Shall we refer to them as the rudimentary principles, let us use the Sanskrit word *Tanmātrā.*

Tanmātrās → Senses → Object

S: What are the rudimentary principles that govern the working of the senses?
A: Between the object and your eye, if there is no light, you cannot see. Similarly between the thunder and your ears, if there is no space, you cannot hear; between the tongue and the eatable if there is no water you cannot taste; between the nose and the rose if there is no air you cannot smell, and lastly it is the presence of the solid earth that gives you a sense of touch.

You should also note that the human capacity to see or hear is limited. It is only within a range of luminosity that we can see. Beyond that we cannot. It is within a range of decibels that we can hear. Beyond that if the decibels are higher we damage our ears. The cat's capacity to see and the dog's capacity smell are more than that of humans. An elephant is said to be capable of sensing underground water seventy kilometres away. A tiger can smell a deer or a prey 40 kilometres away. Our entire lives will be different if we have the sense perceptions of these animals. Again, the capacity varies from individual to individual.

The entire universe consisting of sun, moon, stars, ocean, man, animal, fish, planets, plants, rocks and mountains are all made up of '*Ākāsa*', say Space. The vital energy that has enabled all these to be made is called Prāna (vital energy). The whole universe is one continuous mass in which tree is one point and your eye is another.

S: Yes. The two, the senses and the *tanmātrās* (elements) have to be perfect to perceive things properly.
T: From the object, we come to the senses and from the senses to the powers that constitute the sensory powers, which we referred to as *tanmātrās*. From *tanmātrās* we go to mind. Mind is the governing factor. Mind is superior to the senses and the powers that constitute the sensory organs. If the mind is absent we still cannot perceive the object though the senses may be alright.

Mind → *Tanmātrās* → Senses → Object

S: If the mind is absent, do the objects disappear?
T: No, the objects are always there. For as Patanjali says:

Object, on the mind does not subsist
On mind's absence it ceases not to exist. (4.16)

S: So the mind, the elements and the senses must be working in unison to have a clear vision.
T: Yes.

S: But how does this question of mind working or not working arise? Who makes the mind work or what is the force behind the mind?
A: Another aspect of the mind, the intellect. Even if the mind is present and is in unison with the senses, the object cannot be perceived if the intellect is not working. In the case of the mentally challenged persons the mind is partially working and senses fully. Even then they do not perceive an object. In the case of vast majority of people, their minds may be working alright, but their intellect works at different levels of efficiency and hence the perception of the same object differs from person to person. Not only that, these people are influenced by the triple qualities that operate in them and hence they perceive differently.

S: What is this triple qualities we are talking about?
A: The triple qualities are the qualities of clarity, activity and inertia.

S: These qualities are in the object or in the perceiver?
A: The qualities are present in both.

This world's appearance is a confusion,
Even the blueness of the sky is an optical illusion,
I think it is better not to let the mind dwell on it,
but to ignore it.

Yogavāshishta

S: Are these triple qualities fixed and in same proportion in every perceiver?
A: No, there are variations in each individual and at a given time one or the other is preponderant, while the other two play a smaller role.

S: If there are three different qualities like activity, clarity and inertia in both the perceiver and the object and if there are infinite number of mutations and variations of the three, how is it that instead of perceiving a kaleidoscopic variation of the manifestation, we notice only a single substance or a picture at a given time?
A: The three qualities never act or influence an observer independently. If one is predominant at a time, others subjugate themselves as it were and blend with the predominant quality, lending it a specific orientation. The subsidiary qualities conjoin with the predominant one and help in forming only one specific modification and present only one picture. On account of the coordinated mutation of the three qualities, an object appears as a single unit. Patanjali says:

The object presents a single face
When triple qualities in union surface. (4.14)

S: If the object one sees is a discrete unit, how are we able to see continuity there?
A: It is much like your seeing a film in a theater. Each is an individual shot. In a film strip you can see separate black junctions between two pictures. But when the film is run at a particular speed you see continuity instead of separateness.

S: So, the intellect, mind, elements, senses and the object have to be in unison to be able to perceive and that perception is coloured by the eye of the perceiver who is influenced by the triple qualities?
A: Yes.

Intellect → Mind → Tanmatras → Senses → Object

Patanjali says:

The same appears for several as different
As perception, on the eyes of the beholders depend. (4.15)

On mind's coloured expectation
Depends presence or absence of perception. (4.17)

Commit no wrong but good deeds do,
and let thy heart be pure.
All Buddhas teach this doctrine true,
which will for aye endure.

S: What triggers the action of mind and intellect?
T: It is your feeling of 'I', the false sense of ego. If the 'I' is not present, no object is perceived and neither the intellect nor the mind functions. Patanjali says:

The cause of the emergence of mind
Is ego, one can find. (4.04)

S: So one more new entity is involved?
T: Of course, if you don't have the feeling of 'I' ness, you will not attach yourself to external object at all.

Ego → Intellect → Mind → *Tanmātrās* → Senses → Object

S: If the 'I' ness is absent then what?
T: False ego to object: The whole thing is blanked out.

S: What does one see?
T: The real SELF

S: Just an insignificant presence of the earlier ego?
T: Yes. This state is called a state of absorption with seed.

S: So, it is the Real Self which makes the eye see, the ear hear and the mind perceive?
T: Yes.

S: The Self always knows about the mind?
T: Yes.

The unchanging Self always Knows
Mind's moods and where it goes. (4.18)

Mind, the object of perception
Is not the light, but a reflection. (4.19)

S: So the purpose of the mind is to serve the real Self?
T: Yes.

S: When is the mind de-linked from the object?
T: When it is linked to the real Self.

Those, who try to find the reason for the appearance of optical illusions, are trying to ride on the shoulders of the grandson of the barren woman's son.

S: What is it like to see oneself?
T: It is like looking into a cosmic mirror and realizing your true nature. It is indescribable. Scriptures say that when the external is present, you are object oriented and hence you don't really know who you are. You take the shape and size and colour and quality of the object and hence this veiling does not enable you to see your true nature. When the 'I' ness goes, there is no external veiling and hence you turn your vision inwards and realise your Real Self.

S: So, as long as the 'I' is present, it means thought is present and hence the mind and hence the external object and hence outward orientation and hence inability to see inwards and know oneself?
T: Yes. Hence Patanjali says the objective of yoga is avoidance of mental modifications.

S: So it is the merger of the earlier sense of 'I' and the real 'I' that is referred to as union.
T: Yes.

S: It looks so simple. It sounds logical. All one needs to do is to stop mental modifications. But how is that not even one in a million is able to do so?
T: There lies the trick. Scriptures say that there is an entity called Māyā or illusion that has a sway over you, and because of that you are attached to the object world and hence you cannot see your true Self.

S: That sounds a difficult concept to accept. Can you elaborate?
T: Let us get back to our cine film analogy. Assume that you started your career as a cine screen erector. And you erected the screen in the film theatre. Assume you moved up the organization and were in charge of designing and manufacturing the cine projector. And that you erected the projector too in the film theater. Thereafter, you were the engineer who was responsible for the beamed light and the electricity behind it. Assume you then moved up and became a film baron. You produced the film, wrote the script, directed it and acted as a hero. Assume that after the release of the film you were seeing it. Assume too suddenly in a filmy style you were knocked down by a neighbour. You were rushed to the hospital with a head injury. Doctor treated and operated you, but later it turned out that you lost memory. Everything else up to the moment you were knocked down, were erased from your memory. But somehow you were attached to your film. You go on seeing it again and again. But in the new condition you are unable to recognize the filmy hero. You are affected by the sights there and weep when the heroine weeps, feel bruised when the villain bashes up the hero and feel dead when the hero dies. You are under illusion now.

You don't know that you erected the screen; you were responsible for the beaming light and the power behind. And that the whole thing is not real but only a script and that you were really never bashed by the villain and that you never died either. That is your position now. That is the position of all the teeming millions struggling and dying.

Mind is the cause of bondage
and mind is the cause of liberation.
Mind absorbed in the sense object is the cause of bondage.
Mind detached from the sense objects is the cause for liberation.

Amrita Bindu Upanishad

विशेषाविशेषलिंगमात्रालिंगानि गुणपर्वाणि ॥१९॥

Vishesha_Avishesha_Lingamātra_Alingāni Guna_Parvāni.

The qualities involved:
Gross, subtle, causal and un-evolved.

Vishesha: gross *Avishesha*: subtle *Linga*: mark
Mātra: only(undifferentiated) *Alingāni*: nature
Guna: quality *Parvāni*: appearing

Q: *Are they all physical/gross? How to identify an object?*
A: No. All objects are not physical/gross.
Objects could be 1.Gross 2.Subtle 3.Causal 4.Un-evolved.

The qualities can be broadly categorized as Definable and Un-definable. A further categorization of the qualities could be:

Gunas: Qualities	Definable	Reachable, **Gross** Differentiated	Rose: Its form, petals, etc
		Non-reachable. **Subtle**.	Rose: Its smell.
	Indefinable	Reachable. **Casual**. Manifested.	The vibrating energy that appears as rose.
		Non-reachable. **Un-evolved**. Un-manifested.	The intelligence behind the vibration, God.

The physical eye is able to see only the definable gross objects. If the qualities of the object were to be withdrawn from the object, there will be no object to be perceived.

If you want to see the Real, become the Real.

It is by a process of evolution *Sankhārās* come to be. There is no *Sankhārā* which has sprung into being without a gradual becoming. Thy *Sankhārās* are the product of thy deeds in former existences. The combination of thy *Sankhārās* are thyself. Wheresoever they are impressed thither thy migrates. In thy *Sankhārās* thou wilt continue to live and thou will reap in future existences the harvest sown now and in the past.

Qualities and their experience as Yoga practice proceeds:

Rose Its form	Visible to the seeker even before Practice of Yoga begins, (unless one is physically blind). Only gross is graspable.
Rose: Its smell	As Yoga practice proceeds with vigour and with no interruption, even 'seeing' of smell becomes possible. Subtle is graspable. Advanced stages of *Dhyāna*.
Rose: Its colour The vibrating energy that appears as a rose.	In the absorbed state the vibrating energy is perceptable. Final stages of *Dharanā, Dhyāna, Samādhi* perceived as light, brightness etc.
The intelligence behind the vibration, referred to as God	Final state of merger, Union. There remaining no seer, sight or seen. Un-manifested

Rose Its form	I can see, smell, touch and taste rose.
Rose: Its smell	I can even see ether flowing in to my nose to give me smell and hear the rose petal blooming.
Rose: Its colour The vibrating energy that appears as a rose.	I see rose is nothing but one more manifestation of energy radiating everywhere.
The intelligence behind the vibration, Referred to as God	I am the rose.

Silence, Yogic posture (concentration), practice of meditation, fortitude, living in solitude, desire-less-ness and equableness - are the seven requirements for the single staff carrying monk (the spiritual seeker).

Nārada Parivrājaka Upanishad

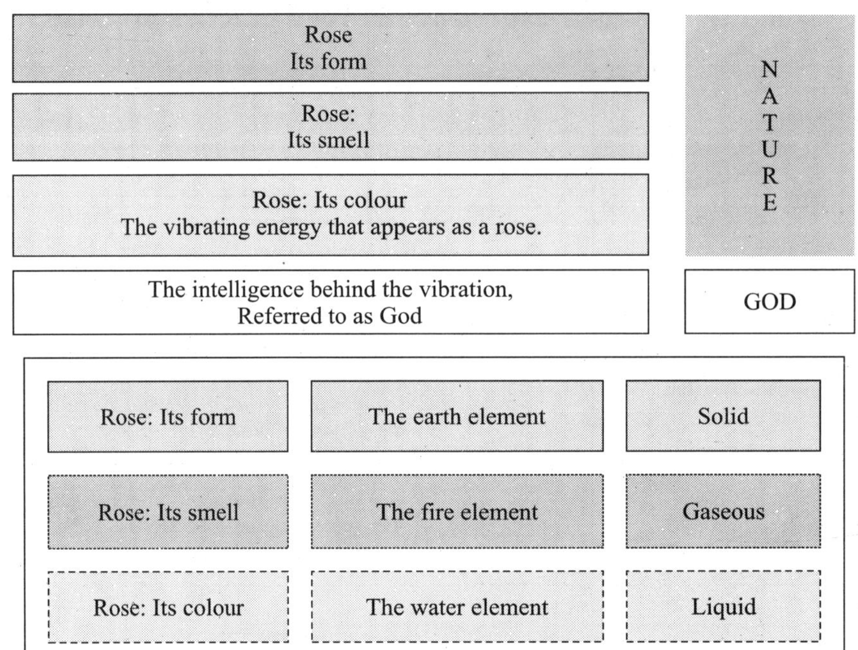

Like the rose that is reduced to its constituents, every object in the world can be reduced to its constituents. The characteristic one sees in an object is because of the threefold presence of the qualities. If these qualities are withdrawn from the objects, there would be no object left at all. If the earth element is withdrawn, one cannot touch and feel the rose. If the fire element is withdrawn, one cannot see the rose or know its color and if the water element is withdrawn, one cannot smell the rose. If one cannot touch, see or smell the rose, where is the rose? The characteristic is the capacity that is present in the object, something structurally, which emits certain vibration causing a perception. The characteristic is only a reaction that is set up in the process of perception. This reaction is caused by the nature of the object. If the threefold presence of the elements are to be withdrawn from the object, there will be no object at all. Millions of objects that one sees are but various dimensions of one single mass of triplicate elements. Because of the difference in dimensions and the proportion of mixing of elements, one distinguishes, rather one mistakes one object to be different from another. Essentially they are the same. The differences in them are notional. One is unable to see the notionality because of his belief in the externality of things. The 'otherness' is the cause for multiplicity. The feeling of separateness of the object from the perceiver, from the object of perception, blinds the connectedness of the subject with the object.

As a boat on the water is swept away by a strong wind, even one of the senses on which the mind focuses, can carry away man's intelligence.

Bhagavadgitā

With respect to an individual, the gross, subtle, causal and primal elements are:

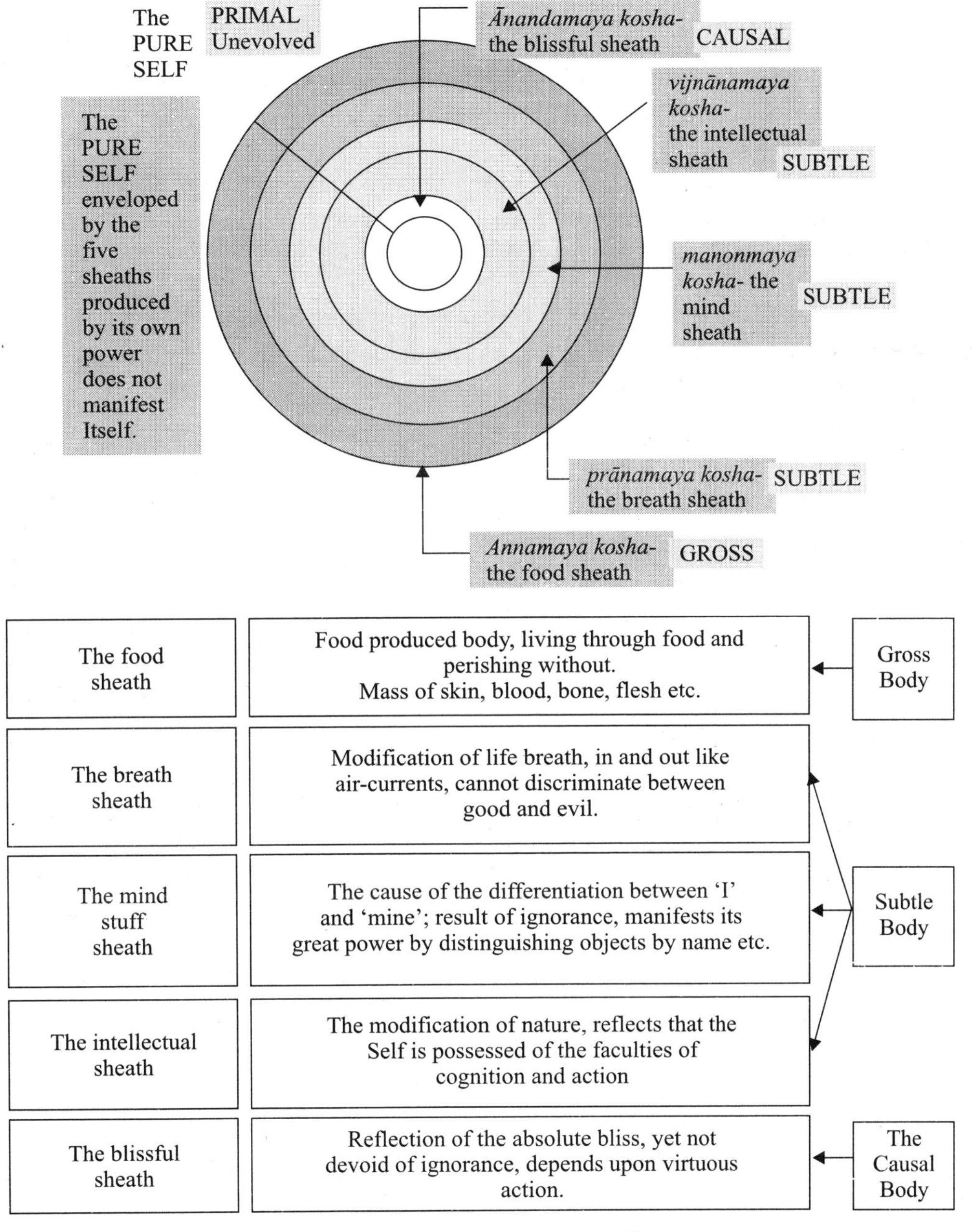

Sheath	Description	Body
The food sheath	Food produced body, living through food and perishing without. Mass of skin, blood, bone, flesh etc.	Gross Body
The breath sheath	Modification of life breath, in and out like air-currents, cannot discriminate between good and evil.	Subtle Body
The mind stuff sheath	The cause of the differentiation between 'I' and 'mine'; result of ignorance, manifests its great power by distinguishing objects by name etc.	Subtle Body
The intellectual sheath	The modification of nature, reflects that the Self is possessed of the faculties of cognition and action	Subtle Body
The blissful sheath	Reflection of the absolute bliss, yet not devoid of ignorance, depends upon virtuous action.	The Causal Body

The "I am" is certain.
The "I am this" is not.

Sri Nisargadatta Mahārāj

द्रष्टा दृशिमात्रः शुद्धोऽपि प्रत्ययानुपश्यः ॥२०॥

Drashtā Drishi_Mātrah Shuddho_Api Pratyaya_Anupashyah.

Seer, the power of seeing, is pure;
Albeit, appearing to be mixed up with the impure.

Drashtā: The seer *Drishimātrah*: existing as pure consciousness only
Shuddho: immutable *Api*: even *Pratyaya*: firm conviction
Anupashyah: experiences accordingly

Q: *If there is an object, there has to be a subject. Who is the subject?*
A: The consciousness, the experiencer is the subject. While the subject, the PURE SELF, is unchangeable, it APPEARS to take on the changing perceptions of mind.

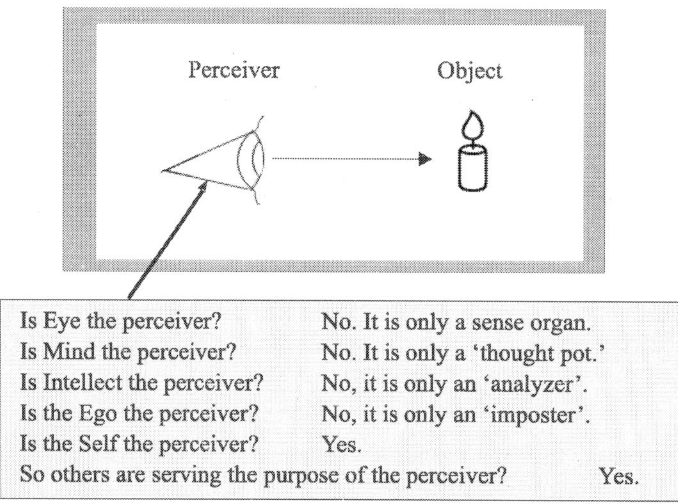

Is Eye the perceiver?	No. It is only a sense organ.
Is Mind the perceiver?	No. It is only a 'thought pot.'
Is Intellect the perceiver?	No, it is only an 'analyzer'.
Is the Ego the perceiver?	No, it is only an 'imposter'.
Is the Self the perceiver?	Yes.
So others are serving the purpose of the perceiver?	Yes.

The understanding that the Self is the perceiver is strictly speaking not right. It appears to be experiencing or perceiving would be more appropriate to say. For no activity like perception can be attributed to the Self. The Self is just as It Is: It is the reflected self that appears to go through the process of experiencing and the pain and pleasure resulting there of and finally appears to be freeing itself from the veil of ignorance.

An object is of two types, the physical and the mental. While observing the mental object results in the ideation, and the observation of physical object in objectification.

By whose commands this mind works? By whose will the life's breath circulates? Who is responsible for man's speech? What intelligence does lead the eyes and the ears? It is the ear of the ear, the mind of the mind, the speech of the speech, the life of all life, and the eye of the eye. The wise abandon the sensory world and become immortal.

Kena Upanishad

At a glance: Aphorism 16-20

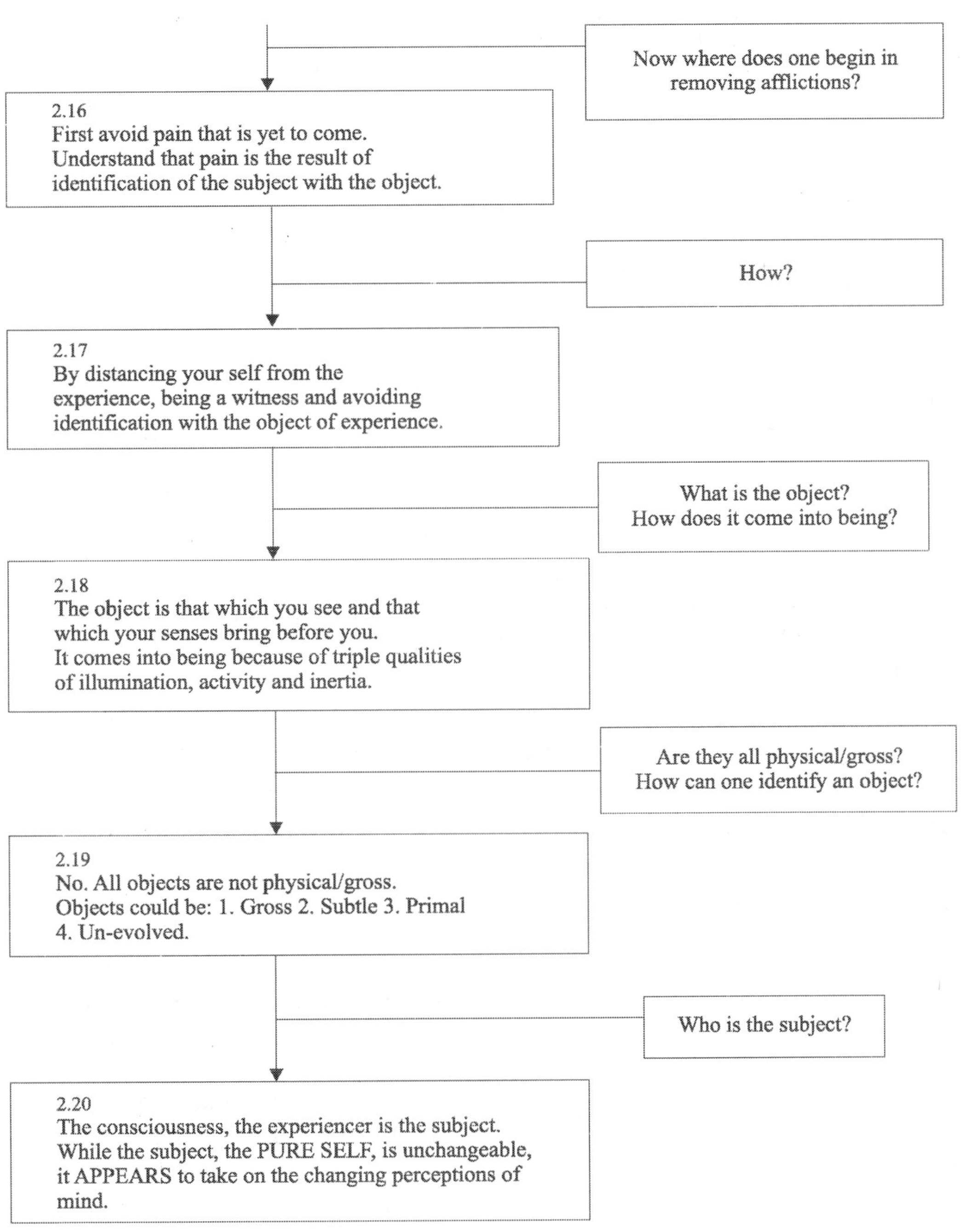

तदर्थ एव दृश्यस्यात्मा ॥२१॥
Tadartha Eva Drishyasya_Ātmā

The purpose of the object, the seen
Is to serve the Self, the seer.

Tadartha: the seer's purpose	*Eva*: only
Drishyasya: the seen	*Ātmā*: Self, essential nature

Q: *Why does the objective world exist?*
A: The objective world exists to serve the Self.

The object could be many and varied. But the perceiver is one.

The objects of experience serve only the experiencer. They are there to provide enjoyment and release. Once the experiencer decides on not having any further experience, the objects of experience cease to operate and influence him. The existence of the intellect and the senses depend on its relation with the perceiver. If the play of experiencing is over, the perceiver recognizes no objects of experience. Absence of perception does not mean that the objects do not exist or they perish.

The purpose of a toy is to provide experience to a child. The child having played decides to move away. It no longer, recognizes the presence of the toy. But the toy is very much there.

After discovering through experience, that all worldly enjoyments offered by Nature (*Prakriti*) are mixed with misery, one gets a distaste towards the impermanent and the illusory and seeks to cling to the never changing and ever blissful.

It should be understood that the Being, the Real Self is not subject to any experiencing or witnessing. It is the reflected Self that experiences and is subject to the stages of realization: ignorance, veiling, distraction, indirect knowledge, freedom from sorrow, and finally satisfaction arising from the merger with the Real Self.

By desire, contact, sight and delusion,
the embodied soul assumes
successively various forms in various places
according to his deeds,
just as the body grows
by food and drink.

Shvetasvatara Upanishad V.11

कृतार्थं प्रति नष्टमप्यनष्टं तदन्यसाधारणत्वात् ॥२२॥

Kritārtham Prati Nashtam_Api_Anashtam Tada_Anya_Sādhārana_Tvāt.

To the one who is absorbed
Objects remain dissolved
But for others in the queue
They remain true.

Kritārtham: one whose purpose has been accomplished
Prati: in respect of towards, with regard to
Nashtam: lost. ceased, dissolved, finished, destroyed
Api: even though
Tada: that
Anya: others
Anashtam: not a loss, has not ceased, not dissolved, not finished, not destroyed
Sādhāranatvāt: being common to others, due to commonness

Q: *Do the objects of perception cease to exist without a perceiver?*
A: No. They exist whether the perceiver is present or not.

The objects of experience remain real for all who have not reached the state of total perception. The existence of the objects of perception is independent of the needs of various individuals.

The purpose of nature is to unfold itself for the perceiver to know, to experience and thence to become free. Nature will continue to exist and perform its functions as long as the process of evolution of beings continue from lower to higher to higher till the last soul is free. Each individual is allowed by this system to realize that he is part of the whole and merge with the whole, losing his separate identity. When all units lose their respective separate identities and merge with the whole, what remains is the whole, the same whole that existed always.

The Bhrahma Sutra says: "Since a man without self-identification with the body, senses etc cannot become an experiencer and as such, the means of knowledge cannot function for him, and since perception and other activities are not possible without accepting the senses etc as his own, since the senses cannot function without the body as the basis, since nobody engages in any activity with a body that has not the idea of Self super imposed on it, and since the related self cannot become a cogniser unless these are all there; and since the means of knowledge cannot function unless there is a cognisership, therefore it follows that the means of knowledge, such as direct perception as well as the scriptures, must have a man as its focus who is subject to illusion"

Live in the present , with your consciousness externalised momentarily, but without any effort; when the mind stops linking itself to the past and to the future it becomes no-mind

Yogavāshishta

स्वस्वामिशक्त्योः स्वरूपोपलब्धिहेतुः संयोगः ॥२३॥

Sva_Svāmi_Shaktyoh Svarupa_Upalabdhi_Hetuh Samyogah.

Nature of the owner and the owned
On their conjunction, is known.

Sva: one's own *Svāmi*: Lord *Shaktyoh*: strength, potential
Svarupa: own form *Upalabdhi*: attainable *Hetuh*: cause
Samyogah: meeting point

Q: *When or how does the experiencer gain awareness?*
A: When he comes into contact with Nature, the process of experiencing occurs. It is then that he identifies himself with the object of experience.

Why this divorce and why this reunion? In reality it is not so. Thanks to the covering of illusion, it appears so, strengthened by the simultaneously following projecting power. But to the un-liberated the fact remains that he does not know that he is only a witness to the play. He thinks he is the character and thus suffers.

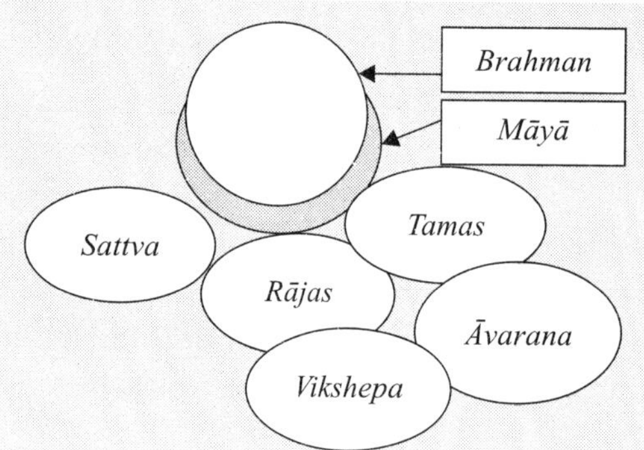

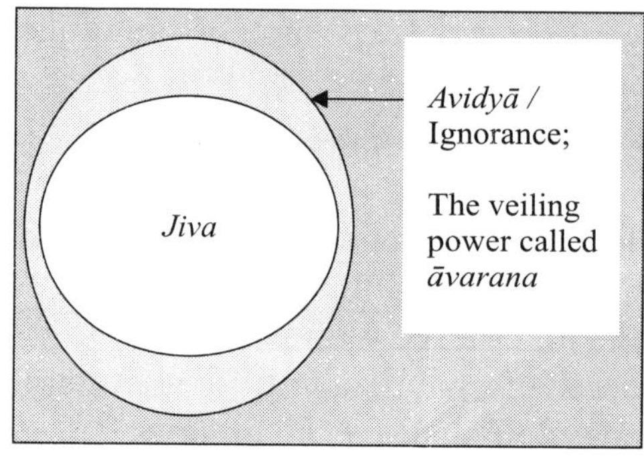

Adhyātma Upanishad says: There are two attributes: *Māyā*, illusion to the universal soul, and *avidyā*, ignorance to the embodied soul. On abandoning the two, what is seen is the perpetually true, Conscious and blissful *param Brahman*, the Ultimate Supreme Reality."

The mind, receiving its capacity for gaining knowledge of objects, basks on the reflected glory and yet thinks that it is by itself capable of knowing. Thus deluded a subject misidentification takes place and a subject-object relationship follows suit.

Scriptures say: "God is the Lord of the *Māyā*. The whole world is filled with beings who form part of his parts."

Q: When will external objects vanish?
A: If the mind, which is the cause of all thoughts and activities vanishes, external objects do vanish.

Shri Ramana Maharshi

तस्य हेतुरविद्या ॥२४॥
Tasya Hetuh_Avidyā

The cause of conjunction
Is misapprehension.

Tasya: for that, of that alliance *Hetuh*: that brings about, the cause, reason
Avidyā: ignorance, veiling, nescience

Q: *Why does the experiencer identify himself with the object of experience?*
A: The identification is caused because of ignorance.

Ignorance is the mistaken identification of the Self with that which is non-eternal; a process by which one superimposes on his real nature, the limitations and imperfections of the finite world. Identifying oneself with the body, one experiences its pain and fears its death as his own. Identifying oneself with his senses, one spends his life running after where the senses lead him on to. Identifying oneself with his mind; one remains victim of its moods, its sorrows and its ever shifting desires. Identifying one-self with all the three-body, senses and mind, one perpetuates the sense of ego and continues to experience indefinitely, the illusion of separateness. The limitations then are not self existent but self imposed.

Plato illustrates the meaning of ignorance by his famous simile of the cave. Think of an enormous cave, dark, uncomfortable and unhealthy, where some unfortunate souls have been huddled together since their birth. Having their backs to the entrance of the cave, which is just a small aperture and bound hand and foot, they do not have any freedom of movement. Nor do they have any knowledge of the outside world of sunshine, joy and beauty except the vague and dim reflection of it as cast upon the wall of the cave in front.

The cave here represents the world of phenomena as registered in one's consciousness through the senses. The fetters that bind the soul are the fetters of body, senses and mind. Ignorantly man believes that he is tied, hand and foot, in the dark cave, caught as he is in the world of phenomena. Knowledge alone can set him free. Once ignorance is removed he will automatically learn that he was never tied, he was never bound and that the he was only seeing reflections and mistaking them to be true and that sunshine and freedom are his real nature.

After being situated in the Yoga practice and vibrating the Sacred syllable 'AUM', the supreme combination of letters, if one thinks of the supreme personality of Godhead and quits the body, he will certainly reach the spiritual planets.

Bhagavadgitā

तदभावात्संयोगाभावो हानं तद्दृशेः कैवल्यम् ॥२५॥

Tadabhāvāt Samyogā_Abhāvo Hānam Tad_Drisheh Kaivalyam.

With ignorance destroyed, identification ceases
With freedom from bondage, clarity increases.

Tadabhāvāt: absence of that (ignorance) *Samyogā*: connection, union, conjunction
Abhāva: non existence, absence, disappearance, dissolution
Hānam: destruction, removal, cessation, abandonment *Tad*: that
Drishteh: of the seer, of the knower, the force of seeing
Kaivalyam: liberation, absolute freedom, enlightenment

Q: *What happens when ignorance ceases?*
A: The identification ceases. One becomes free from the bondage of pleasure pain chain. One remains illumined.

Absence of mental modifications results in:

1. Absence of mind's waves
2. Non accumulation of impurities in the mind
3. Removal of dirt in the mirror of perception
4. Elimination of the coloring agent
5. Removal of disfiguring obstructions
6. Knowing one's true Self

The result: Total clarity of perception.

The freedom that is referred to in this context is the

Freedom from error,
Freedom from bonding arising out of mistaken identity,
Freedom from duality of pain and pleasure,
Freedom from the influence of triple qualities.

Having renounced all mental impressions,
even the state of bliss
which arises from *Nirvikalpa Samādhi*
is dissolved within.

Yogavāshishta

At a glace Aphorism: 21-25

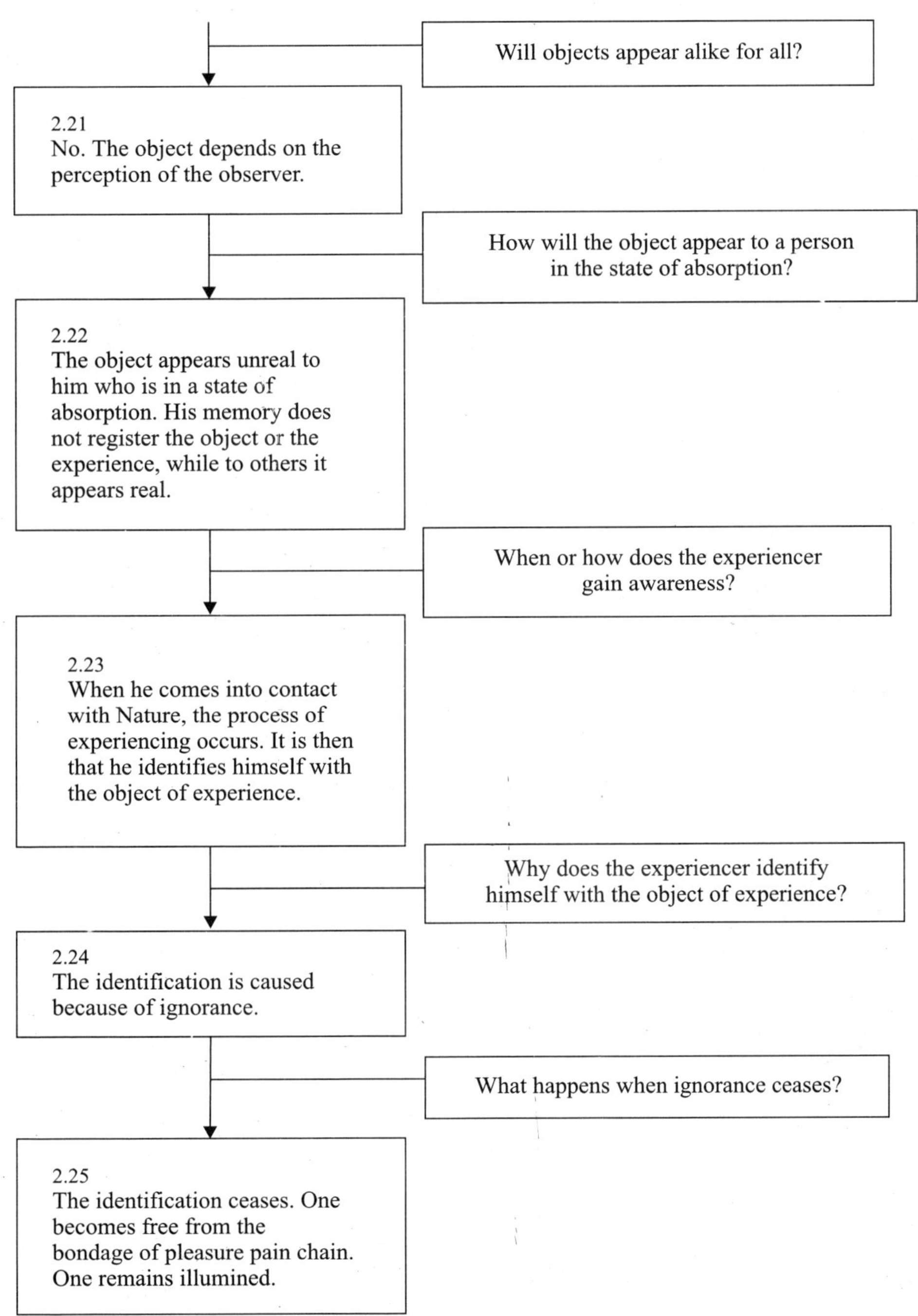

विवेकख्यातिरविप्लवा हानोपायः ॥२६॥
Viveka_Khyātih_Aviplavā Hānopāyah.

Discrimination and awareness, with no confusion
Are the means of removal of illusion.

Viveka: discriminative, discernment
Khyātih: knowledge, correct cognition, clarity, awareness
Aviplavā: with no confusion, undisturbed, without vacillation, uninterrupted
Hana: destruction or removal, of avoidance *Upāyah*: means, method, way

Q: *How to remove ignorance?*
A: By uninterrupted awareness of the truth of false identification, ignorance can be removed.

Discrimination and awareness constitute:

1. Uninterrupted awareness that one is not his body.
2. Awareness that it is the body that is destroyed on death and one assumes new successive bodies after the destruction of one body either being slain or being sick.
3. Awareness that such acquisition of bodies is endless until liberation
4. Understanding that the misery during successive migratory existences is due to actions and inactions done in earlier existences.
5. Repeated reinforcement of the reality that it is due to false identification of oneself with his body that one suffers.
6. Understanding that objects are only name and form and that the real substance in them is the pure Self. Endeavour to go after the real substance in the object, instead of allowing oneself to be led by the senses to run after name and form.
7. Understanding that the mind is covered by the veil of ignorance and is therefore, ideation and object oriented
8. Awareness that death and rebirth, attachment and aversion, misery and pain are inevitable as long as one has not realized the ultimate truth.
9. Understanding that as long as there is mental modification, so long will misery continues and hence efforts to avoid mental modifications should be pursued uninterruptedly.
10. Realisation that it is with God's help that any progress in merging with the Being is possible and hence attitude of surrender is essential.

Books are useless to us until our own book opens
then all the books are as good as they confirm our book.
Swāmi Vivekānanda

तस्य सप्तधा प्रान्तभूमिः प्रज्ञा ॥२७॥

Tasya Saptadhā Prānta_Bhumih Pragyā.

To the discriminative, seven steps
Are the ones that lead to ultimate.

Tasya: to one, to such a person *Saptadhā*: seven steps, sevenfold
Prānta: ultimate, final *Bhumih* : stage, level, degree
Pragyā: knowledge, discrimination, insight, wisdom, cognizing consciousness

Q: *How does one gain this awareness?*
A: One gains this awareness in seven stages, each one leading to the highest.

Seven steps of knowledge

Step 1	Virtuous wish	Preceded by absence of worldly desires.
Step 2	Reflection	Preceded by association with scriptures and practice of dispassion.
Step 3	The state of thin mind	Non-attachment to objects. 'Thin-ness thought' arising out of non-attachment.
Step 4	Entering into being	On practice of above 3 steps, mind becomes pure after cessation of desires.
Step 5	Non union	On practice of above 4 steps shooting up spectacle of Pure Being.
Step 6	Non-ideation of objects	On practice of above 5 steps: Absence of thought of inner and outer objects.
Step 7	Going into fourth state of consciousness	By long practice of above 6 steps and by non cognition of difference.

Matter is motion outside.
Mind is motion inside.

Swāmi Vivekānanda

योगांगानुष्ठानादशुद्धिक्षये ज्ञानदीप्तिराविवेकख्यातेः ॥२८॥

Yoga_Anga_Anushthānāt_Ashuddhikshyaye Gyāna_Diptih Aviveka_Khyāteh.

When Yoga practice destroys impurity
There is correct cognition and clarity.

Yoga: Yoga discipline *Anga*: limbs, steps, parts, members, constituents
Anushthānāt: observance, sustained practice
Ashuddhi: impurities *Kshyaye*: reduction or weakening
Gyāna: knowledge *Diptih*: upsurge, light, brilliance, shining, radiance
Aviveka: ignorance *Khyāteh*: declining

Q: *Now, how does Yoga help in avoiding mental modifications?*
A: There are eight aspects of Yoga.
Adhering to the practice helps one in overcoming ignorance by avoiding mental modifications.

Yoga practice will eliminate ignorance by first ensuring external and internal purity of mind and subsequently enabling one to be absorbed into the Being.

The outward moving nature of the mind and its propensity for object orientation does not allow one to look inward. The practices outlined by Patanjali, enables one to withdraw one's mind from objects and focus attention on the real Self.

The first few aspects of Yoga are aimed at weakening the activity orientation (*Rājasic*) and inertia (*Tāmasic*) of the mind and increase the clarity (*Sattva*) of perception. Once perception is clear, understanding ensues that objects of attention are only distracting elements and in them there is no real substance and focusing inward. Once mind is focused, awareness improves. Improved awareness and continued uninterrupted focusing of mind on a chosen object of meditation leads one to a state of total absorption. All objects dissolve as it were and only the Being is present.

Yoga is union. The union of the outward oriented self with the never changing Cosmic Being. Yoga enables the union.

Through Yoga the illusion of separateness, the false ego and the resulting attachment and aversion as well as fear of loss of body get eliminated.

Knowledge leads to unity,
Ignorance, to diversity.

Sri Rāmakrishna Paramahamsa

यमनियमासनप्राणायामप्रत्याहारधारणाध्यान
समाधयोऽष्टावंगानि ॥२९॥

Yama_Niyama_Āsana_Prānāyām_Pratyāhār_Dhāranā_Dhyāna_ Samādhaya Ashtah Angāni.

Development towards self and external, a right attitude,
adherence to practice of posture and breath control, with fortitude,
withdrawal of senses from objects external and seen,
capacity to remain steadfast and serene,
ability to merge with the object to be known,
and to get united, there remaining nothing unknown,
Are eight limbs or constituents known.

Yama: attitude to external ,codes of restraint, abstinences, self-regulations
Niyama: attitude to internal, observances, practices, self-training
Āsana: placing oneself in, posture *Prānāyāma*: control of vital energy
Pratyāhāra: withdrawal of senses from external objects *Dhyāna*: concentration
Dhārana: contemplation *Samādhi*: state of absorption *Ashta*: eight
Angāni: limbs, rungs, components, steps, parts, members, constituents

Q: *What are the limbs / aspects of Yoga?*
A: The limbs/ aspects of Yoga are: *Yama, Niyama, Āsana, Prānāyāma, Pratyāhāra, Dhāranā, Dhyānā* and *Samādhi.*

Yama	Restraining unhelpful thoughts and impulses	Strengthening mind
Niyama	Cultivating positive habits	
Āsana	Practice to place oneself comfortable	Further regulating mind
Prānāyāma	Regulating the vital energy	
Pratyāhāra	Withdrawing mind from sense objects	Focusing mind
Dhāranā	Fixing mind on an object of meditation	
Dhyāna	Continuing meditation without interruption	Fixing the mind
Samādhi	Total absorption of mind on the object of meditation	Emptying mind

	Yoga with eight limbs ***Ashtānga Yoga***	**Knowledge with eight limbs** ***Ashtānga Jnāna***
Yama	❖ Stands for cultivation of such principles of good conduct such as non-violence, truth, non-stealing, celibacy, and non-possession.	❖ Stands for controlling the aggregate of sense-organs, realising the defects that are present in the world consisting of the body, etc.
Niyama	❖ Stands for the observance of such rules of good conduct such as 1. Purity, 2. Contentment, 3. Austerity, 4. Study of the sacred texts, and 5. Devotion to God.	❖ Stands for maintaining a series of mental modes that relate to the Self and rejecting the contrary modes. In other words, it means love that arises uninterruptedly for the Supreme Self.
Āsana	❖ That which keeps the mind steady and at ease. There are eighty-four main ones. Of these, four are said to be excellent: 1. *Simha* 2. *Badra* 3. *Padma* 4. *Siddha*	❖ That with the help of which constant meditation on the Consciousness is made possible with ease.
Prānāyāma	• Indirect control of mind • It is making the vital air stay firmly in the heart through exhalation, inhalation and retention • Breath control is the means of mind control. • Breath control is done either by absolute retention of breath or by regulation of breath. • Exhalation and inhalation some say is done in equal measure and retention twice that measure.	❖ Direct Control of mind ❖ Exhalation stands for removal of unreal aspects of name and from from the objects constituting the world, the body, etc. ❖ Inhalation stands for grasping the three real aspects: existence, consciousness and bliss, which are constant in those objects; and ❖ Retention is retaining those aspects thus grasped.
Pratyāhāra	• Restraining of mind • The regulating of mind of preventing it from flowing towards external names and forms. • Mind withdrawing from the sense objects and the sense objects from the mind.	❖ Preventing name and form which have been removed from re-entering the mind.

No one, from the Creator down to the smallest insect can attain supreme peace unless he acquires perfect control over his mind.

अहिंसासत्यास्तेयब्रह्मचर्यापरिग्रहाः यमाः ॥३०॥

Ahimsā_Satya_Asteya_Brahmacharya_Aparigrahā Yamāh.

The norms of self-restraint are abstention from:
Violence, falsehood, theft, incontinence and acquisition.

Ahimsā: non violence, non injury *Satya*: truthfulness, honesty
Asteya: avoidance of illegitimate/ needless desires
Brahmacharya: celibacy, continence, walking in awareness of the highest reality, continence
Aparigrahāh: restraint from sense objects, non-ossessiveness, non-holding through senses, non-greed, non-grasping, non-indulgence, non-acquisitiveness
Yamāh: constraints, control, codes of restraint, abstinences, self-regulations

Q: *What is 'Yama'?*
A: Yama refers to our attitude to others, includes abstention from
1. Harming others 2. Falsehood 3. Theft 4. Incontinence 5. Greed.

The five great vows that constitute yama are:

Yama Attitude towards the external	
	Harmlessness towards all beings.
	Truthfulness in thought, action and speech.
	Non greediness. Accepting only what is due.
	Chastity, Continence.
	Abstinence from avariciousness.

"O son of Kunti, the non permanent appearance of heat and cold, happiness and distress and their disappearance in due course are like the appearance and disappearance of winter and summer season. They rise from sense perception, O scion of Bharata, one must learn to tolerate them without being disturbed."

Bhagavadgitā

The great vow 1: *Ahimsā,* **Non Injury:** The principle of *Ahimsā,* stems from the fact of the universal consciousness pervading every life and filling it with energy and vitality. Any injury to the other would mean injuring the Self. Self inflicted injury sure impedes spiritual progress. *Ahimsā* is not any favour done to the other. Non – injury is a by-product of the realization of the seers that every single life be it that of a bird, beast or a man is intimately connected to each other and hence injuring, what is by the ignorant perceived is the other is in effect a self inflicted injury. Practice of non-injury is the first of several steps suggested to strengthen mind and focus it inward. Any injury to another would trigger a reaction. Mind would then be worried about possible reaction and ways to save oneself from the effects of the reaction.

The great vow 2: *Satya,* **Truthfulness:** Truthfulness means mind and speech being well integrated. The wise say that speech being at variance with the mind is untruthfulness. The effort to purify mind fails by untruthfulness. All that does ill is untruthfulness. It is not enough that one speaks to a man what is good for him, one should speak with affection and the one to whom one's words are addressed must find them acceptable. If one speaks harshly nobody will listen to him even if he means well. Thus words that serve no purpose do not constitute a truth. The speech must be beneficial and, at the same time, capable of bringing happiness to the man to whom it is addressed. This is truthfulness. The initial and lowest degree of truthfulness is sincerity and honesty. This is followed by being true in all thoughts, feelings, actions, and intentions. The truthful are those valiant people whose feelings, thoughts, and actions do not contradict one another; the most truthful are those heroes who are absolutely true in all of their imaginations, intentions, feelings, thoughts, actions, and gestures. He, whose way of life is well-established in truthfulness, for him truth is not a matter of prescription or prohibition but a way of life.

The great vow 3: *Asteya*: **Non covetousness:** When one is contended with what he has, where is the need for him to covet what is not his? When one looks outside himself for more, he is neglecting the riches he already has. Practicing non covetousness: this can include fostering a sense of abundance in one's life. Cultivating a sense of completeness and letting go of cravings, gives one such a rich feeling that no one else can be compared with his richness. *Asteya* is not the kind of aggressive competitiveness that is rampant in the business world which is all about elbowing one's way to the top, beating the other guy, using any means necessary to outsmart one's opponent, and winning the game at all costs.

Notions and ideas gradually cease to arise and expand in one who resolutely refrains from associating words with meanings in his own mind- whether these words are uttered by others or they arise in one's own mind

Yogavāshishta

The great vow 4: *Brahmacharya*, **walking in awareness of the highest reality.**

Brahmacharya is a compound word consisting of *Brahma* and *Achara*. *Brahma* is that which contains inexhaustible potential of creativity. It is only all-permeating Supreme Intelligence, because creativity is the characteristic of Intelligence. The other part of the word, *Brahmacharya*, is *Achara*. The word *Acharya* is derived from the root *chara* - to move, to live. *Charya* means the way of living. *Brahmacharya* is the way of living in which you are always aware of the supreme Being. *Brahmacharya* is living a life dedicated to the awareness of Being. *Charya* is also thought of as "grazing" -- in the same way that a cow does her walking and eating at the same time. Thus *Brahmacharya* means living one's life, doing what one has to do or wants to do, and at the same time keeping his mind fixed on God.

The great vow 5: *Aparigraha*, **non-possessiveness**

Aparigraha is non-possessiveness, non-hoarding, not desiring more than one's need. Mind wavers all the time if one were to focus on acquiring things more than what is needed. This wavering is just the opposite of what one sets to do through Yoga, namely avoidance of mental modifications.

Each one of the five great vows of *yama* is to be looked at from the point of view of how it aids in avoidance of mental modifications. Any activity, thought, formation of impression or indulgence in physical activity that helps in restraining the *chitta* is acceptable, everything else is not *yama*.

There are 3 gates which lead to the hell called *'Ātma Nāsham'* (Self destruction)
They are: *Kāma, Krodha* and *Lobha* (Lust, anger and greed).

At a glance: Aphorism: 26-30

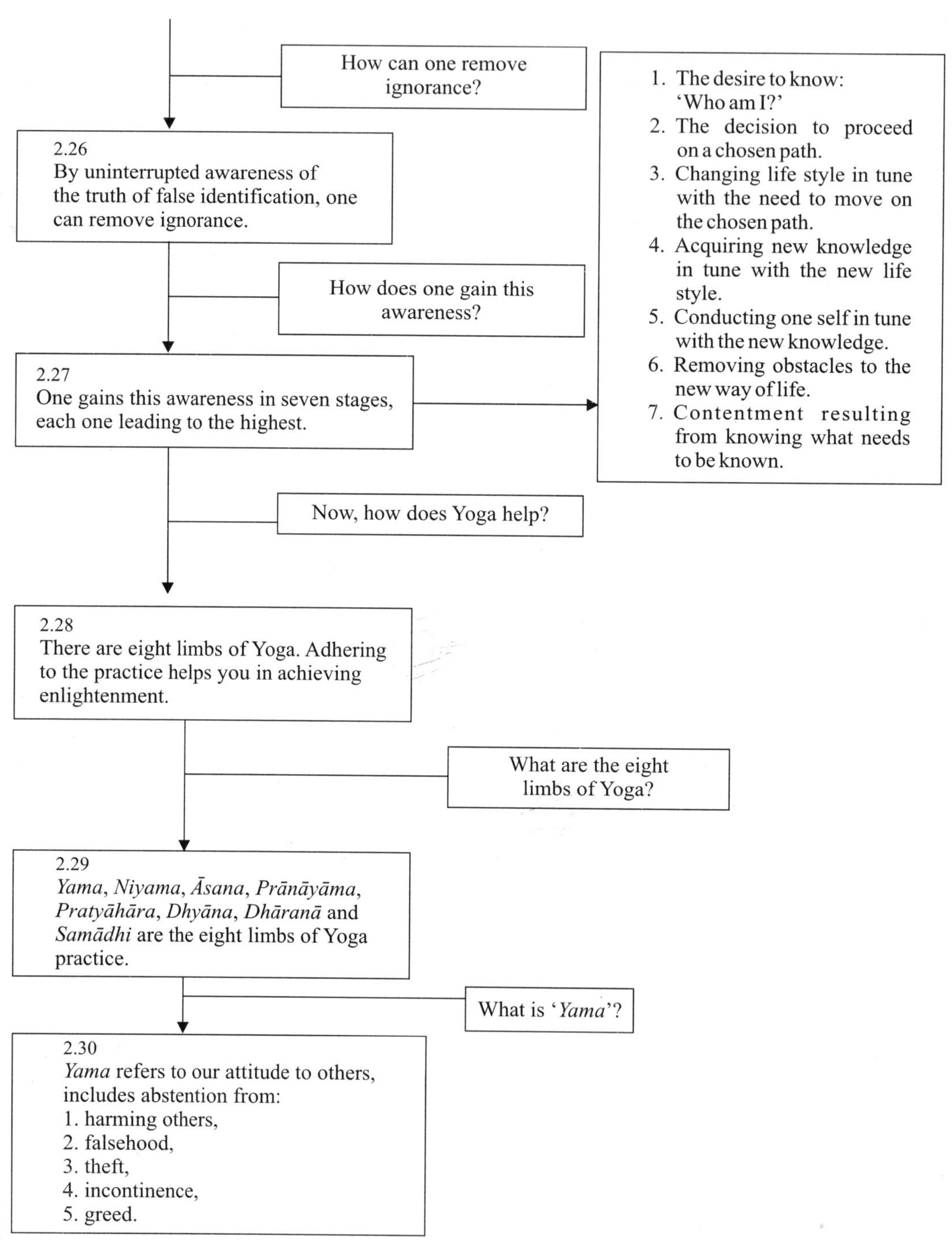

जातिदेशकालसमयानवच्छिन्नाः सार्वभौमा महाव्रतम् ॥३१॥

Jāti_Desha_Kāla_Samaya_Anavachchhinnāh Sārva_Bhaumā Mahāvratam.

The norms to follow
Constitute the Great Vow
Conditioned are they
By class, time, occasion or place nay.

Jāti: class, type of birth, species, state of life *Desha*: place *Kāla*: time
Samaya: fixed time, situation, circumstance, condition, consideration
Anavacchinnāh: unbroken, uninterrupted, not limited by
Sārva Bhoumā: in all states *Mahāvratam*: great vow

Q: *Any guidelines to 'Yama' practice?*
A: They must be adhered to without any reservation as to place, time, person, or circumstances.

Adherence to the five *Yamas*, means observance of great vows towards fulfilling four conditions:

1. They are to be practised universally in relation to all beings of all types of birth, species, or states of life.
2. They are to be practised equally in all places or spaces.
3. They are to be practised continuously at all times.
4. They are to be practised uniformly among all circumstances or situations.

No rule permits deviations. There can be no compromises. Mind's natural tendency is to find excuses to deviate. As practice proceeds one will find it easier to adhere. The veiling power of mind is so great; it helps if the seeker chooses guidance of a committed teacher and has the right motivating company of seekers, to resist the veiling power.

The good is one thing, the pleasant another. Both these, serving different ends, present themselves to man. It goes well with him, who out of the two, takes the good; But he who chooses the pleasant misses the end........Both the good and the pleasant come to man. The calm one examines them well and discriminates. He prefers the good to the pleasant, but the fool chooses the pleasant out of greed and avarice.

Kathopanishad

शौचसंतोषतपः स्वाध्यायेश्वरप्रणिधानानि नियमाः ॥३२॥

Shaucha_Santosha_Tapah_Svādhyāya_Ishvar_Pranidhānāni Niyamāh.

Observances constitute: Purity, Contentment, Austerity
Devotion to God and Self-study.

Shaucha: cleanliness, purity *Santosha*: happiness, contentment
Tapah: fortitude, training the senses, austerities
Svadhyāya: study of scriptures, self-study, reflection on sacred words
Ishvar: God, creative source, causal field, supreme Guru or teacher
Pranidhānāni: dedication, practicing the presence, devotion, surrender of fruits of practices
Niyamāh: observances, practices of self-training

Q: *What is 'Niyama'?*
A: Niyama refers to our attitude to ourselves and includes observances such as purity, contentment, austerity, study and devotion to God.

Purity (*Shaucha*), contentment (*santosha*), austerity (*tapas*), scriptural study (*svādhyāya*), and surrender to God (*Ishvarapranidhāna*) constitute observances. Purity refers to cleanliness of the body and purity of the mind. As the mind and body are interdependent, purification of the body is a means of controlling the mind. By observing cleanliness one becomes less attached to one's own body and loses desire for physical contact with others. When purity is perfected one gains control of the senses and becomes cheerful, one-pointed, and fit for Self-realization.

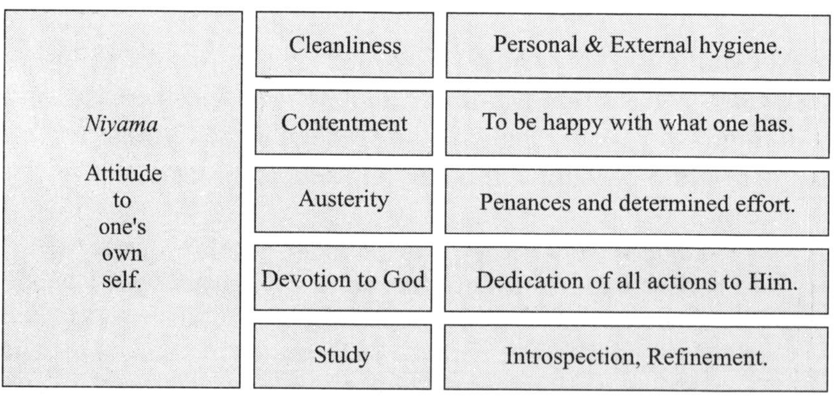

Niyama Attitude to one's own self.	Cleanliness	Personal & External hygiene.
	Contentment	To be happy with what one has.
	Austerity	Penances and determined effort.
	Devotion to God	Dedication of all actions to Him.
	Study	Introspection, Refinement.

The knowledge of an object is gained only by discrimination, by Investigation or by instruction, but not by giving alms or by a hundred retentions of the breath.

Viveka Chudāmani- Crest Jewel of Wisdom- Ādi Shankara

वितर्कबाधने प्रतिपक्षभावनम् ॥३३॥

Vitarka_Bādhane Pratipaksha_Bhāvanam.

When troubled by thoughts ill
Ponder over opposites, well.

Vitarka: troublesome thoughts
Bãdhane: differences, interference, disturbed by, inhibited by
Pratipaksha: opposite view, counter side, to the contrary, opposite thoughts or principles
Bhãvanam: state of mind. cultivate, habituate, thought of, contemplate on, reflect on

Q: *What if one were to be troubled by distracting thoughts?*
A: The antidote for troubled thoughts is to cultivate good thoughts.

The following are treatments as prescribed in the Buddha's teachings:

A calm mind	is an antidote to	a stressed mind.
A benevolent mind	is an antidote to	a malevolent mind.
A trusting mind	is an antidote to	a doubting mind.
A true mind	is an antidote to	a deluded mind.
An open mind	is an antidote to	a narrow mind.
An open mind	is an antidote to	an impulsive mind.
A balanced mind	is an antidote to	a fickle mind.
A non attached mind	is an antidote to	an attached mind.

1. *A calm mind is an antidote to a busy mind*: What can busy people do? How can crowded thoughts go? Crowded thoughts signify restless and inefficient mind. On the other hand a calm mind is an efficient mind. Calm mind looks at one issue at a time, disposes it of and takes up another, whereas a restless mind indulges in fragmented thinking. Never focusing on an aspect, the busy mind gives distracted attention. A few minutes to practice the art of self-healing through mind calming and purification is all that is needed to convert a crowded mind to a calm mind.

2. *A benevolent mind is an antidote to a malevolent mind*: One alternates between being a saint and a sinner, rambling up and down, in between the positive and the negative. One moment everything is hunky-dory and the next moment catastrophe. When the benevolent mind arises, everything goes well; when the malevolent mind arises, millions of defilements result. Therefore, one should train the unwholesome mind, and guard and keep correct thoughts, in order to cultivate a mind of loving kindness and compassion.

3. *A trusting mind is an antidote to a doubtful mind*: Doubt is the dry rot of faith. Many mistakes and tragedies in the world are due to doubt and suspicion, The only way to counter doubt is to develop faith. There are two ways in which one might lose-by doubting and by trusting. Experience shows that loss by trusting is always less than loss by doubting. When one doubts the other he does not delegate, he does everything by himself and he fails to do as efficiently as the other and loses.

4. *A true mind is an antidote to a deluded mind*: Deluding oneself is because of the false identity with the non self. Personal preference and judgments, creating countless illusions and unwarranted responses are all part of the deluded mind's work. The only way to lead a life of truth is to attach oneself with truth.

5. *An open mind is an antidote to a narrow mind*: The parachute flies only when it is open. An open mind is a trusting mind and receives responses not only from without but from within as well. The counter to a narrow mind is naturally to widen it further. Widening is feasible only with effort. The effort includes avoiding prejudices.

6. *A balanced mind is an antidote to a fragmented mind*: Fragmentation is a disease of the mind. A fragmented mind is the by-product of a narrow mind. A perceptive mind that is inclusive and loving and caring is the antidote to a fragmented mind. Balance is the result of right understanding and fragmentation is the result of lack of understanding. Balance comes about by meditation. The right perspective is gained by balance. Balance is harmony, fragmentation is disharmony.

7. *An enduring mind is an antidote to an impermanent mind*: Enduring relationship with the Being is begot by concentration, meditation and focusing on the ultimate truth. Such efforts lead to what is permanent and everlasting. Lack of the same is the cause for trying to hold on to the transient and getting troubled by disappointment resulting from the slippery nature of the transient.

8. *A non-attached mind is an antidote to an impulsive mind*: If ever anyone has lost maximum in terms of money, peace, friendship, health etc it is due to his impulsive nature. The impulsive nature is the result of past karmas. The way to retard the speed of impulsiveness is to cultivate the opposite quality of detachment. Impulsiveness is due to extreme attachment- to the false ego. Detaching oneself from sense objects and attaching to the true Being is the certain antidote to impulsiveness.

All mental statements are limited by
logic, duality and division.

वितर्का हिंसादयः कृतकारितानुमोदिता लोभक्रोधमोहपूर्वका मृदुमध्याधिमात्रा दुःखाज्ञानानन्तफला इति प्रतिपक्षभावनम् ॥३४॥

Vitarkā Hinsa_ādayah Krita_Kāritā_Anumoditā Lobha_Krodha_Mohapurvakā Mridu_Madhya_Adhimātrā Duhkha_Agyāna_Anantaphalā Iti Pratipaksha_ Bhāvanam.

Improper thought and emotion
Its origin; desire, anger or delusion.
Violence done, caused or approved
Mild, medium or intense they prove.
Result always in pain.
Never do they bring gain.

Vitarkā: obstacles *Hinsādayah*: injury etc *Krita*: self inflicted
Kāritā: got done *Anumoditā*: approved *Lobha*: greed
Krodha: hatred, rage, anger *Mohapurvakāh*: misapprehension
Mridu: low *Madhya*: middle *Adhimātrāh*: higher level
Duhkha: sorrow, unhappy, suffering *Agyāna*: Ignorance
Anantaphalāh: endless results *Iti*: these
Pratipaksha: opposing, countermanding *Bhāvanam*: state of mind

Q: *What is the effect of improper thoughts?*
A: The effect is always pain, irrespective of its origin: Desire, anger, delusion, violence caused or approved; the intensity of thought be mild, medium or intense.

This is one of those rarest aphorisms of Patanjali that is clearly very detailed, leaving nothing for the seeker to interpret or misinterpret. Scientifically speaking negative emotions result always in greater drain of energy and overtime work for the heart. The biggest problem faced today by young and old as well as rich and poor alike is stress. This stress is because of negative emotions arising as a result of failed expectations. There is far too much unfulfilled expectation in the society. The increased standard of living is only matched by equally decreased satisfaction levels. The emotions of hatred, lust, greed can only be countered by opposing emotions of love, joy and contentment.

The opposite of hate is not love,
the opposite of hate is non-hate;
on releasing of that hate,
love naturally arises.

अहिंसाप्रतिष्ठायां तत्संनिधौ वैरत्यागः ॥३५॥

Ahimsā_Pratishthāyām Tat_Samnidhau Vairtyāgah.

When one shuns violence,
Hostility ceases in his presence.

Ahimsā: non violence, non injury — *Tat*: that
Pratishthāyām: in a firm state, having firmly established, — *Samnidha*: presence
Vaira : hostility, enmity, aggression — *Tyāgah*: abandonment, abandon, give up

Q: *What is Ahimsa?*
A: *Ahimsā* refers to not hurting or injuring other beings; to respect all life as sacred and to practice non-violence in thought, word and deed, not only relative to people but to animals, plants and all the world of nature.

Violence ceases in the presence of the non-violent. *Ahimsā* or non-injury, of course, implies non-killing. But, non-injury is not merely non-killing. In its comprehensive meaning, *Ahimsā* or non-injury means entire abstinence from causing any pain or harm whatsoever to any living creature, either by thought, word, or deed. Non-injury requires a harmless mind, mouth, and hand. In the words of the Apostle of *Ahimsā* of the modern time, Mahatma Gandhi said,

"Literally speaking, *Ahimsā* means non-violence. But to me it has much higher, infinitely higher meaning. It means that you may not offend anybody; you may not harbor uncharitable thought, even in connection with those who consider your enemies. To one who follows this doctrine, there are no enemies. A man who believes in the efficacy of this doctrine finds in the ultimate stage, when he is about to reach the goal, the whole world at his feet."......

"This doctrine tells us that we may guard the honor of those under our charge by delivering our own lives into the hands of the man who would commit the sacrilege. And that requires far greater courage than delivering of blows."

Ahimsā is disciplined behaviour towards every living being.
- Dashvaikālika Sutra (6/9)

At a glance: Aphorism 31-35

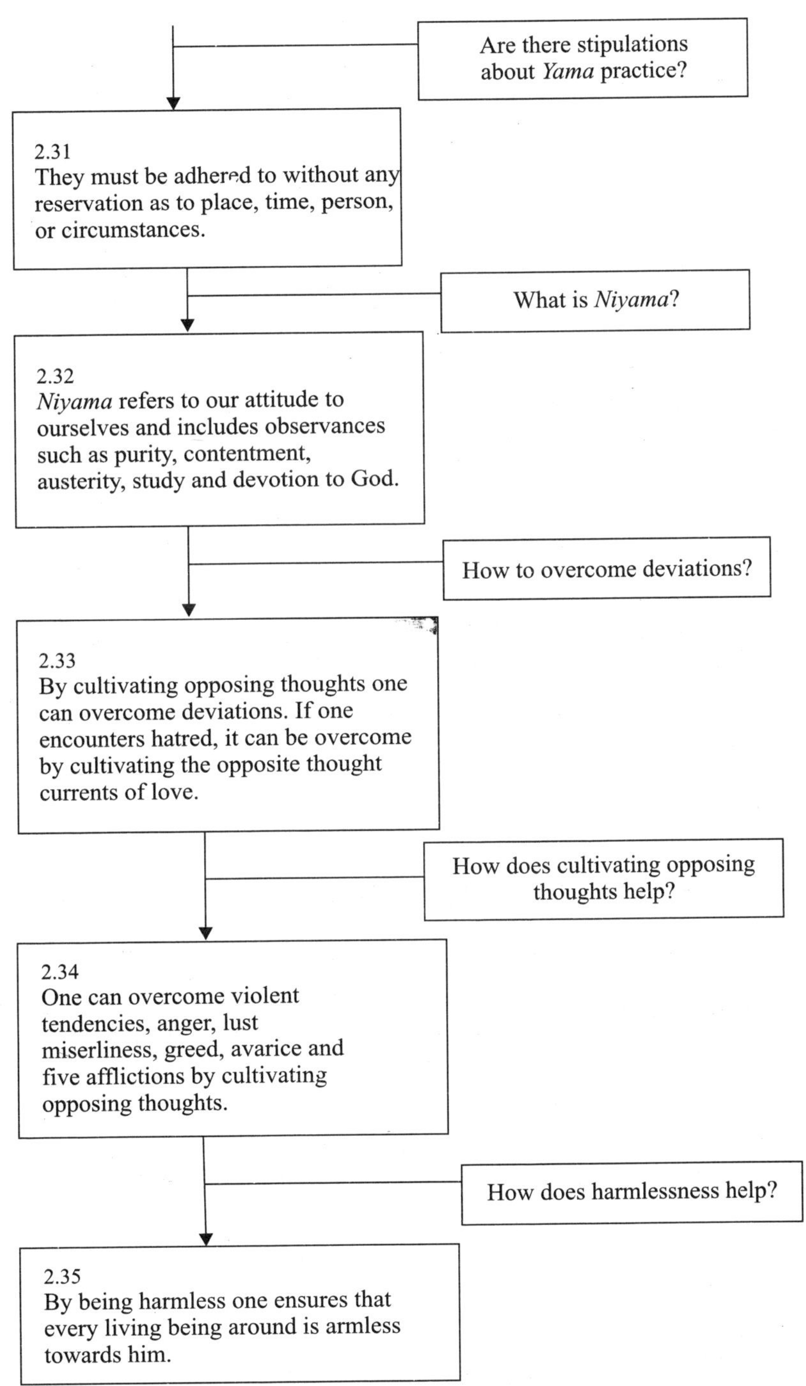

सत्यप्रतिष्ठायां क्रियाफलाश्रयत्वम् ॥३६॥
Satya_Pratishthāyām Kriyāphala_Āshrayatvam.

He who is embedded in truth
Reaps always good fruit.

Satya: truthfulness, honesty
Pratisthāyām: fixed state, a firm state, being well grounded in *Kriyā*: actions
Phala: result of activity, fruition, effects
Ashryatvam: dependent, are dependent on, are subservient to

Q: *Is honesty the best policy?*
A: Yes. The person who is truthful becomes truth himself. Fruits of good deeds reach him effortlessly.

Patanjali says that when an honest and truthful person says something, it will happen. Nature obeys him, for he is nature. As he thinks, so it happens. In the old days, that is the reason some were afraid of being cursed. If a person is well established in truth, whatever he says will happen, if he admonishes, such an admonition will turn true.

The quality or state of being honest includes probity; fairness and straightforwardness of conduct, speech, etc and integrity; sincerity; truthfulness; freedom from fraud or guile. Honesty is the best policy they say. How well said! The mental state when one utters a lie is now well captured by Lie Detector Test. The EEG pattern is highly disturbed when one utters a lie or behaves dishonestly. One has to consider what he says, how he says it, and in what way it could affect others. If speaking the truth has negative consequences for another, then it is better to say nothing, rather than utter falsehood.

Confucius (*The Analects*) says: “Be sincere and true to your word, serious and careful in your actions; and you will get along even among barbarians. But if you are insincere and untrustworthy in your speech, frivolous and careless in your actions, how will you get along even among your own neighbours? See these principles in front of you; in your carriage see them on the yoke. Then you may be sure to get along”

"Speak the truth which is pleasant. Do not speak unpleasant truths.
Do not lie, even if the lies are pleasing to the ear.
That is the eternal law, the dharma."

Mahābhārata

अस्तेयप्रतिष्ठायां सर्वरत्नोपस्थानम् ॥३७॥

Asteya_Pratishthāyām Sarva_Ratna_Upa_Sthānam.

To him, who is ever honest
Reach jewels, best.

Asteya: absence of improper desire, non-stealing, abstention from theft
Pratishthāyām: in a firm state, having firmly established, being well grounded in
Sarva: all *Ratna*: riches, diamonds, jewels, treasures
Upasthānam: reach him, stay with him, come to him, appear, come, present themselves

Q: *What does asteya provide?*
A: When non-stealing (*asteya*) is established, all jewels, or treasures present themselves, or are available to the Yogi. In other words, when the heart is pure, all means will come.

Steya means "to steal"; '*asteya*' is the opposite- to take nothing that does not belong to one. To avoid any kind of misappropriation of material or non-material things, such as acceptance of undeserved praise, is *asteya*. This also means that if one is in a situation where someone entrusts something to him or confides in him, he does not take advantage of him or her. One should refrain from taking that which is not his by right of consciousness and *karma*.

When one does not crave for what rightfully belongs to others and when on the contrary feels happy about others' riches and prosperity, he gets all he needs. This is the law of non-covetousness.

One should cultivate a sense of completeness, self-sufficiency and let go of cravings. If one values material goods too much, this temptation will come upon him at times. If one lets go of that false value, he can attain what he wants through honest means. If one attains what he wants through honest means, he lives without fear.

Asteya is lack of greed, wanting obsessively to have something that somebody else has, even if it is necessary or valuable for one; leads to lack of balance and unhappiness.

Jewels in this context should not be interpreted to mean physical riches or diamonds. The one who is contended is ever rich and the one who is greedy is forever poor.

Give me holy health, but give my brothers more, that I may enjoy my greater health in the greater myself. Give me power, but to my dear ones give it more abundantly, that I may wield the strength of all minds in my united mind.

Paramhansa Yogānanda
Whispers from Eternity A Book of Answered Prayers

ब्रह्मचर्यप्रतिष्ठायां वीर्यलाभः ॥३८॥

Brhmacharya_Pritishthāyām Virya_Lābhah.

He who practices celibacy with rigour
Acquires good spiritual vigour.

Brahmacharya: continence, celibacy
Pritishthāyām: in a firm state
Virya: capability
Lābhah: benefit, attained

Q: *What is Brahmacharya?*

A: Literally '*Brahma*' means the creator and '*Chara*' means movement. *Brahmacharya* can therefore mean moving around the creator, walking in awareness of the highest and absolute reality, remembering the divine, practicing the presence of God and ensuring that the attention of the seeker is always on God. In common parlance, *Brahmacharya* has come to mean celibacy.

Brahmacharya means "to walk on God's path". *Brahman* denotes the Universal Supreme Entity. *Charya* can also be thought of as "grazing", in the same way that a cow does her walking and eating at the same time. Thus, *Brahmacharya* means living one's life, doing what one has to do or wants to do, and at the same time keeping his mind fixed on God. *Brahmacharya* is the key to spiritual success because it converts all actions into acts of spiritual practice. It keeps the seeker on the God's path literally twenty-four hours a day. When mind thinks of everything as Divine, it is no longer the doer of the actions and hence no *karma* accumulates.

In common parlance, *Brahmacharya* has come to mean celibacy. Perfect celibacy is, above all, an attitude of mind; purity of thought, word, and deed. To aid in the practice of celibacy one should eat *sāttvic* food and avoid worldly situations and environments. When continence is perfected, one gains physical, mental, and spiritual strength.

Practice of divine conduct, controlling lust by remaining celibate when single and faithful in marriage, seeking holy company, dressing modestly etc are part of the practice. Abstinence or continence is the corner-stone or foundation on which attainment of Union stands. If one is not established in *Brahmacharya*, his mind is agitated by evil thoughts.

Regard a woman as mother or Devi (goddess). This is *brahmacharya* of the eye. Hear not lustful talks. This is *brahmacharya* of the ear. Speak not of woman. This is *brahmacharya* of the tongue. Entertain not lustful thoughts. This is *brahmacharya* of the mind.

अपरिग्रहस्थैर्ये जन्मकथन्तासंबोधः ॥३९॥

Aparigraha_Sthairye Janma_Kathantā_Sambodhah.

The one of non-greedy nature
Gains knowledge of his past, present and future.

Aparigraha: abstinence from sense objects, non-possessiveness, non-greed, non-grasping
Sthạirye: firmly established *Janma*: birth *Kathantā*: about it
Sambodhah: realisation , complete knowledge of

Q: *How will absence of greed help?*
A: When one becomes steadfast in his abstention from greed, he gains knowledge of the meaning and purpose of his life.

Aparigraha (non-hoarding): means something like 'hands off' or 'not seizing opportunity.' *Parigraha* means 'to take' or 'to seize.' *Parigraha* is the increasing orientation toward material things. If one reduces *parigraha* and develop *aparigraha*, one is orienting himself more inwardly. The less time he spends on his material possessions, the more he has to spend on investigating all that he calls yoga. He will learn to enjoy what he has rather than constantly seek things he does not have.

Aparigraha means to take only what is necessary, and not to take an advantage of a situation or act greedy. One should only take what he has earned; if he takes more it is understood he is exploiting someone else. In addition, unearned rewards can bring with them obligations that might later cause problems. Perfection of *aparigraha* gives dispassion and one gains knowledge of the past, present, and future.

Aparigraha, is to be non-greedy. Greed is a lot more complicated than it seems on the surface. Greed means taking more than what one needs or deserves. It also means hoarding. It means refusing to let go of something when it's time to do so.

Non-greed is generosity, the sharing of power in relationships, resources and ideas--and is interwoven with ingenuity, innovation, cooperation, inspiration, community, invention and spiritual joy. One should have the capacity to shape his world together as well as be shaped by it individually.

Infinite Spirit, teach me to comprehend the utter uselessness of being afraid.
Help me to remember that death, if it must come, does not come twice;
and that when it does occur, through the mercifulness of nature,
I shall not know of it nor care. Thus, I need not tremble
at the thought of death.

Paramhansa Yogānanda
Whispers from Eternity A Book of Answered Prayers

शौचात्स्वांगजुगुप्सा परैरसंसर्गः ॥४०॥
Sauchāt_Svānga_Jugupsā Paraih_Asansargah.

Purity results in aversion
For physical contact, disinclination.

Sauchāt: through purification *Svanga*: own body *Jugupsā*: dislike
Paraih: outsiders, other bodies *Asansargah*: not keeping company

Q: *Why is purity of body and mind insisted upon?*
A: From the practice of purification, aversion towards one's own body is developed and this aversion extends to contact with other bodies. Such purity is necessary to be able to concentrate.

Saucha means cleanliness, purity. *Saucha* has both an inner and an outer aspect. Outer cleanliness simply means keeping oneself clean. Inner cleanliness has as much to do with the healthy, free functioning of one's bodily organs as with the clarity of his mind. Inner cleanliness means getting rid of all impure, unfriendly, hurtful and harmful thoughts. The mind need be rid of hatred, anger, jealousy, fear and other unclean thoughts. Purity operates on many levels. One aspires to cleanliness not only for his body but also for his environment around, eating healthy food and drinking clean water. The purity extends to speech, not talking ill of others and not listening to ills spoken about others in one's presence. The vow to observe purity enables one to constantly reflect and ensure that he entertains no ill will towards any. Naturally, one would get rid of association with others who are observed to be not just unclean but amoral as well. Purity implies the freedom of oneself from everything which cannot be set in tune with, or set in harmony with, the ideal or the aim of Yoga. *Āsana* or *prānāyāma* are essential means for attending to this inner cleanliness. From cleanliness comes non-attachment towards one's own and others' body. By the practice of mental purity one acquires cheerfulness, focused attention and vision of the self. Purity of thought is a consequence of purity of food. Ādi Shankara says that one should receive purity from every sense organ including mind. We must see purity, touch purity, hear purity. That which is compatible with the nature of the Absolute is purity. Every thing else is impure.

The mind is indeed the world.
It should be purified with great effort.
It is an ancient truth that the mind assumes the form
of the object to which it is applied.

Maitrayāni Upanishad

The Rock Sculptor

He was a well-known sculptor in the town. The exquisite work chiselled out by him, made people wonder how he could turn out such master pieces out of rock.

When queried he used to say, "Well, when I look at a rock, I can see a horse, or a beautiful woman or the figure of an elephant inside the rock. All I do is to remove the impure rocks covering the figure. And Lo! the sculpture is ready!"

There after once the sculptor was approached by a follower of Lord Buddha. He wanted a statue of Buddha that he could install in a new temple that he was building. For months the sculptor searched hundreds of rocks to find if Buddha is 'hiding' in the rock, so that he could remove impure stones around. But he was unsuccessful. He could not find even a single rock with Buddha in.

At last he approached the Buddhist monk in a temple and explained to him his difficulty. He asked for the monk's help. He asked the monk, "Can you help find Buddha?" The monk said, "That is no problem, Right here in this backyard, you can find one." Both went to the backyard. But the sculptor found none. The monk asked the sculptor to look into the well. The sculptor found his own image.

He realized that Buddha is inside him and that there can never be a rock with Buddha in, because there can be no impurities surrounding Buddha. The image in him is the pure Buddha. He has to remove his own impurities to see Buddha in him. The sculptor, needless to add became a monk.

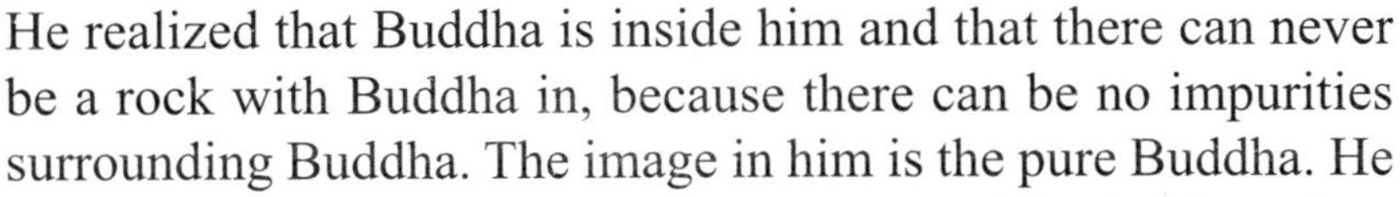

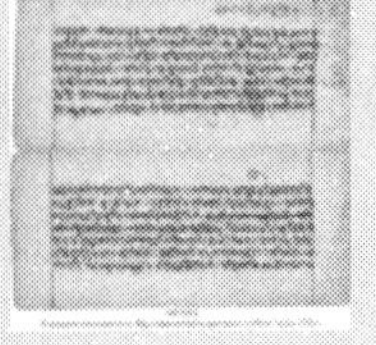

Mind has been described as of two types:
Pure and Impure. The impure is that which is tainted
By desires, the pure is that which is free from desires.

Maitrāyani Upanishad

At a glance: Aphorism 36-40

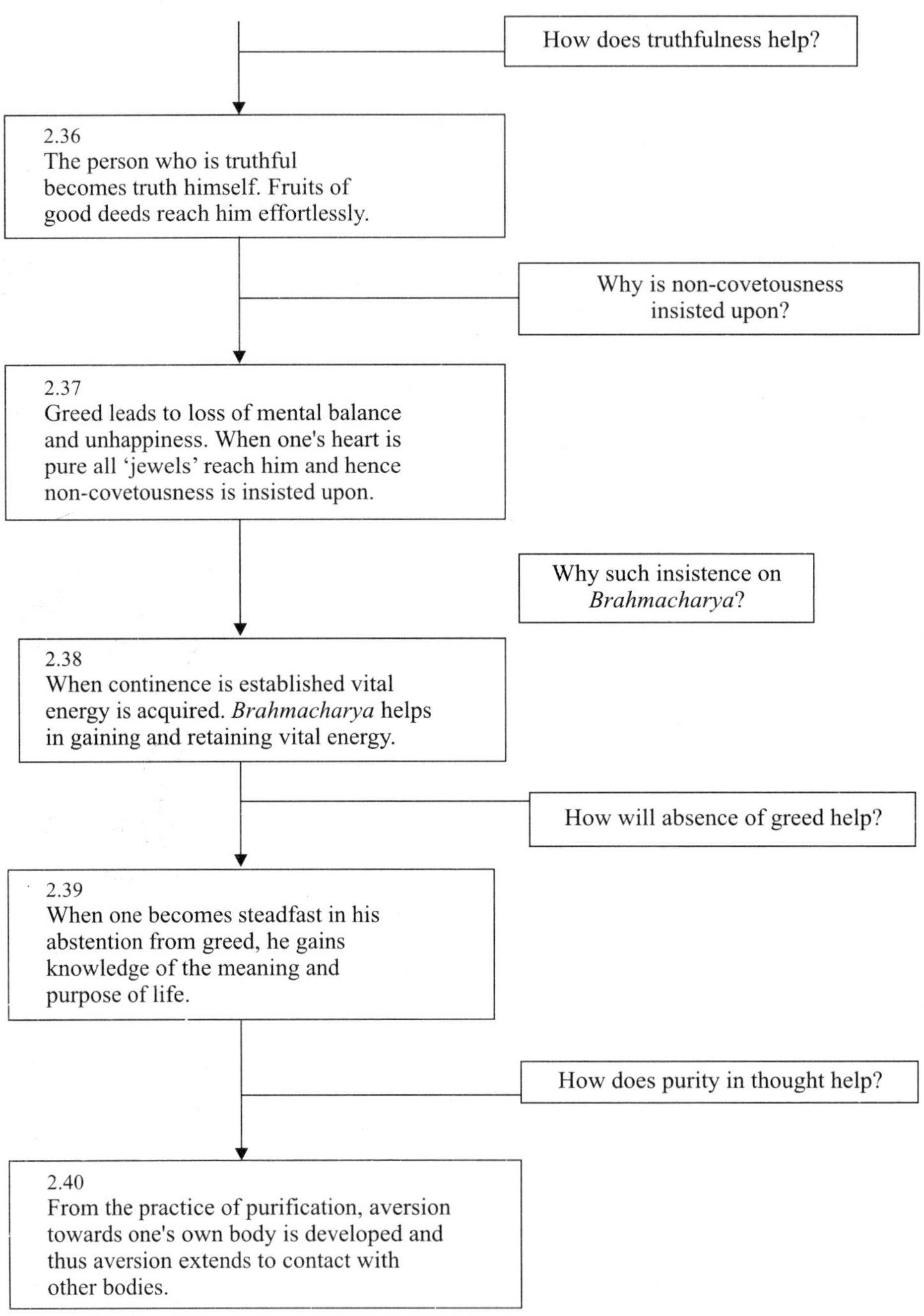

सत्त्वशुद्धिसौमनस्यैकाग्र्येन्द्रियजयात्मदर्शन योग्यत्वानि च ॥४१॥

Sattva_Shuddhi_Saumanasya_Ekāgrya_Indriya_Jaya_Ātmadarshan Yogya_Tvāni Cha.

Cleanliness brings forth cheer and sense control
Thence is one fit to concentrate on inner soul.

Sattva: Purity of heart *Shuddhi* : cleaning
Saumanasya: Cheerful mind
Ekāgrya: Power of concentration
Indriya Jaya: Control of passions
Ātmadarshan: vision of the Self
Yogyatvāni: to be fit, qualified
Cha: and

Q: *What are the gains of being pure?*
A: 1. Purification of the mind 2. Pleasantness of feeling
3. Concentration 4. Control over the senses
5. Ability for self realization are the gains from being pure.

1. **Purification of mind:** Purification of mind is essential for concentration. A mind full of desires and aversion is an unfit mind. The mental modifications will be violent. With such distraction, no spiritual progress is possible.
2. **Pleasantness of feeling:** One can sleep comfortably after a nice shower in the evening, because it washes off the days accumulated thoughts also along with the dirt on the body. The pleasant feeling is the antidote to aversion. Similarly one can shower himself with pure thoughts.
3. **Concentration:** Itching body is no way to focus attention on, the focus will be on the body. Once the body and mind is pure, concentration is easier. The primary purpose of ensuring cleanliness is to be able to concentrate. If the thoughts are over alleged injustices that one could not 'clean' up from his mind, focusing is not feasible.
4. **Control over the senses:** Sense organs get inclined to move and perch itself on internal or external object of interest. Cleanliness means washing out all such objects.
5. **Ability for self realization:** That is the ultimate. While cleanliness in itself does not ensure ability of self realization, in the absence of the same self realization is impossible.

Through the purification of the mind a man destroys the impressions of his good and evil *karma*, and the purified mind abiding in *Ātman* enjoys the un-diminishing Bliss.

Chhāndogya Upanishad

संतोषदनुत्तम सुखलाभः ॥४२॥
Santoshāt_Anuttama Sukha_Lābhah.

Contentment brings forth
Happiness manifold.

Santoshāt: happiness, contentment *Anuttama*: unexcelled, extreme, supreme
Sukha: bliss, pleasure, happiness, comfort, joy, satisfaction
Lābhah: gain, benefit, is acquired

Q: *What happens when one is content with what he has?*
A: One's contentment will lead one to everlasting happiness.

Santosha means happiness, feeling of being content with what one has, to be happy with what one has rather than being unhappy about what one doesn't have, to be at peace within and content with one's lifestyle. Unexcelled happiness comes from the practice of contentment. Happiness is peacefulness with our present situation, whatever it is. This is not stagnation or complacency, both of which have a sense of being stuck. Rather, it is a positive appreciation of what is. This can be a useful foundation for growth from the present. Happiness is not in collecting finite objects, but being in tune with infinite. "I am happy the way I am. I am happy with what I have." These are the thoughts of a contented man. A constant craving and feeling of dissatisfaction with what one has is the result of high body orientation. The senses of the one who is dissatisfied, is in constant turmoil.

Happiness, it is in the tip of your tail !

A small kitten had just retuned from cat philosophy school. He was simply running around in circles, trying to catch his tail. A seasoned old alley cat asked the kitten what he was doing. "I have learnt that happiness is at the tip of one's tail, and I am trying to catch mine, so that I will always be happy". The old cat said, "You have learnt well. I never received any fancy education. But I too have heard that happiness is in the tip of my tail. What I have also discovered is that if you forget about trying to catch happiness, happiness will follow you wherever you go, like the tip of your tail."

My dear Nārada, happiness is not anywhere and yet it is everywhere; it is the completeness of being that you can find happiness.

Sanatkumāra to Nārada

कायेन्द्रियसिद्धिरशुद्धिक्षयात्तपसः ॥४३॥

Kāyā_Indriya_Siddhih Ashuddhi_Kshayāt Tapasah.

Effort to remove impurity
To gain mastery over senses, is austerity.

Kāyā: body *Indriya*: senses *Siddhih*: attainment, mastery, perfection
Aśhuddhi: impurity *Tapasah*: penance, training the senses, austerities
Kshayāt: dissipation, weakening, removal, destruction, Elimination

Q: *What is austerity?*
A: Any practice that helps one to weaken his impurities and get mastery over his senses is austerity.

Austerity is any practice that leads to cleansing up the impurities of mind. It could be fasting, silence, walking on fire, sleeping on a bed of nails or even sitting with both hands up till they are ossified. Many a practice would sound bizarre. It will not be proper to sit on judgment on the austere practices followed by different seekers. It is up to the individual concerned, with the help of the teacher to judge for himself the efficacy of practices followed and decide on its continuation or otherwise.

Yoga practices themselves are good as purification methods. *Prānāyama*, controlling the vital energy enhances the purification process. The austere practices like fasting are done to calm the mind, an objective achieved through Yoga practice. Hence adherence to Yoga practice itself is good enough. *Tapas* should be something simple and small enough to become successful, but should also be difficult and challenging enough to engage the will.

Tapas should be practiced as an act of devotion to God. Performance of *tapas* is not something to be talked about and advertised. It should be ego-less. *Tapas* is intended to transform and purify and enable the conscious awareness and control over unconscious impulses and poor behaviour. The best benefit of *tapas* is that it enhances the will power of the individual.

Tapas is a tool for transformation and should be approached with an attitude of passion and zeal rather than of self-denial and chastisement.

Purify yourself from all the attributes of self,
that you may see your own pure essence.

Rumi: Masnavi 1

स्वाध्यायादिष्टदेवतासंप्रयोगः ॥४४॥

Svādhyāt_Ishta_Devatā_Samprayogah.

Reflection promotes kinship
With chosen object of worship.

Svādhyayāt: self-study, reflection on sacred words
Ishta: that which is preferred, chosen
Samprayogah: connected with, in contact, communion
Devatā: Deity, God

Q: *How does self-study / reflection help?*
A: Self-study / reflection enables communion with the desired deity.

Reflection (*Svādhyāya*):

The fourth *niyama* is Reflection (*svādhyāya*). *Sva* means 'self' or 'belonging to me.' *Adhyāya* means 'inquiry' or 'examination'. The word *svādhyāya* literally means, "to get close to something." It means to get close to oneself, that is, to study oneself.

Svādhyāya could consist of the study of scriptures, listening to lectures from enlightened teachers, participation in discussion-groups that are formed to understand the scriptures, sitting silently in the holy premises of temple, church or mosque etc. Reflection follows such a study or visit to the place of worship. It can be observed by many that while the intended purpose of going to a temple is to have a *darshan* (holy presence) of God; on returning from temple one starts reflecting on his actions and the correctness or otherwise of the same. That is reflection. If the study of scriptures is not followed by reflection on its contents and advocacy, the study becomes useless.

The benefits of reflection can be enumerated as follows:

1. It inspires and elevates the mind and lifts it to higher levels of consciousness.
2. It cuts new spiritual grooves for the mind to move and dwell on, taking thoughts away from mundane matters.
3. It helps mind in withdrawing from being object orientated and thus helps weakening the mind's veiling and projecting power.
4. It helps in acquiring wisdom by digesting the books by sages and saints, philosophers and mystics.
5. It makes one overcome activity orientation and inertia, and become more pure.

Sow a thought and you reap an act.
Sow an act and you reap a habit.
Sow a habit and you reap a character.
Sow a character and you reap a destiny.

समाधिसिद्धिरीश्वरप्ररिणधानात् ॥४५॥

Samādhi_Siddhih Ishvar_Pranidhānāt.

By surrendering to God
Absorption can be had.

Samādhi: union
Siddhih: perfection
Ishvara: God, supreme Guru
Pranidhānāt: surrendering

Q: *How does dedication to God help?*
A: Dedication to God helps in achieving oneness with the SELF, the state of absorption.

Isvarapranidhāna means 'to lay all your actions at the feet of God.' It is the contemplation on God (*Isvara*) in order to become attuned to God and God's will. One should accept the fact that he will not always get everything he wants. Things do go wrong. Having done what is prescribed under the given set of circumstances, it is best to leave the rest to a higher power. In the context of the *niyamas*, one can define *Isvarapranidhāna* as the attitude of a person who usually offers the fruits of his or her action to God in daily prayer. Once again Patanjali suggests surrender to God. In surrender there is peace. Surrender is not to be looked at from the point of view of surrender say after a war where the surrendered is at the whims of the conqueror. When one, surrenders to God, his will is in tact and so is his freedom of exercising the will. What is surrendered is the expectation after every action. When there is no expectation and when an individual leaves all results to God doing his duty, there is peace. It is expectation that brings in disappointment. The failure in turn leads to anguish and anger. Even in the case of attainment of *Samādhi* state, it is better to leave it to God. Do as per scriptures, do adhere to the aspects of Yoga, but don't at every state expect improvement. Leave further progress to God. The chemistry of faith is such that the human effort combined with faith produces faster result, than exclusive dependence on human effort and ingenuity. Surrender means to yield ownership, to relinquish control over what one considers his: his property, his time, his "rights." When one surrenders to God, he is simply acknowledging that what he "owns" actually belongs to Him. God is the giver of all things. One is responsible to care for what God has given him. In surrendering to God, there is an implicit admission on one's part that one is not ultimately in control of everything, including one's present circumstances. Surrendering to God helps one to let go off whatever he has been holding back.

Surrender is
letting false ego, go!

At a glance: Aphorism 41-45

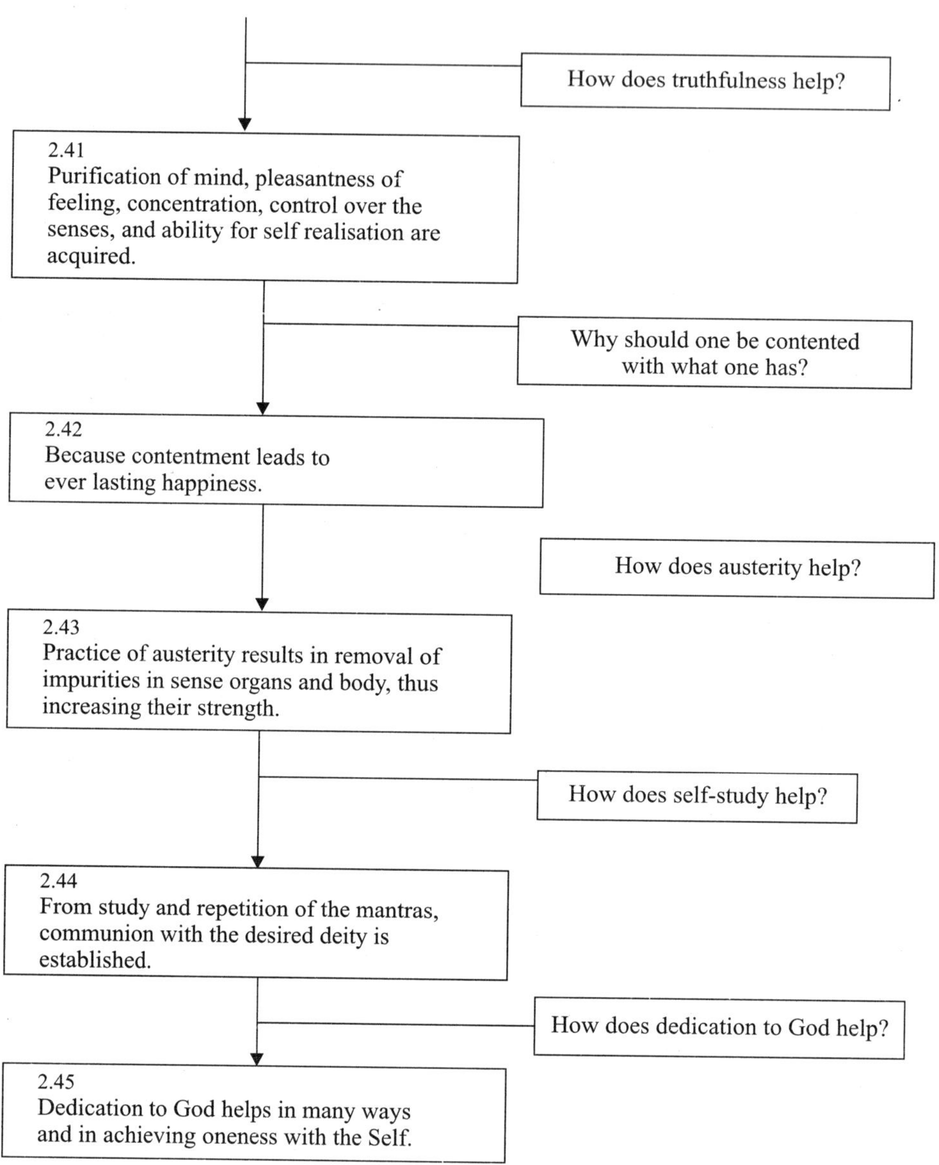

स्थिरसुखमासनम् ॥४६॥
Sthira_Sukham_Āsanam.

Posture is
That which keeps one steady and at ease.

Sthira: steady, firm, attentive
Sukhā: comfortable, happy, at ease
Āsanam: posture, seat

Q: *What is Āsana?*
A: *Āsana* is that posture that permits comfort and steadiness.
Āsana posture should be such that enables one to forget his body awareness.

Āsana is defined as 'posture;' its literal meaning is 'to place oneself' *Āsanas* serve as stable postures for prolonged meditation. More than just stretching, *āsanas* open the energy channels and psychic centers of the body. *Āsanas* purify and strengthen the body and control and focus the mind. *Āsana* is that which is steady and comfortable, firm yet relaxed.

When holding a yoga posture, one should make sure that he breathes slowly and deeply. Swāmi Vivekānanda says;

"Firmness of posture means that you do not feel the body at all. Generally speaking you will find that as soon as you sit for a few minutes, you will feel all sorts of bodily disturbances. But when you have gone beyond the idea of gross, physical body, you will lose all sense of the body. You will feel neither pain nor pleasure. And when you again become aware of it, you will feel completely rested. This is the only real test you can give your body. When you have succeeded in controlling the body and keeping it firm, your practice will be steady; but while you are disturbed by the body, your nerves are disturbed and you cannot concentrate your mind."

It is Prāna that is manifesting as motion; it is Prāna that is manifesting as gravitation, as magnetism, as electricity, as light. It is the Prāna that is manifesting as the action of the body, as nerve currents, as thought force.

Swami Vivekānanda

प्रयत्नशैथिल्यानन्तसमापत्तिभ्याम् ॥४७॥

Prayatna_Shaithilya Anantya Samāpattibhyām.

By effort relaxation
On the infinite, gets one, concentration.

Prayatna: correct effort *Shaithilya*: relaxation *Anantya*: infinite
Samāpattibhyām: concentrating mind on.

Q: *How to perfect 'āsana'?*
A: By relaxation of the effort and meditation on the infinite, one can perfect *āsanas.*

Placing oneself near and at ease is made possible by:

1. *Effort and a relaxed attitude:*

Allowing it to happen is the best policy. Forcing one self and getting tensed up for not being able to sit at ease adds to tensions, the very antithesis of the attempt to calm oneself. *Yoga is not a destination, it is a process*. The benefit is in following the process. It is quite natural for the seeker to compare himself with another aspirant and get dejected that he is not able to be as good as the other. *Yoga is not a competitive activity. It is a self enlightening effort*. Patience and perseverance are two very important qualities that are needed. Relaxed approach to practice is in itself a good ingredient.

2. *Concentration on the infinite:*

Meditating on the Lord and surrendering oneself to Him is essential. As long as one feels the effort is all his and the reward, if not forthcoming, is because of shortcoming in his efforts, there is bound to be disappointment. If on the other hand one surrenders to God and approaches practice with a sense of devotion, results are bound to be better. Effortlessness and the Infinite Being go together. The whole universe is an effortless creation. As part of that creation, all one needs to do is to fine-tune oneself to the vibration that is around. The result follows. Effortlessness is achieved only after hours of practice. It is an apparent contradiction. Effort is needed to become effortless! There is no contradiction if one understands that the effort is in the direction of fine tuning oneself with infinity, thereafter follows the effortless practice of concentration.

"The illusory *Samsāric Vāsanā* that has arisen through the practice of many lives, never perishes except through the practice of Yoga for a long time. It is not possible on the part of one, to control the mind, by sitting up again and again except through the approved means."

Muktikopanishad.

ततो द्वन्द्वानभिघातः ॥४८॥

Tato Dvandva_Anabhighātah.

On acquiring such quality,
One is undisturbed by duality.

Tato: On practice
Dvandva: pairs of opposites, duality
Anabhighātah: unaffected, undisturbed

Q: *What happens when perfection is achieved?*
A: One realizes that he is no longer troubled by the dualities of sense-experience.

When one is steady and easy, he remains undisturbed by the pairs of opposites like pleasure and pain, heat and cold or good and evil. The mental and physical poise one gains by continued practice makes one take a detached look. One does not 'fall at first sight'. With diminished body consciousness the tendency to pamper the body-mind unit decreases sharply. Neither does one bother about pain reported by the body-mind unit. Being centred in himself, he finds he is truly an observer now and remains untouched by experiences.

Says Lord Krishna:

"A centred person is the master
He understands the separateness of sense organs
And their relationship to the
Attractions (rāga) and aversions (dwesha)
Knowing this He wanders
Amongst different sense organs
With happiness and tranquillity.
Such a person is content within himself."

Duality means alternatively being on the left or on the right. Absence of duality means staying at the centre. A centred person is a master says Lord Krishna. *Āsana* practices places one at the centre, right in front of reality. No more wavering, no more vacillations and no more will one be led by the senses. The senses are under total control of the seeker now. He is content with himself.

The wise man should hold his body steady, with the three (upper) parts (the chest, neck, and head) erect, turn his senses, with the help of the mind, toward the heart, and by means of the raft of Brahman (i.e. repetition of OM and meditation on its meaning) can cross the fearful torrents of the world.

Shvetāsvatara Upanishad

तस्मिन्सति श्वासप्रश्वासयोर्गतिविच्छेदः प्राणायामः ॥४९॥

Tasmin Sati Svāsa_Prasvāsyoh Gati_Vichchhedah Prānāyāmah.

Posture practice helps breath regulation
Inhalation, exhalation and suspension.

Tasmin: in that state *Sati*: definitely, certainly *Svāsa*: inhalation
Prasvāsyoh: Exhalation *Gati*: speed, movement
Vichchhedah: interruption, breakages *Prānāyāmah*: regulation of vital energy

Q: *What is prānāyāma?*
A: *Prānāyāma* is control of vital energy. There are of three kinds:
1. External, internal and motionless.

Prānāyāma: is the compound word which consists of *Prāna* and *Āyāma*.
Prāna: Vital energy / Life force. *Āyāma*: Control, extension, expansion.
Prānāyāma: Control, extension, expansion of vital energy

Breath is the first expression of life. Motion of lungs produces breath. It is the motion of breath that produces sound. The Hindu word for God is *Iswara, Svara* is breath. In that sense God is breath. Breath synchronized means God synchronized with the individual self. Through *Prānāyāma* attempt is made to fine tune oneself with God.

Breath is the gross form of mind. Till the time of death, the mind keeps breath in the body; and when the body dies the mind takes the breath along with it. Therefore, the exercise of breath-control is only an aid for rendering the mind quiescent. Like the practice of breath-control, meditation on the forms of God, repetition of *mantras*, restriction on food, etc., are but aids for rendering the mind quiescent.

At the body level, heart, digestive system and others are secondary to the functioning of lungs that produces breath or rather the breath that makes lungs function. If lungs are inoperative heart's function is stopped. Breath at a gross level is oxygen supply and breath at the subtle level is vital energy.

The restraint of *Prāna* (vital air) is equal to the renunciation of mental impressions.

Yogavāshishta

There is an *Upanishadic* hymn: "Oh *Prāna*, stay in your form, do not depart from the body. *You are the Lord who dwells in this body within as speech, ear, eye and mind.*" (*Prashnopanishad*, 2.12). Exit of *prāna* is exit of life. Body the manifest creation would be rendered useless once life force *prāna* leaves the body. The sensory faculties, the mind and its attributes are governed by the life force *prāna*.

Six vital questions concerning the *prāna* are addressed by Ashwalāyan, the disciple of sage Pippalāda and the sage responds (*Prashnopanishad* 3.1). In this context, it would be worthwhile studying the questions and answers,

The questions:

1. From where does the life force *prāna* originate?
2. How does it come into the body?
3. How does it dwell in the body?
4. How does it divide itself into different forms?
5. How is it experienced in the body?
6. How does it leave the body?

The responses from the sage:

1. *From where does the life force prāna originate*? From the Self is born this *prāna*. Much the same way the shadow is inseparable from the man, the vital force *prāna* is inseparable from the Self.
2. *How does it come into the body*? It enters the body through the mind. The causal mind is formed before the body. When mind enters the body, *prāna* follows suit. *Hatha Yoga Pradipikā* states that mind and *prāna* are mixed like milk and water. Where there is *prānic* activity, there is mind and where there is mind there is *Prāna*.

   Body is created by the union of the parents. But mind is not. The causal mind is created in the causal dimension. The mind dwelling and resting in the astral dimension after the death of the earlier body re-enters a new body at the time of conception of a baby in the womb of a mother.
3. *How does it dwell in the body*? After entering the body, life force *prāna*, divides itself into five manifestations and dwells in the body. So, it dwells in the body in different manifestations
4. *How does it divide itself into different forms*?

   The *Prāna*, acting as the Chief regulator, manifests itself as *Prāna*, *Apāna*, *Samāna*, *Udāna* and *Vyāna*.

5. *How is it experienced in the body?*

Prāna and its modifications

Type	Function	Location
Prāna	Respiration	Heart corresponding to the chest region.
Apāna	Excretion	Organs of evacuation corresponding to the lower abdomen region and the function of elimination.
Samāna	Digestion	Area of the navel corresponding to the central region of the body and the function of digestion.
Udāna	Swallowing	Corresponding to the throat region and the function of speech.
Vyāna	Circulation	All pervading corresponding to the distribution of energy into all areas of the body.

6. *How does it leave the body?*

Prāna with its manifestation as *Udāna* leaves the body at the time of death. At the time of death, if *Udāna* is in higher parts, the mind is led to higher planes and vice versa. The mind with its impressions and desires and *Prāna* leave the body at the time of death.

Udāna is the fire or illumination element. Symbolically, it is represented by a burning light. So at death, since the fire element is gone, a lamp is lit and kept by the side of the dead body. With reference to Yoga the vital energy can be described as something that flows continuously from somewhere inside us, filling us and keeping us alive: it is vitality. In this image, the vital energy streams out from the centre through the whole body. When one is troubled, restless, or confused, one's vital energy is more outside the body than within. On the other hand, in a more peaceful and well-balanced person, the vital energy is dispersed less outside the body.

The restraint of all modifications of the mind by regarding all mental states like the *Chitta* as Brahman alone is called *Prānāyāma*. The negation of Phenomenal world is known as *Rechaka* (breathing out), the thought 'I am verily '*Brahman*' is called *Puraka* (breathing in), and the steadiness of thought thereafter is called '*Kumbhaka*' (restraining the breath). That is the real course of *prānāyāma*, for the enlightened, where as the ignorant only torture the nose.

Ādi Shankara

वाह्याभ्यन्तरस्तम्भवृत्तिर्देशकालसंख्याभिः परिदृष्टो दीर्घसूक्ष्मः ॥५०॥

Bāhya_ābhyāntar_Stambha Vrittih Desha_Kāla_Sankhyābhih Paridrishto Dirgha_Sukshmah.

Inhale, exhale and retention process is kept prolonged and subtle
With activity, place, duration and number settled.

Bāhya: external, outside *Ābhyāntar*: inside, internal *Stambha*: retention
Vrittih: action *Desha*: place *Kāla*: time
Sankhyābhih: measured time intervals *Paridrishta*: seen
Dirgha: long, deep *Sukshmah*: subtle

Q: *How is 'Prānāyāma' practised?*
A: *Prānāyāma* is practised by regulating the three components 1. external operation (*bāhya-vritti*) 2. internal operation (*ābhyāntara-vritti*), and 3. suppression (*stambha-vritti*).

The three components (inhalation, exhalation and retention), when regulated by place, time, and number, and further their duration, make three different kinds of *Prānāyāma*. The *Prānāyāma* components are:

1. The breathing cycle, consisting of inhalation, exhalation and suspension.
2. The quality of breath: prolonged and deep, subtle and steady
3. Right mental attitude
4. Duration of the individual inhale, exhale and suspend process
5. Number of cycles

Admittedly the components and variables are many. That is the reason for innumerable combinations and ratios. Since *Prānāyama* means activation of the vital energy, choice of breathing cycle, individual process duration and the right mental attitude are to be very carefully chosen with the guidance of acknowledged experts in the field. Untold damages have been reportedly taking place due to negligence in this regard. Any activity on restraining vital force must have an ennobling effect on mind, for mind and *prāna* are interconnected, they are mixed like water and milk. Both have their activities, where there is prānic movement or activity there is mind (consciousness), where there is consciousness, there is *prāna*.

It is *Prāna* that is manifesting as motion. It is *Prāna* that is manifesting as gravitation, as magnetism, as electricity, as light. It is the *Prāna* that is manifesting as the actions of the body, as the nerve channels and as thought force.

Swāmi Vivekānada

At a glance: Aphorism 46-50

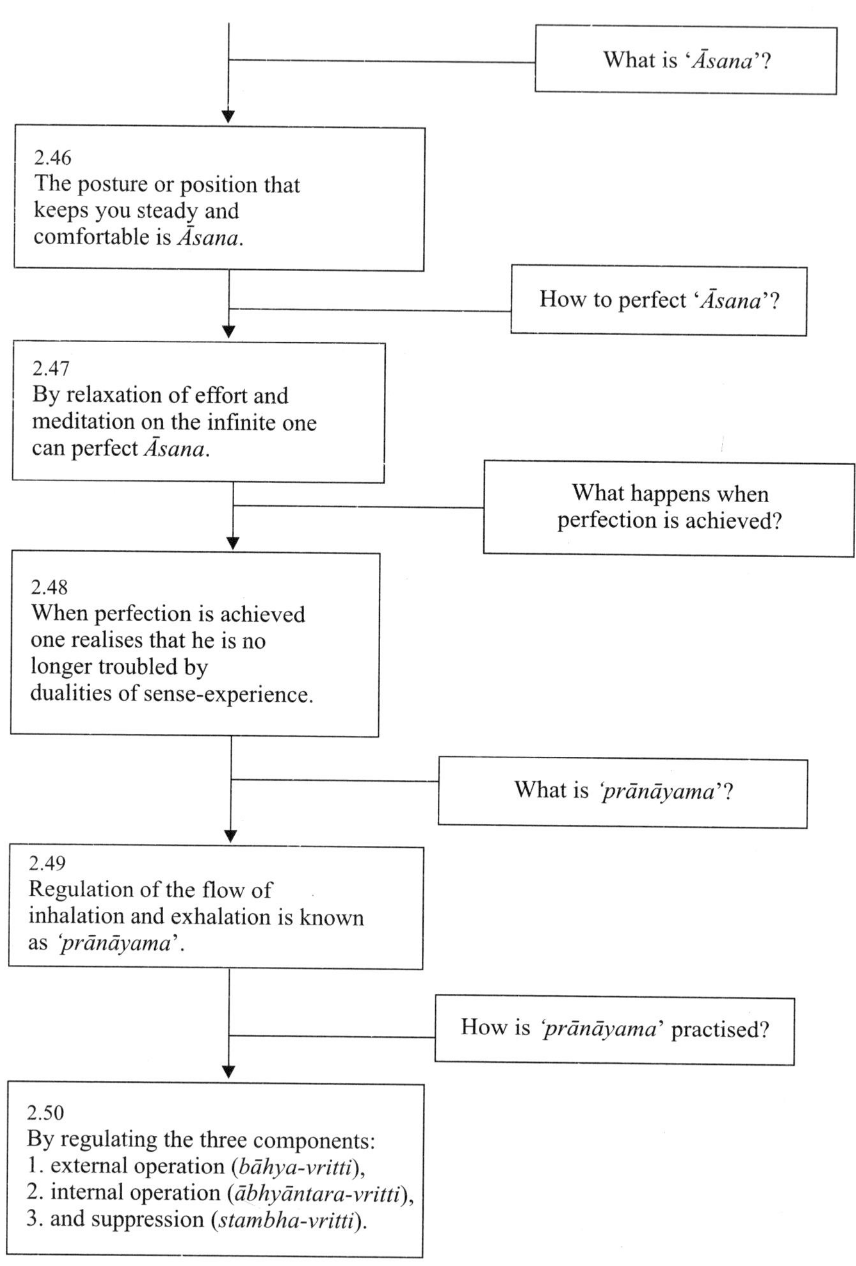

वाह्याभ्यन्तरविषयाक्षेपी चतुर्थः ॥५१॥
Bāhya_Ābhyāntar_Vishaya_Ākshepi Chaturthah.

When inhalation exhalation and retention process one transcends
A fourth state he ascends.

Bāhya: external *Ābhyāntar*: internal *Vishaya*: posture *Ākshepi*: beyond
Chaturthah: the fourth

Q: *What is the fourth type of Prānāyāma?*
A: The fourth transcends external and internal operations. The fourth kind of *prānāyāma* is the stoppage of the breath resulting from absorption.

The first *prānāyāma*:	Exhalation
The second:	Inhalation
The Third:	Retention
The Fourth:	is a happening, it is involuntary. In the state of absorption, there is an automatic cessation of breathing for the period of absorption. The breath returns again on return from the state of absorption.

During the fourth *prānāyāma* one's attention is not on the breath, as he is in a state of absorption. The attention of the seeker transcends the process of coming and going of exhalation and inhalation, as well as the transitions between them. In the fourth *prānāyāma*, one experiences the vital energy as an ever existing force, beyond the surface currents. In that state the veil of ignorance remains removed. Those who have attained that state have described that they have seen the vital energy permeating the entire atmosphere and described rivers and such objects as nothing but a flow of cosmic energy.

The fourth stage of *Prānāyāma* is referred to as *Nishpatti avasthā*, a state of consummation. After attaining this state the seeker feels neither hunger nor thirst, nor sleep nor swoon. He becomes absolutely independent. He can move anywhere in the world. He is free from all diseases, decay and old age. He enjoys the bliss of *Samādhi*.

Once, someone asked Buddha what he gained by meditation. Buddha relied: "Nothing. I have lost much, but I have not gained any thing. I have lost my passion, my thoughts, my struggles, my desires and I have gained what I have always been since time immemorial."

Lord Buddha

ततः क्षीयते प्रकाशावरणम् ॥५२॥
Tatah Kshiyate Prakāsha_Āvaranam.

As practice proceeds, afflictions recede,
Inner light is revealed.

Tatah: on controlling breath
Kshiyate: declines, weakens, dissipates
Prakashā: luminosity, intensity of
Varanam: veil of ignorance

Q: *What effect has the regular practice of Prānāyāma?*
A: Regular practice of *Prānāyāma* removes obstacles to perception. Effect of the veil of ignorance remains diminished.

Prānāyāma helps to develop intensity of concentration, clarity of thought, and a dynamic personality. It brings out the most constructive power latent in a person. A great Achārya Mahāpragyā says "it is not only an exercise of respiration but it is a significant technique of dissociating *karma*. To burn impure particles, fire is needed; similarly, for burning impurity of the sense-organs, it is very essential to practice *Prānāyāma*".

Manu says: "Let the defects be burnt up by *Prānāyāmā*." Vishnu Purāna speaks of *Prānāyāma* as an accessory to Yoga: "He who controls the air known as *Prāna* by practice is said to have secured *Prānāyāma*."

The illusory *Samsāric Vāsanā* that has arisen through the accumulation of tendencies over many lives, never perishes except through the practice of Yoga for a long time. It is not possible to control the mind by sitting up again and again except through the approved means, says Muktikopanishad.

One will be able to concentrate the mind, nicely after this veil on the light has been removed. The mind will be quite steady like the flame in a windless place as the disturbing energy has been removed. The velocity of the mind will be slowly lessened by *Prānāyāma*. It induces *Vairāgya*. Just as fire destroys the fuel, so also *Prānāyāma* destroys the bundles of sins. Tamas and *Rājas* constitute the covering or veil. This veil is removed by the practice of *Prānāyāma*. After the veil is removed, the real nature of the soul is realised. The *Chitta* is by itself made up of the *Sāttvic* particles, but it is enveloped by *Rājas* and *Tamas*, just as the fire is enveloped by smoke. There is no purifying action greater than *Prānāyāma*.

Those alone are freed from conditioned being, who, having transcended all externals, such as hearing, mind, self and egotism, are ready for a state of absorption; not those who simply speak about the mystery.

धारणासु च योग्यता मनसः ॥५३॥
Dhāranāsu Cha Yogyatā Manasah.

Act of concentration
Enables attention.

Dhāranā: act of contemplation
Yogyatā: deserving, capable, achievable
Cha: and
Manasah: mind

Q: *What is the benefit from dhāranā?*
A: *Dhāranā* ensures concentration.

Dhāranā is the act of concentration, the first of the three steps that constitute a state of absorption. Concentration is the first step for the withdrawal of attention from sense orientation to focusing attention in a chosen object.

The concentration process is to the shift of mind from many areas of attention to one area of attention. It is one area, not one specific point in an area. The scriptures always give the example of tied up calf with the help of a long rope. The length of rope signifies the permissible area of mind's operation. The mind is free to move in a larger area of one specific object, say Krishna. But no other subject of attention is permitted. The restriction put on the mind is known as "*Ālamban*". The *Ālamban* is Krishna. With the help of the "*Ālamban*", the mind is fixed and engaged in a particular area. The larger permissible area is Krishna's charm, his flute, his grace, his message, but the field does not include the whole of *Mahābhārata*.

Samādhi equation: Swāmi Vivekānanda outlines a very interesting *Samādhi* equation in which he equates 12 *Prānāyāma* as one *Dhāranā*. His equations:

1. PRĀNĀYĀMA: (2 units in-breath, 2 units Breath retention, 4 units out-breath, 2 units breath retention) Face value for 1 *Prānāyāma* is 2+2+4+2=10 units.
2. DHĀRANĀ : 1 *Dhāranā* = 12 *Prānāyāma*.
   Face value for 1 *Dhāranā* is 10 x 12 = 120 units.
3. DHYĀNA : 1 *Dhyāna* = 12 *Dhāranā* = 144 *Prānāyāma*
   Face value for 1 *Dhyāna* is 10 x 12 x 12 = 1440 units.
4. SAMĀDHI : 1 *Samādhi* = 12 *Dhyāna* = 144 *Dhārana* = 17280 *Prānāyāma*
   Face value for 1 *Samādhi* is 10 x 12 x 12 x 12 = 17280 units.

If the *prāna* does not move, the mind attains a quiescent state, where the *prāna* goes mind follows, even as the rider goes where the vehicle goes.

Yogavāshishta

स्वविषयासंप्रोगे चित्तस्य स्वरूपानुकारः
इवेन्द्रियाणां प्रत्याहारः ॥५४॥

Sva_Vishaya_Asamprayoge Chittasya_Svarupa_Anukārah Eva_Indriyānām Pratyāhārah.

With self to its own nature drawn
Senses from objects seem withdrawn.

Sva: its own *Vishaya*: object *Asamprayoge*: discontinuous
Chittasya: of the mind *Svarupa*: its own basic character
Anukārah: following *Eva*: like *Indriyānām*: of the sense organs
Pratyāhārah: withdrawal of sense organs

Q: *What is Pratyāhārah?*
A: *Pratyāhārah* refers to restraint of senses, a state when senses don't jump to perch on objects, but instead remain steady. *Pratyāhārah* is the liberation of the senses from the objects that attract them. The word means "reversal" or "withdrawal"; it indicates that the normal outward flow of the senses can return to their origin in the mind.

Pratya comes from the word *pratyaya*. *Pratyaya* refers to the basic tendencies. The word *ahāra* means food or nutrition. Normally, our senses are focused on the external objects and hence the mind, the senses and the tendencies receive nutrition from outside, from objects and events. *Pratyāhārah* is the denial of such nutrition to the senses.

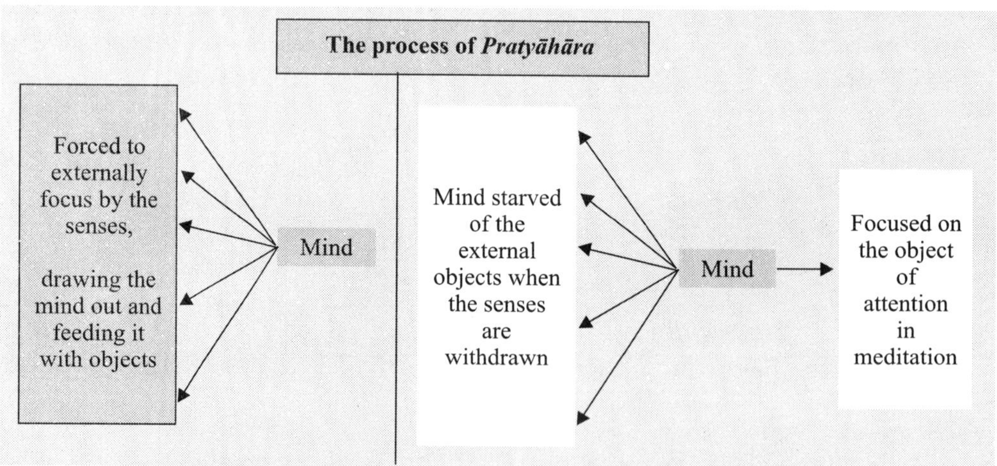

"*Pratyāhārah* is the forgotten fourth aspect of Yoga."

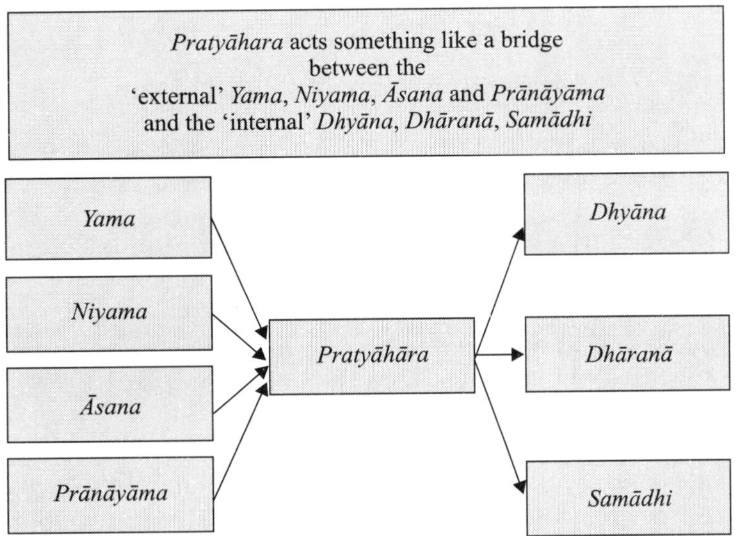

- *Pratyāhāra* is essentially the process of mental control and withdrawal of the mind from sensory functions (a seeker withdraws his mind from the currents generated by the senses).
- *Pratyāhāra* is a process of self-restraint where an individual tries to keep his senses away from the temptations of the materialistic world. In other words, he lives the life of *Vairāgya* (abstaining oneself from all worldly matters) which is an essential pre-requisite for subsequent yogic practices.
- *Pratyāhāra* is the process of withdrawal of senses from its natural tendency to seek food of objects in the external world. This aspect, a crucial one as it is essential for the success of the next three aspects.
- When *Pratyāhāra* is practised in a comprehensive way, then gradually the outer world starts to lose its hold upon the mind. The perceived objects do not impinge on the seeker's mind any more; they pass off like shadows. They do not lodge themselves in the intellect.
- Yoga is concentration. It is the indrawn mind resulting from *Pratyāhāra* practice that makes mind fit for concentration.
- *Pratyāhāra* is not practice, the way *Āsana* and *Prāṇāyāma* are.

The mind of the enlightened one is like the moon in the sky at mid-day. It is illuminated, but its light is not needed in the greater radiance of the Sun which illuminated it.

Shri Ramana Maharshi

ततः परमा वश्यतेन्द्रियाणाम् ॥५५॥

Tatah Paramā Vashyate_Indriyānām.

Thence are senses
Under great clutches.

Tatah: thence *Paramā*: greatest *Vashyate*: controlled, subjugated
Indriyānām: senses

Q: *What is the effect of 'pratyāharā'?*
A: Complete mastery over senses is the effect of *pratyāharā.*

The uninitiated is under the control of senses, while the senses are under the control of the liberated. While other beings get attracted because of one single sense of attachment, man is bewildered by five senses all acting at a time. Hence, trouble for man can be better visualised. Hence constant repetition of the theme that withdrawal from sense objects is necessary for spiritual salvation.

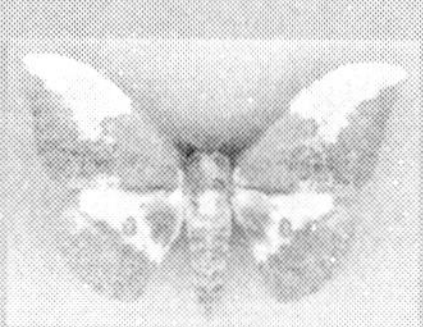

The sense of sight kills the firefly:
The firefly, attracted by the flaming nature of the fire blindly goes close to it and gets killed.

The sense of smell kills the bee:
The bee attracted by the smell of the flower, gets close and gets stuck to the sticky substance. Unable to extricate itself, it gets killed.

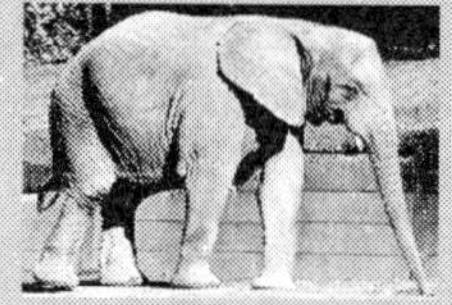

The sense of touch proves problematic to the elephant.
The elephant gets sensory pleasure rubbing itself to a tree. At times, unaware of even the bleeding injury to its skin, it continues to run against the trunk and severely damages its trunk.

Sound is the cause of deer's death:
A deer meets its death at the hands of the hunter who attracts it by its musical call imitating the mating cry of the female.

The sense of taste proves to be the killer of the fish:
Even a well fed fish cannot resist the temptation of biting at the bait offered by the fishermen to attract the fish to the hook. Fish kill themselves by overeating too.

At a glance: Aphorism 51-55

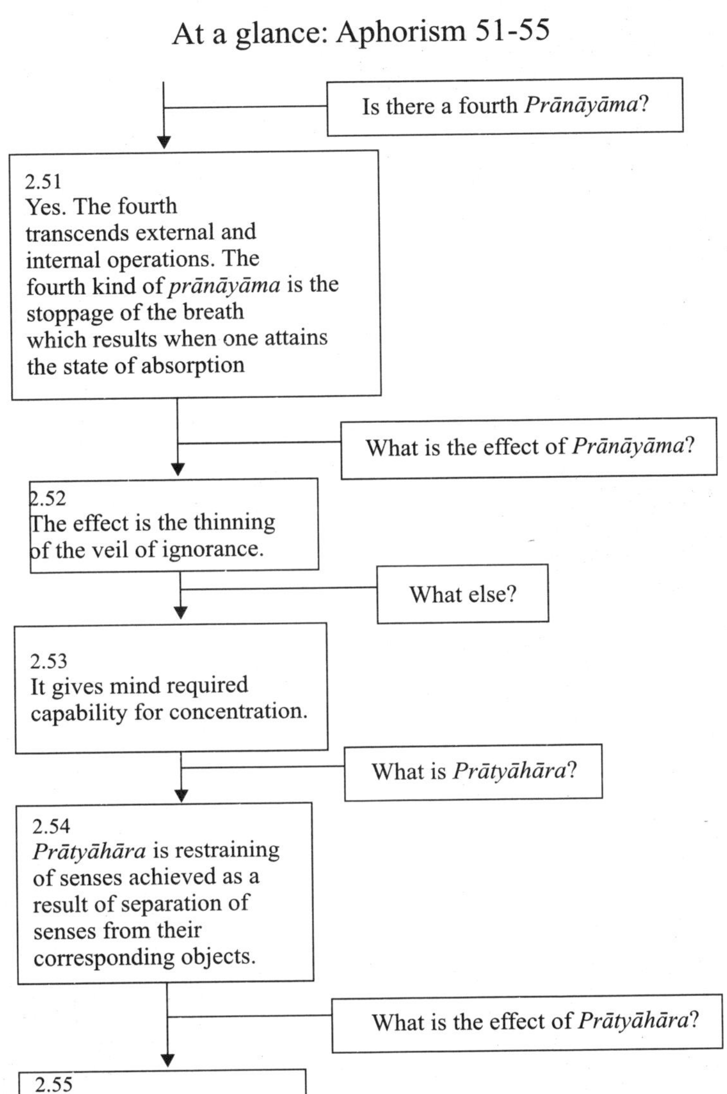

इति श्री पतंजलि योगशास्त्रे साधना निर्देशोनाम द्वितीय पादः।

Thus ends Sree Patanjali Yoga Sutras Chapter 2.

Chapter 3

Vibhuti Pādah

Powers En-route

देशबन्धश्चित्तस्य धारणा ॥१॥

Desh_Bandhah Chittasya Dhāranā.

Concentration is confining attention of mind
To one location.

Desha: place *Bandhah*: fixing *Chittasya*: of the mind *Dhāranā*: concentration

Q. *When is mind said to be concentrated?*

A. When the mind is able to focus attention on the object of meditation permitting no distraction, it is said to be concentrating. Mind is concentrated when its attention does not get diverted to host of other objects that are within its reach.

When the *Chitta*, or mind-stuff, is confined and limited to a certain place it is *Dhāranā*. Engaging the mind in a chosen area is *Dhāranā*. The mind will be free to roam about within the periphery of this area, but it should not cross the boundary. *Dhāranā.* is the 'maintaining of proper concentration' 'Proper concentration' means keeping one's senses withdrawn from outer objects and focusing on any one object of concentration. The word *Dhāranā* is derived from the root *Dhā*, meaning "to hold, carry, support". It refers to the holding of an object in the mind. In *Dhāranā*, mind dwells only on the chosen object.

Concentration is the crucial first step to spiritual absorption. The confinement of mind to a specific location like the navel region, the lotus of the heart, the head, the tip of the nose, the centre between eyebrows, a chosen image of a deity, are some of the external objects for confining attention on. Idol worship fits in eminently as an object for concentration for the idol also assists in developing in oneself all the virtues that the devotee attributes to the image in question.

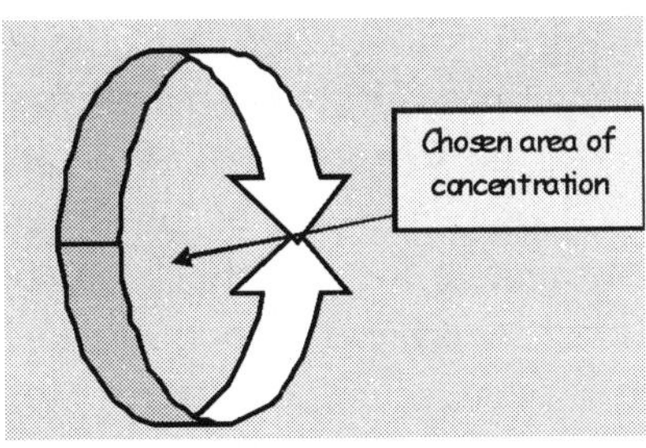

Concentration on elements like earth, water, fire etc is called *external Dhāranā* while, concentration on a chosen object like the light in a candle, scent of a flower, glow of a figure of saint etc is referred to as internal *Dhāranā*.

From the unreal lead me to the real,
From darkness lead me to Llight;
From death lead me to immortality.
Aum! Shāntih! Shāntih! Shāntih!

Brihadāranyaka Upanishad

Dhārnā

External	Internal
	Internal *Dhāranā* develops from the intense practice of External *Dhāranā* when the external support of concentration can be dispensed with in favour of concentration at the point where the unmanifest becomes manifest.
Prithviya Dhāranā or Concentration on Earth Element.	To fix the mind on a flower, a picture of a saint, the statue of a deity.
Jaliya Dhāranā or Concentration on Water Element.	To gaze at the bank of a river or lake, on a waveless water while sitting by the shore of an ocean
Āgneya Dhāranā or Concentration on Air Elements.	To fix the gaze on the flare of a candle, bulb of soft light or fire in the altar etc.
Vāyaviya Dhāranā or Concentration on Air Elements	To steady the mind by constant touch of air by contact with any object, by the feel of heat or cold or *Prānāyāma.*
Shābdika Dhāranā or Concentration on sound Element.	To fix the mind on a loud or semi-verbal *mantra.*

In *Dhāranā*, mind is kept firm at one place instead of letting it wander here and there. This reduces strain on the mind. The mental strength increases. With such habitual concentration, the work is done effectively and efficiently. The daily practice of *Dhāranā* reduces the wavering attitude of mind and a different kind of peace can be observed throughout the day. When the mind holds on to some object, either in the body or outside the body, and keeps itself in that state, it has attained, *Dhāranā*, concentration. When the mind tries to think of one object, to hold itself to a particular spot, such as top of the head or the heart, and succeeds in receiving sensations through that part only and not through any other it is *Dhāranā.*

Meditation is the focusing of the mind on some object.
If the mind acquires concentration on one object,
it can be so concentrated on any object whatsoever.

Swāmi Vivekānanda

तत्र प्रत्यैकतानता ध्यानम् ॥२॥

Tatra Pratyaya_Eikatānatā Dhyānam.

Meditation is continuous attention
With no distraction.

Tatra: there *Pratyaya*: object of concentration *Eikatānatā*: focused
Dhyānam: meditation

Q. *What is Dhyāna?*
A. *Dhyāna* refers to meditation. The uniform flow of cognition to the chosen area of attention is meditation.

Dhyāna is a continuous succession of identical thoughts directed toward one object which happens so quickly that before one subsides another (same thought) takes its place. *Dhyāna* is distinguished from *Dhāranā* (concentration) only by its uninterrupted nature. In scriptures the difference between concentration and meditation is described as the difference between pouring water and pouring oil: both streams fall toward one place, but water fall is a 'broken' stream of drops whereas the stream of oil is smooth, constant, unbroken.

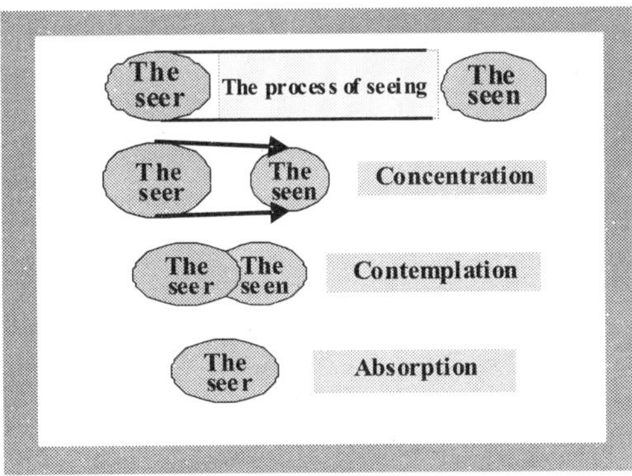

Some opine that in Yoga time-calculation is usually stated in *mātrās*. One *mātrā* is said to be approximately one second. If one's mind remains concentrated on an object for 12 seconds, he is said to be in *Dhāranā*. By continuous practice, if one can increase the concentration period to that of 12 times *Dhāranā* namely, 144 seconds, he is said to be in *Dhyāna*. Again, if one can further increase concentration to 12 times that of *Dhyāna*, he has attained *Samādhi*.

'Earth meditates as it were. The mid-region meditates as it were. Heavens meditate as it were. The waters meditate as it were. The mountain meditates as it were. Gods meditate as it were. Men meditate as it were. Therefore, he who among men, attains greatness here on earth seems to have attained a share of meditation. Thus while small people are quarrelsome, abusive and slandering; great men appear to have obtained a share of meditation.'

Chhāndyoga Upanishad

Benefits of meditation:

The benefits of meditation are threefold: 1. Spiritual 2. Mental, and 3. Physical

Spiritual Benefits	• Realisation that one's self is separate from his body and mind. • Results in awareness of the real self. • Induces a new quality of consciousness. • Freedom from the bondage of ego.
Mental benefits	• Frees us from the fear of death. • Brings about stability in emotions. • Increases capacity of mind to perceive things properly. • Mind becomes rejuvenated and strengthened. • Increases capacity to withstand failures. • Increases capacity of mind's perception.
Physical benefits	• Increases neuromuscular energy. • Good health. Good voice. • Agreeable odour of the body • Good complexion. • Conservation of vital energy.

Effects of meditation on mind

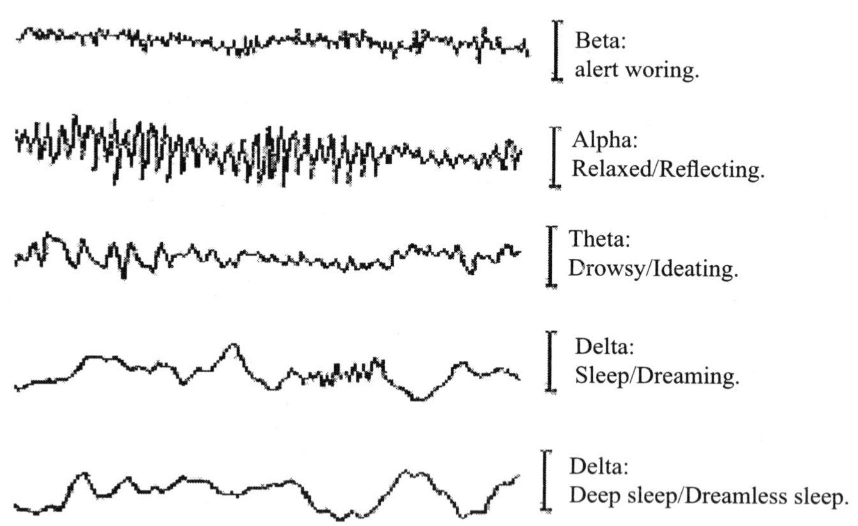

All minds are the same, different parts of one mind.
who knows one lump of clay has known all the clay in the universe.
He who knows and controls his own mind, knows
the secret of every mind, and has power over every mind.

Swāmi Vivekānanda

Obstructions to meditation	Overcoming obstructions
Samasya Bhāvanā Inability to reconcile apparently contrary opinions and statements of different teachers and scriptures. Coming to an erroneous conclusion that since the scriptures contradict, all of them must be wrong.	***Shravana*** Listen to the wisdom imparted by the teacher. Have faith in you and in your teacher, and in the scriptures. Don't indulge in discussions. Logic and reasoning fail, beyond a stage.
Viparita Bhāvanā Persistent feeling that all that is seen is real, that the body is real, that somehow though intellectually one can accept body being different from mind, 'in reality, this body is housing the mind.'	***Manana*** Deeply reflect on the eternal truth. Go on mentally repeating to yourself that you are not the body and that it is the body that decays and withers away and you live forever.
Āsanbhāvanā A sense of hopelessness and a nagging feeling of impossibility to concentrate, not to speak of attaining the state of *Samādhi*.	***Niddyāsana*** The way to overcome obstacles to meditation is to continue it with greater faith and determination, surrendering progress to God.

It is better to avoid too much study and discussion. What is being sought to be done through meditation is to overcome countless births of accumulation of tendencies. Doubts arise due to attachment to the body and the fear of death (*abhinivesha*). The repeated advocacy of triple attempts: Refinement, Reflection and Resignation should be borne in mind. The seeker should have long, uninterrupted and steady practice. The obstructions can be overcome by adhering to Patanjali's injunctions.

One should remember:

1. Meditation is not contemplation.
Contemplation involves thinking about a concept, engaging mind in enquiring about a certain idea. But meditation is to go beyond thought.

2. Meditation is not auto-suggestion.
In autosuggestion to the mind, there is an attempt to manipulate or control the content of the mind. But in meditation one simply observes his mind.

3. Meditation is not a religion.
Meditation does not belong to any culture or religion. It is a simple method of exploring the inner dimensions of life.

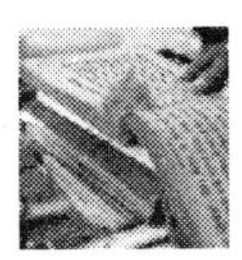

Just like a silk worm is caught in its own cocoon, so also is man caught in this vast net of worldly existence by his own will and tendencies.

Moksha Gītā

तदेवार्थमात्रनिर्भासं स्वरूपशून्यमिव समाधिः ॥३॥

Tadeva_Artha_Mātra_Nirbhāsam Svarupa_Shunyam_Iva Samādhih.

Absorption is then,
When cogniser with cognition, becomes one.

Tadeva: thereafter
Artha: object of meditation
mātra: alone, only
nirbhāsam: shining
Svarupa: its essential form
shunyam: absence, emptiness
Iva: as if
Samādhih: Absorption

Q. *What is Samādhi?*

A. *Samādhi* is the state of absorption, wherein the individual is completely absorbed only with the object, as if he himself has become the object with no thought of his own. The word is derived from *sam* (together) + *a:* (completely) + *dha:* (to hold); thus "to hold together completely". *Samādhi* differs from *Dhyāna* in the sense that there is no succession of identical thought waves, but rather a state beyond mind.

The meanings of the term *Samādhi* are union, totality; absorption in, complete concentration of mind; conjunction. The usual translation is 'concentration,' but this embarks the risk of confusion with *Dhāranā* and. hence the use of the term, absorption. *Samādhi* is the final limb of Ashtānga Yoga. Just as concentration culminates in meditation, so meditation culminates in *samādhi*. In meditation there is consciousness of mind and object only. When meditation becomes intense, the mind and object merge, and the mind is no longer conscious of itself. This dissolution of the subject-object relationship is *samādhi* or more correctly, the first stage of *samādhi*. The term *samādhi* actually refers to several stages of higher consciousness that become progressively more profound, finally culminating in *kaivalya*, perfect Self-realisation. The stages towards *samādhi* reflect the progressive withdrawal of consciousness into its source, the Self. The passage from 'concentration' to 'meditation' does not require the application of any new technique. Similarly, no supplementary yogic exercise is needed to realise *samādhi*. Once the seeker has succeeded in 'concentrating' and 'meditating', *Samādhi*, yogic state just happens. From the state of absorption one does not get back to be his old self. He has discovers nothing but just has uncovered himself completely of illusion. He knows reality. He is.

Seeker: When shall I be free?
Sri Rāmakrishna: When the 'I' shall cease to be.

त्रयमेकत्र संयमः ॥४॥

Trayam_Ekatra Samyamah.

Sustained state of the three
Is perfect mastery.

Trayam : all of the above three *Ekatra* : in respect of one object
Samyamah : self master

Q: What is *Samyama*?
A: When the processes of meditation, contemplation and absorption are continuously and exclusively applied to the one object, it is called *Samyama*.

The application of the combined force of *Dhāranā*, *Dhyāna* and *Samādhi* upon any particular object about which one wants to know everything with a hundred per cent fullness and clarity is *Samyama*. *Samyama* is specifically combining the application of the combined force of *Dhāranā*, *Dhyāna* and *Samādhi* on a chosen object. *Samayama* is a collective term under which the last three steps of the eight aspects of Yoga are grouped together.

One can make *Samyama* say on water, a distant star, fire, whatever and know everything about that object. By *Samyama* on the object, one becomes independent of the object, the object cannot affect the person. Hence, the person can get a very correct knowledge about the object. When one is influenced by the object, that is, he is not independent of the object, the knowledge gained turns out to be imperfect. The deepest truth about an object is revealed to the seeker who combines the force of concentration, meditation and absorption on a chosen object.

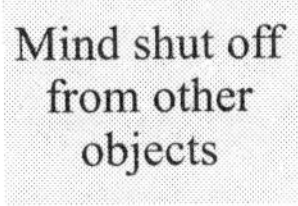

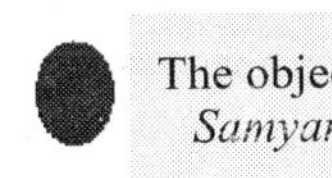

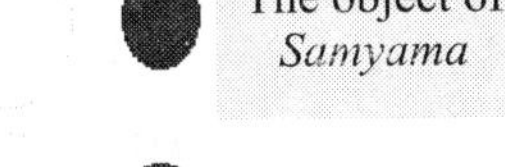

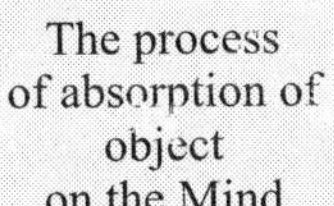

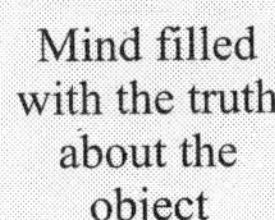

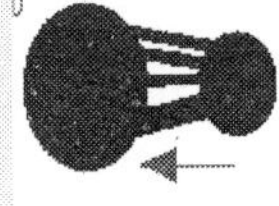

It should however be noted that the ultimate object is union with reality and not knowledge of objects. Patanjali mentions about attainments that are possible in later aphorisms. It is in this context he refers to *Samyama*.

When the mind is free from activity or functioning,
it vanishes and the Self is revealed.
This state has been described by the commentator *Shankara* as ..
"super-sensuous state."

Swāmi Vivekānanda

तज्जयात्प्रज्ञालोकः ॥५॥

Tajjayāt_Pragyā_Lokah.

The three in full flow
Make inner mind glow.

Tajjayāt: that winning over, on attaining *Samyama* *Pragyā*: awareness
Lokah: seeing, to look

Q: *What is Samyama on an object?*
A: *Samyama* on a chosen object leads to a comprehensive knowledge of the object in all its aspects. By mastering that (*Samyama*), the light of knowledge (*prajnā*) dawns.

When concentration, meditation and absorption, together on an object, are directed, it brings in total awareness about the object. What one sees, he 'Knows'.

The word 'look' is derived from the Sanskrit word '*Lokah*'. '*Lokah*' is that which is seen. For a seeker who is absorbed and has directed attention on a specific object, his entire '*Lokah*' is now the object. With such undiluted attention he is focused, the object pours all knowledge about itself on the seeker. He starts seeing the object as It Is and not as he is. In others' case, one sees object influenced by his inherent tendencies and expectations and never as 'It is' Seeing, Looking, Observing and Knowing, all take place instantaneously, as a mirror reflects whatever object is placed in front, to the seeker is now reflected whatever object he chooses to place his mind on. There is no use of faculties of recollection and reasoning for the seeker to know. The recollection and inference, association and reasoning are in any case defective instruments of perception discarded by the seeker.

o *Samyama* is becoming knowledge, not learning.

o In *Samyama* process of knowledge is released by the object, not by the subject.

o In *Samyama* knowledge is not derived from observation and is logic independent. In *Samyama* knowledge is intuitional.

o In *Samyama* the mind is like a mirror: it grasps nothing, it refuses nothing, it receives but does not keep, it adds nothing.

o *Samyama* is becoming one with the Self, not being one with nature.

Herein is the difference between man and the animals—man has the greater power of concentration. The difference in their power of concentration also constitutes the difference between man and man. Compare the lowest with the highest man, the difference is in the degree of concentration. This is the only difference.

Swāmi Vivekānanda

At a glance: Aphorism 3.01-3.05

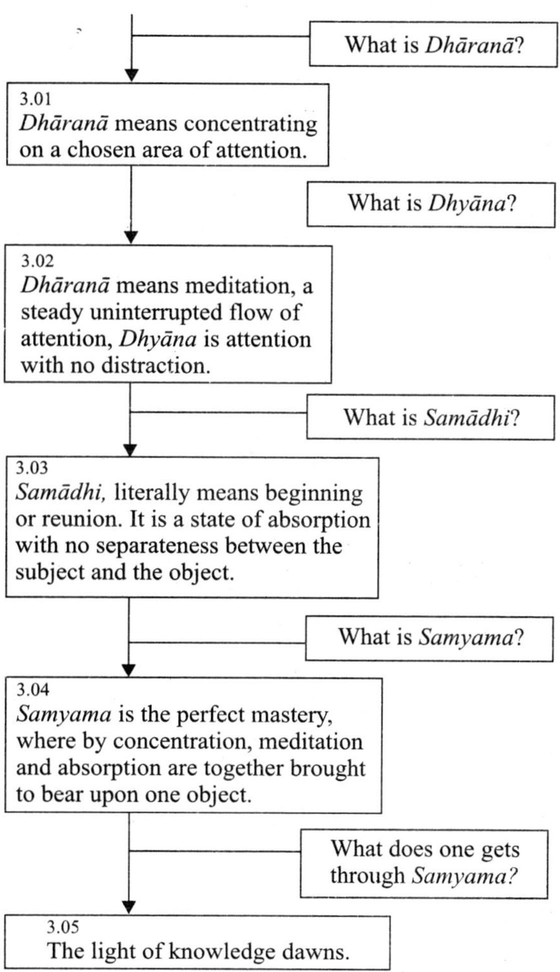

तस्य भूमिषु विनियोगः ॥६॥
Tasya Bhumishu Viniyogah.

Integration of the three
Be deployed in degree.

Tasya: that integration *Bhumishu*: higher degrees
Viniyogah: application, deployment

Q. *How should one practise Samyama?*
A. *Samyama* is to be applied in stages, in slow degrees.

The glow is not to be in one go. One might get blinded. Patanjali does not prescribe instant glory. His prescription asks one to move step by step. When one step is concretised, the next can follow. This way one can be sure that he does not slip up. A state of tranquillity can propel one to sit through focused for days on end. Such an attempt at times might jeopardize the effort. The agony and pain arising out of forced attempts might discourage one in further continuation of practice. On the other hand, a step by step approach will be more enduring and less agonizing. The climb becomes easier with no gasping for breath.

Many a seeker's body may not be just attuned as yet to receive illumination. Just as an electrical bulb will be shattered by excessive electrical voltage, the nerves in the body will get shattered by the cosmic current. Patanjali's practice is meant for those who prefer to go step by step. His is a scientific approach. As a step is taken, one can check back and cross check with the state of awareness that Patanjali says is attained at every step. This cross checking reinforces the belief of the seeker.

On the other hand any attempt to force the pace would hurt the seeker. The advantages in the step by step approach:

1. At each step one gets enough time to understand his changed perception capabilities and can get used to it. Whatever is attained is absorbed.

2. In step by step approach sudden spurt in awareness and associated attainments won't shock and confuse an aspirant and the latent tendencies in him won't push him towards misusing his attainments.

Ātman is verily one and without parts, whereas the body consists of many parts; and yet the people see these two as one! What else can be called ignorance but this?

Ādi Shankara

त्रयमन्तरङ्गं पूर्वेभ्यः ॥७॥

Trayam_Antarangam Purvebhyah.

Internal are these
Than the five that precedes.

Trayam: the threesome *Antarangam*: essential internal
Purvebhyah : earlier ones (the five first angās)

Q: *How do the later three limbs of Yoga, namely Dhāranā, Dhyāna and Samādhi differ from the first five, namely Yama, Niyama, Āsana, Prānāyāma and Pratyāhāra?*

A: Compared to the first five components the next three are more internal. But in relation to the state of seedless absorption, even these three are external.

The first five aspects namely *Yama*, *Niyama*, *Āsana*, *Prānāyāma* and *Pratyāhāra* can be said to be the preparatory steps and the later three namely, *Dhāranā*, *Dhyāna* and *Samādhi* as final steps; although it is not essential that one attains *Samādhi* only if he had perfected *Prānāyāma*. While the focus on the first five are on external activities, that of the last three can be said to be totally self-focused.

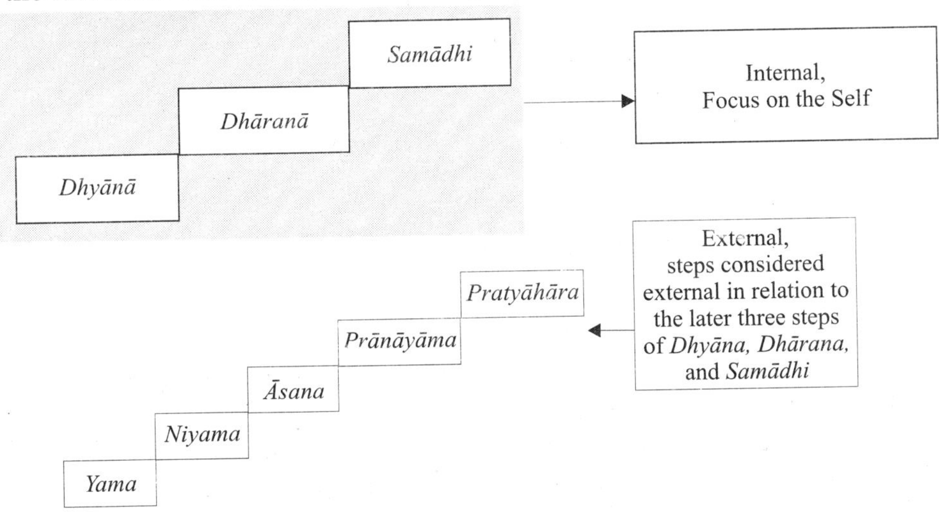

Concentration is the essence of all knowledge; nothing can be done without it. Ninety percent of thought force is wasted by the ordinary human being, and therefore he is constantly committing blunders; the trained man or mind never makes a mistake.

Swāmi Vivekānanda

तदपि बहिरङ्गं निर्बीजस्य ॥८॥
Tadapi Bahirangam Nirbijasya.

External are these
To the state of absorption with no seed.

Tad: that *Api*: also *Bahirangam*: external part
Nirbijasya: absorption with no seed, seedless state of *Samādhi*

Q: *We read in the first chapter about seedless and with seed Samādhi. Is the state of directing mind to an object with no interruption internal or external to the seedless state?*

A: Compared to the seedless state of absorption, even this state described earlier as internal in relation to the first five limbs of Yoga is external.

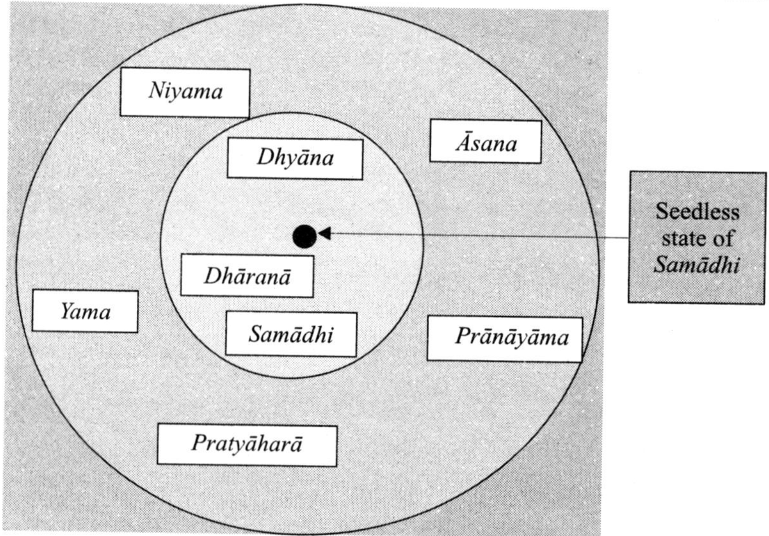

The seeker, now an observer of his own thoughts is the internal.
The thoughts observed become external.
In the ultimate state there is neither external nor internal.
From seedless state of *Samādhi* there is no turning back.
This state is not attained, it happens.

Thou first exponent of "matter exists not as it appears to be," we pay homage to thee. O! Swāmi of Swāmis, thou didst teach us to behold the one ocean of Spirit, hidden beneath the dancing, melting waves of finite forms.

Swāmi Yogānanda

व्युत्थाननिरोधसंस्कारयोरभिभवप्रादुर्भावौ
निरोधक्षणचित्तान्वयो निरोध परिणामः ॥९॥

Vyuthāna_Nirodha_Sanskārayoh Abhibhava_Prādurbhāvau
Nirodha_Kshana_Chitt a_Anvayo Nirodha_Parināmah.

Mind ceases to be in a state of mutation
When between an impression and another impression;
There is a momentary cessation of mental modification.

Vyuthāna: awakened state *Nirodha*: stoppage, blocking
Sanskārayoh: recollections *Abhibhava*: loss *Prādurbhāvau*: manifestation
Kshana: momentary *Chitta*: mind *Anvaya*: connection
Parināmah: modification, change, mutation

Q: *What is Nirodha parināma? When does mind cease to get modified?*
A: *Nirodha* is stoppage. *Parināma* is change or modification. *Nirodha parināma* in this context refers to stoppage of mental modifications. The mind is either concentrated or distracted. It cannot simultaneously be both concentrated and distracted. In the distracted state it is said to be in a state of constant change - from one thought to another, changes taking place in quick succession. Mind is not modified when it is concentrated.

Between one impression that is dying and another that is emerging there is a micro second gap. During this infinitesimal moment there is cessation of thought. One of the methods of meditation suggested is to go on observing this gap, thoughts arising and thoughts subsiding without interfering with the thought process, just being an observer.

Parināma means change. It could also refer to mutation or modification. There are two kinds of changes that can be observed:

a. Irreversible. Like the curding of milk.

b. Reversible like solid gold ornament that could be melted and changed back as solid gold.

Parināma refers to the irreversible change as 'a' above.

Parināma is the property of evolution or change like milk turning into curd. If there is no milk, we cannot change it into curd. *Parināma* is that which changes what is there.

To the one who knows the nature of soul and who enjoys Self-Bliss, there is nothing but silence, void of desire, causing the greatest happiness

Ādi Shankara, Vivekachudāmani, Crest Jewel of Wisdom

There is another kind of material causality. For example, gold is the material cause of an ornament made out of gold. In the process of making the ornament, the metal does not change into something else. It is only drawn into another form, from a lump to an ornament; the gold remains gold. This kind of causality is called *vivarta. Vivarta* is the quality which makes us forget the real thing and makes us impose upon that, some other thing which is not there. It is the effect of *Māyā. Vivarta* is the property which makes us think that there is a change though the substance remains the same. It is made to appear to have a different shape and form. One comes across a rope at night but gets deluded to imagine it as a serpent. On being aware, the snake disappears and the rope appears. Strictly both the rope and the snakes were in the mind. When mind recognizes rope, snake disappeared. In reality the snake does not go and the serpent does not come. It is all an illusion. In order to mistake a rope for a snake, there are three things that should happen.

These three aspects of a misperception is referred to as red, white, and black. Black refers to the darkness of evening twilight; white, to the partial light of twilight (if one hasn't seen the rope, one never would have mistaken it for a snake), and red, to the fact that the perception was coloured by imagination. These three aspects are referred to as the three *Gunas* (*Tamas*, *Rājas*, and *Sattva*). Hence it is also said that one lives under the influence of *Vivarta* and the corresponding triple qualities. Though one is the ever existent consciousness, yet he forgets the supreme reality and he lives with the body consciousness, always identifying himself with his body and thinks that end of the body is the end of the Self. One mistakes the ephemeral existence to be the real existence. One is not afraid of the rope, but is terribly afraid of the serpent. According to the *Vedāntins*, the first cause of physics is *Vivarta*, apparition. It is the mistake of seeing the underlying existence as in time and space. After that, things proceed by *Parināma*, transformational causation, because the underlying existence shows through in the mistake as energy, as gravity, electricity and inertia, which cause the transformations. *Parināma* is what physicists usually think of as causation. It is governed by the conservation laws. The form of the energy may change but the amount of energy, in any change, does not change.

First	Failing to see that it is a rope.	Called the veiling power of the mistake, *Āvarana Shakti.*
Second	Next, one must jump to the conclusion that it's a snake.	Called the projecting power of the mistake, *Vikshepa Shakti.*
Third	Finally, realising that it is only a rope.	Called the revealing power of the mistake, *Prakāsha Shakti.*

'As if, being hidden, through the veiling power of *Tamas*, the nature of *Brahman*, through the revealing power of *Sattva*, shone in the otherness for which, through the projecting power of *Rājas*, it is, as it were, mistaken.'

Panchamahābhuta Sutras

तस्य प्रशान्तवाहिता संस्कारात् ॥१०॥
Tasya Prashānta_Vāhitā Sanskārāt.

When cessation of thoughts becomes a norm,
There is calm.

Tasya: in that restrained state
Vāhitā: flow
Prashānta: peaceful, tranquil
Sanskārāt: from recollections, from memory

Q. *When is mind in a state of total calmness? How can such a state be attained?*
A. Mind is calm when it is concentrated, in a state of attention. By constant and uninterrupted practice, the mind can remain in a state of attention for a long time. Another method of silencing thoughts is to watch the gaps in between thoughts. Thoughts come from and go back to a state of restraint. By noticing the void moments between thoughts, one can silence thoughts. These void moments gradually increase when observed.

As one gets closer to the state of *Samādhi*, one can observe that there is a very great sense of calmness in him. This calmness is the result of frequent cessation of thoughts. When intensity of thoughts wane and when one is seemingly floating in air with the body consciousness missing, there is tranquillity. It is just not the frequency of thoughts that diminish as practice proceeds, but the intensity of thought too. The attachment reduces and results in reduction in intensity of thoughts. As mind's attachment to objects wane, its capacity to get absorbed in the area of focus increases. The object with which mind is preoccupied before practice is not necessarily a physical object, it could be even an impression from the past. Mind is virtually blank-devoid of thoughts after focused concentration, meditation and absorption.

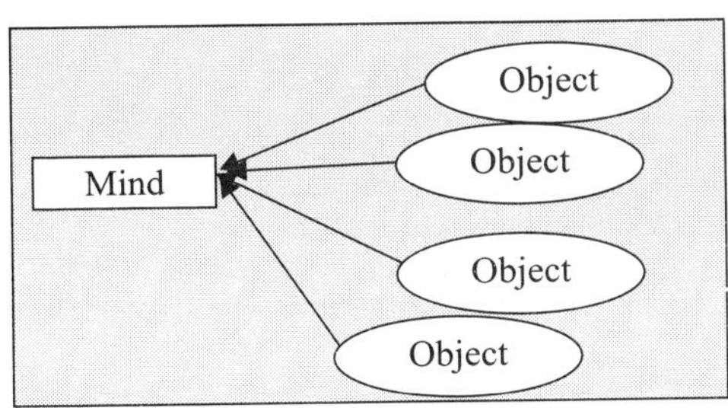

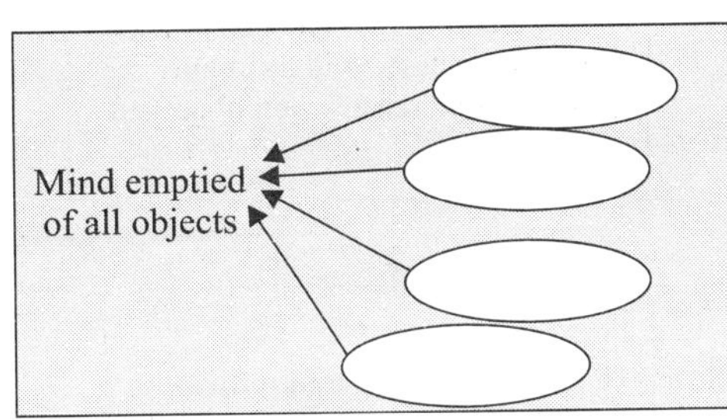

Getting rid of the triple qualities ensures detachment from pleasure and pain.

A Proverb

At a glance: Aphorism 3.06-3.10

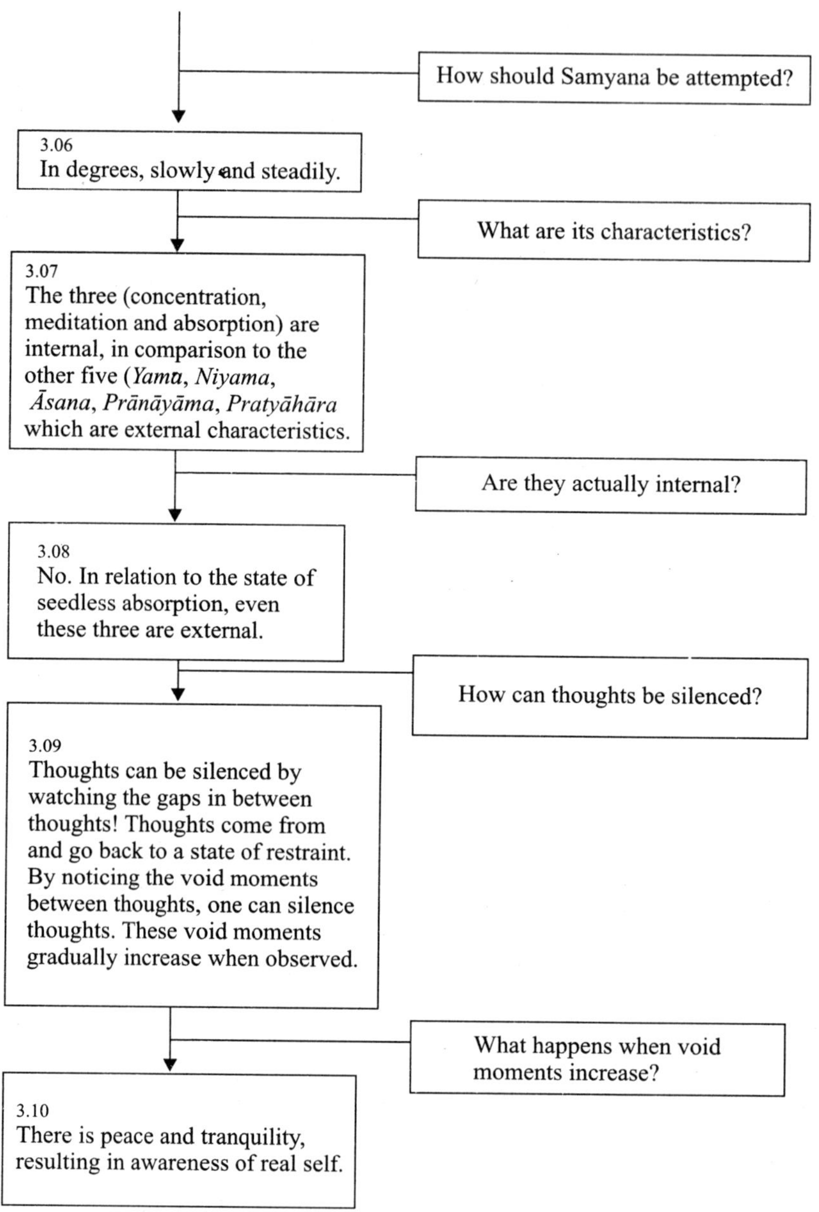

सर्वार्थतैकाग्रतयोः क्षयोदयौ चितस्य समाधिपरिणामः ॥११॥
Sarvārthatā_Ekāgratayoh Kshayodayau Chittasya Samādhi_Parināmah.

With disappearance of distraction
Appears the state of absorption.

Sarvā: all *Artha*: objects *Ekāgrata*: focused, one pointed
Kshaya: dissipation, weakening, *Udaya*: arising
*Chitta*sya: mind *Samādhi*: state of absorption
Parināmah: changing, transforming, mutation

Q. *When is a state of absorption attained?*

A. The state of absorption is attained when there is total concentration and total concentration is attained when there is weakening of mind's distractions towards outside objects and by focusing on the only object of attention. Such a diminution of attention to all and sundry and development of one-pointed-ness is called *Samādhi Parināma.*

The mind in its ordinary state is projected outwards due to the sense organs and their subtle counterparts. This outward orientation of the mind is turned inwards through practice, until the mind gets absorbed in a single thought to the exclusion of all else, and that single thought is its own Self. As the mind tastes calmness and the distractions cease, it slowly gravitates to a state of one pointed-ness called *Samādhi parināma.*

From *Nirodha parināma* (cessation)
to *Samādhi parināma* (absorption).

Nirodha Parināma Beginning of transformation	• Mind becomes permeated by the condition of cessation of thoughts momentarily between one impression that is disappearing and another that is arising.
Samādhi Parināma Reinforcing of transformation	• Mind is getting further transformed with the gradual disappearance of distractions and the resulting state of focused attention. • Further transformation.

In the great forest of worldly existence, mind indeed wanders about. They are led by me by discrimination to supreme tranquillity. Some by disregarding me fall down into hell.

Yogavāshishta

शान्तोदितौ तुल्यप्रत्ययौ चित्तस्यैकाग्रतापरिणामः ॥१२॥

Shāntoditau Tulya_Pratyayau Chittasya_Yekāgratā_Parināmah.

Succession of thoughts, similar in kind
Is the state of focused mind.

Shānta: subsiding, quietening *Udita*: arising *Tulya*: equal
Pratyaya: acts *Chitta*sya: mind *Yekāgratā*: focused, one pointed
Parināmah: modification, changing

Q. *When is mind said to be focused?*
A. Mind is said to be focused when similar thought waves arise in succession, permitting no other thoughts in between.

Yekāgratā Parināma is the state of mind when the mind becomes peaceful and calm even when the impressions of this one pointed *chitta* are arising.

A focused mind can see the object brighter and better.

When the mind is fully concentrated, time passes unnoticed, as if it did not exist. When the mind is focused, there is no time. Time is but a modification of the mind. Time, Space and causation and all external experiences are mental creations. In a focused state, one loses sense of space and time. Mind is said to be focused, when there are no intervening thoughts for 12 continuous seconds (*mātrās*). If the mind starts focusing on say 'Krishna' and after 3 seconds starts thinking about when the next birth day of Krishna is and again after 7 seconds wonders whether the Krishna's birthday is a notified holiday or not, then the mind is distracted. Mind can start with Krishna, after 3 seconds his flute can disappear, after 7 seconds his crown can disappear and only Krishna's charming face should appear. Then one can say his mind is focused on Krishna. 144 seconds of focusing is said to be *Dhyāna* and 12 such 144 seconds of continuous *Dhyāna* is said to be a state of *Samādhi*.

'When the senses are stilled, when the mind is at rest,
when the intellect wavers not - then, say the wise,
is reached the highest stage. This steady control of the senses
and mind has been defined as Yoga.
He who attains it is free form delusion.'

Kathopanishad

Arjuna sees only the eye of the bird, where others see leaves and fruits as well.

During their younger days, the Kauravās and the Pāndavās (protagonists of the Indian epic Mahābhārata) were learning under the tutorship of Dronāchārya. Among them the star pupil was Arjuna, who excelled in archery. One day Dronāchārya decided to test his students. So he fixed a wooden bird on a treetop and asked them to assemble at a distance. He then said: "Each of you must aim to shoot the eye of the bird. The one who does that will be judged as the best among you."

First he called the eldest Yudhisthira to take aim. "Are you ready?" demanded Dronāchārya. "Yes, noble sir," replied the prince. "What do you see?" questioned the teacher, to which the Pāndava replied: "Sir, I see the bird, I see the tree with beautiful leaves, I see you and all the other princes assembled here." Hearing this Dronāchārya replied: "Stop. Don't shoot, you are not ready."

Then he called on Duryodhana, who went through the same routine, and so did all the princes, except the last one, the favoured Arjuna.

Dronāchārya asked him to take aim and put the same question to him. Arjuna replied: "Sir, I see the eye, and nothing else."

"Shoot," said Dronāchārya, and the arrow found its mark.

Arjuna was in the focused state of mind. He was focused on the bird's eye and nothing else. While the other princes were distracted by the trees, the other students had similar possible distractions, Arjuna's senses were in harmony with what the mind was focused on and that was how he found the mark.

Mind alone is the cause for the state of bondage or liberation in man.
It is up to us to use this mind for our liberation, by properly controlling it.

Upanishads

एतेन भूतेन्द्रियेषु धर्मलक्षणावस्थापरिणामा व्याख्याताः ॥१३॥

Yetena Bhuta_Indriyeshu
Dharma_Lakshana_Avasthā_Parināmā Vyākhyātāh.

Thence the explanation of
Property, character and condition;
As also on transformation of
Elements and sensation.

Yetena: by this way *Bhuta*: gross elements *Indriyeshu*: sense organs
Dharma: propriety *Lakshana*: character *Avasthā*: state
Parināmā: changes, mutations *Vyākhyātāh*: explained

Q. *What are the knowable phenomena in relation to an object?*
A. Its characteristics, species and genus, its relation to itself and its relation to the eternal self are the known phenomena in relation to an object.

Dharma, *Lakshna* and *Avasthā* refer to the property, character and state in relation to an object.

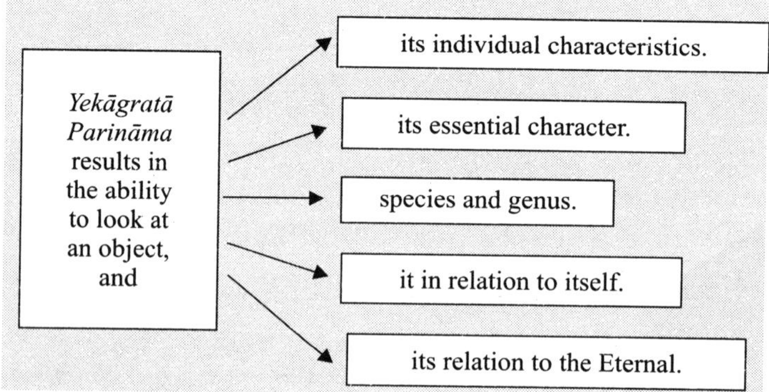

Everything in this world, whether animate or inanimate, man or a monkey, has a definite set of properties. They have their respective nature, both in action and in inaction. In the same way, metals, salts, trees, plants, sun, stars all have different properties. By focused attention, one can get a full picture of the object and understand its properties. When mind is focused, there are no distractions. The distortion presented by the object is also not there, as the object also vanishes, leaving only properties to be known.

Differentiating each genus into its species and each species into its members, the Supreme Being withdraws them once more into their own ground again bringing both the agents of creation, the Great Self holds sway over them all.

Shvetāsvatara Upanishad

"Do you know That, by knowing which everything else is known?" asks sage Uddālaka addressing his son Svetaketu (in *Chhāndogya Upanishad*). Uddālaka continues, "If you know what earth is made up of, you can know everything that is made of earth, pot, plate or glass. Because they are only shapes of the substance called clay." What Uddālaka says is that object forms are inseparable from concepts in the mind. If the objects do not get organically mixed up with the mind of the perceiver, their properties and characteristics can be grasped directly by the perceiver. Ultimately one realises that the object is not there at all. Whatever that is perceived is nothing but consciousness appearing in a particular manner due to certain vibration, a particular density and a movement of the object in a particular manner. On *Samyama*, when the mind is attuned to that vibration, density and movement, all characteristics of the objects become known.

The changes in the gross, subtle matter and the organs result from the threefold transformation in the mind. The *Upanishads* always cite the example of change of solid gold into bracelet and then into a ring.

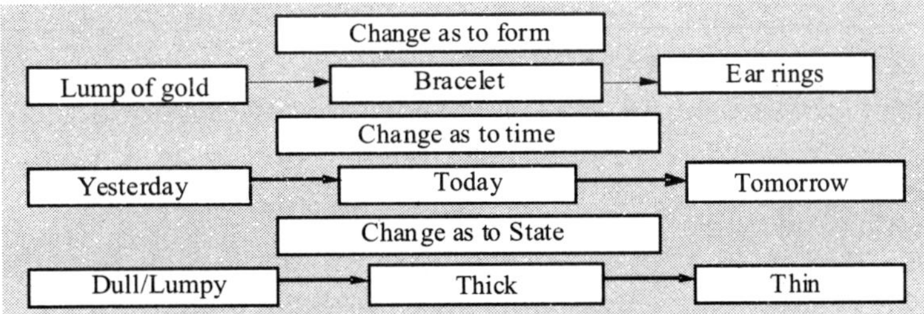

The differences are of three kinds.

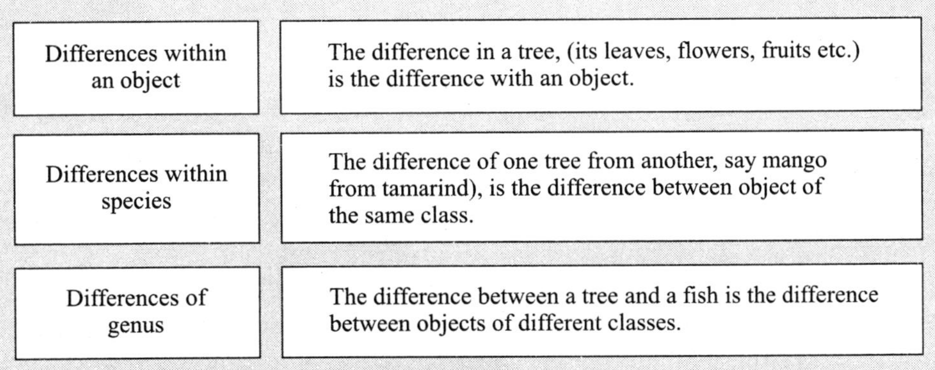

Differences within an object	The difference in a tree, (its leaves, flowers, fruits etc.) is the difference with an object.
Differences within species	The difference of one tree from another, say mango from tamarind), is the difference between object of the same class.
Differences of genus	The difference between a tree and a fish is the difference between objects of different classes.

All the elements can finally be reduced to space. Earth gets dissolved in water, water gets dried up by fire, fire gets extinguished by air, air is absorbed into space. So space is the ultimate visible reality, most comprehensive, very expansive, inclusive of everything almost resembling Omnipresence.

Sanatakumāra to Nārada- Chhāndogya Upanishad

शान्तोदिताव्यपदेश्यधर्मानुपाती धर्मी ॥१४॥

Shānta_Udita Avyapadeshya_Dharmānupāti Dharmi.

Un-manifest, manifest or latent
Have as substratum the same content.

Shānta: latent *Udita*: raise *Avyapadeshya*: indefinable *Dharma*: features
Ānupāti: experienced in succession *Dharmi*: substratum

Q. *What forms the substratum of characteristics?*

A. That which continues its existence all through the varying characteristics, namely
the dormant [appeared in the past],
the arisen (at present apparent),
the potent (a force to be revealed in the future], from its the substratum or the base that comprises all object characteristics.

A substance contains all its characteristics and, depending on the particular form it takes, those conforming to that form will be apparent. But whatever the form, whatever the characteristics exhibited, there exists a base that comprises all characteristics. Some have appeared in the past, some are currently apparent and the others may reveal themselves in the future.

The substratum is the same everywhere, fire, water and earth (gaseous, liquid and solid) and a certain proportion and intensity of consciousness. In a sense, the theory of evolution is right. Not the man has come out of monkey, but that monkey becomes a man, when the degree and intensity of consciousness in the monkey has increased. An ordinary man in a similar way becomes an illuminated and liberated soul when the intensity and degree of consciousness in him reaches to infinity.

Every object in creation can be reduced to its constituents and a law can be stated: There is nothing in an object except its constituents. So all un-manifest, manifest and latent have the same substratum - varying degree of the three elements and varying intensity of consciousness. The redness in the sun is due to its fire principle, the whiteness that dazzles is due to the water principle and the darkness there is due to its earth principle. All objects are a permutation and combination of these three. Thus far what remains unknown to one is due to the incapacity of mind to probe into the structure of the object. If one is not carried away by the features of an object and formation of the structure, he can know the basic structure.

I died as a mineral and became a plant,
I died as a plant and rose to animal,
I died as an animal and I was man,
Why should I fear? When was I less by dying?

Jalalud' D-din Rumi. Sufi Poet

क्रमान्यत्वं परिणामान्यत्वे हेतुः ॥१५॥
Kramānyatvam Parināma_Anyatve Hetuh.

Variation in transformation
Is caused by sequential differentiation.

Kramānyatvam: sequence *Parināma*: change, mutation, transformation, evolution
Anyatve: in other cases, otherness *Hetuh*: is the cause, reason

Q. *What is the cause for these variations in transformation?*
A. Difference in stage is the cause for the variation in transformation.

Modern Science tells us that all substances are consisting of atoms and atoms consist of electrons, protons and neutrons. The difference between one substance and another is because of the difference in the molecular structures. The difference, it should be emphasized is in the difference in the structure, not in the substance. Difference in stage is the cause of difference in development. As a corollary, by changing the order or sequence of structure, characteristics that are of one pattern can be modified to be another. Patanjali begins the explanation on the series of so called attainments that follow.

According to Patanjali there are no miracles. All are normal attainments achieved through a process of *Samyama* that follow law of transformation. This law is not easily understood by the commoner. For the spiritual seeker, the law unfolds.

The variation in transformation is caused by the variation in the underlying process. Everything other than the Being is an effect. The cause is always greater than the effect. If one attunes himself with the cause, effects can be understood, so also chain of effects. If the immediate link in the chain is grasped, the immediate cause for the effect can be understood. This proximate cause, when changed, brings about change in the effect. All attainments are nothing but effecting the law of transformation, whereby the immediate cause behind the effect is understood and the structure of the cause altered so that effect is altered.

All men misconceive themselves to be ignorant or pure, the way they identify themselves with the mental modification, 'I am ignorant', 'I am pure'. It is for this reason they continue to be in transmigratory existence.

Ādi Shankara, Upadesha Sahashri

At a glance: Aphorism 3.11-3.15

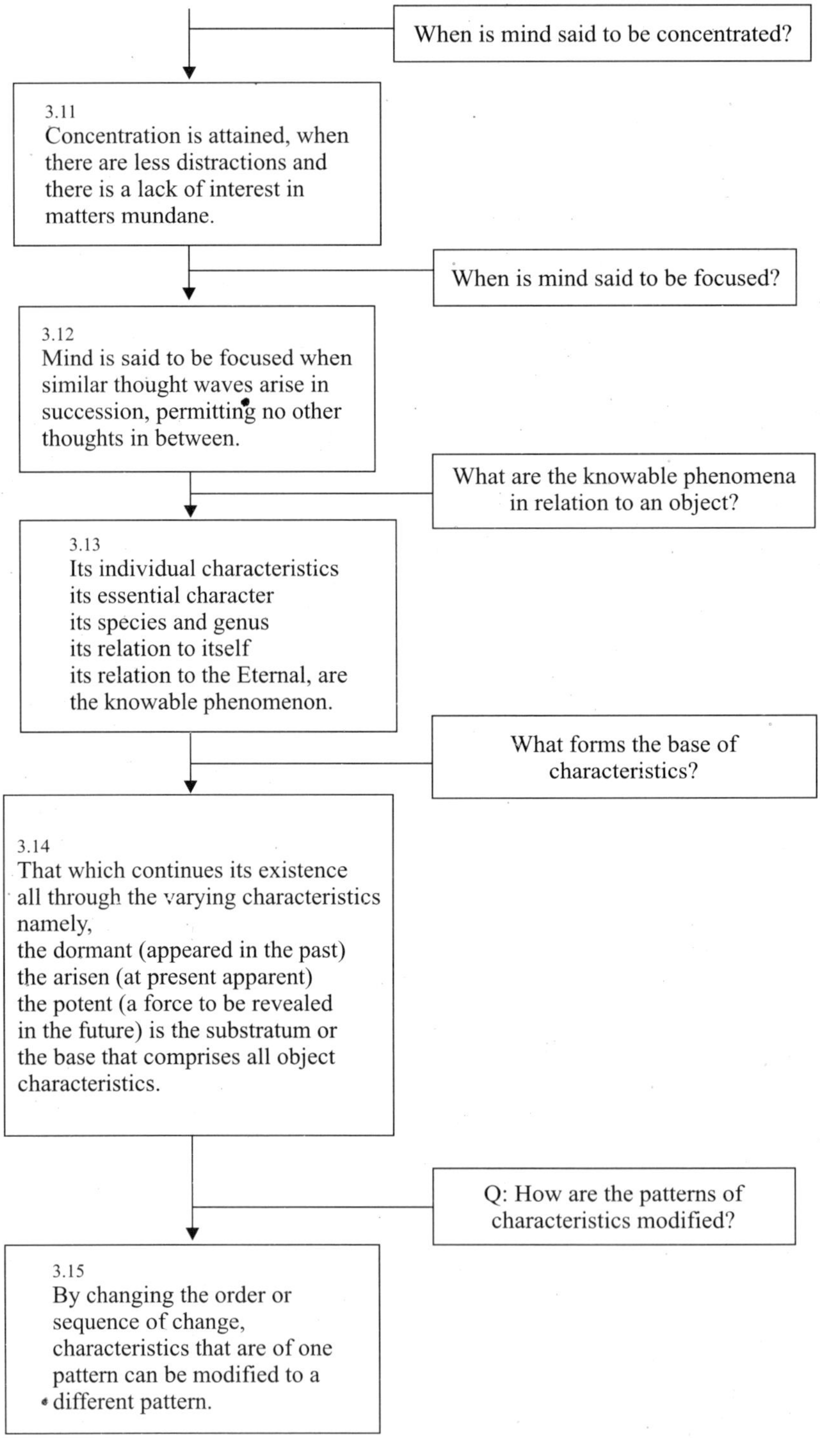

When is mind said to be concentrated?

3.11
Concentration is attained, when there are less distractions and there is a lack of interest in matters mundane.

When is mind said to be focused?

3.12
Mind is said to be focused when similar thought waves arise in succession, permitting no other thoughts in between.

What are the knowable phenomena in relation to an object?

3.13
Its individual characteristics
its essential character
its species and genus
its relation to itself
its relation to the Eternal, are the knowable phenomenon.

What forms the base of characteristics?

3.14
That which continues its existence all through the varying characteristics namely,
the dormant (appeared in the past)
the arisen (at present apparent)
the potent (a force to be revealed in the future) is the substratum or the base that comprises all object characteristics.

Q: How are the patterns of characteristics modified?

3.15
By changing the order or sequence of change, characteristics that are of one pattern can be modified to a different pattern.

परिणामत्रयसंयमादतीतानागतज्ञानम् ॥१६॥

Parināma_Traya_Samyamāt Atita_Anāgata_Jnānam.

On absorption on form, time, condition and their nature
One gains knowledge of past and future.

Parināma: transformation *Traya*: trio (*Dharma*, *Lakshana*, *Avasthā*)
Samyamāt: due to absorption *Atita*: past, that which has already happened
Anāgata: future, that which has not happened yet *Jnānam*: knowledge

Q. *How is knowledge of the past gained?*
A. *Samyama* on the three stages of process of change and how it is affected by time and other factors helps one to gain knowledge of past and future.

Once absorbed, there is no sense of time. The seeker crosses the barrier of time and space. Entrenched as he is in the eternity, the vision of the past and future becomes clear. Living in and absorbed with the present we lose sight of the past. When today's issues dominate, one does not remember last year's incidences. By *Samyama* on form, time and condition, one gains knowledge of past impressions and later stages of evolution, say past lives.

Knowledge of the past is gained when a direct view from the super conscious state is enabled by-passing the conscious state and the current object orientation.

Open terrace Superconscious state	• Free unhindered (unveiled) view • No impressions • Absolute clarity
Living Room Conscious state	• Activity (objects) orientation • View obstructed (veiled) by the windows of attachment, aversion and fear • Forming impressions
Cellar Subconscious state	• Darkness • Old impressions formed out of experiences in all previous births, and until date in this birth

View of the past impression not possible from here as present objective orientation blocks vision.

But of what use is such knowledge for the one inclined spiritually? Imagine the mess one would be in, if he were to know about all his past wives, wealth and children! This one life is messy enough!

Past present and future are all in the eternal.
He who dwells in the eternal knows all the three.

Bhagavadgitā

शब्दार्थप्रत्ययानामितरेतराध्यासात् संकरस्तत्प्रविभाग
-संयमात् सर्वभूतरुतज्ञानम् ॥१७॥

Shabda_Artha_Pratyayānām Itar_Itar_Adhyāsāt Sankarh Tat_Pravibhāga_ Samyamāt Sarva_Bhuta_Ruta_Jnānam.

When sound, meaning and idea merge
Mix up and confusion emerges;
But with absorption on sound
Its purpose and meaning is found.

Shabda: sound, spoken word *Artha*: meaning, import
Pratyayānām: the mental reaction on hearing the spoken word and understanding its import
Itar: one for the other *Adhyāsā*: by super imposition
Sankarah: admixture *Tat*: that *Pravibhāga*: dividing *Samyamāt*: absorption
Sarva: all *Bhuta*: beings *Ruta_Jnānam*: Knowledge about sounds

Q. *How is knowledge of sounds produced by even birds and beasts understood?*
A. Word, meaning implied, and the idea thereof overlap and produce one unified impression. If by separating sound apart *Samyama* is practised on the sound, knowledge of the meaning of the sound produced by all beings – be it a bird or a beast, can be acquired.

Knowledge comes out of comparison. Mind acts like a dictionary. One hears a word and the implied meaning. The association of the word and the meaning together becomes knowledge stored in the memory. If at a later day similar sound is heard an understanding is arrived at. Ordinarily the three: word, meaning and knowledge are mixed together. When the three are separated and *Samyama* is made on the sound alone, one can understand the meaning implied, it does not matter if the sound is made by a bird or a beast. This understanding is arrived at, not by referring to the dictionary of memory.

Word	• An audible sound. • External vibration, hitting the auditory nerves in the ear.
Meaning	• Internal vibration. • Travels to the brain through the sensory organ • Conveys external impression to mind.
Knowledge	• Represents reaction of the mind • If earlier a similar sound was heard and a meaning found, the comparison and understanding takes place. Otherwise the vibration makes no sense.

The Billy Goat and the King

[Punjabi story, Major Campbell, Feroshepore, from The Olive Fairy Book , by Andrew Lang)

Once there lived a certain king who understood the language of all birds and beasts and insects. This knowledge had of course, been given to him by a fairy godmother; but it was rather a troublesome present, for he knew that if he were ever to reveal anything he had thus learned he would turn into a stone. How he managed to avoid doing so long before this story opens I can not say, but he had safely grown up to manhood, and married a wife, and was as happy as monarchs generally are.

Well, one day the king was eating his dinner in just such a nice, clean, mud-plastered spot, and his wife was sitting opposite to wait upon him and keep him company. As he ate he dropped some grains of rice upon the ground, and a little ant, who was running about seeking a living, seized upon one of the grains and bore it off towards his hole. Just outside the king's circle this ant met another ant, and the king heard the second one say, 'Oh, dear friend, do give me that grain of rice, and get another one for yourself. You see my boots are so dirty that, if I were to go upon the king's eating place, I should defile it, and I can't do that, it would be so very rude.'

But the owner of the grain of rice only replied, 'If you want rice go and get it. No one will notice your dirty boots; and you don't suppose that I am going to carry rice for all our kindred?'

Then the king laughed. The queen looked at herself up and down, but she could not see or feel anything in her appearance to make the king laugh, so she said, "Why did you laugh?"

'Did I laugh?' replied the king. 'Of course you did,' retorted the queen; 'and if you think that I am ridiculous I wish you would say so, instead of behaving in that stupid way! What are you laughing at?'

'Well, I'm afraid I can't tell you,' said the king. 'You must tell me,' replied the queen impatiently. 'If you laugh when there's nothing to laugh at you must be ill or mad. What is the matter?'

Thought- reduction is freedom; thought-assertion is bondage. The seeker must learn to rise above his desire-promptings. There is no other escape.

Yogavāshishta.

The more the king refused to say the more the queen declared that she must know. For days the quarrel went on, and the queen gave her husband no rest, until at last the poor man was almost out of his wits, and thought that, as life had become for him hardly worth living while this went on, he might as well tell her the secret and take the consequences.

'But,' thought he, 'if I am to become a stone, I am not going to lie, if I can help it, on some dusty highway, to be kicked here and there by man and beast, flung at dogs, be used as the plaything of naughty children, and become generally restless and miserable. I will be a stone at the bottom of the cool river, and roll gently about there until I find some secure resting-place where I can stay for ever.'

So he told his wife that if she would ride with him to the middle of the river he would tell her what he had laughed at. She thought he was joking, and laughingly agreed; their horses were ordered and they set out. But the king knew that he will soon turn into a stone. On the way they came to a fine well beneath the shade of some lofty, wide-spreading trees, and the king proposed that they should get off and rest a little, drink some of the cool water, and then pass on. To this the queen consented; so they dismounted and sat down in the shade by the well-side to rest.

It happened that an old goat and his wife were browsing in the neighbourhood, and, as the king and queen sat there, the nanny goat came to the well's brink and peering over saw some lovely green leaves that sprang in tender shoots out of the side of the well. 'Oh!' cried she to her husband, 'Come quickly and look. Here are some leaves which make my mouth water; come and get them for me!'

Then the billy goat sauntered up and looked over, and after that he eyed his wife a little crossly. 'You expect me to get you those leaves, do you? I suppose you don't consider how in the world I am to reach them? You don't seem to think at all; if you did you would know that if I tried to reach those leaves I should fall into the well and be drowned!'

'Oh,' cried the nanny goat, 'why should you fall in? Do try and get them!' the nanny goat wept and entreated.

'I am not going to be so silly', replied the billy goat.

'Look here,' said her husband, 'there are many fools around, but don't count me amongst them. I am not like that stupid king here, because he can't cure his wife of asking questions, is going to throw his life away. But I know how to cure you of your follies, and I'm going to.'

And with that he butted the nanny goat so severely that in two minutes she was submissively feeding somewhere else, and had made up her mind that the leaves in the well were not worth having.

Then the king, who had understood every word, laughed once more.

The queen looked at him suspiciously, but the king got up and walked across to where she sat.

'Are you still determined to find out what I was laughing at the other day?' he asked. 'Of course yes' retorted the queen angrily. 'Because,' said the king, tapping his leg with his riding whip, 'I've made up my mind not to tell you, and moreover, I have made up my mind to stop you mentioning the subject any more.'

'What do you mean?' asked the queen nervously. Well,' replied the king, 'I notice that if that goat is displeased with his wife, he just butts her, and that seems to settle the question.'

'Do you mean to say you would beat me?' cried the queen. 'I should be extremely sorry to have to do so,' replied the king; 'but I have to persuade you to go home quietly, and to ask no more silly questions when I say I cannot answer them. Of course, if you will persist, why?'

And the queen went home, and so did the king; and it is said that they are both happier and wiser than ever before.

You may control a mad elephant
You may shun the mouth of a bear and tiger
Ride on the lion and even play with the cobra
By alchemy you may earn your livelihood
You may wander through the universe incognito
Make vassals of gods; be ever youthful;
You may walk on water and live on fire,
But control of the mind is better and more difficult.

South Indian Saint Thāyumānavar
(Translation by *Swāmi Yogānanda*)

संस्कारसाक्षात्करणात् पूर्वजातिज्ञानम् ॥१८॥

Sanskāra_Sākshāt_Karanāt Purva_Jāti_Jnānam.

Through perception of latent impressions
Comes knowledge of past incarnations.

Sanskāra: recollection *Sākshāt*: realisation *Karanāt*: being done
Purva: previous, earlier *Jāti*: birth *Jnānam*: knowledge

Q. *How does one gain knowledge of past lives?*
A. *Samyama* on one's tendencies and habits, on past thoughts and propensities; will lead one to their origins. Consequently, one gains knowledge of one's past.

Where do I come from? Why am I here? Where am I going? These age-old questions are the link to the deepest yearnings in Man. There is an order to the universe and the surrounding world. There is purpose to life and an order to its seemingly disjointed string of the idea of pre-existence of soul. Reincarnation has settled the questions relating to life and death amongst ancient philosophers like Plato and Pythagoras as also amongst poets like Wordsworth, Tennyson, Walt Whitman and others.

Walt Whitman said: "As to you life, I reckon you are the leavings of many death. No doubt I died myself ten thousand times before."

The objective of Yoga is to wipe out all impressions and not add on further problems by remembering past lives.

During his enlightenment experience, Siddhārtha attained three types of knowledge. First he saw that he had died and been reborn many times: 'I recollected my manifold past lives, that is, one birth, two births, three births...a hundred thousand births.' Each birth was seen in some detail: 'There I was so named, of such a clan, with such an appearance...and passing away from there, I reappeared here.'

Krishna to Arjuna: "O Arjuna, both you and I have passed through many births. You know them not, but I remember them all."

There are arguments advanced against the possibility of past incarnations and rebirth. The main argument is that since one does not remember previous birth there is no likelihood of an earlier incarnation. This argument is fallacious. It would mean negation of everything that one does not remember. Even in the present birth, several incidences and childhood memories remain suppressed in the sub-conscious and one is unable to recollect them, it cannot therefore be said that one did not exist as a child! It would be absurd. Equally absurd it is to negate earlier births.

Past impressions get constantly pushed into the subconscious. Since new impressions are constantly being formed they blur and prevent past impressions being recollected. It is much like our inability to see the TV channel that is on, when through the windows, rays of light fall on the TV screen. The rays in this context are the '*impression rays*'. The windows are the '*sense windows*.'

The TV screen is the '*memory screen*.'

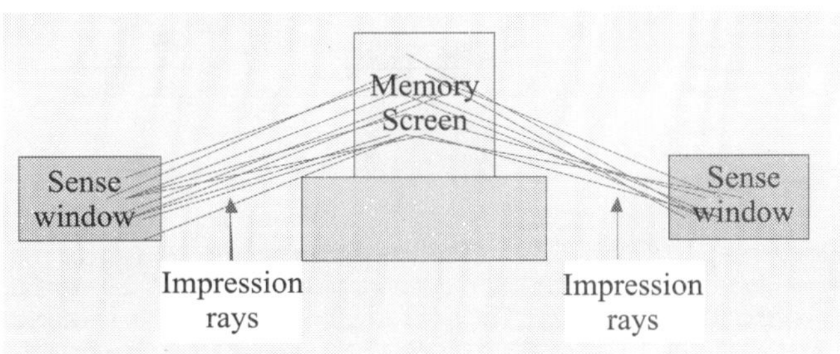

Knowledge of past lives can be had, if the impressions are no longer formed now and the sense windows are shut. Once sense organs are shut and mind is not allowed to become object oriented, no longer are fresh impressions formed. Since no fresh impressions are formed, old impressions can be read, if attention is focused on the same.

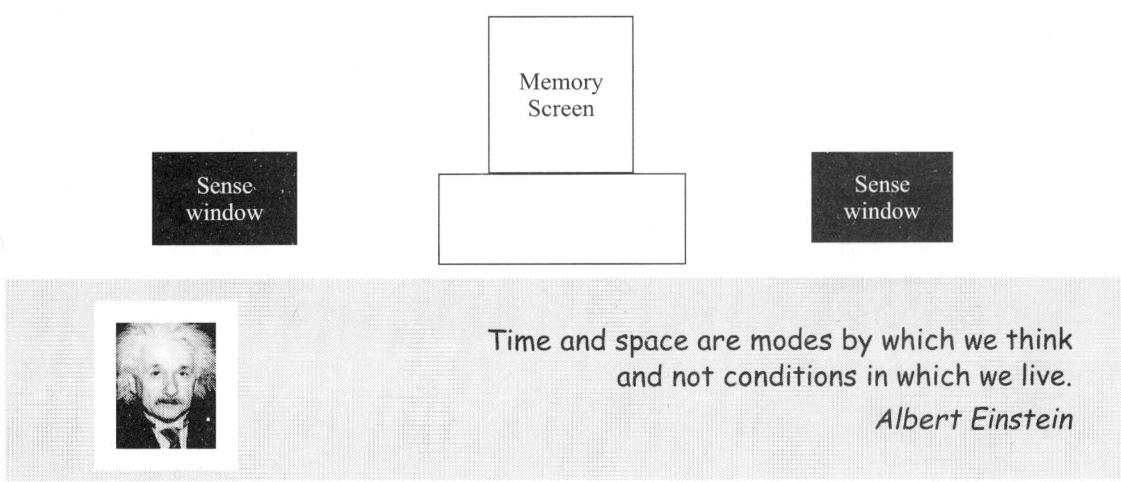

Time and space are modes by which we think and not conditions in which we live.

Albert Einstein

SPOTLIGHT

4-year-old claims to be father of 3 in previous life

By AMITA VERMA

Lucknow, Nov. 2: Four-year-old Anekesh claims he has from a "previous birth" a wife and three daughters in a neighbouring village in Bahedi, in Uttar Pradesh's Bareilly district. He insists on visiting "his wife" and wants to take on the responsibility of "his three children" too.

Anekesh is the only son of Babu Ram of Piparia village. About a year ago, Anekesh suddenly told his father that his name was Chhotelal and that he lived in the nearby village of Gursauli. He said he had a wife and three children. Babu Ram did not pay heed to his son's claims and thought the child had been tutored to make such statements by someone in the village.

However, Anekesh continued to repeat his statements and began calling himself Chhotelal. He claimed he had been killed by a speeding truck about nine years ago and had been "reborn" because he wanted to go back to his family and ride his old Luna moped.

"In the beginning we did not take the boy

from page one...

4-year-old claims

■ Continued from Page 1

seriously. But when he began giving out other details, we could not ignore it either. I sent some of my relatives to Gursauli village to check out whether Anekesh was telling the truth. My relatives had no difficulty in tracing Chhotelal's house and his mother confirmed that her son had been killed in a road accident about nine years ago," says Babu Ram.

Two months later, Babu Ram took Anekesh to Gursauli and the boy seemed to know the village like the back of his hand. "He guided us through the roads and as soon as entered the village, he directed us to Chhotelal's house where he immediately recognised 'his mother, his wife' and 'his children'. He even gave us their names," says the boy's father.

Chhotelal's family was taken aback when Anekesh began relating past incidents and Chhotelal's wife fainted with shock when Anekesh claimed he had been Chhotelal in his "previous birth".

Chhotelal's family does not seem too keen to accept Anekesh as the son "who died nine years ago", but the latter insists he wants to stay with them. Babu Ram is determined not to let his son go, but has to live with the fact that Anekesh is more attached to the family he claims was his in his "previous birth" than his current family.

"We have done several pujas at home and consulted several astrologers, but no one seems able to help us. The only solace is that a psychologist in Bareilly has told my uncle that as Anekesh grows older, his memory of his previous birth will probably fade. This is now our only hope," says Babu Ram.

प्रत्ययस्य परचित्तज्ञानम् ॥१९॥
Pratyayasya Parachitta_Jnānam

By concentration one can find,
What runs in others' mind.

Pratyayasya: the state of mind associated with like, dislike etc.
Parachitta: other's mind
Jnānam: knowledge

Q. *How can one read others mind?*
A. The nature of the mind of another person becomes known to the ascetic when he concentrates his own mind upon that other person.

How does one recognize that the other train on the railway platform is moving? Naturally, when the train in which he is seated is still. Much the same way, when one's own thoughts are still, he can read the other's thought. Perceiving mind must be stilled, before the mind-image projected by the other mind can be seen. This is the essence of thought reading. One is not different from another. It is the same consciousness that pervades through every being in the universe. It is the degree and intensity of consciousness that varies. When one raises his level of consciousness through *Samyama*, he can easily know (read) what runs through in another's mind. Even in our normal life, we can notice that a mother easily reads through the child's mind and a committed teacher can easily understand what troubles his student. Once the degree of involvement in the other person increases, the capacity to read his thought also increases. This supernatural ability to comprehend sentient beings' intentions and inclinations arise when a seeker has achieved clarity of mind through *Samyama*. Practising and applying compassionate intention to daily life activities, when well versed to the point of constant empathy and sincere caring into details of others' needs, it would not be much different from possessing the ability to know others' minds, but would be even superior to that by its altruistic aspect of benefiting others.

The ability to read other's mind need be shunned. There is every possibility of getting embroiled in other's lives and thoughts. Misuse of such powers drag one down.

In the illumined one, who sees no 'other', all thoughts are his thoughts. He is not influenced by such thoughts. He sees such thoughts come and go and hence remains unperturbed by them.

Language is only a medium for communicating one's thoughts to another. It is called in after the thoughts arise; the 'I' thought is the root of all conversations. When one remains without thinking one understands another by means of the universal language of silence.

Sri Ramana Mahārishi.

न च तत्सालम्बनं तस्याविषयीभूतत्वात् ॥२०॥

Na Cha Tat Sa_Ālambanam Tasya_Avishayi_Bhutatvāt.

While others' mind one can read
Knoweth not the reasons that precede.

Na: No *Cha*: and *Tat*: that *Ālambanam*: with attachment
Tasya: its absorption *Avishayi*: non- object *Bhutatvāt*: being the cause thereof

Q. *The capacity to read others' mind can be gained alright. But can one know the reasons behind the thinking of the other individual?*

A. No, the cause of the state of mind of the other person cannot be known because he does not perform '*Samyama*' with that object before him.

But since that on which the thought in the mind of another rests is not objective to the thought-reader's consciousness, he perceives the thought only, and not also that on which the thought rests. One may be able to perceive the thoughts of some one at a distance; one cannot, by that means alone, perceive the external stimuli of that person, which arouse these thoughts.

ESP is most commonly called the "sixth sense." It is sensory information that an individual receives which comes beyond the ordinary five senses sight, hearing, smell, taste, and touch. It can provide the individual with information of the present, past, and future; as it seems to originate in a second or alternate reality.

Telepathy literally means "distant feeling". The term is often a shortened version of mental telepathy and refers to mind reading, discerning another person's thoughts through ESP. Clairvoyance or second sight: Clairvoyance is an alleged psychic ability to see things beyond the range of the power of vision. Clairvoyance is usually associated with precognition or retro cognition. The faculty of seeing into the future is called "second sight" if it is not induced by drugs, trance, or other artificial means. People can predict the future. We do it all the time, but we usually, if not always, do it by taking into account our experience, knowledge and surroundings. Some predictions by psychics come true. So do some predictions by non-psychics. No doubt much of our anticipation of the future is unconscious and second nature, but it is based on quite natural and mundane abilities not on mysterious or supernatural powers.

What is important and what is trivial?
Principle is important while technique is trivial.
Basic is important while application is trivial.
What is permanent is important, while what changes is trivial.

At a glance: Aphorism 3.16-3.20

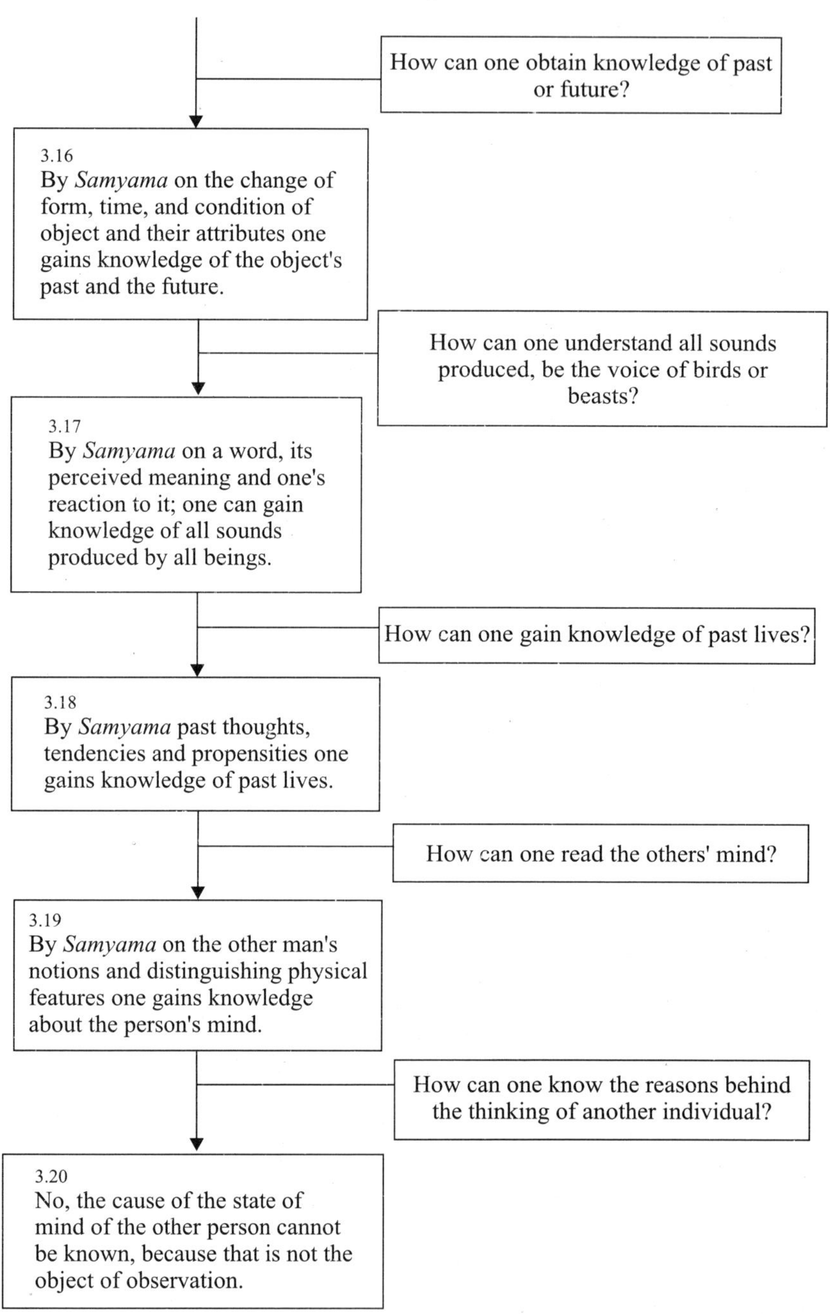

कायरूपसंयमात् तद्ग्राह्यशक्तिस्तम्भे चक्षुःप्रकाशासंप्रयोगेऽन्तर्धानम् ॥२१॥

Kāya_Rupa_Samyamāt Tada_Grāhya_Shakti_Stambhe Chakshuh_Prakāsh_ Asamprayoge Antardhānam.

When on one's own body form, there is absorption,
There is suppression of others' capacity of comprehension.

Kāya: body *Rupa*: form *Samyamāt*: absorption in *Tada*: that
Grāhya: comprehension *Shakti*: capability *Stambhe*: being lost
Chakshuh: eye of the beholder *Prakāsh*: perceived
Asamprayoge: devoid of contact *Antardhānam*: disappearance

Q: *How can one become invisible, though standing in front of another?*
A: When perceptibility of the body is suppressed by Practising *Samyama* on its visual character, disappearance of the body is effected. The relationship between the features of the body and what affects them can give one the means to merge with one's surroundings in such a way that one's form is indistinguishable.

Rosicrucianism is the science of becoming invisible. A brother in the Rosicrucian fraternity wrote a paper on how to walk invisible among men, and there is evidence that this was being taught in those early days. H. Spencer Lewis, the founder of the Ancient and Mystical Order Rosae Crucis in San Jose, California, stated that one can gain invisibility with the use of clouds. He says that clouds or bodies of mist can be called out of the invisible to surround a person and thus shut him out of the sight of others.

According to Lewis, this secret practice is still taught in the mystical schools of today. The written literature on this subject supports the statement that the cloud is the basis of the Rosicrucian invisibility secret.

The knowledge that objects are visible because light bounces off the objects was well known to *Yogis* of the past. That a body is but an object was also their understanding. So they concentrated on their bodies and ensured that the light does not bounce off their bodies. That was the way the *yogis* made themselves invisible. The purpose of their making themselves invisible was to make sure that no body disturbs them during their meditation.

Oh! Well for him, whose will is strong;
He will not have to suffer long.

Scientists to make invisible cloaks

London, March 3: A cloaking device that makes objects invisible is being developed by researchers — bringing the magic of Harry Potter into the world of scientific fact.

Electronic engineers at the University of Pennsylvania in the US are working on a real invisibility shield called a "plasmonic cover", which works by preventing objects from reflecting and scattering light. The cloak could have widespread use in the military as it would be more effective than current stealth technology, reported Scottish daily *Scotsman*.

Although no final product has been made, the engineers claim their proposal "does not obviously violate any of the laws of physics".

According to Andrea Alu and Nader Engheta, the engineers behind the project, objects are visible because light bounces off them. If this could be prevented and the objects would not reflect any light, and become invisible. *(IANS)*

Rāmalinga Adigalār

In the 19th century, in southern India lived a saint named Sri Rāmalinga Adigalār. It is reported that he posed for group photograph with his disciples. The photographer on washing and printing the film in his laboratory observed that only a spot existed where Sri Adigalār stood. He was not visible in the photo. On being queried by his disciples, he dismissed their query off saying that such invisibility on his part is not a willful act, but due to divine transformation in him.

Except ye see signs and wonder
Ye shall not believe.

सोपक्रमं निरुपक्रमं च कर्म तत्संयमादपरान्तज्ञानमरिष्टेभ्यो वा ॥२२॥

Sopakramam Nirupkramam cha Karma
Tat_Samyamāt_Aparānta_Jnānam Arishtebhyo Vā.

On absorption on past and possible future reactions of one's past actions,
Gains one knowledge of his body's end by watching inauspicious portent.

Sopakramam: immediate reaction *Nirupkramam*: delayed reaction *Cha*: and
Karma: action *Tat*: that *Samyamāt*: from absorption
Aparānta: of death, of end *Jnānam*: knowledge
Arishtebhya: from inauspicious portents *Vā*: or

Q. *How can one know about exact time of death?*

A. By *Samyama* on past actions some of which will soon fructify and yet others later, one gains knowledge of exact time of his separation from his body, observing inauspicious portents.

Foreboding of death is guessed by ordinary Hindu folk by observing inauspicious events. A rotten coconut observed by the individual on being broken in front of a favourite deity with a prayer for well-being of a diseased is considered inauspicious portending death of the diseased. Camphor lit in front of the deity being blown off by wind is also considered inauspicious.

The Aittareya Upanishad introduces some omens of death as in Brihadāranyaka and elsewhere. It is however not advisable to the uninitiated to know these and get influenced by auto suggestion. When the fairly advanced spiritual seeker notices such omens as are introduced prepares to 'leave off' his body.

Jesus knew for certain he would die.

By seeing himself as the Servant of Jehowa and the smitten shepherd,
Jesus apparently came to grips with the fact
that the prophets had predicted his death.
Driven by this insight and sense of mission,
he confidently asserted that the scriptures must be fulfilled
that predicted his death.
R. T. France says, "The servant figure provided a 'blue-print' for his ministry,
which he must follow."

What do the scriptures say with regard to prediction of death?

Shivapurāna Umā Samhitā says:

Death may occur within fifteen days:

- When the eyes see the sun without rays, sees only red blob.
- He who sees his own shadow without the head, or he cannot see at all his own shadow.

Death may occur within one month:

- When the organs of the body cease functioning and start pulling, when the upper part of the mouth feels dry all the time.
- When a man's left hand continuously keeps shaking for seven days.

Death may occur within six months:

- When the rainbow is being seen at night.
- When a person cannot see his or her reflection in water, oil, *ghee* (clarified melted butter), or in the mirror; otherwise sees the reflection in the mirror in a distorted form or sees only flesh, or
- When the tongue thickens, and the teeth remain coated with greasy substance.
- The mouth, ear, eye or the tongue suddenly freeze-up.
- When the body suddenly becomes pale and the face turns red.
- When vultures and crows seem to surround the person.

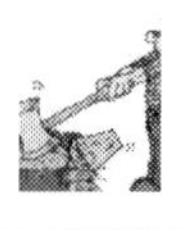

An old woodcutter, too weary to pick up his load of sticks, exclaimed: "I wish that Death would take me!" Even as he spoke, Death appeared, but seeing him, the old man changed his mind. Now his only request was: "Would you help me lift this load to my shoulders?"

Aitareya Upanishad:

The Upanishad enlists number of signs of approaching death:

- When the sun appears like the moon, sky like red madder, the wind is not retained and the head smells like a raven's nest.
- Sun appearing pierced and looking like the navel of a cart wheel.
- One's own shadow being pierced.
- Sight of one's image in a mirror or in water with a crooked head or no head.
- Pupils of the eye seen crooked or inverted.
- Threads appearing in group when the eyes are covered and when looked, not seen so.
- Seeing no lightening in a cloudy sky where it actually takes place.
- Fire appearing blue like the neck of a peacock.
- Lightening seen in a cloudless sky.
- Dreaming as though one is being slain by a dark man with black teeth or by a boar.
- Dreaming as if one self is being carried away by swift winds.
- Dreaming as if one is carrying a single lotus.

The Upanishad follows up listing of signs of possible death, with advice on what needs be done in the event of the signs being perceived or dreams being dreamt.

Signs of approaching death: (The Mahābhārata)

Addressing King Janaka, Yājnavalkya said: "I shall now tell thee the premonitory indication, as laid down by the wise of those who have but one year to live. One, who having previously seen the fixed star called Arundhati, fails to see it, or that other star called Dhruva (the Pole Star), or one that sees the full moon or the flame of a burning lamp to be broken towards the south, has but one year to live. Those men, O king, who can no longer see images of themselves reflected in the eyes of others, have but one year to live. One who, being endued with lustre, loses it, or being endued with wisdom loses it, indeed, one whose inward and outward nature is thus changed, has but six months more to live. He, who disregards the deities, or one, who, being naturally of a dark complexion becomes pale of hue, has but six months more to live. One, who sees the lunar disc to have many holes like a spider's web, who sees the solar disc to have similar holes, has but one week more to live. One, who, when smelling fragrant scents in place of worship, perceives them to be as offensive as the scent of corpses, has but one week more to live. The depression of the nose or of the ear, the discolouring of the teeth or of the eye, the loss of all consciousness, and the loss also of all animal heat, are symptoms indicating death that very day. If, without any perceptible cause a stream of tears suddenly flows from one's left eye, and if vapours be seen to issue from one's head, that is a sure indication that the man will die before that day expires.

मैत्र्यादिषु बलानि ॥२३॥

Maitri_Ādishu Balāni.

Concentration on qualities like compassion
Strengthens such disposition.

Maitr: friendship, compassion *Ādishu*: similar states *Balāni*: strengthening

Q. *How does one beget a friendly disposition?*
A. By *Samyama* on qualities of kinship one can beget a friendly disposition.

Mother Teresa

- Compassion is a deep awareness of and sympathy for another's suffering.
- Compassion is the humane quality of understanding the suffering of others and wanting to do something about it.
- Compassion is a sense of shared suffering, most often combined with a desire to alleviate or reduce such suffering.
- Compassion transcends both natural human sympathy and enables one to sense in others a wide range of emotions and then provide a supportive assistance.

Realisation, that one is not apart and different from others around, is gained by *Samyama* on attributes such as compassion. Compassion is the keen awareness of the interdependence of all things. This realisation leads one to be friendly and helpful to every being around him. One rejoices by helping. One realises that his consciousness expands by giving; and contracts by withholding and withdrawing.

The eminent Tibetan scholar Geshe Kelsang Gyatso states that compassion is the root of a Buddha because all Buddhas arise form the mind of compassion, it is the root of *Dharma* because Buddhas give *Dharma* teachings out of compassion for others, and it is the root of the *Sangha* (the community of Buddhist practitioners) because it is impossible to become *Sangha* without practising compassion. Buddhist teachings on compassion are extremely practical. Their immediate purpose is to lessen the stress on oneself and those around him by making him more peaceful, understanding and patient. Ultimately, they reduce the negative imprints in one's mind that turn the obstacles to liberation.

Where there is no passion,
there is compassion.

बलेषु हस्तिबलादीनि ॥२४॥

Baleshu Hasti_Bala_Ādini.

Through concentration one can gain
Strength elephantine.

Baleshu: among the strong *Hasti*: elephant *Bala*: strength *Ādini*: similar to

Q. *How can one gain elephantine strength?*

A. By *Samyama* on any type of strength such as that of an elephant, one can gain elephantine strength.

This is a pretty image. Elephants possess not only force, but poise and fineness of control. They can lift a straw, a child or a tree with perfectly judged control and effort. So the simile is a good one.

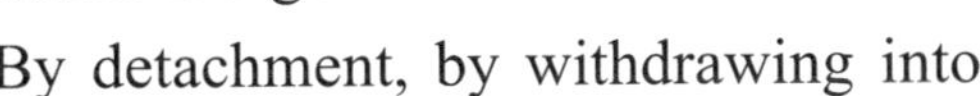

By detachment, by withdrawing into the soul's reservoir of power, one can gain all these, force and fineness and poise; the ability to handle with equal mastery things small and great, concrete and abstract alike. Of course, the Greek God Atlas is here only symbolically carrying the world on his shoulders.

The strength of body is that of the strength of mind. Patanjali says that by concentrating on the strength of the elephant it is possible to get that animal's strength and dexterity.

It is common to observe trained men being able to break up stacked bricks with one single blow. These men explain that their achievement is based on training their mind and not on building their body. Gripping a rope in the teeth, and dragging a car or a truck with the strength of the teeth is also witnessed by many and reported in several news and TV channels. All those who achieved such feats have reported about need to train mind to do such acts. It should be clear however, that a spiritual seeker has a higher goal than proving muscular powers.

Filling the *Kundalini* (referred to as coiled serpent) through the practice of *Pooraka* (inhalation) when one stays evenly he remains firm, stable and strong like the Meru mountain.

Yogavāshishta

प्रवृत्त्यालोकन्यासात् सूक्ष्मव्यवहितविप्रकृष्टज्ञानम् ॥२५॥

Pravritti_Āloka_Nyāsāt Sukshma_Vyavahita Viprakrishta Jnānam.

Concentration on inner light
Gives one knowledge of things beyond sight.

Pravritti Āloka: on the inner light
Nyāsāt: being absorbed
Sukshma: subtle
Vyavahita: veiled
Viprakrishta: far away, far removed from sight
Jnānam: knowledge

Q. *How can one, gain knowledge of something far away?*
A. By *Samyama* on inner light one gains knowledge of objects that are subtle, invisible or placed far away.

In these days of television, it may appear rather normal to observe, say Olympic games played in one part of the world, all over the world. But ability to observe things and hear words spoken in a far off place in the days bygone was one of the attainments bestowed on the faithful.

Sanjaya was a trusted counsellor and confidant of King Dhritarāshtra. He was often employed by the King as a messenger. When the war of Kurukshetra was about to be fought, he was given the gift of divine insight by the sage Vyāsa. He saw the events unfolding on the battlefield and described them to King Dhritarāshtra. The entire battle of Kurukshetra, is narrated from the perspective of Sanjaya in the epic Mahābhārata.

Sanjaya means complete victory. i.e. a complete mastery over senses. Such a one, is endowed with vision extraordinary. For such a one, everything subtle, hidden and distant; is in his grip. Detachment from sense objects, collapses in such a one the distance between the subject and object. He sees himself in everything as he is everything.

"................for all things are possible with God."
Mark 10.27

At a glance: Aphorism 3.21-3.25

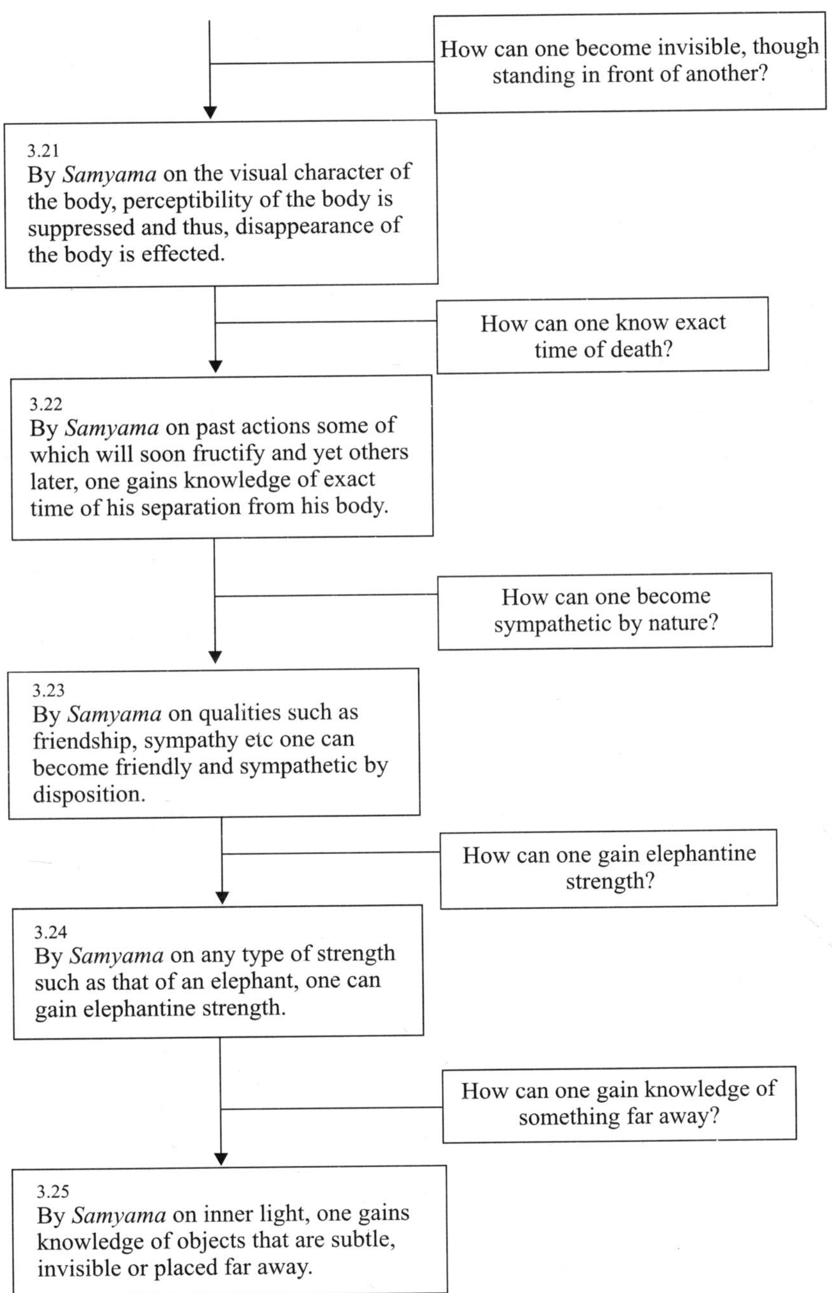

भुवनज्ञानं सूर्ये संयमात् ॥२६॥

Bhuvana_Jnānam Surye_Samyamāt.

By absorption on the sun,
One gains knowledge of cosmic region.

Bhuvana: about the earth
Jnānam: knowledge
Surye: sun and around, solar system
Samyamāt: by absorption

Q. *How can one get knowledge of the cosmic regions?*
A. By practising *Samyama* on the sun (the point in the body known as the solar entrance), the knowledge of the cosmic regions is acquired.

When one considers sun and applies the triple of concentration, meditation and absorption on the sun, one should keep in mind three aspects of sun.

the first, the physical aspect;
the second, the life force aspect
and third, the light aspect.

The first:	Physical aspect governs the material world.
The second:	Life force aspect, is the Om-nipotent, Om-niscient and Om-nipresent vitality, which, when awakened, gives the experience of the three faculties of cognition: the seer, the process of seeing and the seen.
The third:	The Light aspect, is that which dispels darkness and removes ignorance, due to which one is subject to fears and hallucinations, whereby one mistakes the rope as a snake.

It is said that one should learn during the *prānāyāma* training to close the solar plexus centre to the entrance of forces from the astral plane, and open it to the entrance of forces from super conscious level, via the head centre. One should also learn to function more powerfully from the centre between the eyebrows, the *Ājnā* centre. One can then have visions of solar region. The heart centre and the solar plexus centre are the two centres which are the most important centres for concentration and next in order is the throat centre.

He who inhabits in the sun, but is within it,
whom the Sun does not know, whose body is the sun,
and who controls the sun from within,
is the internal ruler, your own immortal self.

Brihadāranyaka Upanishad

चन्द्रे ताराव्यूहज्ञानम् ॥२७॥

Chandre Tārā_Vyuha_Jnānam.

Through concentration on moon and star
Begets one, knowledge of objects far.

Chandre: moon and around
Tārā: stars
Vyuha: view, galaxy
Jnānam : knowledge

Q. *How to know about moon and stars around?*
A. By *Samyama* on moon one gains knowledge of the moon and the stars around.

Today, it is common for man to land on moon. But what one learns about the moon is very little as the samples for analysis are small and physical observatory and analytical instruments are of limited capacities. Yet, one cannot understand such factors like influence of moon on man.

Knowledge of moon and lunar influence on man and his mind were well-known to ancient seers for they acquired such knowledge through *Samyama*. Positions of moon in relation to sun were calculated with precision by Rishis, seers and astrologers of those days.

Moon in the scriptures is always given as an example to convey the message that mind is only a reflected consciousness. Mind and object being co-terminus, object perception, near or far is linked to mind.

In this world of many,
he who sees the One,
in this ever-changing world,
he who sees Him,
who never changes,
as the Soul of his own soul,
as his own Self,
he is free, he is blessed,
he has reached the goal.

Swāmi Vivekānanda

ध्रुवे तद्गतिज्ञानम् ॥२८॥

Dhruve Tada_Gati_Jnānam

Through concentration on the Pole Star
One gains knowledge of stars afar.

Dhruv: Pole Star *Tada*: that *Gati*: movement *Jnānam*: knowledge

Q. *How to know about the movement of stars?*
A. By practising *Samyama* on the Pole-Star, motion of the stars is known.

The movements of stars are observed with reference to the Pole Star. Different patterns or configurations of stars can be observed at different seasons like summer, spring, winter and fall. Pole Star is considered as an unmoving star. Actually, it is a very slow moving star and hence thought to be non moving. And since there is no movement, there is no time and hence, eternal.

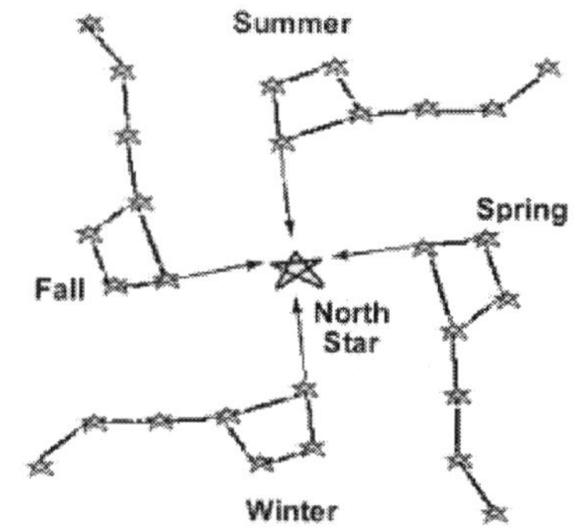

Hence, by concentrating on the Pole Star, one can gain knowledge about all stars and their movements. Concentration is not gazing intently at the star, but keeping the star as a mental object and practising *Samyama* on the same. It should be noted that movement can be known only in relation to a fixed one.

According to the boon granted in his boyhood by Lord Nārāyana, Dhruva became as it were, the crowing of the entire galaxy of stars. He became the lord of stars. To this day when Indians see the Pole Star they remember Dhruva, the devotee with perfect purity of mind. His fame is deathless.

He who inhabits in the sun, but is within it, whom the Sun does not know, whose body is the sun, and who controls the sun from within, is the internal ruler, your own immortal self.

Brihadāranyaka Upanishad

नाभिचक्रे कायव्यूहज्ञानम् ॥२९॥

Nābhi_Chakre Kāyavyuha_Jnānam.

On concentration on navel region
One gains knowledge of physical regime.

Nābhi: navel region
Chakre: plexus
Kāyavyuha: view of limbs of the body around
Jnānam: knowledge

Q. *How to know about one's body system?*
A. By *Samyama* on one's own navel plexus, one gains knowledge of the systems and constitution of the body.

Knowledge of organs and their functioning around the navel region could be obtained by *Samyama* on the navel region, says Patanjali. An explanation is possible, that by focusing on the region gives a sort of X-Ray of the region to the naked eye and knowledge about the functioning or mal-functioning is obtained by concentration.

One of the manifestations of *Prāna*, namely *Samāna* dwells in the middle of the body in the region between the heart and the navel and governs digestive system, liver, small intestines, pancreas, stomach, gall bladder etc. and the various secretions which they supply for digestion of food. *Samāna* also activates the heart and circulatory system. *Samāna* is responsible for equal assimilation and distribution of nutrients to sustain the body. Upanishads figuratively say that seven flames energise the system. Some opine and associate the flames with the digestive secretions such as **peptin, rennin, hydrochloric acid, pepsinogen, amylase, lipase and tryspin** released by the stomach, gall bladder, pancreas and liver to assist the food assimilation.

Yoga aims at knowing the body and its functions while the body is alive. It is unlike modern science that dissects the body to know how it would have worked while it was alive.

When the currents of bio energy flow unevenly,
their channels (*Nādis*-Nerves, arteries, veins)
attain an improper condition.
Because of the unevenness in the flow,
the food that is eaten causes
harm by bad digestion or indigestion.

Yogavāshishta

कण्ठकूपे क्षुत्पिपासानिवृत्तिः ॥३०॥

Kanthakupe Kshut_Pipāsā_Nivritih.

By absorption on the hollow of one's throat,
One gains freedom from thirst.

Kanthakupe: depth of throat *Kshut*: depth *Pipāsā*: thirst *Nivritih*: removal

Q. *How to gain freedom from hunger and thirst?*
A. By *Samyama* on the hollow of one's own throat (trachea), one gains complete freedom from hunger and thirst.

One is hungry when the water element in him liquefies the physical food, draws the essence of it inwards and exhausts the content of the food that one takes.

In a similar way, when the fire principle, in one, dries away the water, one feels thirsty. What is called thirst is the absorption of the water element in the system by the fire principle within one. By *Samyama* on the absorption process one can slow down the effect of fire principle to gain freedom from thirst. Yogis in the past did not want their concentration and contemplation disrupted by hunger or thirst. By *Samyama* on the hollow of one's own throat (trachea) they gained complete freedom from thirst.

There is absorption of the grosser element of earth (solid food) into the finer element of water, the finer element of water into the subtler element of fire and ultimately the fire element into the ultimate reality. The ultimate cause is that which is not absorbed into a higher cause. The absorption process ceases when the ultimate cause (from the empirical point of view) is reached.

Though, initially there is effort in ensuring lack of hunger and thirst, once the seeker attains the state of absorption, with the vanishing of the body consciousness, hunger and thirst vanish too. The illumined need no physical food to sustain themselves.

Kahola, son of Kausitaka: Which is within all, Yājnawalkya?
Yāgyawalkya: That which transcends hunger and thirst is within all.

Brihadāranyaka Upanishad

At a glance: Aphorism 3.26-3.30

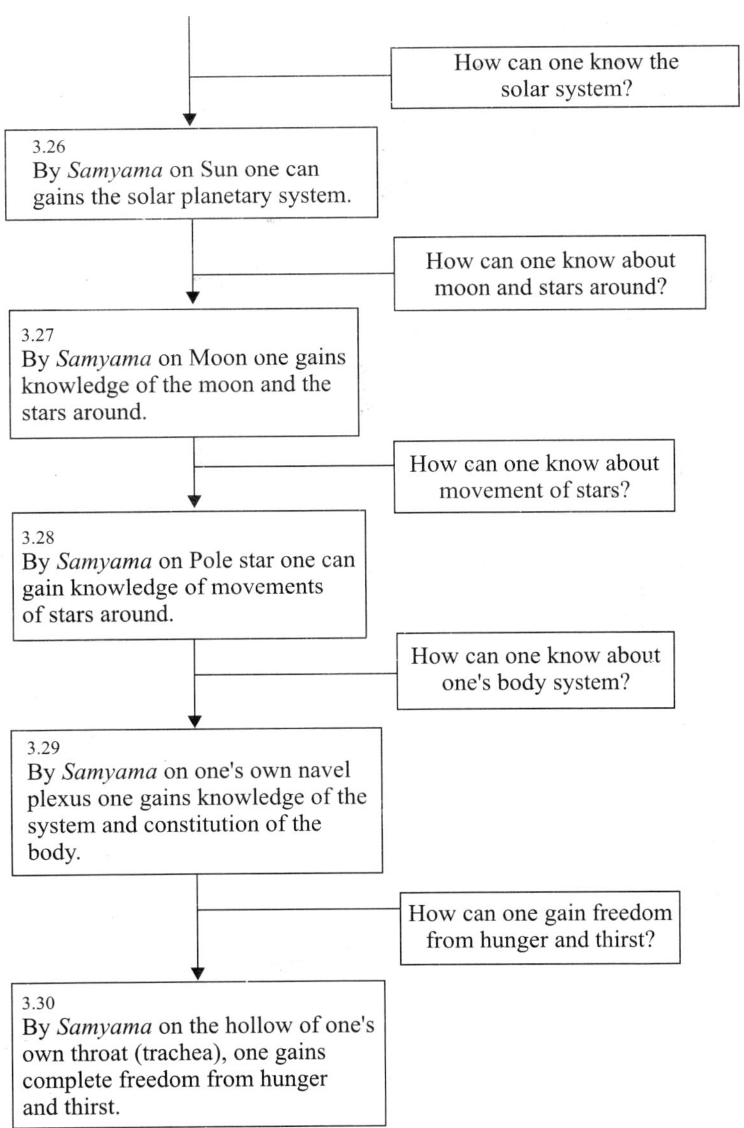

कूर्मनाड्यां स्थैर्यम् ॥३१॥

Kurma_Nādyām Sthairyam.

On concentration on throat and cavity,
One becomes calm and steady.

Kurma: tortoise (shaped) *Nādyām*: nerve *Sthairyam*: steadiness

Q. *How can one acquire qualities of calmness and tranquillity?*

A. By *Samyama* on one's own bronchial tube one gains qualities of calmness and tranquillity.

Samyama on *Kurma nādi* (the astral tube in the chest, below the throat) gives steadiness to the body. We shall have to remember here from physiology that there are two kinds of action of the nerve currents, one afferent or sensory, which carries the sensations inward to the brain, and the other efferent or motor, from the brain outward to the body.

There are ten subtle nerve tubes through which the nerve currents or *prāna* moves. Out of these ten *nādis*, the principal *nādis* are three: *idā*, *pingalā*, and *sushumnā*. Again, among these three *nādis* the *sushumnā* located in the spinal column is the most important for Yogis. *Sushumnā* plays a great part in *prānāyāma*. Through certain *prānāyāma* and concentration, Yogis withdraw *prāna* from the *idā* and *pingalā* consciously and take it to *sushumnā*, which will become active. When the *idā* and *pingalā nādis* are devitalized by the operation of *sushumnā nādi* there is no night or day for the Yogi. When the *sushumnā* is in operation, the Yogi can transcend the limitation of time and space.

The meaning of the Sanksrit word '*nādi*' is to be understood correctly. *Nādi* is generally translated as nerve, but nadis are not nerves. Nerves are physical matter, while *nādis* are astral matter. *Nadis* are visible like currents of light to the one who is illumined.

Just as myrobalans (plum like fruits) produce purging by their very nature,
the mind attains to purity on account of contemplation, chanting of *Mantras*,
doing rituals and by service to the virtuous.
Then happiness grows.

Yogavāshishta

मूर्धज्योतिषि सिद्धदर्शनम् ॥३२॥

Murdha_Jyotishi Siddha_Darshanam.

On the head when there is absorption,
Begets one, of saints vision.

Murdha: head
Jyotishi: brightness
Siddha: realised people
Darshanam: visibility, appearance

Q. *How can one see saints or the realised souls?*
A. By concentrated absorption (*Samyama*) on the spinal area back of one's head, one sees all saints and celestial beings.

There are three planes of existence, the physical, astral and causal. Some saints and sages, living in the astral plane communicate through vibrating energy. On *Samyama* on the concerned area, one can synchronise his vibration with that of the saint or the sage he wishes to communicate and establish a channel of communication.

It is believed that saints and angels live amidst men, but in a subtle unrecognizable form, invisible to one. One's communication to them or for that matter their communication the other way, remain shut, since one's mind is focused on the objective world. Once, the seeker makes good progress, the spiritual path opens up. Thus, visions of chosen deities and saints are obtained.

Several saints and prophets have claimed that what they say is truth because they have directly heard it from the 'heaven', meaning thereby that they have established communication with higher forces and that the message delivered to them is what is being conveyed by them. The hearing of *Asharira-vāni*, the voice of the one who is un-embodied is common folklore in India. The realised souls who have attained the state of *Samādhi* and have voluntarily left their bodies are stated to be living in the astral plane. By *Samyama* the seeker hears from them.

Controlling exhalation (*Rechaka*) thus restraining the interior of *Nādis* (Nerves, veins and arteries), when the energy of the *Kundalini* flowing ırough the *Brahma Nādi*, gets established for a *muhoorta* (48 minutes) then there is the vision of the celestial beings.

Yogavāshishta

प्रातिभाद्वा सर्वम् ॥३३॥

Pratibhādvā Sarvam.

On concentration and absorption,
Everything gets known by intuition.

Pratibhād: due to intuition *Vā*: or *Sarvam*: everything, all knowledge

Q. *How can one have all the powers described thus far?*
A. All powers described thus far can come about with *Samyama* to the seeker who has risen to the state of highest illumination.

'*Pratibhā*' means flashing of inner light. It is an intuitive knowledge that comes about in reaction to any object presented before the seeker. This intuitive knowledge is always faultless.

There are three kinds of knowledge:

Instinctive
Deliberative
Intuitive

1. The animal kingdom operates with instinctive knowledge. For instance, if an animal smells a poisonous flower or seed, it will instinctively withdraw and avoid eating the same.
2. The deliberative is the normal man's knowledge, based on reason and logic.
3. Intuition is letting intelligence speak with no hindrance.

   Intuitive knowledge is always better than inferential one. In the later case it is the logical mind that infers based on information stored and fed into it. Intuitive knowledge just occurs. Often we hear people saying that it just occurred to them that they decided to act one way or the other because of their instinct. On continuous practice, seekers rely more on intuitive knowledge and less on inferential.

The pure Self is the universal intelligence. Universal intelligence pervades every being. It is because of ignorance, the intelligence is veiled. Once ignorance ceases, automatically intelligence operates.

Like the sharp edge of a razor,
that path is difficult to cross and hard to tread;
thus say the wise.

Katha Upanishad

हृदय चित्तसंवित् ॥३४॥

Hridaye Chitta_Samvit

Through absorption on heart,
Knowledge about mind can be had.

Hridaye: heart *Chitta*: of the mind *Samvit*: knowledge

Q. *How can knowledge of consciousness be gained?*
A. By concentrated absorption (*Samyama*) on one's heart, knowledge of consciousness can be gained.

The brain, the neck and the heart are three centres of consciousness. '*Hridaya*' literally means 'Here inside is He' The heart here means, as it so often does in the Upanishads, the interior, spiritual nature, the consciousness of the spiritual man. It is mortal, not physical. Patanjali tells us that inside the heart is all the mystery of things. Every object of one's desire is in his heart. Through *Samyama* when one dwells deep into one's heart, he understands how his mind works and thinks the way it does.

Knowing tendencies helps one in cutting out tendencies. That is the reason some sages suggest that one must watch the way his mind moves. Watching it would calm it. One of the best ways to avoid mental modification is to watch the tendencies in a dispassionate manner.

The heart centre is considered extremely important. There is a lotus flower with eight petals in the heart centre (figuratively speaking). Before meditation it is in the form of a bud with the petals closed and drooping; but during meditation it stands erect and blossoms.

Avidyā, Kāma and *Karma*, ignorance, desire and action, are known as the knots of the heart. By *Samyama* on the heart centre the knots are loosened. One understands one's desires and causes thereof and thus cuts at the root of his ignorance.

Beings endowed with life are superior to gross matter;
superior to the later are creatures with breath;
superior still are those endowed with a rudimentary consciousness;
still superior are those with sense organs.

Bhāgavata

सत्त्वपुरुषयोरत्यन्तासङ्कीर्णयोः प्रत्ययाविशेषो भोगः
परार्थत्वात् स्वार्थ संयमात् पुरुषज्ञानम् ॥३५॥

Sattva_Purusayor Atyanta_Asankirnayoh Pratyaya_Avishesho Bhogah Para_Arthatvāt Swārtha_Samyamāt Purusha_Jnānam.

The Self and the quality of clarity,
Each is a distinct entity.
The qualities, the Self does not make.
Self exists for its own sake.
By absorption on the Self
Gains one awareness of the same.

Sattva: purity, clarity
Purusayoh: consciousness
Atyanta: totally, completely
Asankirnayoh: distinct, unmixed
Pratyaya: idea, concept
Avishesho: with no distinction
Bhogah : experience
Pararthatvāt: for the purpose of another
Swārtha: for its own, self interest
Samyamāt: absorption
Purusha: consciousness, Self
Jnāna: knowledge

Q. *Is pure consciousness and quality of clarity one and the same?*
A. No. The Self is independent of any quality. The qualities like clarity exist for serving the Self. The Self and the quality are different entities. In the Self there is no ego. By *Samyama* on the Self one can get clear knowledge about the Self.

Patanjali cautions the seeker that it is easily possible that the seeker misunderstands and confuses the serenity and calmness of the state of clarity to be that of the state of realisation of the Self. These two states are quite distinct. The Self, the pure consciousness is independent of the state of clarity, referred to as *Sattva*. The Self exists on its own, for its own sake. *Samyama* on the consciousness gives one awareness of the Self. Due to ignorance one mistakes the joy inspired by quality of clarity to be the Bliss of the Self. The *Sāttvic* joy pales into insignificance in comparison with that of the Bblissful state of *samādhi*. In that blissful state, there is no false ego left. In the blissful state on attaining the awareness of Self, there is neither an experiencer nor an experience.

The inability of science to solve life is absolute.
This fact would be truly frightening,was it not for faith?
The mystery of life is certainly the most persistent problem
ever placed before the thought of man.

Marconi

At a glance: Aphorism 3.31-3.35

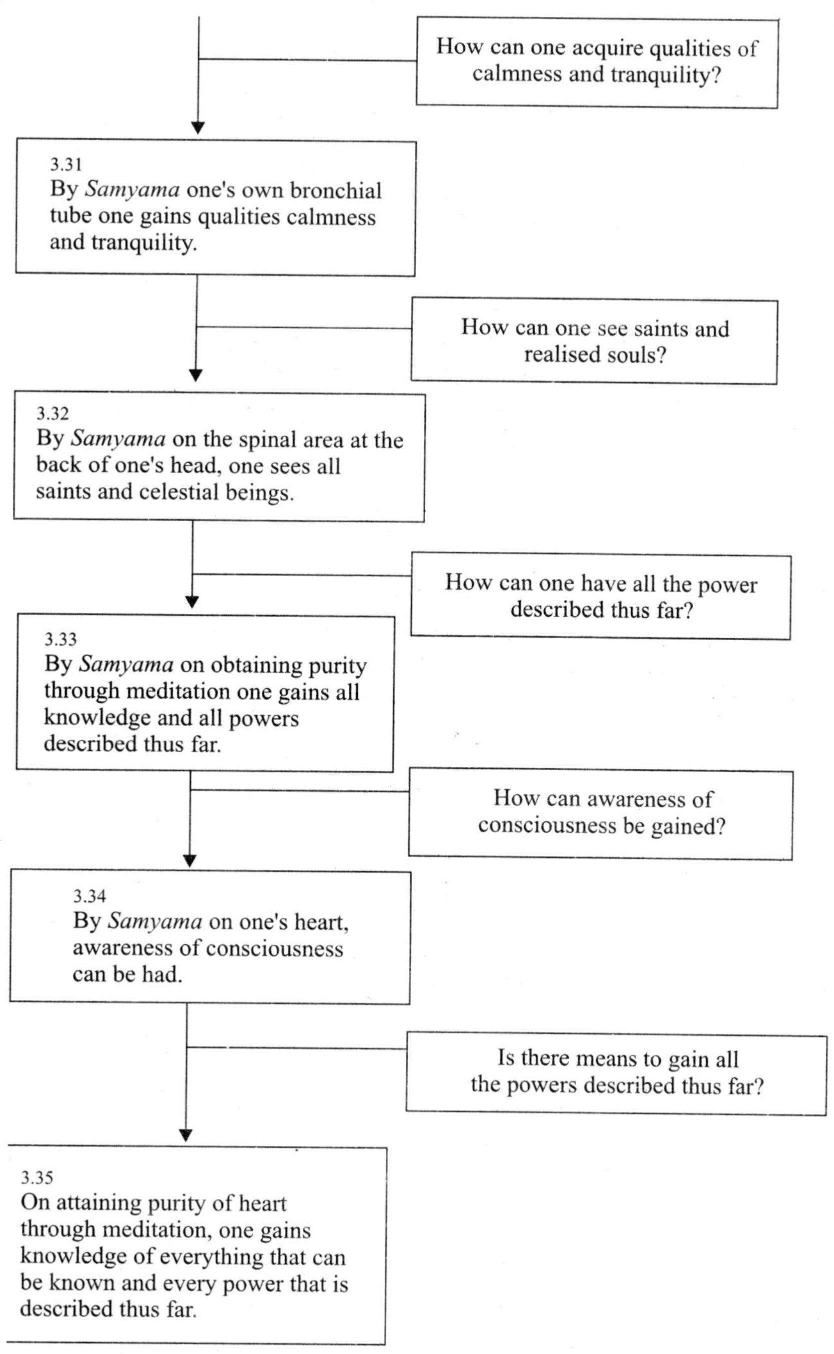

ततः प्रातिभश्रावणवेदनादर्शास्वादवार्ता जायन्ते ॥३६॥

Tatah Prātibha_Shrāvan_Vedanā_Ādarsha_Āsvāda_Vārtā Jāyante.

Thence arises knowledge intuitive
When one becomes supra sensitive.

Tatah: thence (from realisation of the self)
Prātibha: intuitive knowledge
Shrāvan: listening
Vedanā: feeling (through touch)
Ādarsha: through the sense of sight
Āsvāda: through the sense of taste
Jāyante: arise

Q. *On gaining awareness of the SELF, what happens?*
A. On gaining awareness one gains extraordinary sense perceptions. One can see without seeing, hear without listening, smell without the use of his nose.

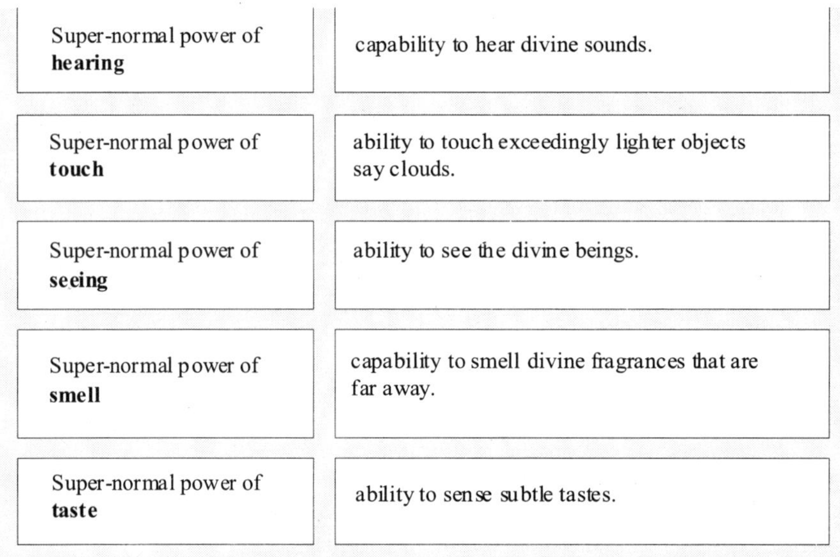

Super-normal power of **hearing**	capability to hear divine sounds.
Super-normal power of **touch**	ability to touch exceedingly lighter objects say clouds.
Super-normal power of **seeing**	ability to see the divine beings.
Super-normal power of **smell**	capability to smell divine fragrances that are far away.
Super-normal power of **taste**	ability to sense subtle tastes.

It should be noted that even as the seeker continues to practise and attempts at the withdrawal of his senses from the external objective world, his sensory perceptions become stronger. Here lies the danger. Since perceptions are stronger, temptations to yield to the senses are also strong. Hence vigilance is needed.

The Realm of Reality is there, from where the mind along with speech returns disappointed.

Taittiriya Upanishad

ते समाधावुपसर्गा व्युत्थाने सिद्धयः ॥३७॥

Samādhāv_Upasargā Vyutthāne Siddhayah.

Absorption is attainments,
In the waking state, obstacles.

Te: they *Samādhav*: in the state of absorption *Upasargā*: obstacles
Vyutthāne: in the waking state *Siddhayah*: attainment

Q. *Are these attainments unmixed blessings?*
A. No. They are double edged weapons. The attainments in the state of absorption can turn into obstacles in the waking state.

Knife can be used to cut a fruit or a throat. In the hands of the undisturbed one, the knife damages not, but helps. On the way to attaining the ultimate, the road is infested with many attractions. If one stays behind, he may stray from the chosen path.

Attainments are signposts en route. Patanjali pauses and cautions the seeker again not to stray but stay steadfast.

Even the mighty Shankara stays behind, lost in the new found royalty and family, when he enters the body of the about to die king Amaraka. The sensory pleasure provided by the kingdom and two wives of Amaraka was too much for even Shankara to resist and forsake. When Shankara used his attainments to enter the body of Amaraka, he was taking the risk of allowing himself to be deluded. Not until he was reminded of who he really was, did Shankara wake up and move away from the body of Amaraka. Not every body is gifted with that capacity. Countless seekers slide down deeply.

Only a dispassionate seeker can remain indifferent to the attainments and let them pass. Such a one is neither enamoured of them nor detests them.

The subtler the power, the greater is the difficulty of not using it. Knife can be thrown away. *Attainments have to be lived with until one merges with eternity.*

Live in that delight.
That Delight-Consciousness, is the God in you.
He is in every heart.
You need not go anywhere to find Him.
Find your own core and feel Him there.
Peace, bliss, felicity, health - everything is in you.
Trust in the Divine in you.
Entrust yourself to His Grace.
Be as you are, off with past impressions.

Thāyumānavar

बन्धकारणशैथिल्यात् प्रचारसंवेदनात्च चित्तस्य परशरीरावेशः ॥३८॥

Bandha_Kārana_Shaithilyāt Prachāra_Samvedanāt_Cha Chittasya Para_Sharira_Āveshah.

Continuous absorption
Causes bondage disintegration.
Thus freed mind
Can with another bind.

Bandha: binding *Kārana*: causative *Shaithilyāt*: on disintegration
Prachāra: being used *Samvedanāt*: by absorption *Cha*: and
*Chitta*sya: mind *Para*: others *Sharira*: body *Āveshah*: entry

Q. *How can consciousness be transferred to another body?*
A. When the cause of bondage gets weakened by regular practice, the movements of the mind are known and then the mind can get into another body.

Shankarāchārya, the saint philosopher par excellence chanced to debate with a famous scholar named Mandana Mishra, Many learned persons gathered for the debate and Bhārati, the saintly wife of the scholar, was chosen to be the judge and moderator. At the outset of the debate Bhārati placed a garland of flowers around the neck of each of the two contestants. She proclaimed that at the end of the discussion whoever was wearing the garland which had not withered would be the winner.

Mandana, who had never known defeat, opened the debate by stating: "I accept the authority of the Vedas. Their main teaching is that merit can be acquired by the performance of the prescribed rituals in the prescribed manner. When the merit is exhausted, he will return to earth so that he can acquire more pious credits for a longer stay in the world of the gods." The audience, consisting of many of Mandana's admirers and disciples, applauded his statement.

Shankarāchārya then responded, "I also accept the authority of the Vedas. Their main purpose, however is this: Brahman alone is real; the phenomenal world is an illusion; and the individual soul is identical with Brahman........ Rituals can only lead to *Karma*, both good and bad, which prevents one from attaining self-realsation. *The only goal of the Vedas is Brahman.*"

When the vital air is established outside the nostrils
for a long time by the practice of exhalation of breath,
one enters into another body.

Yogavāshishta

Both the scholars showed profound knowledge of the Vedas in various ways, Finally however Shankara won. Mandana Mishra had to admit defeat. In a final attempt to save her husband, Bhārati said, "Oh Great *Ācharya*, you are certainly victorious in the debate with my husband and he will have to become your disciple. However, I, the wife of Mandana Mishra, am his better half. Before your victory is complete you will have to defeat me also." Shankarāchārya was somewhat surprised, but he accepted the challenge.

Addressing Shankarāchārya, Bhārati said, "I can not admit that you are the master of all learning unless you can prove that you have a good understanding of sex education also. Now, tell me, what are the various forms and expressions of love? What is the nature of sexual love? What is the effect of the waxing and waning moons on sex urge in men and women? You must answer all these questions."

Being a celibate monk and only sixteen-year-old, it appeared as though Shankarācharya had been bewildered by-his opponent. He then asked for forty days additional time since he was not prepared to speak on the subject immediately. Bhārati granted the request and Shankarāchārya and his disciples left the assembly. Through the powers of mystic Yoga Shankarāchārya entered into trance. He left his body and entered the body of a sensuous king named Amaraka. Shankara asked his disciples to take care of his body. In the body of the king, Shankara experienced erotic love and acquired knowledge of all its intricacies.

The new king "Shankara Amaraka" proved to be a brilliant and just ruler, winning admiration of all in the kingdom. But the king's two wives soon realised that something extraordinary had happened. For the new Amaraka showed not only youthful energy but seemed a novice in the art of love and was learning the same. They realised that some great saint had entered their husband's body. They instructed their private soldiers to look for any dead body and immediately burn the same. Meanwhile Shankara had lost knowledge about who he really was and was too preoccupied with the affairs of the kingdom to think of anything else. He began to believe he was Amaraka and not Shankara. The disciples of Shankara realised that Shankara seemed to have forgotten about himself and showed no inclination to return. Since monks were not allowed in the king's court, they disguised themselves as musicians and got Shankara's audience. Then they began to sing a poem called, "*Moha Mudgaram*" which runs thus: "Strange are the ways of the world and vast thy ignorance. Who is thine wife and who thy son? What art thou, and where cometh thou from? Ponder this in thine heart and bow to God." Shankara realised and quickly re-entered his original body. Before the forty days had ended he returned to debate with Bhārati. After a brief discussion, Bhārati conceded that Shankara was the undisputed winner.

"Rāghava! Know that as the mind which perceives reality in unreality; on account of mental impressions solely of objects, the mind which is of firm habit and extremely fickle, becomes the cause of birth, old age and death."

Yogavāsishta

उदानजयाज्जलपङ्ककण्टकादिष्वसङ्गः उत्क्रान्तिश्च ॥३९॥

Udāna_Jayāt Jala_Panka_Kantaka_Ādishu_Asangah Utkrāntih_Cha.

Controlling vital air within,
One can begin
To walk on thorn or water
Or move in space outer.

Udāna: the vital air within called "*Udāna*" *Jayāt*: conquering, controlling
Jala: water *Panka*: mire *Kantaka*: thorn
Ādishu: etcetera, and so on *Asangah*: having no connection
Utkrāntih: movement in space (occurs) *Cha*: and

Q. *What powers are attained by controlling Udāna?*
A. By controlling vital air within called '*Udāna*', one can get powers to levitate (waken the gravitational forces), move in outer space, walk on water or on a thorny surface without hurting one's feet.

The parts of the body above the larynx are controlled by *Udāna*. The eyes, the nose, the ears are activated by this vital force *Udāna*. The ascension of *Kundalini* is ascribed to *Udāna*. Without this vital force, one would not be able to think or be conscious of the outer world.

Udāna	
	Vital air *Udāna* is the vehicle of transport for all.
	It helps swallowing of food.
	It takes one to consciousness during deep sleep.
	Its abode is the throat.
	Vital air *Udāna* draws out the subtle body from the gross body at the time of death.

The vital air *Udāna* moves out with the subtle body from the gross body at the time of death. It is this subtle body that goes to heaven and works in the dreaming state. By controlling the *Udāna* one can move to the higher worlds, even as not controlling could result in one getting back to the objective world. The liberated beings with their minds purified by renunciation and with knowledge of the imperishable *Ātman* are completely absorbed at the time of death. There is no return to this world for them.

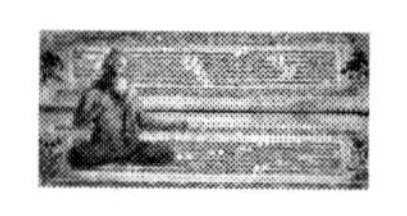

From the whole, when the whole is negated,
what remains is again the whole.

Upanishadic Shānti Pātha

The Prashnopanishad states: "Now, by one of the *nādis* (astral nerves) *Udāna* flows upwards. By performing righteous actions men are carried to virtuous worlds. By sinful (those acts that are binding one further to this earthly world), one is carried to the sinful world (world of unsatisfied desires). By combining both sinful and virtuous acts, one is carried to the human world.

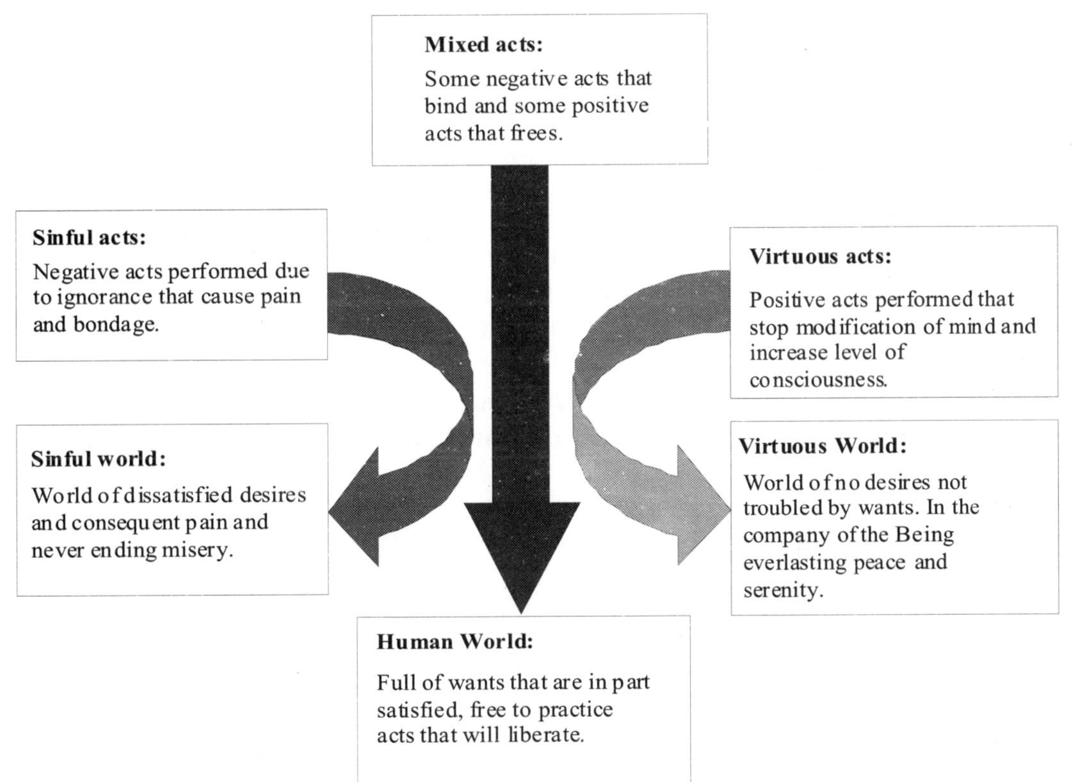

When the vital air *Udāna* is filled in restrained within, after filling up through inhalation, then one floods the body in entirety with *Prāna* or vital energy. Through exercises such discipline gravitational forces and their effect on the body is nullified. Since gravitational forces do not work, there is no pulling down. In the absence of forces pulling down, the corollary possibilities are like walking on water, moving through the sky and walking on a thorny surface. Going higher up could also be interpreted to mean rising to higher levels of consciousness. The gravitational pull down is due to attachments that pull one down. When freed from attachments / ignorance, rising to higher levels of knowledge (gaining higher knowledge) automatically happens. *Avidyā* is a pull down factor, while Yoga is the release factor att ained on negating the pull down factor. The thorny surface referred to in the aphorism could be interpreted to mean the thorny surface of *Avidyā*, *Asmitā*, *Rāga* and *Dwesha*. Freed from these pulling down entities, the Self can fly high.

Totāpuri, a *digambara* monk, is reputed to have lived to be 300-year-old. Totapuri was the guru that initiated Sri Rāmakrishna's enlightenment. Totāpuri, as an orthodox wandering monk never remained more than three days in one location. However, he became so awed by Rāmakrishna's ability in *Samādhi* to remain 'rigid as a corpse for days on end', that he broke his longstanding rule, resulting in him staying eleven months at Dakshineswar hoping to learn from the man who had previously been his disciple.

During this long stay he contracted serious dysentery. There was prolonged and severe pain, which was distracting Totāpuri during meditation. Since, he considered the body just a medium, essentially unnecessary after the realsation of the Absolute, he decided to give up his body by drowning in the Ganges. He walked out into the river, but, even though the river should have been extremely deep, at least in the middle, no matter how far he went the water never got above his knees. He ended up without ever reaching deep water. Eventually he came upon the bank on the far side and when he turned to look back, he saw the Kāli temple gleaming in moonlight and experienced a sudden deep awakening. He recognized sheer divine power and consciousness, moving through all beings and controlling all events, including his own attempt to discard the body. Totāpuri thus accepted the manifest universe and its energy as a radiant expression of the Absolute. The demarcation between form and formless no longer existed for him.

Arthur Osborne, Ramana's biographer writes in *Ramana Maharshi and the Path of Self-knowledge* (York Beach: Samuel Weiser, Inc., 1995, pages 96-97):

About a year after his first meeting with Sri Bhagavān, Ganapati Muni experienced a remarkable outflow of his Grace. While he was sitting in meditation in the temple of Ganapati at Tiruvottiyur he felt distracted and longed intensely for the presence and guidance of the Bhagavān. At that moment Sri Ramana entered the temple. Ganapati prostrated himself before him and, as he was about to rise, he felt the Maharshi's hand upon his head and a terrifically vital force coursing through his body from the touch; so that he also received Grace by touch from the Master. Speaking about this incident in later years, not Ganapati Muni, but the enlightened sage himself, Sri Ramana Maharshi said: "One day, some years ago, I was lying down and awake when I distinctly felt my body rise higher and higher. I could see the physical objects below growing smaller and smaller until they disappeared and all around me was a limitless expanse of dazzling light. After some time I felt the body slowly descend and the physical objects below began to appear. I was so fully aware of this incident that I finally concluded that it must be by such means that sages travel over vast distances in a short time and Appear and Disappear in such a mysterious manner. While the body thus descended to the ground it occurred to me that I was at Tiruvottiyur though I had never seen the place before. I found myself on a high road and walked along it. At some distance from the roadside was a temple of Ganapati and I entered it."

We have forgotten the prayers you taught us

The great Leo Tolstoy wrote a delightful folktale, *The Three Hermits*.

His friend Nocholas Roerich summarized it as follows.

On an island there lived three old hermits. They were famous for their simplicity, devotion and dedication to God. They were embodiment of honesty, truth and sincerity. All people in the island respected them and admired their simplicity and honesty. They were so simple the only prayer they used was: "We are three.

Thou art three. Have mercy on us!." Great miracles were manifested during their naive prayers. The local Bishop came to know about the three hermits and their inadmissible prayer and decided to visit them in order to teach them the canonical invocations. He arrived on the island, told the three hermits that their heavenly petition was undignified, and taught them many of the customary prayers.

The satisfied Bishop was returning in a ship. The Bishop did not wish to sleep, but sat alone at the stern, gazing at the sea where the island was no longer visible, and thinking of the good old men. He thought how pleased they had been to learn the Lord's prayer; and he thanked God for having sent him to teach and help such godly men.

Suddenly he saw something white and shining, on the bright path which the moon cast across the sea. The Bishop fixed his eyes on it, wondering as it approached he discerned that the three hermits, who were holding hands and running upon the waves in an effort to overtake the vessel. The Bishop fixed his eyes on them, wondering. The Bishop exclaimed, "Oh Lord! The hermits are running after us on the water as though it were dry land!"

All three were gliding along upon the water without moving their feet. Before the ship could be stopped, the hermits had reached it, and raising their heads, all three as if in one voice, said: "We have forgotten your teaching. As long as we kept repeating it we remembered, but when we stopped saying it for a time, a word dropped out and now it has all gone to pieces. We can remember nothing of it. Teach us again."

The awed Bishop shook his head. "Dear ones," he replied humbly, "Dear ones, continue to live with your old prayer."

Mind is like a forest with thought forms for its trees and cravings for its creepers.
If the mind ceases to be, body ceases to be too on account of the cessation of thought force and mental conditioning, but mind does not cease to be when the body dies.

Yogavāshishta

समानजयाज्ज्वलनम् ॥४०॥

Samāna_Jayāt Jvalanam.

On controlling vital air
One radiates.

Samāna: the vital air within called *Samāna* *Jayāt*: conquering
Jvalanam: radiance

Q: *What is the effect of controlling Samāna?*
A: By mastering *Samāna* one dazzles with radiance.

The word *Samāna* is derived from *samam* which means equal and balanced. It is responsible for equal and balanced assimilation of foods and nutrients to sustain the body. *Samāna* abides *in the middle of the body, in the region between the heart and navel.*

Samāna	The vital air called *Samāna:* • *Samāna* resides in the middle of the body. • The heat in the bodies of living creatures which is circulated all over the system by the breath is controlled by the vital air called *Samāna.* • When vital air *Samāna* becomes extinct all the life-winds become extinct in the bodies of living creatures.

Samāna relates to the *sushmnā nādi*. "*Samāna* is the priest, *hotā*. He maintains the equilibrium between the inhalation and exhalation: the two oblations. The mind is the sacrificer. *Udāna* is the fruit of the sacrifice", says Prashnopanishad. The strength provided to the body through natural breathing is due to the effect of the vital force *Samāna*. *Samāna* dwells in the middle of the body in the region between the heart and the navel and governs digestive system, liver, small intestine, pancreas, stomach, gall bladder etc. and the various secretions which they supply for digestion of food. *Samāna* also activates the heart and circulatory system. *Samāna* is responsible for equal assimilation and distribution of nutrients to sustain the body.

'The wind nursed by *Prāna* afterwards takes birth in *Apāna*.
The wind nursed in *Apāna* then becomes developed into *Vyāna*.
Nursed by *Vyāna*, the wind is then developed into *Udāna*.
Nursed in *Udāna*, the wind is then generated as *Samāna*.'

Upanishads figuratively say that seven flames energise the system. Some opine and associate the flames with the digestive secretions such as **peptin, rennin, hydrochloric acid, pepsinogen, amylase, lipase** and **tryspin** released by the stomach, gall bladder, pancreas and liver to assist the assimilation of food. But in the context of Upanishads, seven flames mean the power of strength gained by the two eyes, two ears, two nostrils and the mouth. Without nutrients, the power to recognize and perceive would gradually diminish and the organs will become weak.

Patanjali says that by *Samyama* on *Samāna* one can radiate. By regulation of the vital force *Samāna* begets one, strength to direct the flame of energy. The luminosity of a seeker increases with *Samyama* on *Samāna*.

Ramana Maharishi's biographer Arthur Osborne,

in *Ramana Maharshi And The Path of Self-Knowledge*

(York Beach: Samuel Weiser, Inc., 1995, pages 144-145)

writes:

Ramana would turn to the devotee, his eyes fixed upon him with blazing intentness. The luminosity, the power of his eyes pierced into one, breaking down the thought-process. Sometimes it was as though an electric current was passing through one, a vast peace, a flood of light. One devotee has described it: "Suddenly Bhagavān turned his luminous, transparent eyes on me. Before that I could not stand his gaze for long. Now I looked straight back into those terrible, wonderful eyes, how long I could not tell. They held me in a sort of vibration distinctly audible to me."

What is seen as you and I and what is seen as the dialogue
between us, are like two waves colliding
in the ocean and making a sound

Yogavāshishta

At a glance: Aphorism 3.36-3.40

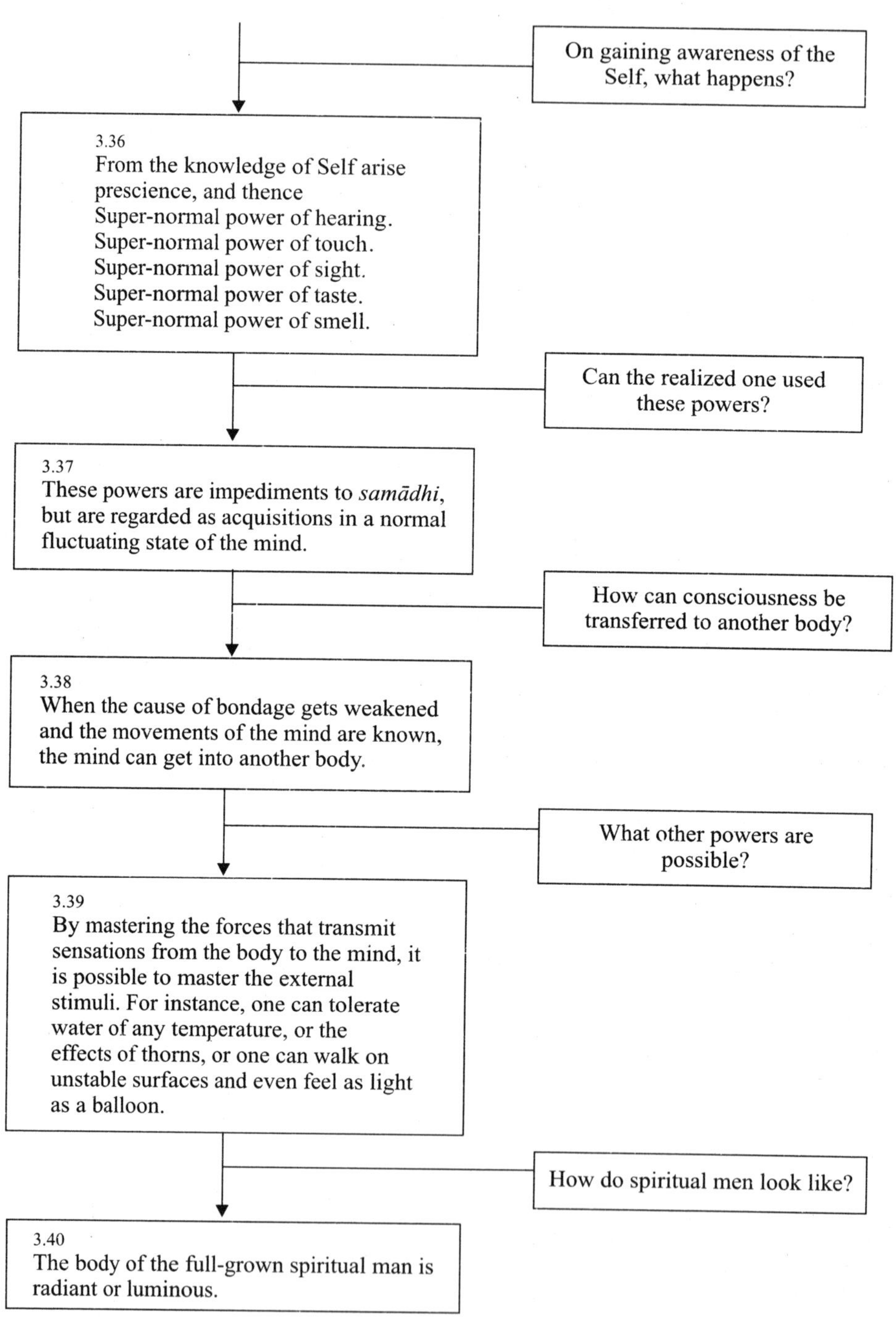

श्रोत्राकाशयोः संबंध संयमात् दिव्यम् श्रोत्रम् ॥४१॥

Shrotra_Ākāshayoh Sambandha_Samyamāt Divyam Shrotram.

On absorption on the link between ears and space
One attains the capacity to hear distant and subtle voice.

Shrotra: ears *Ākāshayoh*: space (both these together) *Sambandha*: association
Samyamāt: through absorption (on these) *Shrotram*: ears
Divyam: having capacity to hear distant, subtle and latent sounds

Q. *How is abnormal hearing capacity obtained?*
A. From perfectly concentrated meditation on the correlation of hearing and the ether, comes the power of spiritual hearing.

The transfer of a word by telepathy is the simplest and earliest form of the "divine hearing". From the Mahābhārata one notes that it is the divine seeing and hearing capacity of Sanjaya that enables him to describe what was happening at the Kurukshetra to the King Dhritarāshtra.

He is blessed indeed who can through *Samyama* fine tune himself with the celestial forces and divinely hear what they say. Knowledge so begot is unfailingly true. By *Samyama* on the link between ear and space, one attains capacity to hear the subtlest of the voice emanating through space. 'Speech is a distortion of truth' says a Sanskrit proverb. This is true in relation to speech of the humans. But hearing 'unspoken' and unseen voices is knowing the truth.

Scriptures claim authenticity and authority by saying, "It is God's word, directly heard from the celestial world. No permission is given to alter or modify what is claimed to have been the God's word."

The revelation 22:18-19 says: . . . 'If any man shall add to these things (or delete) God shall add unto him the plagues written in this book. 'Such is the faith in the truth of the 'heard'.

All which have form are false; the formless is the changeless.
The world of names and forms is only
the imagination of the total-mind.
It has no existence what-so-ever.
The Self is Undisturbed, Profoundly Peaceful and Ever -formless.

कायाकाशयोः संबन्ध संयमाद लघुतूलसमापत्ते आकाशगमनम् ॥४२॥

Kāyā_Ākāshayoh Sambandha_Samyamāt
Laghu_Tula_Samāpattey Ākāsha_Gamanam.

On absorption on the link between body and space
One attains lightness of cotton to move in space.

Kāyā: body
Akāshayoh: The space too
Sambandha: association
Samyamāt: arising from absorption
Laghu: light
Tula: cotton
Samāpattey: on attaining
Cha: and
Ākāsha: space
Gamanam: movement

Q: *How can one pass through sky?*

A: By practising *Samyama* on the relationship between the body and *ākāsha* and by concentrating on the lightness of cotton wool, passage through the sky can be secured.

Hindu mythology describes Lord Hanuman as Vayu's son,

Son of the Wind Deity, Ānjaneya can move about in space with even a mountain on his palm. Heaviness weighs down. Earth element, which is the last of the three elements to evolve, represents quality of inertia. Heaviness means gravitational pull. On the other hand lightness is *Sattva*, the quality of purity. By *Samyama* on the link between space and body, one can gain antigravity quality. The body consciousness in such a one is not there. Hence, he can move up and move about.

Mother, of the Aurobindo Āshram, while she was very sick, was reported to have 'moved around in space' to watch and observe things going around in the hermitage at Pondichery in India. The process of such moving by her is to remain still (thoughts totally stilled) and sending the consciousness around to watch and see.

Swāmi Yogānanda reports that he could move to his home town in India and watch the proceedings at home, while being physically present in California, on a lecture tour.

We are not punished for our sins
we are punished by our sins.

Gautama Buddha

बहिरकल्पिता वृत्तिर्महाविदेहा ततः प्रकाशवरणक्षयः ॥४३॥

Bahir_Akalpitā Vrittih_Mahāvidehā
Tatah Prakāsha_Āvarana_Kshayah.

State of awareness beyond the body one attains
And the veil on light dissipates.

Bahir: external to the body
Akalpitā: beyond imagination
Vrittih: mental mode
Mahā: great
Videhā: disembodied state
Tatah: thence
Prakāsha: brilliance
Āvarana: envelope
Kshayah: dissipation

Q. *How is veil over darkness removed?*

A. Veil of ignorance is removed by illumination. Darkness can only be removed by light. When one attains a state of awareness losing body consciousness altogether then dawns the lightness that dispels darkness of ignorance.

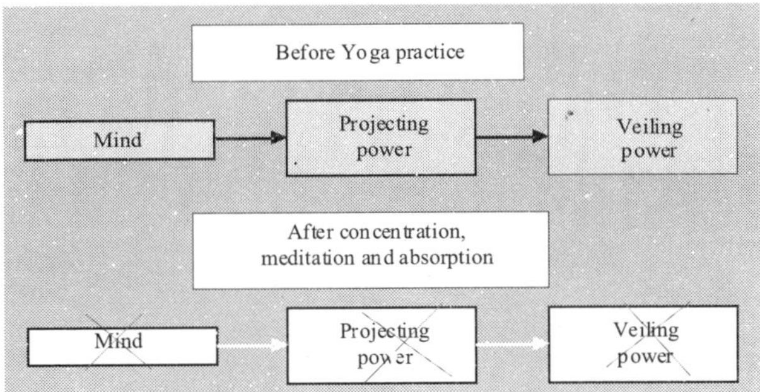

The veiling power vanishes on absorption, as the ability of objects to attract the senses vanishes. The veiling, the ideation and object orientation is the refraction. In the normal state, because of the entanglement with the complexity of perception, one sees many where there is only one. Because of the veiling, resulting from the projecting power of the mind, one remains under the illusion that there are millions of objects. On absorption, the *swa-rupa* is revealed and the *vritti-rupa* is gone. With the becoming gone, Being remains.

"I knew a man in Christ above fourteen years ago, (whether in the body, I cannot tell; or whether out of the body, I cannot tell: God knoweth;) such a one caught up to the third heaven. And I knew such a man, (whether in the body, or out of the body, I cannot tell: God knoweth;) how that he was caught up into paradise, and heard unspeakable [or, unspoken] words, which it is not lawful for a man to utter."

St. Paul

स्थूलस्वरूपसूक्ष्मान्वयार्थवत्त्वसंयमात्भूतजयः ॥४४॥

Sthula_Svarupa_Sukshma_Anvayaya_Arthavattva_Samyamāt Bhuta_Jayah.

On absorption on elements, gross and subtle
One attains over them, total control.

Sthula: gross elements *Svarupa*: form, basic characteristics *Bhuta*: elements
Anvayaya: all pervasive, the essential constituting principles
*Artha*vattva: meaningful *Samyamāt*: absorption *Jayah*: victory

Q. *How is mastery over elements obtained?*

A. Mastery over elements comes from concentrated absorption (*Samyama*) on their five forms: the gross, the elemental, the subtle, the inherent and the purposive. These five forms are analogous to those recognized by modern physics: solid, liquid, gaseous, radiant and ionic.

GROSS ELEMENTS

1. Ether/Space (Ionic), *Ākāsha*;
2. Air (Gaseous), *Vāyu*;
3. Fire – *Agni*, (radiant)
4. Water – *Jala*, (liquid)
5. Earth, - *Prithvi*, (Solid)

This body is organized and systematized by the atoms of these gross elements. A permutation and combination of these gross elements constitute the entire Gross World that we perceive. Our body too is a part of this world and hence made up of the 5 gross elements.

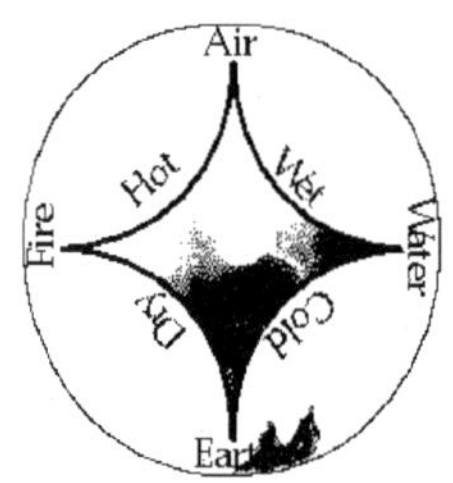

The Four Elements
according to Aristotle and Western Alchemy

SUBTLE ELEMENTS

1. Sound or *Shabda* (Ether. Space); 2. Touch or *Sparsha* (Earth); 3. Form or *Roopa* (Radiant); 4.Taste or *Rasa* (Water) ; 5. Smell or *Gandha* (Air). The subtle body is formed by the atoms of these subtle elements

"Inquire of the earth, the air, and the water,
of the secrets they hold for you.
The development of your inner senses
will enable you to do this."

ततोऽणिमादिप्रादुर्भावः कायसंपत् तद्धर्मानभिघातश्च ॥४५॥

Tatah_Animādi_Prādurbhāvah
Kāya_Sampat Tat_Dharma_Anabhighātah_Cha.

Thence becomes one minute
Body, unaffected by any attribute.

Tatah: after total control over elements — *Animā*: minuteness — *ādi* : etc
Prādurbhāvah: appearance — *Kāya*: body
Sampat: body's attributes — *Tat*: that — *Dharma*: features
Anabhighātah: not affected by — *Cha*: and

Q. *What follows the acquisition of power over elements?*
A. Thereupon will come the manifestation of being able to become minute. Body now not affected by the elements, reaches perfection and begets extraordinary capabilities.

Venerable Pindola Bharadvāja, one of the Buddha's sixteen disciples named in the *Amitābha Sutra*, attained the holy fruit of *Arhat*. Once, when in a jubilant mood, he said to the faithful:

"Do you think flying in the sky is magical?
I will show you some spectacular acts."
He then jumped up into the sky. He flew all around and performed many miraculous acts. The faithful were all impressed and praised him without ceasing.

The Buddha was very displeased upon learning of this incident. He asked the Venerable to come forth and admonished him, "My teaching uses morality to change others and compassion to save living beings. It does not use magic to impress and confuse people. You have misused magic today. As punishment you stay in this world to work for more merits and repent for this misbehavior."

When the five elements-earth, water, fire, air and space-
have been acquired and when yogic powers
(of becoming minute etc) have started functioning,
then the aspirant,
who has acquired a body by the fire of Yoga,
there is no disease, no decrepitude, no death."

Swāmi Vivekānanda

The eight attainments (powers)

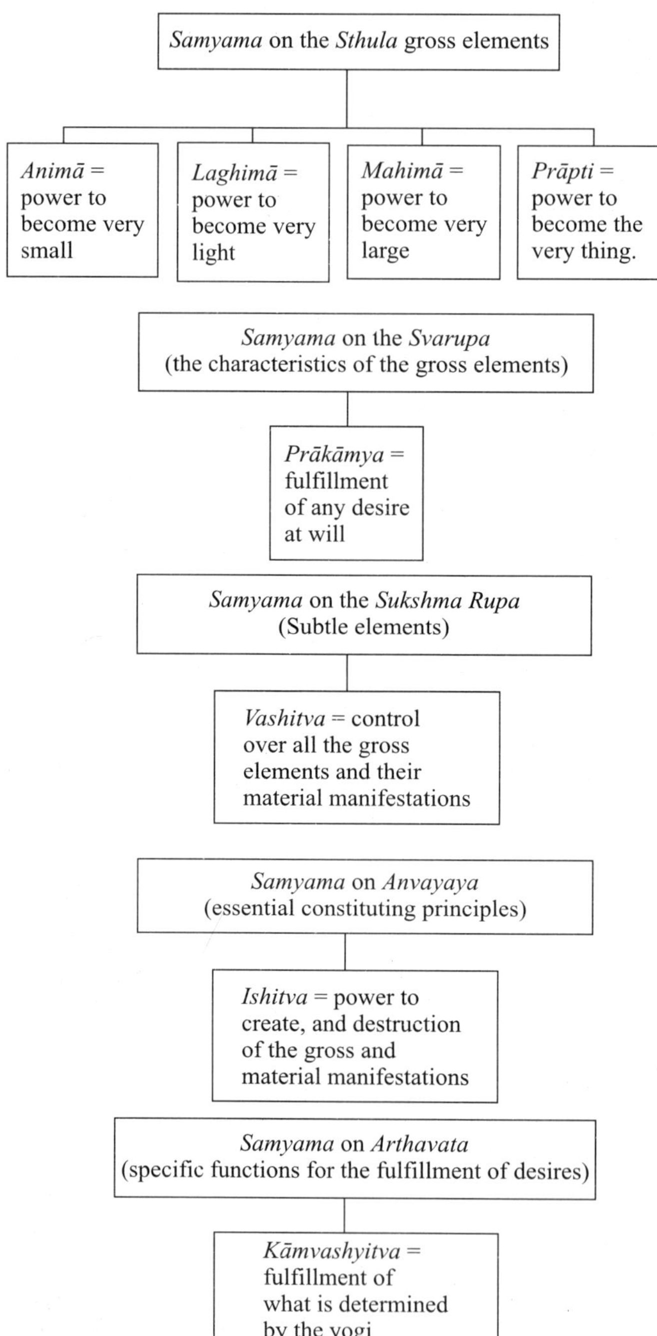

The Eight Attainments Ashta Siddhis:

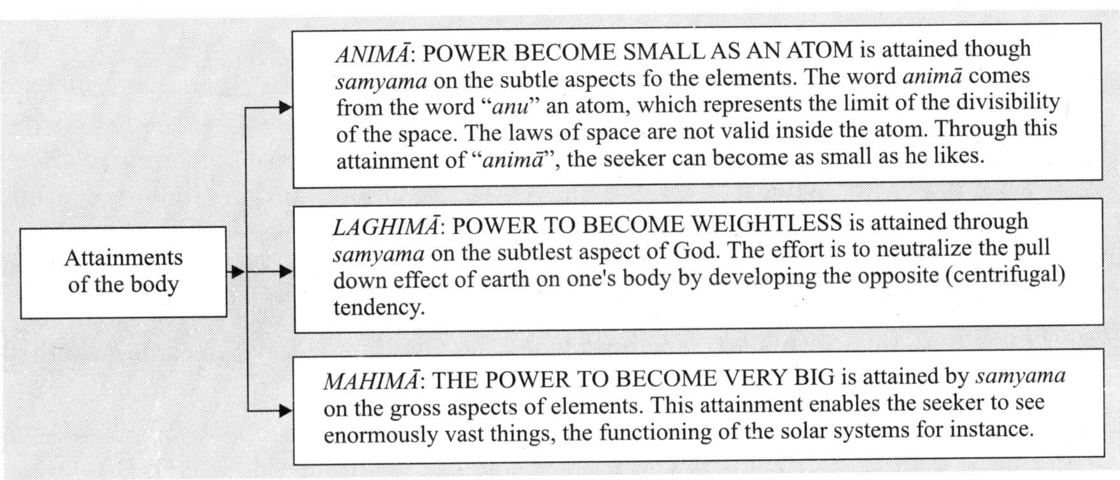

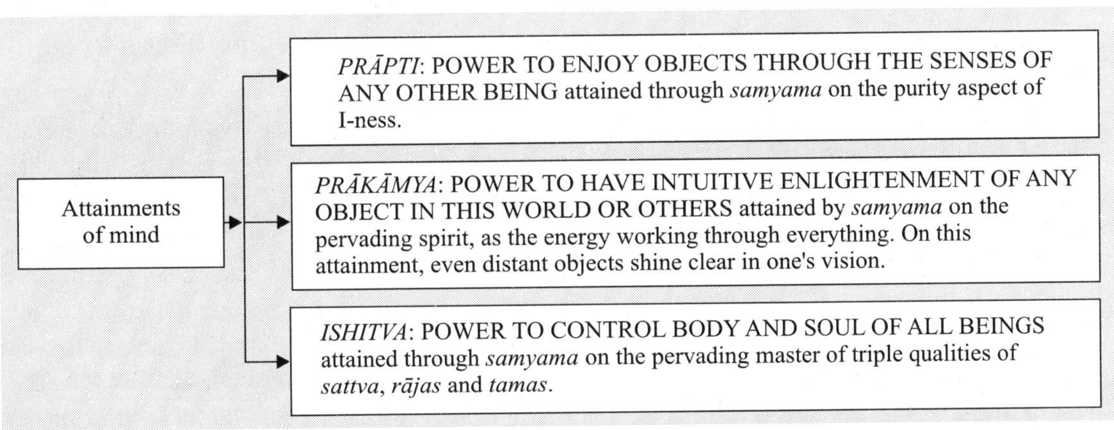

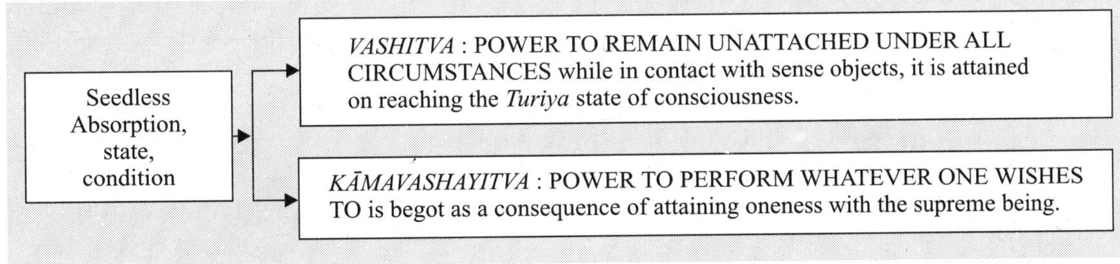

Hanumān humbles Bhima by his spiritual strength.

Once, Bhima and Draupadi were enjoying a day together during their *vanavāsa* (exile in the forest). Draupadi finds *Saugandhikam,* a flower of unusally sweet fragrance brought there by the wind. She expressed her desire to obtain more of them to Bhima, who promises to bring them to her, whether from the tops of the high mountains or from the worlds of the gods.

Bhima sets out into the forest in search of the *Saugandhikams,* beating a path often through the thick of the forest using his mighty *gadā* (mace). He approaches the Gandhamādana mountain in this pursuit.

Gandhamādana is the seat of meditation of Hanumān. Hanumān and Bhima are also half-brothers. (Vāyu, the wind-god, is their father). The meditating Hanumān is disturbed by the noise from the forest and is unable to concentrate. When he finds his brother Bhima is the cause, Hanumān decides to test Bhima's strength and to reduce his pride. He transforms himself into a frail old monkey and lies blocking Bhima's path.

Bhima approaches the old monkey and dares him to move away. The monkey replies he is too old to move but Bhima could move his tail out of the way and proceed. Bhima decides to tease the monkey by the tail and tries to move it using his club. He not only fails to move the monkey's tail, but also finds himself unable to extricate the club that got tied up with the tail, even with his legendary strength. Realizing this is not an ordinary monkey, Bhima requests him to reveal himself. Hanumān tells him who he was and Bhima pays all respects to his older brother. Bhima wishes to see the colossal form Hanumān assumed before jumping across the ocean to see Sitā. Hanumān cautions it might frighten Bhima, but Bhima insists, driven by the pride in his own strength. Hanumān displays his *vishwaroopam* (universal figure) which scares Bhima and chastens him. Hanumān later blesses Bhima, promising to help the Pandavas in their eventual war with the Kauravas. He also advises Bhima on where *Saugandhikams* were available. The brothers part with great affection for each other.

True wisdom never arises to a person who acts in consonance with what the people of the world will say or to a person who is concerned about his knowledge of the scriptures or who is subject to delusion about his body.

Ādi Shankara, Vivekachudāmani

At a glance: Aphorism 3.41-3.45

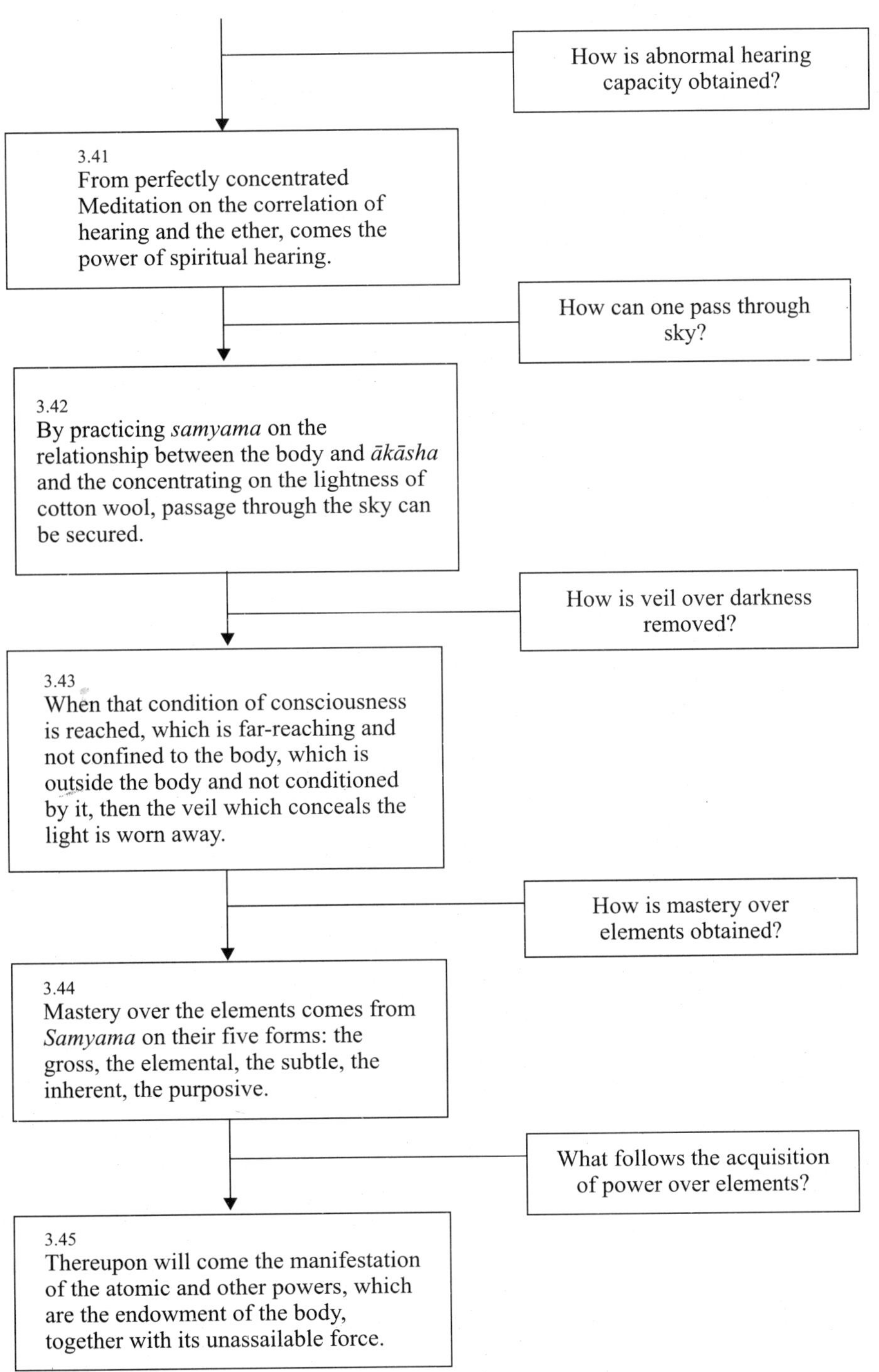

रुपलावण्यबलवज्रसंहननत्वानि कायसंपत् ॥४६॥

Rupa_Lāvanya_Bala_Vajrasamhananatvāni Kāya sampat.

Temper of a diamond, good form and beauty
Are the endowments of that body.

Rupa: form, shapeliness *Lāvanya*: charm, beautiful *Bala*: strong, forceful
Vajrā: temper of the diamond *Samhananatvāni*: association of limbs
Kāya: body *Sampat*: endowments

Q. *How will the body of the realised one be?*
A. Form, grace, beauty, force, the temper of diamond: are the endowments of that body.

The one personality that immediately comes to our mind as a personification of all qualities that Patanjali attributes to an enlightened one- fine form, grace, beauty and temper of diamond - is Swāmi Vivekānanda. In him, one can see the gracefulness of Rāma, the charming nature of Krishna, The compassion of Buddha and the loving nature of Jesus. He is determined and detached, bold and beautiful and fearless and desireless.

Of course, one should not read too much in the description of realised personalities as described by Patanjali. Sri Rāmakrishna Paramahamsa, Chaitanya Mahāprabhu, Sri Ramana and others, all enlightened beings were yet not so strong physically. He is strong who is endowed with faith. Beautiful form he begets who is desireless. Loving is he who is fearless. Graceful is he who has divinity in him. Adamantine is he who is detached. He has temper of a diamond who is not tempted by diamonds.

Ādi Shankara says: "A knower of God is like a bright light set within a pot which is full of holes. The inner illumination in such a one pours through every pore. His very presence is dazzling. The brilliance that radiates from such a one immerses the seeker with cool comforting light."

Be who you are and say what you feel,
because those who mind, don't matter
and those who matter, don't mind.

Dr. Theodor Suess Giesel.

ग्रहणस्वरूपास्मितान्वयार्थवत्त्वसंयमादिन्द्रियजयः ॥४७॥

Grahana_Svarupa_Asmitā_Anvaya_Arthavattva_Samyamāt_Indriya_Jayah.

By absorption on sense perception,
Its nature and underlying causes,
Governing principles and specific functions,
One gains control over senses.

Grahana: perception *Svarupa*: essential nature *Asmitā*: egoism
Anvaya: qualities, ttributes *Artha*vattva: intent, specific functions
Samyamāt: absorption *Indriya*: senses *Jayah*: control

Q. *How does mastery over perception come about?*
A. Mastery over the senses is achieved through concentrated absorption (*Samyama*) on sense perception, its nature and underlying causes, governing principles and specific functions.

The mastery over sense perception is attained by focusing attention on:

The ability of the senses to observe their respective objects,

How the objects are understood,

How the individual identifies himself with the object,

Nature of relationship between the perceived object, the perceiving senses and mind, and the Perceiver are related to each other, and

The net result of such a perception.

In the ordinary state of mind, the influence of the constituting principles, namely, clarity, activity and dullness erects a smokescreen as it was, preventing correct cognition. On absorption, this smokescreen vanishes. The obstructions to vision recede.

A correct understanding of who the real seer is, helps in avoiding identification of one self with his mind and senses. The ability to look at the mind and senses as objects of perception also increases.

Camels in a caravan kneel down in the evening
and the camel-driver un-loads their burdens.
In the morning, the camels kneel down again,
and the camel-driver puts the burdens back on.
It's the same with prayer:
we get on our knees to unload at night,
and in the morning we get on our knees again.
God gives us just the load
we are able to carry that day.

Dr. Bob

ततो मनोजवित्वं विकरणभावः प्रधानजयश्च ॥४८॥

Tato Manoja_Vitvam Vikarana_Bhāvah Pradhāna_Jayah_Cha.

Thence speed of mind one attains
And 'senseless' perception he gains
On nature total control he obtains.

Tato: on gaining control over senses *Manoja*: mind *Vitvam*: speed
Vikarna: without the sense organs *Bhāvah*: perception *Pradhāna*: nature
Jayah: control *Cha*: and

Q. *What after gaining the power of perception?*

A. After gaining the power of perception the senses become as swift as the mind. The perception is not limited to the limitation of the sensory organs and the individual gains control over the elements.

A story in the Skanda Purāna illustrates this: After the battle of Kurukshetra, Dharmarāja contemplates on performing the *Ashwameda Yagya*. Krishna who wanted Bhima to know the importance of *Mantra Japa* asks him to bring *Purusha Mriga* who lives in Himalayas for the *Yagya*.

Krishna warns Bhima that *Purusha Mriga* travels at the speed of mind and to bring him he has to travel at that speed failing which the *Purusha Mriga* would kill him. Bhima who could travel at the speed of wind (*vāyuvega*) thinks he could bring him.

Bhima goes in search of *Purusha Mriga* and happens to meet his brother Hanumān and tells him about his mission. Hanumān tells Bhima that the only way to keep pace with *Purusha Mriga* is to place thousand *Lingas* through the route. Being a devotee of Shiva, *Purusha Mriga* would halt at each *Linga* to chant the thousand names of *Shiva,* thus allowing Bhima to keep pace with him. *Bhima* succeeded in the mission, his *vāyuvega* could match *Purusha Mriga*'s *manovega* since it was slowed down with *Mantra Japa*

Just as the dream experience of two people
sleeping side by side are not the same,
and one does not know what the other is dreaming about
one's understanding and inner experience
are personal and unique.

Yogavāshishta

सत्त्वपुरुषान्यताख्यातिमात्रस्य सर्वभावाधिष्ठातृत्वं सर्व ज्ञातृत्वं च ॥४९॥

Sattva_Purusha_Anyatā_Khyāti_Mātrasya Sarva_Bhāva_Adhishthātritvam Sarva_Gyātritvam Cha.

The one who is clear
That Self and purity differ
Gains omnipresence
And omniscience.

Sattva: purity *Purusha*: Self *Anyatā*: distinctive
Khyāti: connection *Mātra*sya: onfined to *Sarva*: all
Bhāva: states *Adhishthātritvam*: mastery
Gyātritvam: the state of awarenes *Cha*: and

Q. *What happens after gaining the state of awareness?*
A. When the state of awareness is gained: There is clear separation between the perceiver and the mind, the various states of mind and what affects them is known and the mind perceives flawlessly everything that needs to be known.

The quality of purity permeates all manifestations in varying degree. The Being exists for its own sake. To the one who is well established in the knowledge of the distinction between the purity aspect of the Being and the Being itself, there arises mastery over all states of awareness. The Being has no attributes. Attributes are the result of the apparent becoming. The liberated ones are grouped in a graduated series depending upon the degree of *Sattva* still present in them and are called:

Brahman-vid, Brahman-vidvara, Brahman-vidvariya and *Brahman-vidvarishta.*

Brahman - *vid*	• In a state of *Sattvapatti* • Where there are flashes of reality • Attainment of pure *Sattva*
Brahman - *vidvara*	• In a state of *Āsamshakti* • Where in one is spontaneously free from all attachments.
Brahman - *vidvariya*	• In a state of *Padārthabhāvana* • In which there is only perception of reality in everything • There is no perception of materiality.
Brahman - *vidvarishta*	• In a state of *Sattvapatti* • Where there are flashes of reality • Attainment of pure *Sattva*

तद्वैराग्यादपि दोषबीजक्षये कैवल्यम् ॥५०॥
Tat_Vairāgyāt_Api Dosha_Bija_Kshaye Kaivalyam.

Such gains, when renounced,
Seeds of evil get weakened,
One is now awakened.

Tat: the attainments *Vairāgyāt*: by detachment *Api*: also
Dosha: faulty, ignorance *Bija*: the seed, the root, the causative factor
Kshaye: wakening, dissolving, dissipation *Kaivalyam*: Liberation

Q: *What happens when the attainments are renounced?*
A: When attainments are renounced by the rejection of even the extraordinary powers, the source of all bondages is dissipated and the seeds of bondage to sorrow are destroyed. One is now liberated.

Freedom, the last goal of Yoga, is attained only when the giving up even this knowledge arising from the state of total awareness, one becomes liberated. Knowledge of the Ultimate is not an acquisition process, but a negation and elimination process. All acquired knowledge, even those through concentration, meditation and absorption, are but seeds that can sprout. Giving up even such knowledge one becomes truly liberated. The causative factor for bondage is ignorance. Dispassion even towards the new awareness weakens the causative factor. When a seeker gives up even omnipotence and omniscience, after grasping it, in effect he rejects the ultimate temptation. Thought is bondage and action follows thought. In him who gives up even the awareness of his omnipotence, the last link of the false ego is snapped. The final extinction of tendencies is the dissolution of mind. Such a state is called a *Jivanmukti*.

Rabi'a and Hasan were well known Sufi Sanits in Arabia. Rabi'a, a woman was greater of the two. Junayd was the greatest amongst them all. Once Hasan saw Rabi'a at the river banks of the Eupheamerates river. Hasan threw his prayer-rug on the river and invited Rabi'a: "Come, let us pray together on the river." Rubi'a replied: "Good Hasan, you should show your spiritual powers amongst these worldly people. And, if you do, the powers should be greater than anything ordinary creatures can display. She then threw her own prayer-rug in the air and told Hasan, "Let us together pray in the mid air." But Hasan could not match the powers of Rabi'a. Hence he kept quiet. Rabi'a tried to console Hasan and said," What you suggested we do, every fish can do. "What I suggested we do, even an insect can do. Our real spiritual purpose is beyond both."

As gold, properly purified by fire, attains its essential quality, abandoning all dross; so the mānas, abandoning the impurities Sattva, Rājas, and Tamas, through meditation attains the supreme reality.

Ādi Shankara in Viveka Chudāmani, Crest Jewel of Wisdom.

At a glance: Aphorism 3.46-3.50

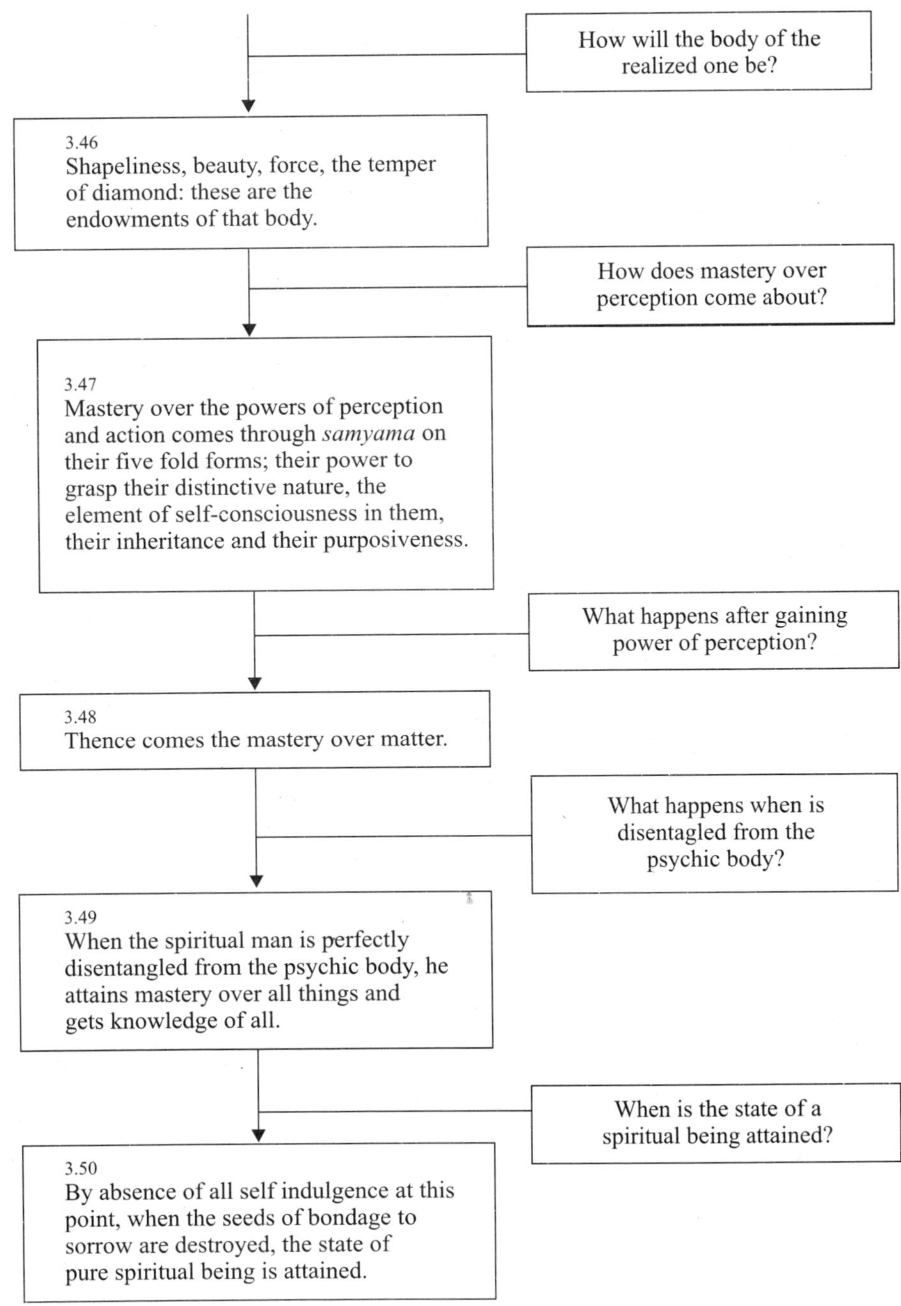

स्थान्युपमन्त्रणे सङ्गस्मयाकरणे पुनरनिष्टप्रसङ्गात् ॥५१॥

Sthāni_Upamantrane Sangasmaya_Ākarane Punah_Anishta_Prasangāt.

When the celestials tempt one with gain,
Devoid of pride, one should refrain.
Lest unwelcome thoughts resurface again.

Sthāni: the celestial beings *Upamantrane*: prayed for, on invitation
Sanga: association *Maya*: false ego *Ākarane*: attracted, tempted
Punah: again *Anishta*: undesired *Prasangāt*: apprehension

Q. *Is there still any risk of resurfacing of unwelcome thoughts?*
A. There is the possibility that the beings higher up tempt the seeker to use and abuse powers so acquired. Should the false ego of the seeker is kindled unwelcome thoughts will resurface again.

The celestials are fallen beings who are trapped by their own attainments that were misused. Such a one is said to be jealous and hence desirous of tempting the new seeker with gains so that the aspirant fails in his mission of achieving liberation.

Categories of seekers		
	The entrant **Yet to know**	In the Unknown zone
	The entered **In the realm of allurenment**	In the Danger zone
	The housed **In total control**	In the Secure Zone
	The merged **Undifferentiated**	In the Borderless

The aspirant enters the twilight area of ignorance and knowing in the second phase of spiritual journey. He is earnestly advised to ignore powers that come by, like the capacity to read other's mind, and move on. The initial control over mind and matter could tempt the seeker to try and demonstrate to others. That would be a trap and a definite obstacle to union.

Satan tempted Jesus with dominion over the whole world.
But Jesus said, "Get thee behind me Satan."
Jesus was not the one to be tempted.

Lord Death Yama tempts Nachiketā

Nachiketā, the young lad of sixteen, was determined to know the truth about death. He reached the gates of the God of Death, Yama. But Yama unfortunately was not available as this lad was not expected there then, and Yama had a previous appointment with his boss, Vishnu. For three full days, until the return of Yama, Nachiketā waited for him. After the preliminaries, apologies for having made Nachiketā wait and enquiries about his mission, Yama grants Nachiketā three boons. After utilising the first two boons for his father, Nachiketā reserves the third boon for something Yama did not expect.

Nachiketā had a fundamental doubt. Nachiketā wanted to know from 'the horse's mouth' what death is. What is permanent and what is transcient? What is everlasting and what is fleeting? Nachiketā beseeches Yama to tell it all.

Lord Death Yama knows that to teach Nachiketā about death is to teach him about life, the creator, the created and the process. Yama decides to tempt and test and know whether Nachiketā deserves to know Truth. Here is how their conversation went on:

Nachiketā: "There is doubt when a man is dead: some say that he is and some say that he is not. This I would like to know, taught by thee. This is the third boon I seek from thee."

Yama: On this point even the gods of olden times have doubted. Verily it is not easy to understand it as subtle is its nature. Oh Nachiketā, choose some other boon. Do not press me on this. give up this for me.

Nachiketā: Oh! Lord Death, none but you can tell me the purpose of life and the secret of death. Please let me know.

Yama: Young boy! Much older people than you, retired Kings and Generals, saints and sages, philosophers and poets have tried and failed. Ask me something else don't waste time. What about beautiful girls? Gold? Exotic wine with women? Dancing girls who will keep you happy every way? How about thousand horses and elephants? If you want all these together with.........

If the world is real, let it appear in the state of dreamless sleep also. As it is not at all perceived in dreamless sleep, it is false like a dream.

Ādi Shankara, Vivekachudāmani

Nachiketā: Lord Death, please stop. It is not me who is wasting time. You are wasting time talking about fleeting things. Instead of luring me with riches, comes to the point straight. Tell me what is death?

Yama: I understand that you don't understand how difficult it is to understand life and death. That is why I am saying that you better enjoy wealth and woment and spend time happily. If you want I will give strength to enjoy. I assure you that none can compete with you and none can snatch your wealth. You will eb the lord over everything you see.

Nachiketā: Yama, tell me what after all these enjoyments that you promise?

Yama: Of course, you will perish and so will all the damsels. You know death is unavoidable.

Nachiketā: Yama, now do you understand why I don't want those perishables and why I am looking for the permanent?

Yama: Oh! I see you point. OK, I will grant you and your damsels thousand years of youth and beauty. Is that OK?

Nachiketā: Death! You are wasting time in tempting me. What after thousands years?

Yama: Of course, you will all die. None can escape death. You should know that. But while every one dies before turning even eighty, in your case I am giving thousand years.

Nachiketā: Death, can't you stop fooling around. I am not interested in your thousand years life with whatever else you promise. I want here and now, knowledge about Truth. Do you want me to exchange knowledge of truth for those fleeting objects?

Yama: But those fleeting objects that you say you don't want are really sweet, tasty, pleasurable, and joyful and in you case a thousand times more than others.

Nachiketā: And yet perishable. I don't want that. I want to know the permanent. I am not going to leave this place until then.

Yama: I am pleased Nachiketā. You are not tempted. With much less, others were tempted. I will be honoured to have you as my student. Here straight away, I am going to begin the lessons on the purpose of life and the secret of death.

> Seeing this world as pure illusion, and devoid of any interest in it, why should the strong minded person feel fear, even at the approach of death.
>
> *Song of Ashtāvakra*
> (Translation by John Richards, Stockpole Elidor, UK)

क्षणतत्क्रमयोः संयमाद्विवेकजं ज्ञानम् ॥५२॥

Kshana_Tat_Kramayoh Samyamād Viveka_Jam Jnānam.

Absorption on moments and their succession
Brings about absolute clarity through discrimination.

Kshana: moment, infinitesimal time *Tat*: its *Krama* : sequence, succession
Samyamād: absorption *Viveka*: discrimination
Jam: born of *Jnana*: knowledge

Q. *What brings about absolute clarity in understanding?*
A. By *Samyama* on moments of time and their succession, discrimination arises, which brings about absolute clarity in understanding.

Succession of thoughts, similar in kind, is the state of focused mind. This focusing, the subsequent meditation and absorption on a single moment of time and the previous and succeeding one as well as the succession of moments of time brings about discrimination. In order to be able to stay away from allurements referred to in the earlier aphorism, discriminative knowledge that clearly distinguishes the impermanent and fleeting from the permanent and everlasting is necessary. The allurements are temporary, time bound. The everlasting and the permanent is the Being. Choosing the company and merging with the Being, instead of the misery of becoming is a decision arising out of the discrimination.

Samyama on the moments of times gives discrimination that these moments are all of fleeting nature and any attempt to identify oneself with the fleeting is futile. The desire to cling to the eternal giving up the ephemeral follows such discrimination.

Whenever there is temptation towards the sensation, the seeker would realise on discrimination that what is to be sought after is the Eternal Bliss and there can be nothing greater than, nothing more pleasurable and nothing everlasting as that arising out of elimination of mental modifications.

It is these modifications that are impressions. The tendencies or impressions constantly drag the seeker towards misery. Whatever may be the allurements that the celestial beings offer, there can never be peace with them. Such temptations are only to drag the aspirant out of his spiritual path.

Righteousness and unrighteousness, pleasure and pain
are purely the product of mind and are of no concern of yours.
You are neither the doer nor the reaper of the consequences,
so you are always free.

The song of Ashtāvakra
(Translation by John Richards, Stockpole Elidor, UK)

जातिलक्षणदेशैरन्यतानवच्छेदात्तुल्ययोस्ततः प्रतिपत्तिः ॥५३॥

Jāti_Lakshana_Desaih Anyata
Anavachchhedāt Tulyayoh Tatah Pratipattih.

Such discrimination delivers
Knowledge of objects similar
That otherwise is not clear
By its position in space, class or character.

Jāti: class, category, type *Lakshana*: characteristics *Anyata*: distinction
Desha: place, position in space *Anavachchhedāt*: undefined, indistinguishable
Tulyayoh: similar objects, the same category *Tatah*: thereby, from that
Pratipattih: distinguishable knowledge

Q. *What happens after getting such discrimination?*
A. On such discrimination, even those things that cannot be differentiated by class, category, place or features can be understood.

From such discrimination referred to in the previous aphorism, arises knowledge of the difference between two very similar objects that are not normally cognizable by their difference in class, category, place or features.

The superimposition of the false self over the real Self is not easy to identify. On discrimination, one is able to get out of the grip of ignorance. The mix up of the name, form and substance, the cause of ignorance ceases. Leaving the name and form aside, the seeker is now able to be aware of the substance alone. The discrete entities give way to the 'indiscrete' continuum. The body and mind are the impure instruments and yet one mistakes them to be pure and clings on to them. Discrimination helps one to know the reality that body-mind unit is only a disintegrating stuff and it is the pure Self that is real and ever Blissful.

In everyone and in everything one sees the Real One only. Hence, to look for anything else is now impossible. There is no other, other than the Self. When there is no other, what is there to seek?

Who is there to tempt?

"The wise who knows the Self as bodiless within the bodies,
as unchanging among changing things,
as great and omnipresent,
does never grieve".

Katha Upanishad.

तारकं सर्वविषयं सर्वथाविषयमक्रमं चेति विवेकजं ज्ञानम् ॥५४॥

Tārakam Sarva_Vishayam Sarvathā_Vishayam_Akramam Cheti Vivekajam Jnānam.

Such discrimination
Gives knowledge through intuition,
There is always comprehension
About all objects and all their modifications.

Tārakam: star like, intuitional
Sarva: all
Vishayam: objects
Sarvathā: always, ever
Vishayam: objects
Kramam: in regular order
Cha: and
Eti: thus, in this way
Vivekajam: arising out of discrimination
Jnānam: knowledge

Q. *What is knowledge of discernment like?*
A. Knowledge of discernment is star like or intuitional, is comprehensive of all things and of all times, is not restricted to any object or any specific situation, is not the result of sequential logic and is spontaneous.

Why is knowledge of discernment called star like?

Because it sheds light, nothing can hide it, nothing is hidden from it, it rises high, illumines all things and is ever present, in the single light of the Divine. This power has been beautifully described by Columba:

"Some there are, though very few, to whom Divine grace has granted this: that they can clearly and most distinctly see, at one and the same moment, as though under one ray of the sun, even the entire circuit of the whole world with its surroundings of ocean and sky, the inmost part of their mind being marvellously enlarged."

A mind that is crowded is sick
A mind that is stilled is sound.

सत्त्वपुरुषयोः शुद्धिसाम्ये कैवल्यमिति ॥५५॥

Sattvapurushayoh Shuddhisāmye Kaivalyamiti.

When perceiver and the perceived attain equal purity,
There is Samādhi.

Sattva: mind *Purushayoh*: Self *Shuddhisamye*: pure, unblemished
Kaivalyam: Liberation, Samadhi *Iti*: this, end

Q. *When is the Samādhi state said to be attained?*
A. When the seeker loses his individuality and merges himself with the Being, then he is said to have attained a state of *Samādhi*.

Finally, when the purity aspect of the triple qualities has become as untainted as the Being, there is liberation. During the meditative process, inertia gives way to activity, activity to mixed purity and mixed purity to untainted purity. With this all impressions cease. Modifications of mind come to an end. The mind which was '*Vritti-Rupa*', activity oriented, is now centered in itself.

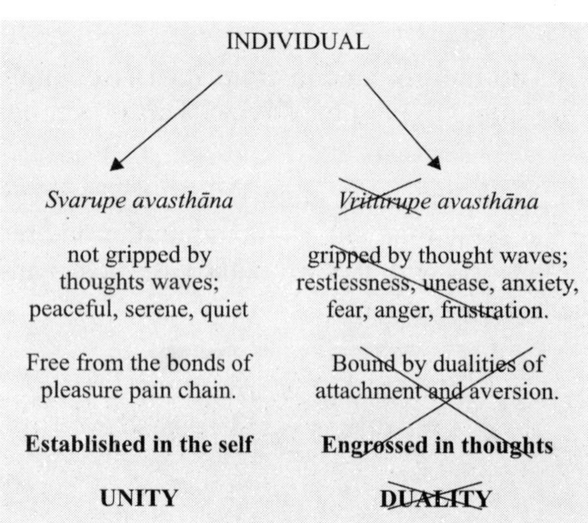

The distinction that an individual is different from pure consciousness is an illusion. With the merger of the individual self with the pure Self, the distinction is removed. The absence of illusion is liberation. The bonding with the body – mind unit is freed. This freeing is the liberation. The liberation is thus the freedom from the illusion of separatedness.

This aphorism ends with the word '*iti*'. 'Iti' means this or end. Patanjali defined Yoga as end of mental modification, '*Chitta vritti nirodha*'. *Vritti* is from the root word *Vru*. *Vru* refers to the Being. *Vritti* is the end of Being, that is becoming. Strictly speaking there is neither a beginning nor an end to the Being. In this limited context of the mental modifications, it is the absence of perception of the Being that is the cause of becoming. Becoming therefore, ends in the awareness of Being. On attaining the state of *Samādhi*, this false ego merges with the universal ego.

At a glance: Aphorism 3.51-3.55

Will attachment show up even at this stage?

3.51
Yes, it can. There should be complete overcoming of allurement or pride in the invitations of the different realms of life, otherwise attachment to evil things arise once more.

How does knowledge of difference between self and the non-self come about?

3.52
Differentiating knowledge of the self and the non-self comes from practicing *samyama* on division of time and its sequence.

How is picture of Reality obtained?

3.53
Sequence, time and space are creations of mind that distort and refract objects, preventing a view of reality. The power of spiritual discernment and illumination now presents objects as they are and not as the mind thinks.

What is knowledge of discernment like?

3.54
The knowledge of discernment is star-life or intutional, is comprehensive of all things and of all times, and has no sequence.

When does spiritual man enter perfect spiritual life?

3.55
When the vest and the wearer of the vest become alike pure, the spiritual man enters into perfect spiritual life.

इति श्री पंतजलि योग शस्त्रे विभूति निर्देशोनाम तृतीय पादः।

Thus ends Sree Patanjali Yoga Sutras Chapter 3.

Chapter 4

Kaivalya Pādah

Liberation

जन्मौषधिमन्त्रतपः समाधिजाः सिद्धयः ॥१॥

Janma_Aushadhi_Mantra_Tapah_Samãdhijãh Siddhayah.

Absorption state, attains one, by birth or incantation
Or practices ascetic or concentration.

Janma: birth *Aushadhi*: medicine *Mantra*: incantation
Tapah: observances *Samãdhijãh:* arising out of trance *Siddhayah*: attainments

Q: How is perfection and illumination attained?
A: Perfection and illumination is attained:
By birth (consequence of efforts made in previous births)
By use of special medicines as prescribed in the texts/Vedās
By constant repetition of mantras
By following rigid ascetic practices and austerities
By concentration/ *samãdhi*

Patanjali is not dogmatic. He agrees that there are several other methods of realsation. The Bhagavat Gitã broadly categorises four different paths to realsation:

1. *Bhakti Yoga*, Devotional 2. *Karma Yoga*, Service without expectation

3. *Gyãna Yoga*, enquiry orientation 4. *Rāja Yoga*, the systematic royal path of Patanjali

Bhakti Yoga Path of devotion	• Designed to take care of the emotional • Responds easily to love and affection
Karma Yoga Path of right action	• Takes care of people who believe in the dictum that service to main is service to God. • Suits the activity oriented
Gyāna Yoga Path of rational enquiry	• Appeals to people who go by reason rather than faith • Suits those endowed with sharp intellectual skills
Rāja Yoga Path of mind control	• Ideal for those of introspective kind • Suits those who look for systematic way to approach the reality

Strive to enter in at the straight gate,
for narrower is the gate and straight is the way that leads to life,
and few be they who find it.

All paths lead to divinity. All religions are equally true. All saints and scriptures say the same thing. But all men are not the same. They have different modes of thinking. Some are rational, some emotional, some logical and some are intellectual. Ones' way of approach naturally does not impress the other. Each can therefore choose his path. En route of course, all will realise that their final destination is the same and that there is difference only in the method of approach, but not in the destination.

State of illumination is attained	By Birth	Example: Christ, Krishna
	By use of special medicines	Psychedelic drugs like LSD
	By practices ascetic and austere	Example: Devas, Rāvana
	By mantra	Eample: AUM
	By concentration	Eight limbed Yoga

1. By Birth:

Personalities like Jesus and Krishna belong to this category. They were born with Yogic stature. They were born divine. They had extraordinary aura and illumination about and around them. Krishna's exhibition of powers as a child, are household tales in India.

Yoga is Krishna's gift to humanity. The resurrection of Jesus moved millions and has impact amongst his millions of followers till this day.

By virtue of the practice of spiritual enquiry in a previous birth, Saint Vāmadeva had realsation even while in his mother's womb. While yet inside his mother's womb, Vāmadeva declared thus (Rig Veda IV 27.1) "Ah! Dwelling inside the womb I understood all the births of all the gods. A hundred bodies as strong as steel restrained me, but like a hawk I broke them by force and came out swiftly."

Buddha said that neither the repetition of scriptures, nor self-torture, nor sleeping on the ground, nor the repetition of prayers, penances, hymns, charms, mantras, incantations and invocations can bring the real happiness of *Nirvānā*. Instead, he emphasized the importance of making individual effort in order to achieve spiritual goals.

2. By Drugs:

Patanjali says that through the use of certain herbs it is possible for a partial awakening to be brought about. Through drugs either the awakening of *Idā* or *Pingalā*, or the awakening of *Sushumnā* takes place. The method of awakening through herbs is called *Aushadhi* and an Awakening thus achieved, can, under the right circumstances and conditions, albeit short term, replicate at least partially, the level of consciousness.

Use of psychedelic drugs is widespread over the centuries. Patanjali acknowledges over many millenniums back that extraordinary psychic powers can be obtained by use of special drugs made of herbs as prescribed in the Vedas. "The overall results of testing with psychic drugs are inconclusive, but some striking experiences have been reported recently after the subject took LSD, mescaline or PSILOCYCIN" reports Herbert S Greenhouse in his wonderful "Book of Psychic Knowledge". His other observations: "When South American Indians drink Yage they go into a deep trance and become both telepathic and clairvoyant. During this period they know what is going on, hundreds of kilometres away."

Gateway to Heaven: A Sadhu smokes Sannabis at the Pashupatinath Temple in Kathmandu

Dr. Margaret Paul was a psychiatrist who experimented with the Ananitha Pnthaina mushroom, which has a psychedelic effect. While she was enjoying a three hour fantasy, one of her patients went into an irrational state while another lost three hours during which he could not think straight and had the impulse to eat mushrooms for the first time in his life. Neither patient was aware of what was happening to Dr. Paul.

"Many tribes use drugs to stimulate psychic powers. Natives in Latin America tool OLOLINQUI, a morning glory seed, before the arrival of Spanish missionaries. These missionaries have told of American Indians who used PEYCITE so that they could predict when enemies would attack or to find hiding places of stolen goods. The danger with the drugs are that they can deceive and push a seeker into a make believe world. Getting out of the drug habit can be extremely painful and destabilizing. Realisation is attained not by drugging but by meditating. Short cuts can be a short way to a steep fall. Every higher experience through drug is bound to be followed by deep depression and dejection.

Your right is to work only, but never to the fruit thereof.
Be not instrumental in making your action bear fruit,
nor let your attachment be to the action.

Bhagavatgitā

3. By Mantra:

Mantras are the composition of a few letters, words, sounds in such a manner that they build up to produce effects on specific places, people or things. There are a lot of mantras given to us by our ancestors. Since the mind wanders so much, the music of a mantra easily rescues the mind and brings it back to the object of one's meditation. Both the rhythm of it and the meaning of it, combine to guide the mind safely back to the point of meditation, the higher consciousness or the specific spiritual focus. The practice of mantras are specific sound formulae, in many cases used in conjunction with rituals and geometric symbols called *Yantra*s to bring about specific results.

Mantra is a compound word, combining *man* and *tara*, meaning deliverance of the mind. *Tara* is also translated to mean protection. Mantra therefore is also referred to as protection of the mind. A Mantra is a pure sound vibration intended to deliver the mind from illusion and inclination towards material objects. Chanting is a process of repeating a Mantra. Mantra Yoga meditation involves chanting a word or phrase until the mind and emotions are transcended and the super conscious is clearly revealed and experienced.

4. By *Yantra:*

Yantra is a visual representation of Mantra in a geometrical form. *Yantra* helps one in focusing the mental energy. Such focusing facilitates the communion with cosmic energy. Gazing at a *Yantra* intently and chanting the appropriate Mantra results in increased brain wave coherence. *Yantra*s are steps to higher levels of consciousness.

The *Yantra* provides a focal point that is a window into the absolute. When the mind is concentrated on a single, simple *Yantra*, the mental chatter ceases. Eventually, the object is dropped when the mind can remain empty and silent without help. In the most advanced phases, it is possible to attain union with God by the geometric visualization of a *Yantra*.

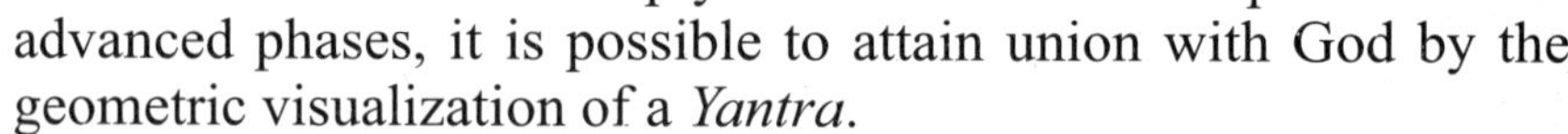

The *Yantra* is like a microcosmic picture of the macrocosm. It is a focusing point and an outer and inner doorway. The *Yantras* are often focused on a specific deity and so by tuning into the different *Yantra*s you can tap into certain deities or creative force centres in the universe.

If a person merely repeats the name of a medicine without taking it, he is not cured of his disease.
So, a person cannot find realisation by reciting the scriptures.

Ādi Shankara, Crest Jewel of Wisdom

4. By Ascetic Practices: An ascetic is a person who renounces material comforts and leads a life of austere self-discipline, as an act of religious devotion. He leads a life of self-discipline and self-denial, for spiritual improvement. The ascetic practices in the past sometimes turned even bizarre with ascetics indulging in self inflicted bodily torture.

Tapa is a way of asserting one's will and break the sensual nature which craves for comfort and indulgence. Mortification means undergoing hardships and conditions which makes one realize the ultimate truth. Mortification involves reining in of senses from their external orientation. Fasting, forgoing sleep, walking on fire and lying on a bed of nails are different mortification practices indulged by different groups.

There is no society anywhere in any part of the world where a group of people do not follow some ascetic practice or other at some point of time in their life. But these practices, sometimes called rituals are in no way meant to gain realization.

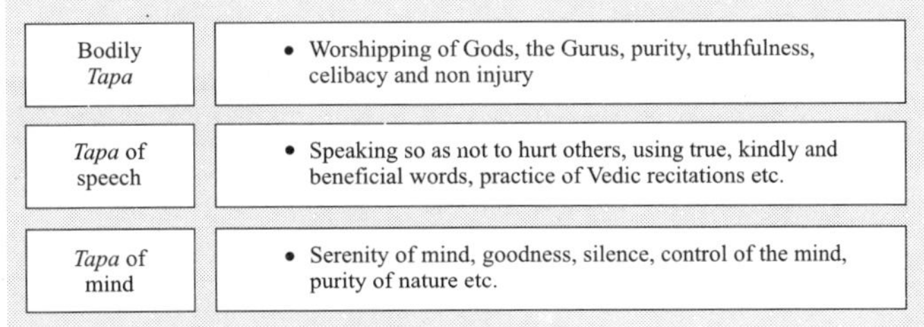

Bodily *Tapa*	• Worshipping of Gods, the Gurus, purity, truthfulness, celibacy and non injury
Tapa of speech	• Speaking so as not to hurt others, using true, kindly and beneficial words, practice of Vedic recitations etc.
Tapa of mind	• Serenity of mind, goodness, silence, control of the mind, purity of nature etc.

The objective of the ascetic practices according to Buddhism is to make Improper motive become Proper Intent, whereby;
Greed becomes generosity,
Anger becomes patience and endurance,
Stupidity becomes wisdom,
Conceit becomes embracing of the precepts with humility, and
Doubt and distraction becomes mental (meditative) concentration.
Austerity is essential, but it should be within one's ability to withstand the negation. Austerity should therefore, be within rational limits. One needs not copy the ascetic practices of another.

Ceremonials and sacrifices lead men round and round but not to the ultimate goal to which an understanding of Self-alone can lead.

Mundakopanishad

Vālmiki was not the name that his parents chose for the poet. His real name was Ratnākara. The word 'Vālmika' in Sanskrit means an ant-hill. Since he came out of an ant-hill, he got the name of Vālmiki. But how strange! How did he come out of an ant-hill? Now, that is a wonderful and delightful story.

Vālmiki also lived in the age of Sri Rāma - called the 'Tretā Yuga' (the Age of Tretā). In those days, there was a thick forest all along the banks of the river Ganga. Many sages built their hermitage in that forest for their '*tapa*'; that means they meditated on God. Among them was a sage by the name of Prachetās. He had, a son called Ratnākara. When he was a very young boy, one day, he went into the forest. While playing he lost his way and began to cry. Just then a hunter came there looking for a prey. He saw the chubby boy and fondled and pacified him. The hunter had no children. He took the boy to his hut in the midst of the jungle.

Ratnākara's father searched for his son all around the hermitage, but could not find him. Finally he and his wife thought that the boy had become the prey of some wild beast. Both wept at the loss. The hunter and his wife brought up the lad with great love. Ratnākara forgot his parents. He took the hunter for his father and the hunter's wife for his mother. He was taught how to hunt. Ratnākara was a clever boy and learnt it quickly. He became a hunter with a sure aim.

To the birds and beasts of the forest, he became verily Yama, the God of Death. When he came of age, his foster father searched for a bride and celebrated his marriage with a beautiful girl from a hunter's family. In a few years she gave birth to some children. Thus, Ratnākara's family grew in size. It became very difficult for him to provide food and clothing to his large family. So, he took to robbery. He began to attack people going from one village to another, frighten them and to take away all that they had. If they opposed him, he killed them.

One day Ratnākara was sitting by the side of a road waiting for a victim. It happened that the great sage Nārada was passing that way. Nārada had his favourite musical instrument, a Veenā, in his hands. As he played on the Veenā, he was singing a song in praise of God. When he was thus lost in joy, suddenly, Ratnākara rushed at him. He lifted the stout staff in his hands and shouted, "Look here! Hand over all you have or else I'll break your head."

But Nārada was not an ordinary man. He was a divine sage, and one who wandered all over the Earth, the Heaven and the Underworld. He was not frightened by the loud shouts of Ratnākara. He smilingly said "My dear man, all that I have is only this old

Veenā and the rag cloth I am wearing. If you want them, you can certainly take them. Why should you break my head for these?"

Ratnākara was astonished at these words. He looked up at Nārada's face. There was neither fear nor anger; there was only peace. And how bright was that face! He was surprised to see a face tender and innocent like that of a child. He had never seen such a lovely face. As he gazed, his cruel mind melted into tenderness. Nārada sat beneath a tree and as played on the Veenā, sang a song in praise of God. It was sweet like the song of a cuckoo. Ratnākara was deeply moved. Noticing the change, the sage Nārada paused in his song and said, "Brother, stealing is a sin. Killing animals is also sinful. Why do you do such evil?"

"Sir, what can I do?" Ratnākara replied, "I have a large family. There are my old parents and my wife and children, They partake of my happiness and my troubles. I have to provide them with food and clothing. Hunting and stealing are all I know. What else can I do?"

The sage smiled and said, "My friend, will any member of your family partake of your sin also ? Go and ask them, and bring back their reply."

Ratnākara thought that Nārada was trying a trick to make his escape. Nārada understood it and again said, "Well, child, if you do not trust me, you can tie me to this tree and then go."

Ratnākara thought that it was all right. He tied Nārada to a tree and went home.

On reaching home, he first went to his father and said, "Father, I rob people to get food and clothing for you all. It seems that it is a sin. Do you not share in that sin?"

His father was angry and said, "You sinner, you should not do such bad things. Am I to share your sins? No, never. You have to suffer for what you do."

Ratnākara went to his mother and said, "Surely, mother, you will share my sin, won't you?" But she also scolded him and sent him away. He then went to his wife and said, "Do you know how I earn to provide you and your children with food and clothing? It is by robbery. But I steal for your sake. Therefore, you are also partners in my sin. Isn't that so?"

The wife was displeased and said, 'What are you saying? What have we to do with your sin? You are my husband, and my children are your children. It is your duty to look after us and give us food and clothing."

Ratnākara's eyes were opened. He realized that he alone was responsible for all his sins no one else would share his sin. As soon as it was clear to him, he ran back to Nārada. He untied the sage and amidst weeping, narrated to him all that had happened in his home. Falling at Nārada's feet, he asked the sage, "Oh, sir, now what of me? How can I atone for all the sins I have committed? You are my only saviour."

Nārada lifted him up and wiped his tears. He consoled him saying, "Do not be afraid. I shall teach you a way to wash off your sins." So he taught Ratnākara the sacred name of Rāma 'Rāma Nām'. He made him sit beneath a tree and asked him to go on repeating the sacred name of Rāma. He said, I shall come here again, Till then you should not get up and go away." Then the sage departed.

Ratnākara continued his '*tapa*' chanting the name of Rāma. His eyes were closed. His whole mind was concentrated on the chanting of the name of the Lord. He forgot his existence. He had neither food nor sleep for days and days. And in this way quite a few years passed. An ant hill grew all around and above him. He could not even be seen by anybody.

At last one day, the sage Nārada again came that way. Of course, he knew that Ratnākara was inside the anthill. Very carefully he cleared that anthill. Ratnākara was wholly lost in his '*tapa*' and did not wake up to the world around him. Nārada chanted the name of Rāma in his ears. Then he opened his eyes and saw the sage standing before him. He saluted him from where he was sitting. Nārada helped him to get up. He also gently touched him all over. Ratnākara felt new life flowing through him.

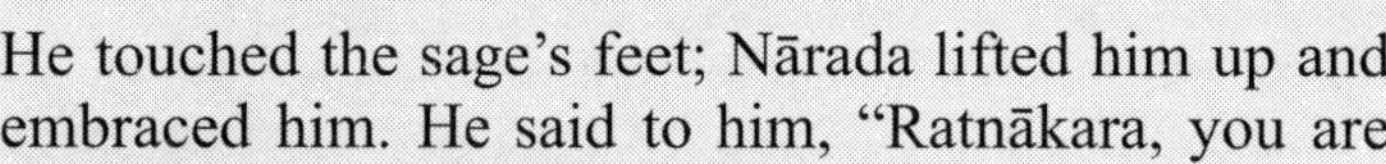

He touched the sage's feet; Nārada lifted him up and embraced him. He said to him, "Ratnākara, you are blessed. God is pleased with your '*tapa*'. You are now a sage of the highest order, a *Brahmarishi*. As you are now reborn from a Vālmika (the ant-hill), from hereafter, you will be famous as Vālmiki."

Tears of joy welled up in Vālmiki's eyes at these words. He prostrated before Nārada again and said, "Sir, all this is your kindness. The company of good men uplifts man. I am myself a proof of this." Nārada blessed him and went his way.

Later on Vālmiki composed "Rāmāyana", the greatest epic in the world.

If you keep admiring the creation,
you cannot see the creator.

जात्यन्तरपरिणामः प्रकृत्यापूरात् ॥२॥

Jāti-Antara-Parināmah Prakrityā-Purāt.

Transformation within a class
Is brought about by filling in the subtlest cause.

Jāti: class *Antar*: internal *Parināmah*: transformation
Prakrityā: of the nature, btlest material cause *Apurāt*: entry of, filling of

Q: *How is transformation achieved? What is the cause of permanence of attainment through the practice of dhyāna / dhārana / Samādhi?*

A: Change from one set of characteristics to another is essentially an adjustment of the basic qualities. Such an adjustment is brought about by exceptionally attuned mind, when the subtlest of the causes are filled in.

Due to the efforts of the Yogi, there is a metamorphosis of the very nature of the individual from the ordinary to the supreme.

In the beginning there was nothing. There was and is only the Being. The Being multiplied itself. In the language of religion, God said let me be many. The being fills the space with nature and beings. Hence even space and time are objects. Originally there was neither external variation nor internal variation. In scriptural language, there was neither *Sajātiyabheda* (internal variation) nor *Vijātiyabheda* (external variation). Strictly speaking there is nothing internal. In relation to the Being, everything is both internal and external.

From the beginning there is Being. Then came Space, Fire. Air, Water and Earth. The triple element of fire, water and earth, the permutation and combination of objects from out of these three, permeated by the varying degree and intensity of consciousness is what one sees as multiplicity. Behind the apparent millions of objects, there are the triple elements; behind the triple elements is the Being. Through awareness of the being one gains clear insight into the formations and hence the capacity to change the same. It is the filling in of nature that makes for the difference. The mind attuned to the Being sees through this difference.

So long as ignorance facilitates the operation of the gunas
this multiplicity is experienced as a hard reality,
and so long as multiplicity is experienced due to ignorance,
Time generates the fear of death.

Maharishi Vālmiki- Rāmāyana

Fire principle is the cause for Water, water the cause of Earth. The combination of the three is the cause for the millions of formations. The triple elements; fire, water and earth are the cosmic, super-physical subtle elements, called the *tanmātrās*. They are not the physical fire, water or earth that one sees. From out of the subtle elements came the grosser elements. The process is the three fold mixing of original subtle principles. The mixing is in such a way that each one of the three contains the other two in certain smaller proportion. The solid content in a human body is known to be a transformation of earth; the liquid part consists of water, and heat, vibration and channels through which food, drink and the mind move in the body. They are linked to fire, air and ether respectively. The senses of touch, smell etc are again transformation of earth etc. These are called the organs of knowledge. The sense organs and the motor organs and the mind are all transformations of the subtlest of the triple visible principles of earth, water and fire and the invisible principle of air and ether. The cause of the gross body-mind unit is the subtle triple qualities. The difference in the body-mind units is the result of change in the proportion of the triple principles. The consciousness permeates every part of the universe and so also every person, who is but part of the universe.

Every object in creation can be reduced to its constituents. There is nothing in an object, bar its constituents. This is the universal law. The difference in the contour or the shape of the object is not relevant. What is important is the substance out of which the object is made up of. A person is also an object. If now transformation is sought to be brought about in the person, it is done by 'filling in' the subtlest cause. The filling in of nature, expressed as triple qualities, is the cause for transformation. Such transformation is brought about within a class. Man can become an angel. But a plant cannot be made a man. Through meditation, when the mind is attuned to the vibrations of the pure beings, transformation is brought about. Transformation is the weakening of activity orientation and inertia and the strengthening of purity. Transformation is the uncovering of the veil of ignorance. The uncovering takes place when the gross yields to the subtle. The first stage of transformation is absorption of the senses into the mind, called *Pratyāhāra*. The second stage of transformation is the absorption of the mind into the *prāna*, vital energy. When this transformation takes place, there is breathing process but no thinking process.

Ādi Shankara says in the Vivekachudāmani (Crest Jewel of Wisdom): "As gold, properly purified by fire, attains its essential quality, abandoning all dross; so the *mānas* (mind), abandoning the impurities *sattva, rājas* and *tamas* (clarity, activity and inertia) through meditation attains the Supreme Reality."

Success is certain for him with faith endowed,
In its absence one is not with bliss bestowed.

निमित्तमप्रयोजकं प्रकृतीनां वरणभेदस्तु ततः क्षेत्रिकवत् ॥३॥

Nimittam_Aprayojakam Prakriteenãm Varana_Bhedah Tu Tatah Kshetrikavat.

Removal of barriers make mind glow
As cutting a dam, makes water flow.

Nimittam: efficient
Aprayojakam: without much force
Prakriteenãm: causes, for nature
Varana: obstacles
Bhedah: to break, differences
Tu: but
Vat: similar to
Tatah: from that, thence, thereafter
Kshetrika: farmer, cultivator

Q. *How can such a power of mind for transformation be realised?*

A. Transformation can be realized by removing barriers blocking the latent powers. Even as a farmer cuts a dam to cause water-flow; removal or cutting aside the known and unknown obstacles, brings up the hidden powers of mind over matter. It is not the good or bad deeds that bring about the transformation. The process of evolution is inherent in creation. Yogic practices break the obstacles to evolution and smoothen the path of evolution.

The control over the veiling power is not achieved through struggle. The effort involved on the part of a farmer to let water flow into his tilled soil is very small; that of cutting a small dam (a mound of soil) blocking the passage of water to the desired area. The reference to cutting a dam is in the context of ancient agricultural practices of initially blocking flow of water by erecting a 'dam' and letting it flow by cutting, i.e. removing the mound of soil with agricultural implements.

The dam in the context of Yoga is the dam of ignorance. Once the false identity of self with the body-mind syndrome is cut or snapped, illumination flows automatically and engulfs the being. The false sense is gone, the True Self is revealed. Acquisition of knowledge of sciences is an addition-process that requires effort of memory, logic, equation, reason and what not. But obtaining spiritual knowledge, i.e. being internally illumined, is a subtraction-process involving of cutting down blocks/dams such as propensities, sensations, and impressions and eventually the egoism as well as eliminating the false identification of one with the impermanent body, name and form. When such an elimination or subtraction takes place ignorance gives way to awareness of the rudimentary principles that govern mind and matter.

As long as one does not realise the distinctiveness of the *Ātman*
From the body, the senses and the *prāna*, so long will one be subject to
the sufferings of the transmigratory life, including death.

Adhyātma Rāmāyana

निर्माणचित्तान्यस्मितामात्रात् ॥४॥

Nirmāna_Chittāni Asmitā_Mātrāt.

The cause for the emergence of mind
In ego one can find.

Nirmāna: created *Chittāni*: minds *Asmitā*: ego, egoism
Mātrāt: from, alone, only from, limitation, boundary

Q. *What causes the emergence of mind?*
A. Awareness of the individuality (*Asmitā*) is the cause of manifestation.

"*I think, therefore, I am*". This statement of the French philosopher Descartes is wrong. Thinking cannot be equated to Being. One of the important affliction is Asmitā, false ego, the 'I' ness. Mind's modifications start as soon as 'I' ness appears. The subtler form of ego is thus the cause of creation of mind. In order to be able to control the modifications of mind, one should be able to understand how mind comes into being and how mind itself draws its illumination from the Being, and has no separate existence of its own. That which is created can be controlled. Mind is also a created unit and hence can be controlled.

When false sense of ego is controlled, mind gets subdued. Through meditation 'I' consciousness gets dissolved and gets merged with the cosmic consciousness and as a corollary mind's false identification with the world of objects ceases. In day to day life, when one refers to himself, he refers to his mind. 'Me' and 'Mine' notify his mind. If the 'Me' and 'Mine' are absent, mind is de-notified. The moment the 'Me' and 'Mine' arise; the whole conglomeration of objects connected with that thought appears at one stroke in its presence. That presence signifies the modifications of mind.

It is the ego that veils the ultimate Reality. It is this veiling power that is responsible for this projection of mind. It is the projecting power that makes mind attach itself to myriad objects and it is this attachment that is referred to as the modifications of mind. It is the internal thought that shows its effect as external act. The effect grows by the growth of tendencies and by the growth of the effects, the tendencies also grow. Hence the seeker should burn these two completely.

Like the cloud brought in by the wind in the rainy season,
even though completely rooted out,
if the ego is awakened in the mind even for moment,
coming to life again,
it creates hundreds of perplexities.

Ādi Shankara, Vivekachudāmani

प्रवृत्तिभेदे प्रयोजकं चित्तमेकमनेकेषाम् ॥५॥

Pravritti_Bhede Prayojakam Chittam Yekam Anekeshām.

Mind's activities, varied and many
Have but one cause only.

Pravritti: actions *Bheda*: difference, distinctions *Prayojakam*: inspiring, cause
Chittam: mind *Yekam*: one *Anekeshām*: many

Q. *What is the root cause of so many mental activities?*

A. Though the activities of different minds are different, but it is one Supreme Mind which controls all.

All actions of mind are inspired by the false sense of 'I'. It is this wrong identification with the impermanent that causes many variations of mind. All mind's activity, looking like many minds at work have but one director, the Ego. The root aspect of mind that emerges from individuality or asmitā is the core out of which there may emerge many clusters of mental identity. All of the mental constructs of one thinks what he is, and the false identities are secondary to that central mental identity of associating with the transitory mistaking it to be permanent. All modifications of the mind are just the aspects of Ego. The fragmentations of the mind are but different conditioned responses. Shri Ramana Maharshi says, "The first and foremost of all thoughts, the primeval thought in the mind of every man, is the thought 'I'. It is only after the birth of this thought that any other thoughts can arise at all. It is only after the first personal pronoun, 'I' has arisen in the mind that the second personal pronoun 'You', can make its appearance. If you could mentally follow the 'I' thread until it lead you back to its source you would discover that, just as it is the first thought to appear, so it is the last to disappear. This is a matter which can be experienced." All kinds of thoughts that spring from one mind can be categorized as arising from either as a result of attachment or of aversion or out of fear. These three mental states to which many kinds of thoughts can be attributed to are but caused by false sense of Ego.

That which is seen is different, one from the other and all from the seer. Moreover, the seen is the product of the seer's likes and dislikes, his imagination and feelings, his impulses and tendencies. When the lamp is brought in, the "snake" disappears and the rope alone remains and is understood as such. When the world is examined in the light of *Brahma Jnāna*, the illusory picture which attracted and repelled, the picture of duality disappears.

Brahmānubhava Upanishad

At a glance: Aphorism 4.01-4.05

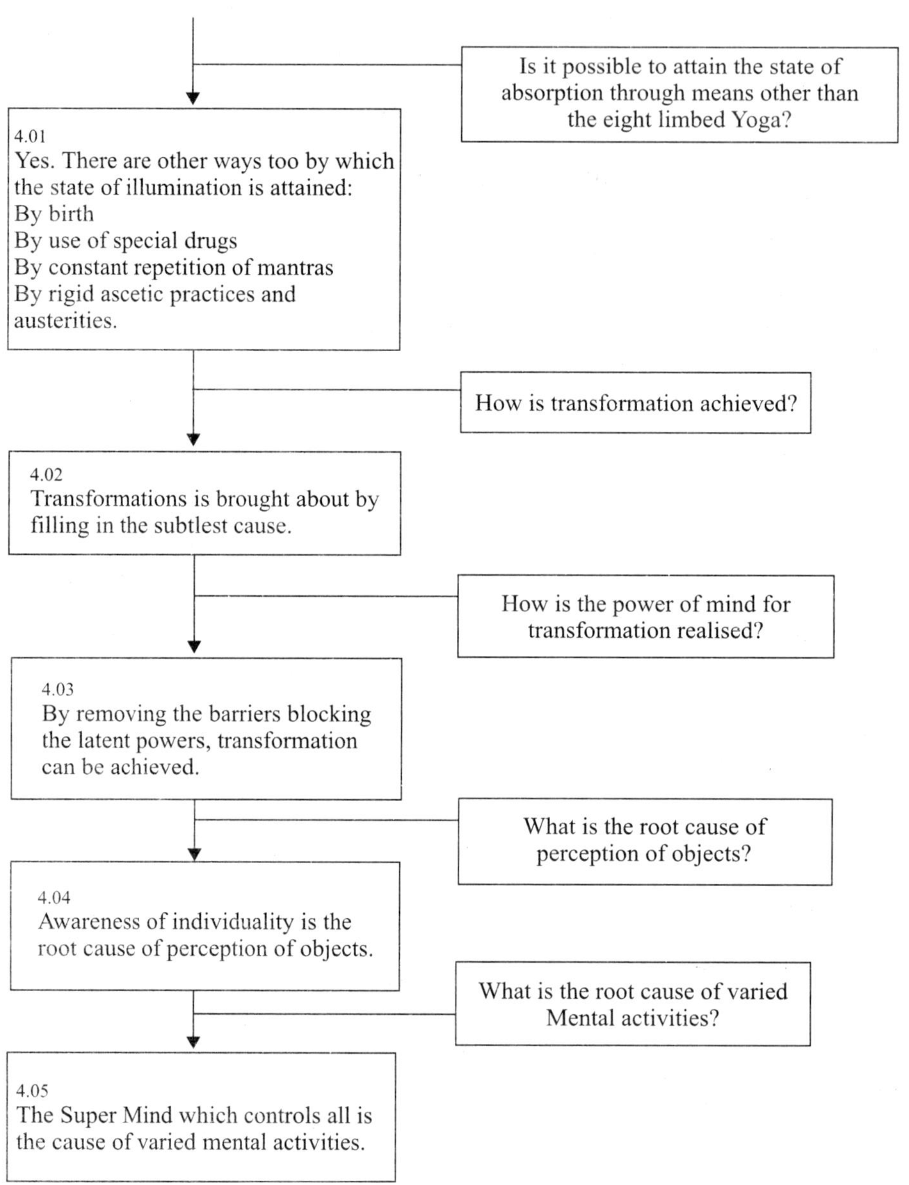

तत्र ध्यानजमनाशयम् ॥६॥

Tatra Dhyānajam Anāshayam.

Those of the meditative kind
Exert influence benign.

Tatra: there, among the settled minds
Dhyānajam: born out of trance, born of meditation
Anāshayam: devoid of tendencies of action and ignorance, free from propensities, past impressions

Q. *From amongst many of these mental activities, which is best to be held on to?*
A. The meditation oriented is the best to be held on to. These activities help erase mental modifications and tendencies that are born out of ignorance.

There are two kinds of activities, those that bind and those that free. The freeing actions are those that free one from the effect of accumulated tendencies and ensure no further accumulation. The binding ones are those that reinforce the tendencies and impressions and make one object-bound. Having said that ego is the root cause of several activities of mind and having identified that these activities need be curbed, the next logical thing to do is to hold on to that activity of mind that is directed to removal of ignorance. While every kind of action done or contemplated to be done binds one and causes further actions, meditation and contemplation eases the vigour of the binding forces.

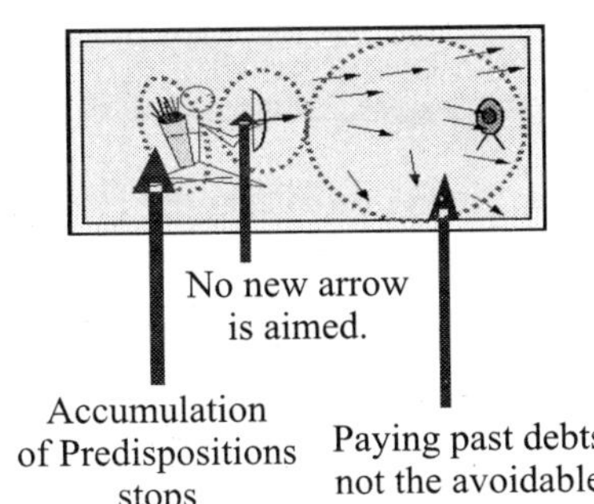

The accumulated predispositions and the actions that will bind one in future can both be nullified by those activities born of meditation. There will then be no debts that will accumulate to be paid in a later life. After attaining a state of *Samādhi* (absorption), whatever are the past debts accumulated, that need be experienced.

As you sow, so you shall reap.
With whatever measure you give,
with the same measure, it shall be given unto you.

Brahmānubhava Upanishad

कर्माशुक्लाकृष्णं योगिनस्त्रिविधमितरेषाम् ॥७॥

Karma_Ashukla_Akrishnam Yoginah Trividham Itareshām.

Yogi's actions not bound by dualities;
Others, influenced by triple qualities.

Karma: activity *Yoginaha*: of the Yogi *Itareshām*: for others
Ashukla Akrishnam: neither positive nor negative actions, done without desire for any results
Trividham: three fold –positive, negative, externally positive but internally negative, Hippocratic.

Q. *How can one distinguish the actions of a Yogi from that of others?*
A. The one, who has attained a state of illumination acts without expectations. He is beyond the binding dualities of pleasure and pain; good and bad; gain and loss and well or ill. Actions of others are tainted with anticipation and experiences of good, bad or worst or a mix.

For the first time Patanjali uses the word Yogi. Yogi is one who has united with the Reality. The actions of a Yogi are neither white nor black, whereas the actions of others are of three kinds. Words like good, bad or black or white cease to have any meaning for a yogi. Each one of his actions automatically proves beneficial to the society. He does not reason out to act. He acts spontaneously as if he were an automate machine. In such a machine one needs to insert a coin to make it act, but in the yogi machine even that is not necessary. His thoughts, words and actions are all beneficial to all. His actions have no anticipations or expectations. They do not leave the imprint of tendencies in him. One should not judge a Yogi by his actions. He may even be seen enveloping himself with luxuries. But he is not touched by them. If a follower thinks that such luxuries are OK for him too, he is mistaken. While the yogi is in them, he is not aware of them. But the seeker in them will be aware of nothing other than the luxuries.

Krishna is a *Yogapurusha*. He was in the thick of actions in the Mahābhārata. But he was untouched by them. Until one becomes a Krishna, one should be careful enough to distinguish as to which actions of him bind him down and which set him free. Meditation and constant awareness of God sets one free. All actions done with expectation bind one down. Even meditation is to be done without expecting liberation. God again should be sought for His own sake, not for boons.

A human being fashions his consequences
as surely as he fashions his goods or his dwelling.
Nothing that he says, thinks or does is without consequence.
Just as there is no loss of basic energy in the universe,
so no thought or action is without its effects,
present or ultimate, seen or unseen, felt or unfelt.

Norman Cousins

The Sage and the King

There was a wise king. One day, he strayed into deep forest after his hunting mission. He came across a sage. Impressed by the sage's learning and wisdom, the king requested him to accompany him to the royal palace and be with him. But the sage said, "Look, noble king, my place is this forest and my dwelling is this cottage. Not for me the palace or luxuries." But the king won't listen. He kept persuading the sage. At last the sage relented as he did not want to offend the king. But the sage decided, he would test the king and teach him what detachment means.

When the king said, 'Let us go', the sage did not move. He wanted the king to arrange the king's chariot. For a moment the king was intrigued at the demand. But he kept quiet as he did not want to offend his new guest. Both rode to the palace in full public view, the sage sitting as majestic as the king.

Once, at the palace the sage insisted on living in the palace itself. He rejected the outhouse reserved for saints and sages. Not only that every day, he insisted that he be provided new dress like that of the king, food like that of the king, servants at his disposal, dancers to dance and musicians to sing. With his every demand the king wondered whether the sage was a genuine one or a fake. As days passed by, the king noticed that there was no difference between him and the sage, in terms of comforts or respect shown. The king was wondering whether the sage will ever quit the palace and leave him free. His subjects found that there was almost another king for them to obey and be dictated upon.

The sage was watching the king and his reaction. He waited for the King to ask. One day, the sage wanted the King to arrange for his tour of the town, with all soldiers, orderly, the horses and elephants and all other retinue in place. That was a little too much for the king to digest. He got exasperated and asked the sage, "Oh sage, I doubt your credentials now. Are you really a sage? What is the difference between you and me now?". The sage did not respond. He just said, "O, king, now come along with me, let us go to the end of your Kingdom". The sage and the king went to the border. The sage said,

"Let us go to the forest and stay there." The king said, "no way, how can I leave my Kingdom, family and friends and come along with you?" The sage moved on. The king realised the difference. The sage had no attachment. He was not bothered about all the luxuries the king thought he was enjoying.

*A holy man is one who is full of fellow feeling,
who is a friend of all, who looks upon none as enemy,
who is overflowing with peace, who has virtue alone as his ornament
and who has deep rooted love for Me (God).*

Bhāgavata

ततस्तद्विपाकानुगुणानामेवाभिव्यक्तिर्वासनानाम् ॥८॥

Tatah Tad_Vipāka_Anugunānām Eva Abhivyaktih Vāsanānām

Propensities from past actions,
Remain in memory deep,
Manifest they when conditions ripe.

Tatah: thence, arising out of tendencies, latent impressions, propensities *Tad*: that
Vipāka: result *Anugunānām*: corresponding to *Eva*: only
Abhivyaktih: manifestation *Vāsanānām*: tendency, propensities

Q. *Don't tendencies die out?*

A. In the one, who has attained state of illumination through the yogic way, tendencies do not resurface, in others the latent tendencies will resurface and bind one with actions. In the others, because the tendency of the mind to act on the basis of five obstacles such as misapprehension has not been erased they will surface in the future to produce their unpleasant consequences.

Latent tendencies and propensities in the forms of compulsions, negative habits, reflexive patterns, etc. are like a computer programme which performs a task. It sits in wait, waiting for the programme to be executed. Past actions create tendencies. They are to be eliminated through meditation. The tendencies are a result of nature of actions undertaken.

- **White**: Born out of *Sattva* / purity aspect of mind: Actions that are white (good, useful) result in deep impressions that are also white (good, useful).
- **Black**: Born out of *Tamas* / inertia / thoughtlessness: Actions that are black (bad, not useful) result in deep impressions that are also black (bad, not useful).
- **Mixed**: Born out of *Rājas* / activity orientation: Actions that are mixed (shades of grey) result in deep impressions that are also mixed (shades of grey).

But whatever may be the action, corresponding result and the binding force cannot be avoided, while it is straight away essential to avoid actions based on inertia and activity orientation; eventually, one will be performing even actions based on clarity without expectations. As long as there is the body, so long will actions continue. In the illumined, all actions are born of *Sattva* but with no expectation. Expectation means seed generation.

Your bad attitudes have led to bad habits, which are hard to break;
You had allowed an ant of sensuality, to become a serpent;
You must slay the serpent now, or else it will grow into a dragon;
But like most people you probably think that your serpent is still an ant.

Rumi. Masnavi 2

जातिदेशकालव्यवहितानामप्यानन्तर्यं स्मृतिसंस्कारयोरेकरूपत्वात् ॥९॥

Jāti_Desha_Kāla_Vyavahitānām_Api
Ānantaryam Smriti_Sanskārayoh Yekarupatvāt.

Latent impressions, linked with memory remain.
Cease they not due to intervals of time, space or by a birth again.

Jāti: birth
Desha: place
Kāla: time
Vyavahitānām: removed from
Api: even though
Ānantaryam: subsequent happening
Smriti: memory, recollection
Sanskārayoh: latent impressions too
Eekarupatvāt: in appearance

Q. *Why don't tendencies die out?*

A. Because there is a very strong link between the latent impressions and memory. There is an uninterrupted relationship between the two even if separated by state, space, time or a new birth. Only when one is awakened to realize his true self, the afflictions, tendencies and modifications are destroyed.

On account of similarity between memory and corresponding latent impressions, the subconscious impressions of feelings appear simultaneously even when they are separated by birth, space, and time

Human beings are born with fully developed consciousness, but only in potential. This means that nothing needs to be added to human consciousness in order for an individual to realize the highest wisdom. Instead, something needs to be removed.

Human beings do not realize the full potential of their awareness because their consciousness is clouded by the residue of previous experiences, acquired through the long course of the soul's evolution. This residue is deposited in the storehouse of impressions as latent impressions or sanskāras. These impressions must be cleared away before an individual can realize the full potential inherent in human consciousness.

Abandoning vain talks know the supreme *Ātman*,
The Self by whom heaven, earth and nay, even the mind and
the vital powers are permeated.
This is the way to attain immortality- the eternal life.

Mundaka Upanishad

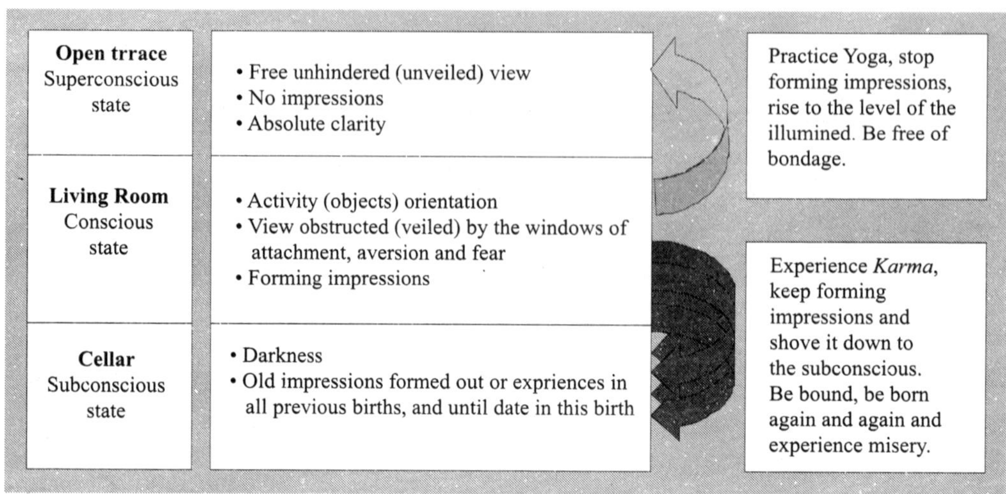

It should be understood that there are no divisions in consciousness. It is only for the purpose of understanding that we are differentiating as subconscious, conscious and super consciousness. Once the degree of consciousness reaches the highest state, it is described as super-conscious state. This degree of consciousness is in direct proportion to the level of awareness attained. This level in turn is directly proportional to the extent of practice on the part of the seeker and the extent of grace of the Supreme Being.

The heightened degree of awareness and consciousness results in the development of the quality of pure *sattva*. That is an indication of the attainment of Super Consciousness. The pure *sattva* can be distinguished from mixed *sattva*:

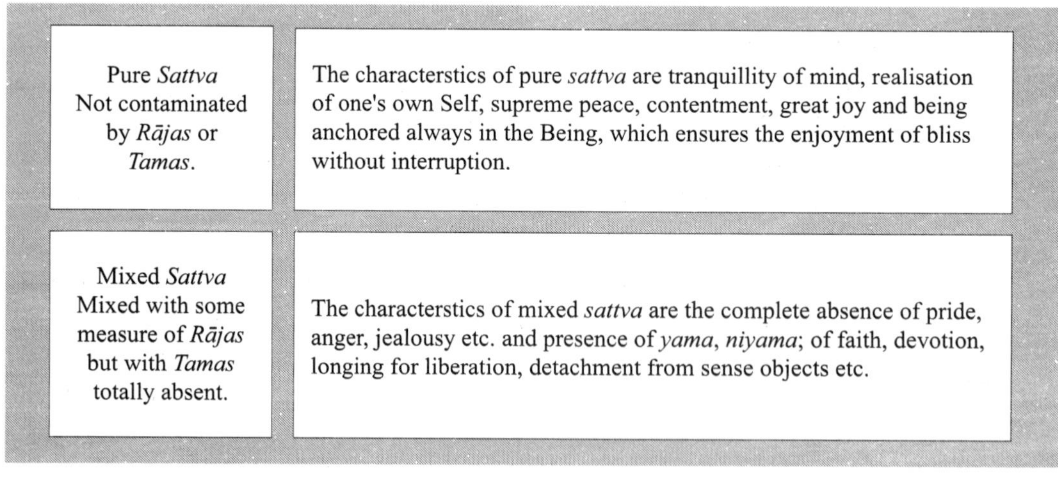

Pure *Sattva* Not contaminated by *Rājas* or *Tamas*.	The characterstics of pure *sattva* are tranquillity of mind, realisation of one's own Self, supreme peace, contentment, great joy and being anchored always in the Being, which ensures the enjoyment of bliss without interruption.
Mixed *Sattva* Mixed with some measure of *Rājas* but with *Tamas* totally absent.	The characterstics of mixed *sattva* are the complete absence of pride, anger, jealousy etc. and presence of *yama*, *niyama*; of faith, devotion, longing for liberation, detachment from sense objects etc.

तासामनादित्वं चाशिषो नित्यत्वात् ॥१०॥

Tāsām_Anāditvam Cha_Āshisho Nityatvāt.

Tendencies are origin less
Even as desire for life is endless.

Tāsām: those impressions *Anāditvam*: beginning less, no ultimate cause *Cha*: and *Āshisha*: present ever, living, eternal desire for beneficence *Nityatvāt*: permanently

Q. *What is the origin of these tendencies, say, when does it begin?*

A. These tendencies and instincts have no beginning, especially the desire for life. There is a strong desire for immortality in all beings and at all times. Thus, these impressions cannot be ascribed to any time.

The binding has ignorance as its source. It is without a beginning and without an end (until destroyed by awareness). It is beginning-less because it is the effect of ignorance, which is beginning-less. It cannot be known or said as to when begun.

Desire for self-welfare being everlasting, it follows that the subconscious impression from which it arises must be beginning-less. The assertion that 'the mind is a blank tablet at birth' has time and again been proved wrong. The cause-effect chain stops when one goes back to the beginning. What is the first cause that produced the effect of desire for life? The basic tendency of every single living being; be it man, beast, bird or a microbe is to protect and procreate. The other tendency of fight or flight results from this basic tendency to cling to life. The need to protect oneself and further its generation results in activity.

The instinct for self preservation results in keeping in memory incidents that has caused danger to existence as well as the presence of objects like food that resulted in satisfaction. The waking, sleeping and dreaming state automatically means the presence of triple quality of activity, clarity and inertia. So the tendencies are origin-less.

Luckily, the process of removing tendencies is well explained and well instructed by saints and sages. So, one need not despair and throw up his arms saying since tendencies are origin-less, there is nothing that can be done except to endure and suffer. The very awareness that one is subject to the influence of tendencies makes one get caught in them.

Be lamps unto yourselves....... do not depend on any external help. Rely on yourself. The more you depend on your self the more will your potentialities be realized.

Lord Buddha

At a glance: Aphorism 4.06-4.10

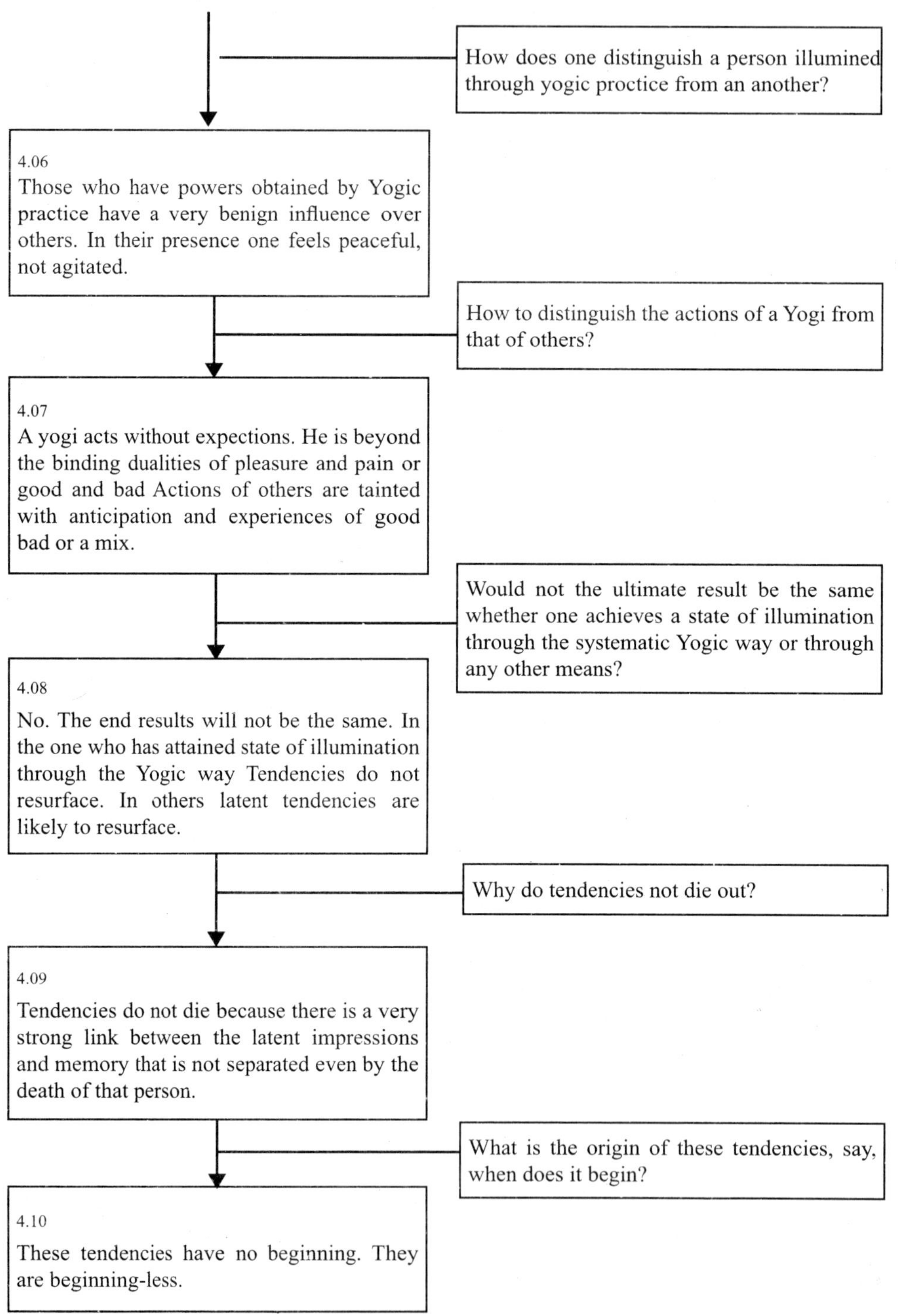

हेतुफलाश्रयालम्बनैः संगृहितत्वादेषामभावे तदभावः ॥११॥

Hetu_Phala_Āshraya_Ālambanaih Sangrahitatvāt Eshām Abhāve Tad_Abhāvah.

Causes, actions and the fruits that bind
Disappear when tendencies are not to find.

Hetu: reasons, causes
Phala: fruit, result
Āshraya: prop, base, abode
Ālambanaiha: support
Sangrahitatvāt: being held together
Eshām: these causes
Abhāve: in the absence of
Tad: that, that tendency
Abhāvah: absent

Q: When do desires disappear?
A: Desire, actions and the fruits that bind
Disappear when tendencies are not to find.

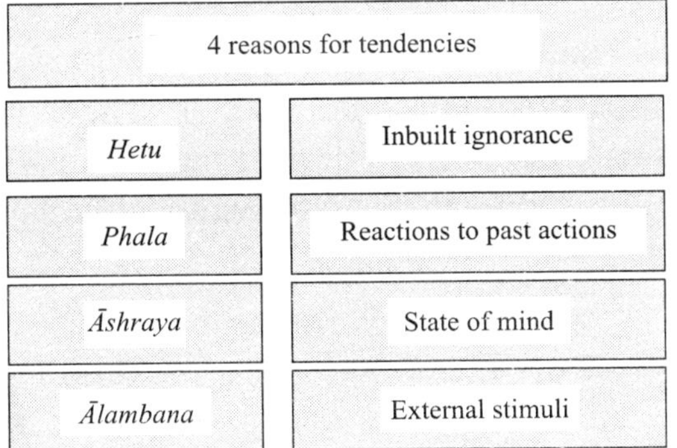

Tendencies are maintained and sustained by

Misapprehensions
Attachment to the fruits of actions
The quality of mind that permits instinctive activity
Devoid of reflection, and
External stimuli

How can one ensure that tendencies do not recur?

We can stop recurrence of tendencies by:

Being aware that ignorance is the root cause for misery
Following the dictum, "Action but no anticipation."
Adherence to *Āsana*, *Prānāyāma* and meditation practice.
Recognition that one cannot control external environment, but one can control own reactions to it.
Knowing that one is not the body, not the mind, not the intellect but the Pure Being.
Being devoted to God, thinking and chanting His name and seeking forever only His company.

Hold fast to the truth as a lamp.
Look not for refuge in anyone other than yourself.
Work out your salvation with diligence.

Lord Buddha

Since the desire to live is eternal, impressions are also beginning-less. The impressions being held together by cause, effect, basis and support, they disappear with the disappearance of these four.

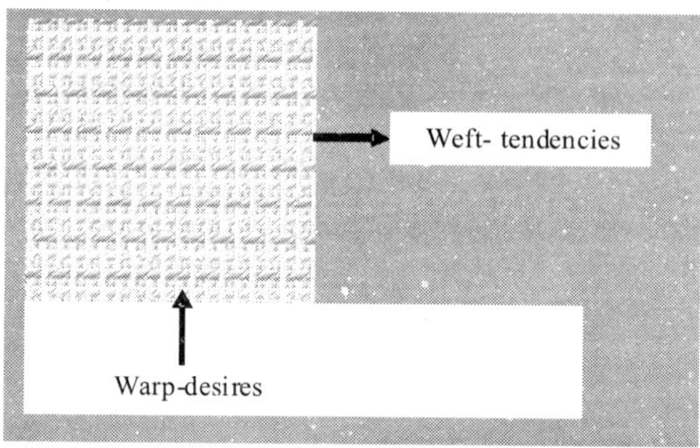

The cause and effect; the desire and tendency are interwoven as the very warp and weft of a fabric. If one pulls aside yarn by yarn, what will be left? nothing. That is how it is. If one removes desire after desire and tendency after tendency the fabric will loosen out. At the end when all threads / yarns are pulled out, there is nothing left. There will be no mind left out. Mind constitutes theses warps and wefts of desires and tendencies. There is no mind and hence there are no modifications. If theses constituent parts of mind are pulled out, mind will have no support base thereafter.

The warp and weft of desires and tendencies are so tightly woven that the fabric does not let light in. The closer the weave, the lesser the lights that it lets pass through. As one pulls a thread here and a thread there, the weave is weakened. As further and further the warp and weft threads are pulled out, there remains no fabric at all. Now, it is all light. Mind now gives way to light. There is just no mind to be seen anywhere. Everywhere there is light.

The tendency to love, hate, judge, accept, reject, control, compare, gravitate towards objects of pleasure, criticize, scrutinize etc belongs to different aspects of the mind. These are the modifications of mind.

When the tendencies/modifications are gone,
Then only one lets light of knowledge dawn.

Duality problems resolve,
when mind and memories dissolve.

The wheel of suffering

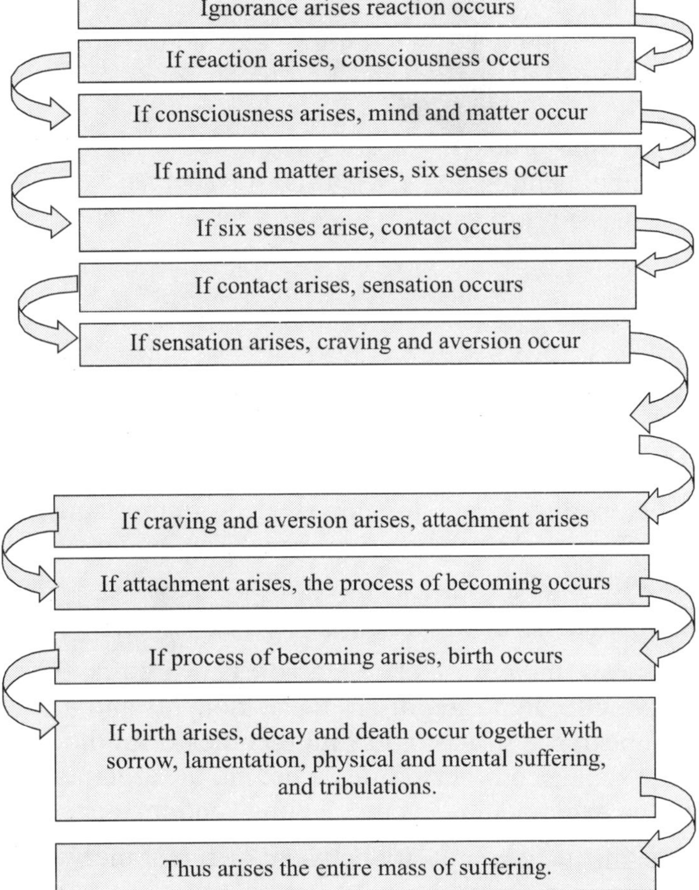

From a person's contemplating objects
Is born attachment to them
From attachment is born desire;
From desire is born anger:
From anger comes delusion;
From memory wondering, loss of intuition
From loss of intuition one perishes.

Man's suffering lasts only until he sees the Supreme Being
that dwells within himself.

Mundakopanishad

अतीतानागतं स्वरूपतोऽस्त्यध्वभेदाद्धर्माणाम् ॥१२॥

Atita_Anāgatam Svarupatoh_Asti Adhva_Bhedāt Dharmānām.

The past and the future exist in the present
Their evidence arises when given conditions ascend.

Atita: the past, the transpired
Anāgatam: that which is to come
Svarupatoh: essential nature
Asti: is, stays, exists
Adhva: the three divisions of time
Bhedāt: seen as different
Dharmānām: in the effects of action.

Q. Don't past impressions fade out?

A. Nothing old disappears for ever. Nothing new presents afresh.
All past impressions remain buried in the mind as tendencies. Future tendencies are caused by what already is lying buried, what is already experienced. Hence, past and future are both present in the present.

All of the characteristics, forms, memories, deep impressions, etc., exist in the 'here and now', whether in active or potential forms. The evidence of their presence can be felt when conditions are ripe.

The substance of what has disappeared, as well as what may appear always exists.

All tendencies, forms, memories, characteristics etc are present in the present. It is the rearranging in sequence that categorizes these thoughts and incidences as past, present or future. The appearance of past and future comes from the condition, path, or order in which they are sequenced. The rationale behind the argument that past tendencies do not die out, can be explained by events, feelings and incidences such as:

Difference in the instinctive capacity between different individuals.

The subconscious mind which survives death is the cause for fear of death, since one would have experienced the pain from separation of body.

Love at first sight is a certain feeling of a previous life lived together.

The seed of a banyan tree can only produce a banyan tree, not a mango tree.

At the time of separation of mind from the body, past tendencies and memories are encapsulated and stay frozen, until the soul finds a new body to sprout and experience. Until minds modifications are totally subdued with no seed (tendency) left out, the process of birth and death continues.

Those who do not show any revulsion
to unpleasant experiences and do not get elated by any pleasant ones,
and those who look upon the whole universe as *Māyā*, a mere
appearance and remain devoted to Thee alone,
their heart forms a fitting residence to Thee.

Ādhyātma Rāmāyana

ते व्यक्तसूक्ष्मा गुणात्मानः ॥१३॥

Te Vyaktasukshmā Gunātmānah.

Be they gross or subtle
Both have qualities in the middle.

Te: They (all effects) *Vyakta*: clear (present time) *Sukshmā*: subtle (past time)
Gunā: the three gunas, triple qualities *Atmānah*: have as the core

Q: *Do all objects have triple qualities?*
A: Yes. All manifested subtle things are *guna* oriented.
All have the triple qualities as its core.

The Being, manifests Itself as the fire, water and earth principles, Consciousness permeates them.

They are present always either in subtle or in gross form, the visible or invisible form. In whichever form they are, the triple qualities are always present in them. In connection with the object, the intellect gets transformed into the form of the object. This transformation is the modification of the mind. Modifications cease in meditation, when the thought patterns of propensities, tendencies, actions etc dissolve.

It is worth noting in this context what the well known Physicist, Dr John L Dobson says about the triple qualities and manifestation:

"If, in time and space, the changeless didn't show through, we wouldn't have inertia. If the infinite didn't show through, we wouldn't have electricity. And if the undivided didn't show through, we wouldn't have gravity and the attraction between opposites. Also, if the duality didn't keep up the plurality, we wouldn't have the atomic table. And if the plurality didn't keep up the duality, we wouldn't have atoms at all. That's how I see it.

"Space is not that which separates the many, but that which seems to separate the one. And in that space that oneness shines, therefore falls whatever falls."

Every object in the world, and every event which occurs in the world,
is a snare for the fool, but a means of violation for the wise.

Rumi. Masnavi 6

परिणामैकत्वाद्वस्तुतत्त्वम् ॥१४॥

Parināma_Yekatvāt Vastu_Tattvam.

The object presents a single face
As the triple qualities, in union, surface.

Parināma: change, transformation
Yekatvāt: state of being one
Vastu: things
Tattvam: real nature, as it is

Q. *Should the transformation be not many?*
A. The transformation is only one as the changes are brought about by the triple qualities act in unison. The essential substance of things comes about from the unification of mutation.

If there are three different qualities like clarity, activity and inertia and if there are infinite possible mutations and variations of the three and if the perception is always clouded by the three; how is that instead of observing a kaleidoscopic variation of manifestation we notice only a single substance or picture at a given time? The three qualities never act or influence an observer independently. The effect of their admixture is one. If one is predominant at a time, others subjugate themselves as it were and blend with the predominant quality, lending it a specific orientation. The subsidiary qualities conjoin with the predominant one and help in forming only one specific modification and present only one picture. On account of the coordinated mutation of the three qualities, an object appears as a unit. The triple qualities should not be looked at as three distinctive and different ones. The qualities merge and a single personality emerges. The Cosmic *Tamas* (inertia) divides itself into the veiling and projecting powers. The projecting powers appear as five forms as the principles of sound, of touch, of taste and of smell. These principles have in them again the subsidiary qualities of clarity, activity and inertia. The *Sattva* of sound becomes the sense of hearing, the *sattva* of *Rupa* (form) becomes the sense of touch etc. These *Sattva* properties taken together form the internal organ, which has four aspects- mind, will, ego and intellect. Similarly the *Rājas* aspect of the five principles becomes the organ of action and the *Tamas* aspect the gross universe.

Whoever sees the six transformations of one's being beginning with birth as occurring to the body and not to the Self, whoever sees hunger, thirst and fear as also happiness and misery as belonging to the *Prāna* and not *Ātman*, and whoever is by such knowledge free from involvement in the process of *Samsāra*- the heart of such a person forms a fitting residence for Thee.

Ādhayātma Rāmāyana

At a glance: Aphorism 4.11 – 4.14

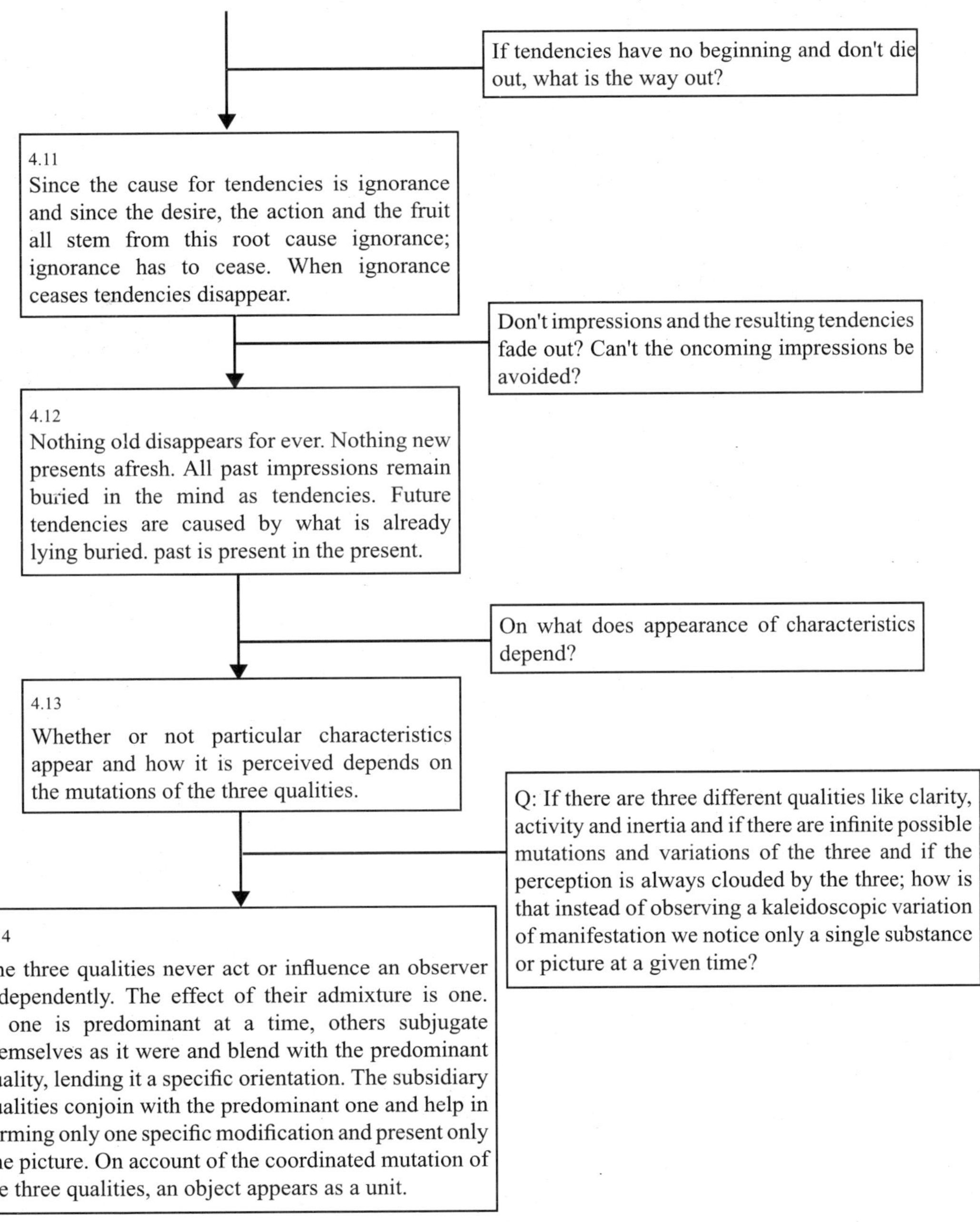

वस्तुसाम्ये चित्तभेदात्तयोर्विभक्तः पन्थाः ॥१५॥

Vastu_Sāmye Chitta_Bhedāt Tayoh_Vibhaktah Panthāh.

The same object appears for several as different
As perception, on the eyes of the beholders depend.

Vastu: things *Sāmye*: similarity *Chitta*: mind *Bhedāt*: difference
Tayoh: their (knowledge of things) *Vibhaktah*: separation *Panthāh*: path

Q: *But is the object perceived the same, the reality, a single entity or is it always different?*

A: The object is the never changing reality. But the observer influenced by ever changing mix of qualities, perceives the object differently; until, with ignorance gone, he realizes that he is the observer, the observed and the process of observation.

Mind is divided on even just one single object, resulting in different paths to knowledge. Brahman is everywhere and therefore all are One Thing only. But things are perceived as plural because of lack of perception of unity. The characteristics of an object appear differently, depending upon the different mental states of the observer. Consciousness becomes individualized due to ego. As a consequence perception of the same object varies from one person to another. Until 'ego' ness is removed, one cannot perceive the reality within the things. Since mind is influenced by triple qualities, the same object is perceived differently at different points of time by the same mind. Similarly different minds perceive the same object at the same time differently. The same incident is reported by different people differently as their observation of the incident is influenced by the triple qualities.

An international company was engaged in the business of manufacturing and selling shoes. They had a global presence, except in some parts of Africa. The sales director sent a sales manager and asked him to explore business opportunity. The sales manager visited the country and noticed that no one was wearing shoes. He therefore returned and reported to the Director that there is no potential since no one wears shoes. Not quite impressed with the report, the Director sent another sales manager to study the same market. The second sales manager visited the country and retuned with excitement. He reported that there is huge potential. The Director told him; "But your colleague has reported that no one wears shoes". The second sales manager answered:"That was exactly I am also saying. No one wears shoes there. Therefore we can sell shoes to each and every one of them. There is a huge potential."

Mind is the source of the sense of difference,
When the mind does not function there is no difference.
Therefore, concentrate the mind on the inner most Supreme Being.

Ādi Shankara, Crest Jewel of Wisdom

न चैकचित्ततन्त्रं वस्तु तदप्रमाणकं तदा किं स्यात् ॥१६॥

Na Cha Yeka_Chitta_Tantram Vastu
Tad_Aprmānkam Tadā Kim Syāt.

Object, on the mind does not subsist
On mind's absence it ceases not to exist.

Na: not Cha: and *Yeka*: one *Chitta*: mind *Tantram*: dependent
Vastu: things *Tad*: that *Apramānkam*: invalid *Tadā*: then
Kim: What *Syāt*: will be there

Q. *Is the object a reality or is it just an imagination or fantasy?*
A. The object is an apparent reality. Will the object cease to exit just because the mind does not observe?

When there is lack of awareness that all things and subjects are but one Consciousness, there is perception of multiplicity due to the presence and influence of tendencies/*vāsanās*.

As far as the object is concerned, it is the same. The object does not depend on the eye of the beholder. It exists. Its existence is independent of the mind. It does not subsist on the mind.

It is an ever changing mind which thinks the object is changing. If the object were indeed the conception of a particular individual's mind, then in the absence of his perception, would it cease to exist?

There are philosophical debates about the presence or absence of objects. Such debates are only sterile. From the point of view of the seeker, in his present state of awareness it is not possible to conceive an objectless world. Suffice it is to note that he better avoid debates and idle enquiry. It is useful to remember the saying that 'Wisdom begins where word ends' as also the saying 'Speech corrupts truth" Patanjali here answers the nihilists and the Buddhists, who held different view.

People know a magical show to be unreal, but this knowledge does not involve the destruction of the show. So it is possible to know the unreality of external object without causing their disappearance or the cessation of enjoyment from them.

> Many doors opened of themselves before me because of Thy coming. O Lord, everything shone with life when Thou comest. The temple's marble floor, on which I stood, thrilled me because of Thee. Everywhere dumb matter spoke, spirit-resurrected by Thy touch. Everywhere throbbed the incense-breeze of stillness, bearing to me Thy perfume of bliss.
>
> *Paramhansa Yogānanda*
> *Whispers from Eternity A Book of Answered Prayers*

तदुपरागापेक्षित्वाच्चित्तस्य वस्तु ज्ञाताज्ञातम् ॥१७॥

Tad_Uparāga_Apekshitvā Chittasya Vastu Gyāt_Agyātam.

On mind's coloured expectation;
Depends, objects perception or absence of perception.

Tad: that *Uparāga*: coloured *Apekshitvā*: expecting, anticipating
Chittasya: for the mind *Vastu*: things, objects *Gyāt*: known, perceived
Agyātam: unknown, not perceived

Q: *On what does the perception of an object depend?*
A: It depends on whether the object generates an interest in the mind of the observer.

If an object does not generate interest in the observer, his mind does not see the object. This situation happens when one is so engrossed or so lost in solitary thought as to be unaware of one's surroundings. In the first instance how can the mind know whether the object has generated interest in the object unless the mind sees the object? The mind does not even see it, because it is preoccupied with some other "internal" object, a thought. So, when one predominant thought is gripping one's mind, his faculties are so absorbed in the thought, eyes don't see and ears don't listen.

It is everyday experience for many that while they are physically present and even their eyes are wide open; they do not recognize and see events or observe others who are right in front of them. They are said to be 'absent minded'. Only when the mind is present is the object cognized. When 'mind is absent', that is, when the mind 'is present elsewhere', though eyes are wide open, one does not see objects. It is the condition of being so lost in solitary thought as to be unaware of one's surroundings.

"Where mind sees the creation, it does not see the creator". If one is lost in the objective world, he does not see reality. And when one has seen the reality and is lost in thought of God, he does not see the objective world.

Material object	Cognised by the mind-being modified by the form of material object
Mental object	Cognised by the Witness-consciousness

Observances void of purity of heart! To what end are they? To what end is preparation of food without cleansing the vessel? Void of purity of mind, to what end is the worship of God?

Vemana (South Indian mystic and poet)

The Absent Minded Professor

The professor was very famous for his lectures as well as his forgetfulness. Many days his wife will give him some instruction or other like wanting him back home early, or his need to visit the doctor etc, but he will invariably forget and then get back home.

One day the professor's family were shifting their residence to another street in the same neighbourhood.

The professor's wife told him: "Darling today don't get back to this home. By afternoon we would have shifted all our belongings to the new home. There will be no one here if you return here in the evening."

He replied, "Don't worry I can remember well." Yet the loving wife left many pieces of papers with the new address. She wanted to make sure that the gentle professor should not forget the new address.

As usual the professor was busy at the university and needless to add all the bits of papers with the new address were scribbled with notes on the reverse side and thrown away.

When the professor returned to his old home, he found a big lock and a note that they have shifted. Now, he was in a dilemma. He forgot the new address and not even one bit of paper that his wife gave him was in his pocket.

Any way the professor thought, "I am intelligent enough. After all I am a famous professor in this area. I can ask anyone here and they will be able to tell me where my family has shifted"

So thinking, the professor was walking along. There were four teen aged girls coming from the opposite direction. The professor approached one of them and asked her, "Will you please tell me, where the professor's family has shifted?"

The young girl replied, "Don't worry dad. I will take you home."

How can one be healthy,
if there is even a trace of poison in the body?
Such also is ego (*ahamkāra*)
in respect of the liberation of a seeker.

Ādi Shankara, Crest Jewel of Wisdom

सदा ज्ञाताश्चित्तवृत्तयस्तत्प्रभोः पुरुषस्यापरिणामित्वात् ॥१८॥

Sadā Gyātah Chitta_Vrittayah Tat_Prabhoh
Purushasya Ā_Parināmitvāt.

The unchanging Self always knows
Mind's moods and where it goes.

Sadā: always *Gyātah*: known, revealed *Chitta*: mind
Vrittayah: movement, modifications *Tat*: that *Prabhoh*: experience
Purushasya: experience *Āparināmitvāt*: due to immutability, changeless nature

Q. *Who is the perceiver of the mind's modifications?*
A. Mind's activities are always known to the changeless and immutable Self. Hence, for the Self mind is the seen.
The seer is the Self, while the seen is the mind.

That which moves can only be witnessed by that which is still. From the state of equilibrium, movements and changes can be observed. The seer is always the one that perceives changes in the seen. With reference to the mind, the one that perceives movements/thoughts in mind is the unchanging Self. The witness for the consciousness can be the consciousness itself. Since, there is no movement in the consciousness, it can be recognized or seen only by itself.

The seer	The seen
Seer: Eye organ →	Seen: The tree (the external object)
Seer: The senses of sight →	Seen: Eye organ
Seer: The mind →	Seen: The sense of sight
Seer: The Self →	Seen: The mind
Seer: Consciousness →	Seen: The self
Seer: Consciousness →	Seen: Consciousness

Mental modifications in the form of objects of knowledge produced through the instrumentality of the other organs and also those in the form of memory, attachment etc which are only within the mind and then again in dream are witnessed by one different from all of these. Knowledge therefore of the Knower is eternal, pure, infinite and without a second.

Ādi Shankara, Upadesha Sahashri

At a glance: Aphorism 4.15-4.18

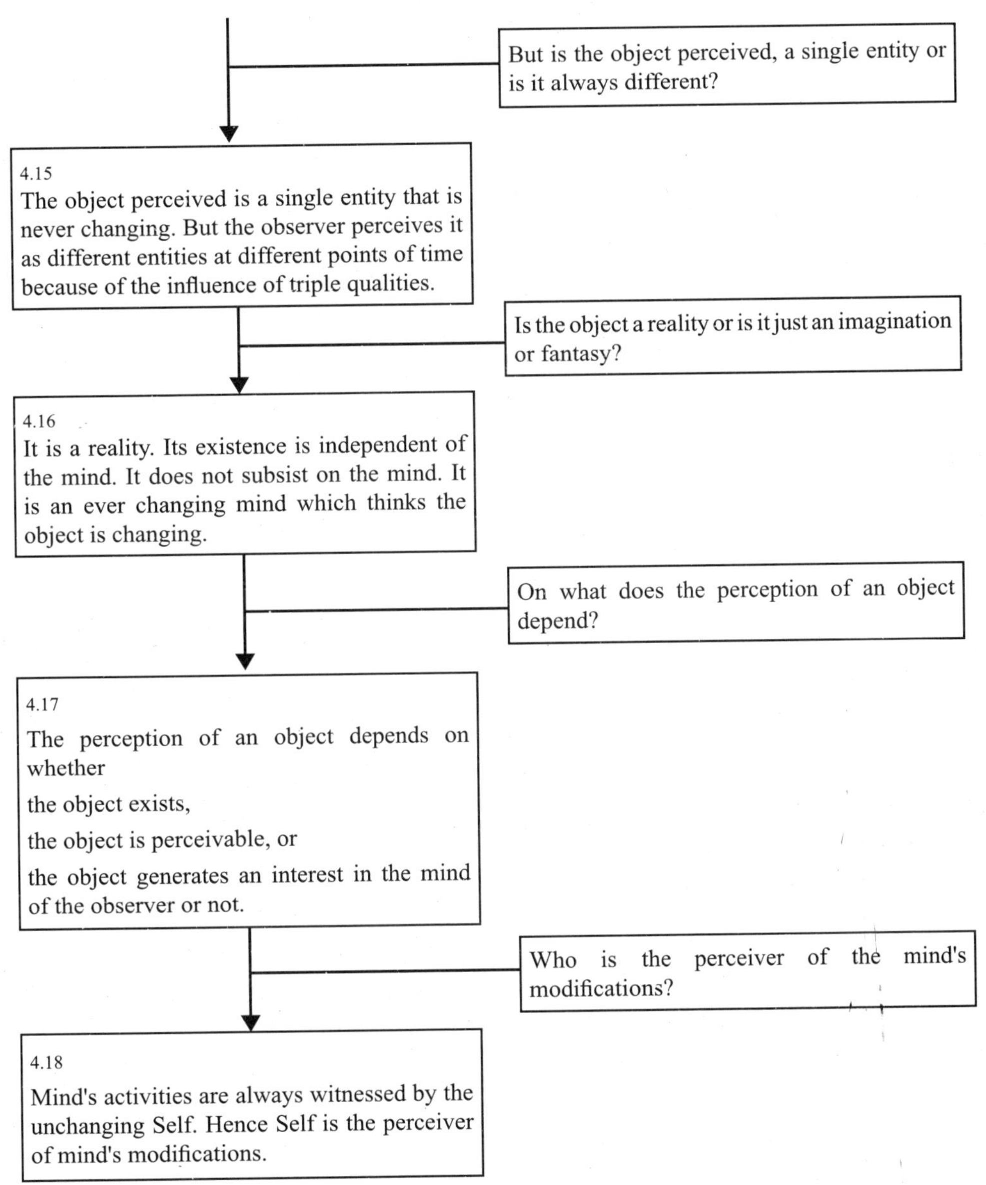

न तत्स्वाभासं दृश्यत्वात् ॥१९॥

Na Tat Sva_Abhāsam Drishyatvāt.

Mind, the object of perception
Is not the light, but a reflection.

Na: no, does not become *Tat*: that state of mind *Sva*: on its own, by itself *Abhāsam*: shining nature, illuminating *Drishyatvāt*: because it is comprehensible

Q. *Can the Brahman and the objects be perceived simultaneously?*
A. No. The mind is a part of what is perceived and has no power of its own to perceive. Brahman and objects (as real) cannot be cognized at the same time.

Mind is not self luminous. It derives its luminosity from the Consciousness. Mind is not the light, but a reflection. Unless Seer wills, the mind cannot function. Being an imperfect instrument influenced by prejudices it cannot see properly unless cultivated to avoid getting coloured.

Mind, intellect and the senses are illumined by the Consciousness. Consciousness, much like sun, lightens up everything, but receives no light from any where, as it is self illuminating. Consciousness is a witness to the varying states of mind such as waking, dreaming and sleeping. The three states keep rotating much like a Persian wheel, while Consciousness remains as it is. The street light is a witness to the drunkard who blabbers, the villain who cheats an innocent caught in the night, and the young couple who express their desire for each other. But the street light has no role to play in any of the incidents happening right under its nose!

It is wrong to think of the mind as playing a dual role of being a witness as well as the player. Mind is a changing entity. A changing entity should not be mistaken to the never changing pure Consciousness.

When one sees the creation, the creator is not perceived.
When one sees the creator (realizes Brahman) the creation is seen as unreal.

Yoga, i.e., detachment and self-discipline, purifies the mind and enables it to perceive the Truth. Those, whose understanding has been thus enlightened as well as purified become one with the Universal Spirit. They join the Supreme Being and lose themselves in Him even as all the rivers join and lose themselves in the great ocean.

Mundakopanishad

एकसमये चोभयानवधारणम् ॥२०॥

Yeka_Samaye_Cha Ubhaya_Anavadhāranam.

Mind functions not in two different role;
To see and to fabricate is an impossible goal.

Yeka: One	*Samaye*: time	*Cha*: and
Ubhaya: both	*Anavadhāranam*: incomprehensible	

Q: *Is it possible that mind simultaneously perceives and fabricates the object of perception?*

A: No, that is impossible. Mind cannot simultaneously see and produce the image being seen. The premise that the mind can play a dual role is untenable. Mind cannot simultaneously fabricate and see what it fabricates. When Brahman is everywhere the mind becomes still.

If the mind is assumed to be the perceiver, it should perceive the object always in the same way. But mind presents different pictures of the same object at different points of time depending upon the changes to its nature brought about by tendencies. Hence, mind cannot be the perceiver.

If the mind is presumed to be the perceiver, then who is presenting the picture in front of the mind for it to perceive? Senses are only organs of perception. Even if the eye is looking at an object, the mind may not perceive since it may be engrossed in some other thought. Therefore, one comes across an untenable situation that some times the mind perceives and at other times it does not. Perceiver should always exist.

The Perceiver is the never changing entity. Mind along with senses and objects are the perceived. The meditator can easily watch thoughts raising up and vanishing away. The meditator can experience the reality of the mind being an object, coming into existence only if there are thoughts and disappearing the moment thoughts melt down. If a cognition has to be known by an entity other than itself, that second one in turn has to be known by another and the third by yet another. This leads to infinite regress. A cognitor is an illuminator like a lamp. If cognition is assumed to be a lit-lamp and if one were to imagine a second cognition, then both the cognitions are similar, then there will no revelation of one by another. Hence, such assumptions turn fallacious.

Can a man be possessed of two identities, two selves? To understand this matter it is first necessary for a man to analyse himself. Because it has long been his habit to think as others think, he has never faced his 'I' in the true manner. He has not a correct picture of himself; he has too long identified himself with the body and the brain. Therefore, I tell you to pursue this enquiry, "Who am I?"

Raman Maharishi

चित्तान्तरदृश्ये बुद्धिबुद्धेरतिप्रसङ्गः स्मृतिसंकरश्च ॥२१॥

Chitta_Antar_Drishye Buddhi_Buddheh Ati_Prasangah Smriti_Samkarah Cha.

If first mind were to on a second prevail
Disorder ensures and memories fail.

Chitta: mind *Antar*: another *Drishye*: perception, sight
Buddhi: intellect, cognition *Ddheh*: of cognitions
Atiprasangah: disorder, confusion *Smriti*: memory *Cha*: and

Q. Could it be that there are two minds, one observing and the other fabricating?
A. No. If the premise of a succession of mind is assumed, there will be utter confusion and lack of comprehension and memory.

Could it be that there are two minds, one observing and the other fabricating? Possibly one is referring to the observing mind as the Self and the fabricating one as the mind? No, says Patanjali. If the premise of a succession of mind is assumed, there will be utter confusion and lack of comprehension and memory. If one mind were to be illumined by another mind then there would be repetition *ad infinitum* of illumining minds and intermixture of memory.

If one were to dismiss the reality of an unchanging Perceiver, ever observing and experiencing; he has to substitute the Perceiver with another mind; one mind to experience and another to provide the experience, are simultaneously in action, at the same moment of time. Immediately there after another set of minds have to take over to create and observe the next experience. A succession of double minds in action! This would involve the argument of *regress ad infinitum*. To expect each of these successions of double minds to recall the experience of experiencing and fabricating would be futile. Only lunacy and confusion can prevail.

An imagination of a succession of double minds can come about only from lack of comprehension. Series of minds is the snake that the uncomprehending mind sees where there is a rope. The perceiver alone can recognize rope always as a rope.

"Apart from the mind there is no ignorance. The mind itself is the ignorance which is the cause for the bondage of rebirth. When the mind is destroyed, everything else is destroyed. When the mind manifests, everything else manifests"

Ādi Shankara

चितेरप्रतिसंक्रमायास्तदाकारापत्तौ स्वबुद्धिसंवेदनम् ॥२२॥

Chiteh_A_Prati_Samkramāyāh Tad_Akāra_Āpattau Sva_Buddhi_Samvedanam.

Mind, delinked from object it sees
Reflects perceiver as it is.

Chiteh: of the consciousness *A_Pratisamkramāyāh*: self being changeless
Tad: that *Akāra*: form *Āpattau*: possibility being present
Sva: one's own *Buddhi*: intellect *Samvedanam*: experience

Q. *What is the purpose of mind? When does it function effectively?*
A. The mind has a dual purpose, presents the external to the perceiver and presents the perceiver to itself for its own enlightenment.

When the mind is not linked to external objects and it does not reflect an external form to the perceiver, then it takes the form of the perceiver itself. Understanding improves if mind is not linked to objects. Such a de-linking comes about by the grace of God or by practice. It requires training, to get the mind to turn away from the external objects to internal.

It is worthwhile recollecting that:

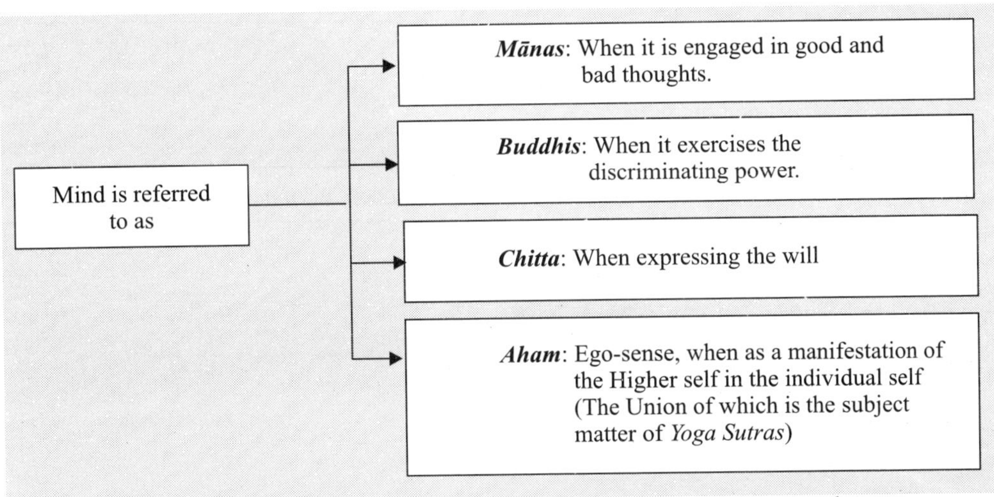

The reflection of the self in the mind is mistaken by the mind as the true self due to ignorance.

At a glance: Aphorism 4.19-4.22

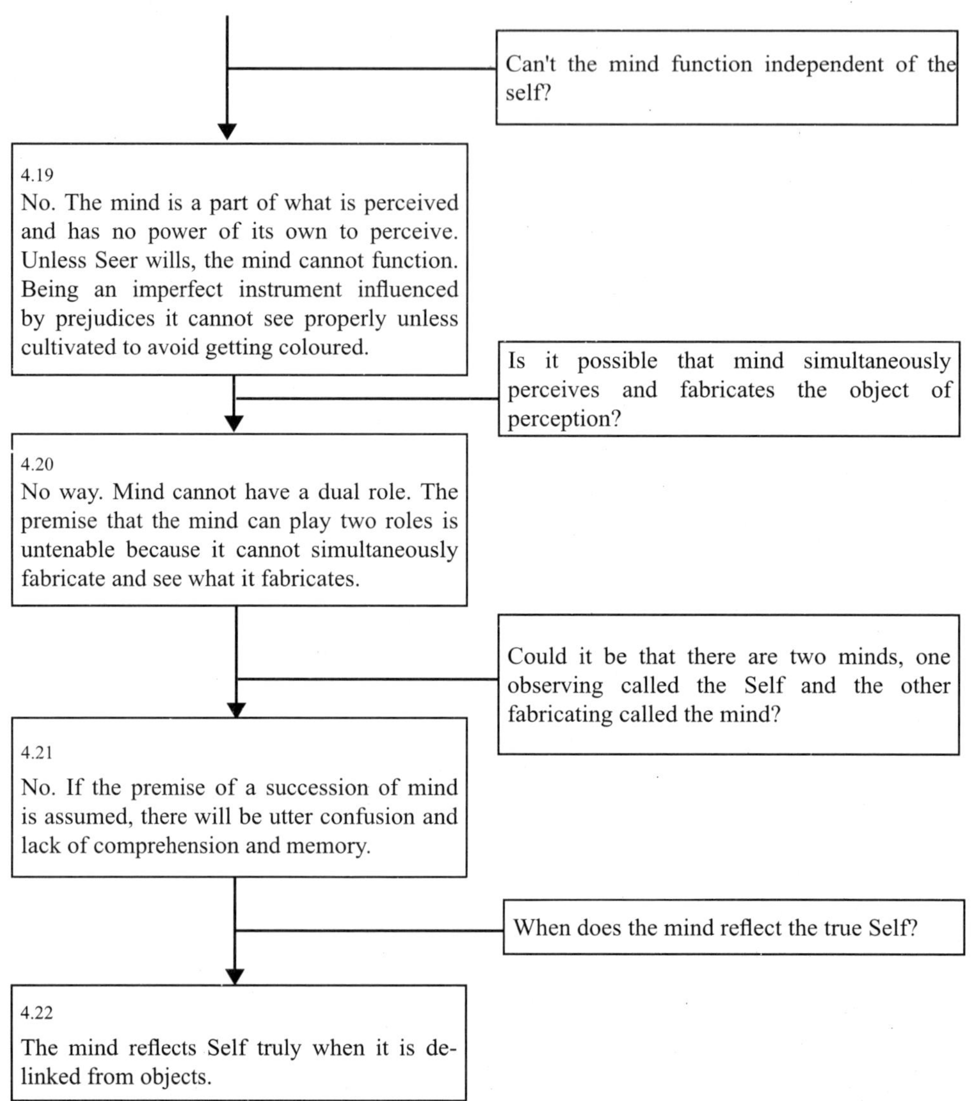

द्रष्टृदृश्योपरक्तं चित्तं सर्वार्थम् ॥२३॥

Drishti_Drishya_Uparaktam Chittam Sarvārtham.

Mind presents objects to perceiver
Reflects the perceiver to itself.

Drishti: seer	*Drishya*: seen	*Uparaktam*: together in the same company
Chittam: mind	*Sarvā* : all	*Artham*: understands

Q. *What is the purpose of the mind?*

A. The mind has a dual purpose, the first to serve the perceiver by presenting external objects to it. (while performing this role it is referred to as ***mānas***) and the second to Reflect the perceiver to itself for it's own enlightenment (while performing this role it is referred to as ***chitta***). At a given time it performs only one or the other of the two functions.

As all our sense organs are projecting outwards, our vision is outward-oriented. The attempt in meditation is to develop the inward-look.

Mind is the link between the eternal and the ephemeral.

The field of knowledge
- Eternal
- All pervading
- Non caused
- Beyond time and space Freedom

The field of Energy
- Beginning of time and space
- Alternating waves and particles
- Fluid

The field of Matter
- Ephemeral
- Subject to decay and death
- Known through senses.
- Time is linear

Bound, Rigid

The Lord is not to be apprehended by the senses,
but only by the mind into which all the senses have been drawn in.
All thought is inter-woven with the senses,
and it is only when the mind is released from all this
and is in a state of perfect freedom and tranquillity,
that the Lord reveals Himself.

तदसंख्येयवासनाभिश्चित्रमपि परार्थं संहत्यकारित्वात् ॥२४॥

Tat Asankhayeya_Vāsnābhih_Chitram_Api Para_Artham Samhatya_Kāritvāt.

Mind, though tainted in many ways
Serves the cause of the Perceiver always.

Tat: that, (the mind) *Asankhayeya*: Innumerable, countless
Vāsnābhihi: propensities, tendencies *Chitram*: pictures, variety of
Api: though *Para*: outer, other *Artham*: meaning, concept
Samhatyakāritvāt: in view of action in association with

Q. Is the mind independent of the Self, since it acts on impulses and tendencies from past memory?

A. No. Mind is a tool of the perceiver. Although mind is filled with its own impressions it can always be at the disposal of the Self. Even though the mind has accumulated various impressions of different types it is always at the disposal of the Perceiver. This is because the mind cannot function without the power of the Perceiver.

Though innumerable tendencies influence mind and make it a defective instrument, it is still an instrument always at the disposal of the Perceiver. Without the power of the Perceiver the mind cannot function even for a moment.

Mind differs from the sense organs. Mind has the capacity to reflect an inferential presence of the unseen Being, the ultimate Reality. Mind when not distracted by the senses has an integrating power. Such a mind with the integrating power receives illumination from the Consciousness. Once illumination is received, the darkness of ignorance is removed. Then the *karmas*, tendencies, propensities, whatever name one wishes to call, are weakened. Those who abide in the Consciousness having been illumined, reside in the blissful Being and are not the least affected by the three kinds of *Karmas* (*Prārabdha*, *Sanchita* and *Āgama*). In them they are destroyed by the fire of knowledge.

So long as the notion continues that body is the self, *prārabdha* exists.
When that notion is not cherished, *prārabdha* is abandoned.
Even the notion that *prārabdha* belongs to the body is a delusive one.

Ādi Shankara, Crest Jewel of Wisdom.

विशेषदर्शिन आत्मभावभावनाविनिवृत्तिः ॥२५॥

Vishesha_Darshina Ātma_Bhāva_Bhāvanā Vinivrittih.

The desire to know the reality
Ceases in one with clarity.

Vishesha: discrimination *Darshinah*: perceiver *Ātma*: self
Bhāva: expression, matter relating to self *Bhāvanā*: perception
Vinivrittihi: culmination

Q. Is the curiosity to know Reality an idle one?
A. No. It is as natural as wishing to quench the thirst. It is an effort on one's part to know his true self. It ceases the moment true knowledge dawns.

But such a desire automatically disappears in the one who has realised. The one with total perception is devoid of curiosity. A person of extraordinary clarity is one who is free from the desire to know the nature of the Perceiver.

Patanjali suggests that the polemical discussion about the nature of mind, its relationship between the seer and the seen; better cease. The fact remains that human mind is ignorant. It is bound by dualities. Attachment and aversion creates a constant state of anxiety, fear and unhappiness. What is needed is freedom from ignorance, not debates or discussion about ignorance. Freedom cannot be gained from discussion about the nature or the need for freedom, but from actions towards freedom. Discussions are good in so far as they reinforce desire for freedom. Such a discussion provides an intellectual basis for what is an intuitive craving. It is an idle mind that fantasies on scenes outside the prison gates. The determined mind will attempt and get out instead of indulging in futile interpretations. The mind that alternates as intellect is inadequately equipped to attain freedom by contemplating on freedom. Unless the mind is silenced it cannot hear!

On realizing the ultimate Reality, Wisdom and Bliss through freedom from connection created by the bond of ignorance, arguments cease. The only authority then is Self acquired. Neither scriptures nor teachings have any validity if they contradict acquired authority.

"There is a seeking until there is a knowing
When there is a knowing, there is no longer a seeking."

Carl Jung

तदा विवेकनिम्नं कैवल्यप्राग्भारं चित्तम् ॥२६॥

Tadā Vivekanimnam Kaivalya_Prāgabhāram Chittam.

The discriminating mind gravitates there
Where freedom is seen in full glare.

Tadā: then, after such awareness
Vivekanimnam: discrimination, awareness
Kaivalya: liberation, freedom
Prāgabhāram: having the final result
Chittam: mind

Q. What do the discriminating aspire for?

A. Nothing. The discriminating mind stops not to analyse but gravitates to freedom. They are inclined towards discriminative knowledge and naturally move towards the state of liberation and aim to remain there.

When discrimination dawns, by which the seeker casts off his delusions, He does not regard even his own personality as anything meaningful, but seeks to be in touch with reality only. Dawning of discrimination is akin to one tasting the nectar. After enjoying the taste of nectar none would like to taste anything else.

Once a person realizes that he had mistaken a piece of rope for a snake, he feels sorry for his act of having run away from it. The fearing and trembling in the person who has mistaken a rope as snake may continue for couple of minutes more, even after he realizes it is only a piece of rope. If he revisits the site again after an interval and he may again for moment see a snake where there is a rope. Realisation dawns on him not abruptly, but slowly. When in contact with the objects of the world, he would see them again with his senses, but would be unaffected by the sight. The senses would remain neutralized in him.

A holy person would not mix with infidels, having performed penance for all the impurities he might have come into contact with, due to association with them previously. The awakened one, entrenched in his new home as it were, takes a detached look. He recognizes that he is one with the rest and that he is not apart from the rest.

In the case of the discriminating one, experience of pleasure and pain is like the experience of that of audience in a theater or a magic show. He is a witness to the drama. He is not a player.

He witnesses the magic with no awe as he knows that it is only a magic.

Arm yourself with the shield of discrimination
and the sword of dispassion.

At a glance: Aphorism 4.23-4.26

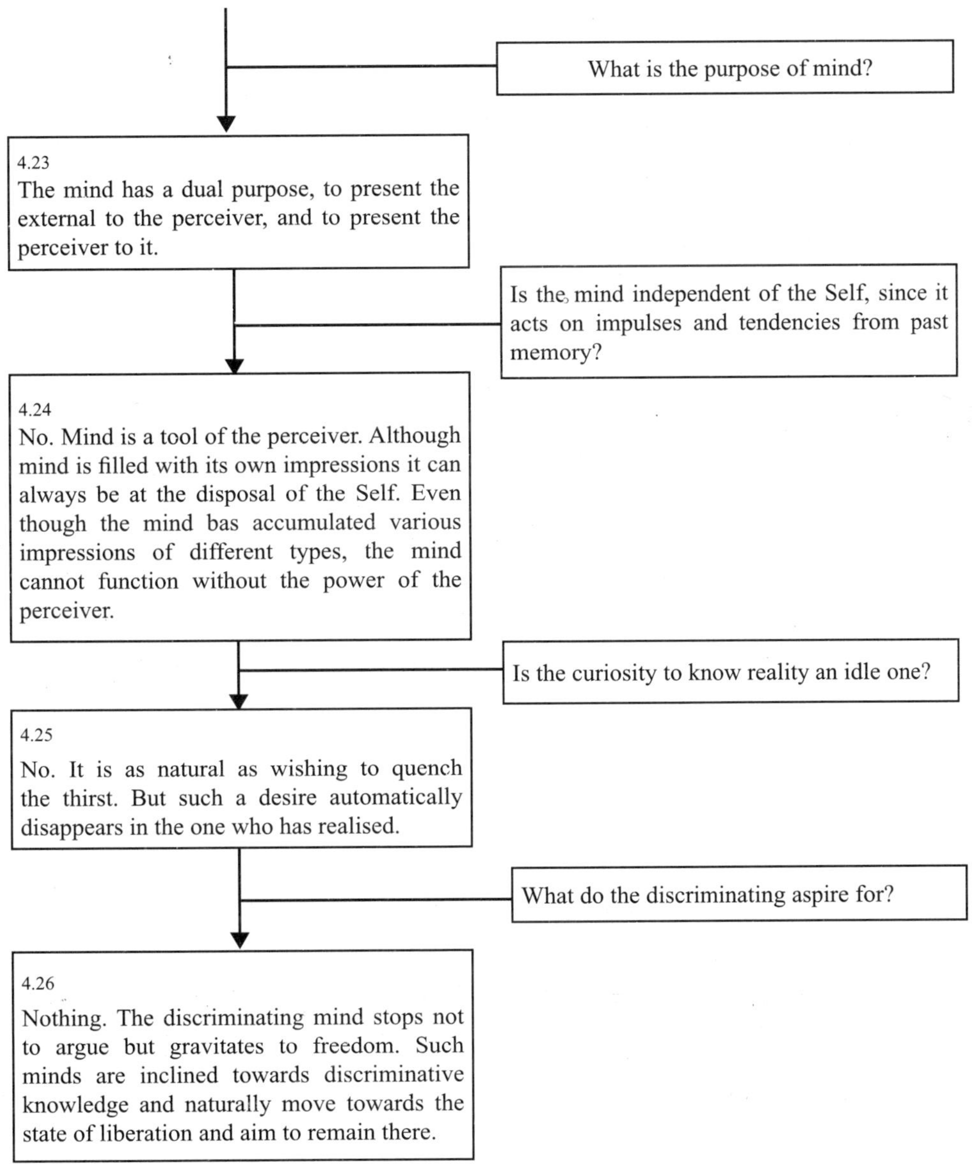

तच्छिद्रेषु प्रत्ययान्तराणि संस्कारेभ्यः ॥२७॥

Tat_Chhidreshu Pratyaya_Antarāni Samskārebhyah.

Thoughts pour in, where there is regress.
Tendencies resurface blocking progress.

Tat: that (the state of awareness)
Chhidreshu: gaps
Samskārebhyah: from past impressions
Antarāni: differentiated
Pratyaya: knowledge, field of consciousness

Q. *What when there is regress in the path to liberation?*
A. When there is regress in the path of liberation, tendencies resurface blocking progress, disturbing past impressions trouble the seeker again and breaks in discriminative knowledge result in fluctuations of the mind due to latent impressions.

Yet another caution for even at this stage there is a possibility of regression. Eternal vigilance is what is called for. The discriminating should ensure that traces of past impressions are also erased. *Pratyaya* is the secondary condition or conditions pre-existing allowing primary causes to function. The preexisting condition is the latent tendencies. As the external objects present their forms to cognition, so do the internal objects like pleasure, pain and hatred; thus they too become inferable. While there is less risk of external objects distracting the seeker at this stage, there is greater risk of internal objects like past memories and tendencies resurfacing, however wise one may be.

Samskārās are past impressions. *Vāsanās* are the tendencies, the forces deep within everybody that shape one's emotions and thoughts. They are un-manifest while emotions and thoughts are manifest, perceived. *Vāsanās* are only inferred. Any indulgence that is done consciously can cause a *Vāsanās*. It is sure to be generated when such an indulgence is repeated several times. *Vāsanās* can be eliminated when the intellect clearly sees no value in an object of desire. This clear seeing can be made possible by study, thinking and meditation. One can drop one's identification with one's mind, which will amount to freedom from the *Vāsanās*. The means to destroy the three, tendencies, thought and action, is to see everything as the Being under all conditions, always, everywhere and in all ways. By strengthening the wish to be forever with the blissful Being, these three are avoided.

As moss on the water pushed aside does not stay away even for a moment, so māyā also covers a man however wise he may be, if the senses are outward bound.

Ādi Shankara, Crest Jewel of Wisdom

हानमेषां क्लेशवदुक्तम् ॥२८॥

Hānam_Eshām Kleshavat_Uktam.

Means of removal of latent impressions
Are like that of afflictions.

Hānam: total release
Eshām: the latent impressions
Kleshavat: afflictions like ignorance
Uktam: spoken of earlier

Q. How are interfering thought patterns removed?

A. Interfering thought patterns are removed the same way as removal of afflictions are performed.

Single biggest obstruction at this level is the tendency to enjoy fruits resulting from heightened awareness. The means to remove obstructions remain the same as elucidated earlier. The afflictions like Ignorance, (*Avidyā*), false sense of ego, (*Asmitā*), Attachment *Rāga*, Aversion *Dwesha* and Fear (*Abhinivesha*) arising out of attachment to body though mitigated remain dormant.

Until their roots are burnt out it is essential practice is not given up. Patanjali gives indications of several sign posts on the way to the destination of liberation. These sign posts are meant to reinforce one's conviction in the course chosen. En route there will be more kinds of temptations to enjoy fruits of penance thus far and relax. It is such a tendency to stop and enjoy that it is a regress. Mythology gives us several case histories of saints who were struck by attachments en route and got stuck. Austerity (*Tapa*), Self-study / introspection (*Svādhyāya*) and Surrender to God (*Iswara Pranidhāna*) are not only the first steps, they are also the last steps to liberation. The fruits of efforts put in thus far also need be surrendered to God. Accumulation of new *Karma* will result if even the thought of enjoying such fruits arises. Much the same way a diseased man avoids unwholesome diet, one should avoid thinking sense objects.

The *Dhāranā*, *Dhyāna* and *Samādhi* aspects of the eight limbed Yoga need be adhered to fast. The cure for ills arising in spite of Yoga practice is more practice. The rising of tendencies is an indication in lacunae in adhering to the rigid guide lines enunciated by Patanjali.

Sense objects recede from the abstinent man but the taste for them lingers still, with the realisation of the supreme Being, even that taste disappears.

Bhagavatgitā

The Saint and his pot

Ubhaya Bhārathi and her husband Mandana Mishra were an enlightened couple.

Once in a debate with Ādi Shankara, Mandana Mishra was defeated. Thereafter both renounced worldly activities and took to the life of a recluse and decided on propagating wisdom.

Ubhaya Bhārathi set up a hermitage on the banks of the river Ganges. Many women became her disciples. She was teaching a number of women disciples. The lady Saint taught her disciples the need to remove the soot of ego that covers one's mind.

Every day Ubhaya Bhārathi and her women followers used to go to the river Ganges to have a bath. On the way there lived a Sage, called Brahma Gyāni. Truly he was a learned one, oozing out wisdom. However, somehow he was attached to a small earthen pot, in which he used to preserve water. He was afraid someone may steal it while he is asleep; hence he used his pot as a pillow while sleeping.

Noticing this desire for the pot in the Gyāni, Ubhaya Bhārathi remarked one day on her way to the river, "Though he is a man of wisdom and knowledge, one small defect still persists in him. He cannot be free from his attachment to the pot. He has renounced the world, but not his pot."

The sage overheard this remark of Ubhya Bhārathi. He became so angry he immediately crushed the pot on the spot and threw it on the passage. He wanted to prove that he had no attachment to any object.

On her way back, Ubhaya Bhārathi noticed the crushed pot strewn around and the angry *Sanyāsi* looking at the broken pot. Now Ubhaya Bhārathi remarked, "I thought this *Sanyāsi* has only one defect of attachment to pot left in him. But now I notice he has actually two. His ego has not left him yet. How can this one with attachment and ego be called a man of wisdom?"

The *Sanyāsi* learnt his lesson. Immediately thereafter all his ego vanished and so also his attachment to the sense objects.

Just as in the sky, the clouds, darkness and light appear by turns, So do the qualities of nature (*pravritti*) like tamas, *rājas* and *sattva* appear and disappear in the Being (*Ātman*).

Ādi Shankara, Crest Jewel of Wisdom

प्रसंख्यानेऽप्यकुसीदस्य सर्वथा विवेकख्यातेर्धर्ममेघः समाधिः ॥२९॥

Prasankhyāne_Api_Akusidasya Sarvathā
Viveka_Khyāteha Dharma_Meghah_Samādhih.

On the one who discriminates and desires not even the highest truth
Is showered rain clouds of virtues as tribute.

Prasankhyāne: in the state of omniscience
Akusidasya: for the desireless one.
Sarvathā: always, permanently, forever
Dharma: righteousness *Meghah*: cloud
Api: even
Viveka: discrimination
Khyāteh: arises
Samādhih: trance, absorption

Q. *What is the effect of attainment of awareness?*

A. On attaining awareness there arises a state of mind full of clarity concerning all things at all times. It is like a rainfall of pure clarity. Old habits, tendencies and fluctuations do not resurface.

Even the terse and prosaic Patanjali cannot help becoming poetic when it comes to describing the state of the one who overcomes all temptations on the way, avoids all possible pitfalls and progresses towards liberation. He says the discriminating ones who are disinterested in the benefits thrown in en-route is showered cloud of virtues. A rain cloud of never changing clarity and a constant downpour of knowledge is his for ever.

There arises a state of mind full of clarity concerning all things at all times. It is like a rainfall of pure clarity. Old habits, tendencies and fluctuations do not resurface.

In the Maitrayāni Upanishad, sage Sakayanaya says when all the modifications of the mind subside, it reverts to its source, even as fire is extinguished when it is devoid of the feeding material. Such a mind is established in truth. Turned away from all objects of senses, the seeker sees this world of objects and actions as senseless.

Clarified butter extracted out of milk does not become milk again. Even so the mind that has attained the state of self-effulgent bliss does not get attached to things that are non-Being.

"I am neither ego nor reason, I am neither mind nor thought.
I cannot be heard nor cast into words, nor by smell nor sight ever caught:
In light and wind I am not found, nor yet in earth and sky.
Consciousness and joy incarnate, Bliss of the Blissful am I."

Ādi Shankara, Ātma Shatakam.

ततः क्लेशकर्मनिवृत्तिः ॥३०॥

Tatah Klesha_Karma_Nivrittih.

Thence are removed afflictions
And so are actions.

Tatah: from that state of trance
Klesha: afflictions
Karma: action
Nivrittih: removed. Inactivated

Q. *How can one describe that state of trance?*
A. The state of trance can be described as the state free from actions based on the five obstacles, a state where afflictions remain removed.

Patanjali earlier described God as a special person unaffected by affliction or action. The seeker too is now a special person. He is beyond the afflictions and actions. All his past tendencies remain burnt out. There is no return to the state of misapprehension. It is a state of *nivritti*, non mental modifications.

This journey from ignorance to illumination can take one ten or thousand births. But the ultimate goal of *Samādhi* is worth aspiring for, worth striving for and worth waiting for even thousand births. The Yogi now rests in his own true nature. *Samādhi* is the end of the seeker's quest.

At the peak of his meditation, he passes into the state of *Samādhi*, where his body and senses are at rest as if he is asleep, his faculties of mind and reason are alert as if he is awake, yet he has gone beyond consciousness. The person in a state of *Samādhi* is fully conscious and alert.

In him duality comes to an end. Non-duality becomes stable. He perceives the world like a dream. Abiding in non duality with all distinctions and divisions extinguished, he is seen as one asleep. He dwells without knot of ignorance or the knot which binds the spirit to matter. Ultimately he reaches a state of liberation.

I have no name, I have no life, I breathe no vital air,
No elements have molded me, no bodily sheath is my lair:
I have no speech, no hands and feet, nor means of evolution .
Consciousness and joy am I, and Bliss in dissolution.

Ādi Shankara, Ātma Shatakam

At a glance: Aphorism 4.27-4.30

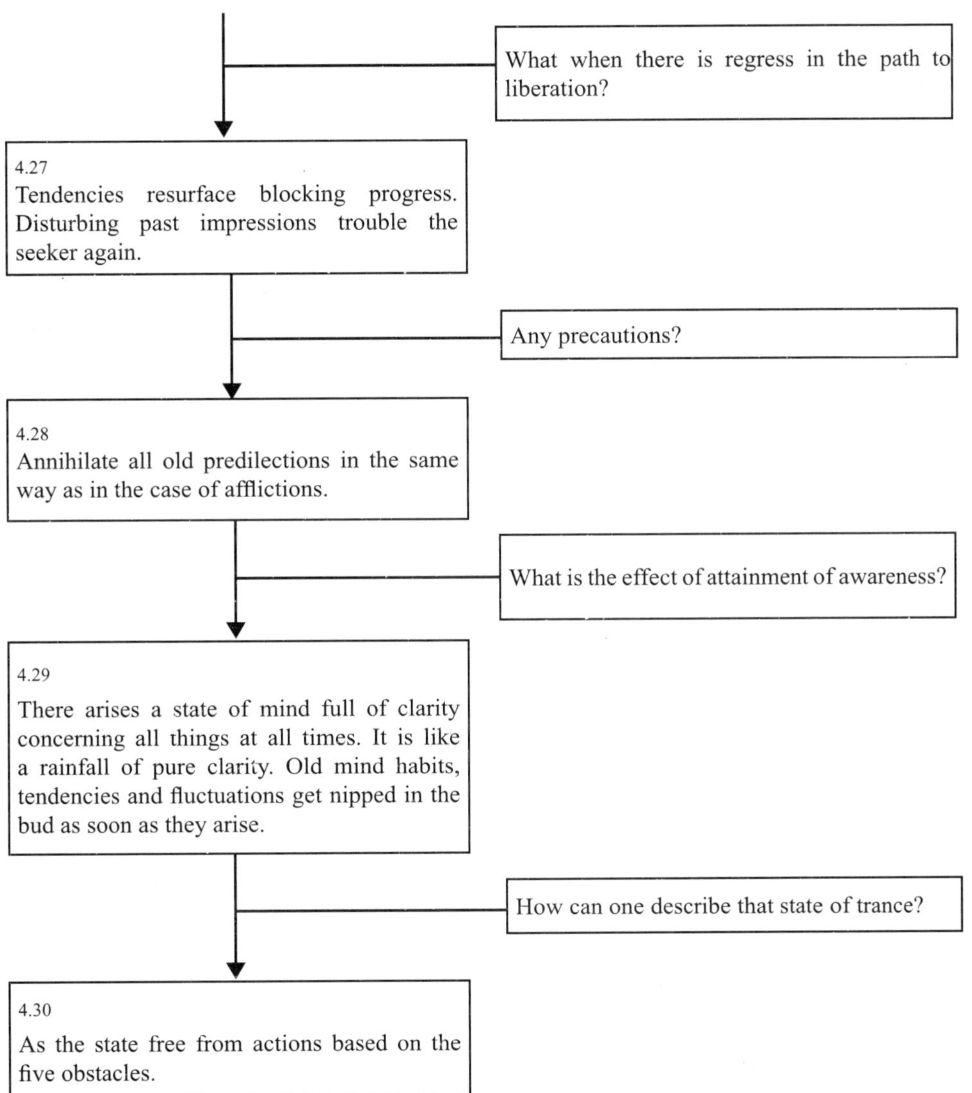

तदा सर्वावरणमलापेतस्य ज्ञानस्यानन्त्याज्ज्ञेयमल्पम् ॥३१॥

Tadā Sarva_Āvarana_Mala_Apetasya Jnānasya_Ānantayāt_Jneyam_Alpam.

With the overpowering impurities gone
There remains nothing to be known.

Tadā: In that state of detachment *Sarva*: all *Āvarana*: encircling, enveloping
Mala: impurities, confusion, false identification, afflictions
Apetasya: the one with the impurities removed *Jnānasya*: for the knower
Ānantayāt: because of infiniteness *Jneyam*: to be known *Alpam*: nothing

Q. *What on attaining the state of detachment?*
A: On attaining the state of detachment there remains nothing to be known.

Questions like 'Who am I' remain vanished. The afflictions being removed, the knower, the to be known and the process of knowing remain merged. There are no more questions to ask nor answers to seek. In him who is liberated there is only a residual effect of *karma* getting worked out. He has no more actions to perform for a consideration. He seeks not, wants not and craves not.

Ādi Shankara in the *Vivekachudāmani* (Crest Jewel of Wisdom) explains how a liberated while living (*Jivanmukta*) is:

A liberated is one,
whose mind is transcended,
whose Bliss is continuous,
whose awareness is free from desires,
who although is possessed of a mind is yet free from mind,
who has no sense of 'I' or 'mine',
who does not ponder over the past, does not worry about the future and who is indifferent to the present,
who looks at both evil and good with equal eye, and
who is liberated from the bonds of desires and tendencies.

I cast aside hatred and passion, I conquered delusion and greed;
No touch of pride caressed me, so envy never did breed:
Beyond all faiths, past reach of wealth, past freedom, past desire,
Consciousness and joy am I, and Bliss is my attire.

Ādi Shankara , Ātma Shatakam.

ततः कृतार्थानां परिणामक्रमपरिसमाप्तिर्गुणानाम् ॥३२॥

Tataha Kritarthānām Parināma_Krama_ Parisamāptih_Gunānām.

With attachment eased out
And purpose served
With qualities worked out
Sequence of change is severed.

Tataha: in that state of detachment
Krit: having done, having achieved
Arthānām: What needs to be achieved
Parināma: change, transformation, mutation
Krama: sequence, order
Parisamāptih: ceases, remains fulfilled
Gunānām: triple qualities

Q. *What else after attaining the state of detachment?*

A. After attaining the state of detachment tendencies/ *Gunas* remain detached too. The three basic qualities cease to follow the sequence of alternating pain and pleasure.

In that state of detachment, having achieved what needs to be achieved, namely having attained the state of bliss, the mutations that occur due to the triple qualities remain erased. No more is such a one, subject to dualities. He sees not two. He is one, remaining one with all. Where there is no two, there is no attachment or aversion or fear. When there is no other, with whom should one get attached or from whom should one be detached. Whom is one to be afraid of? when there is none other than the one present! When one sees himself everywhere and in everything there is no other to be seen or feared. The play of triple qualities ends. Birth after birth, endlessly the seeker had to suffer ignorance because of the superimposition of the non-self over the Self. The super imposition ceases on attaining illumination. The sequence of changes that one is subjected end too. The objective world is seen by the enlightened simply as it is, with no meaning beyond that.

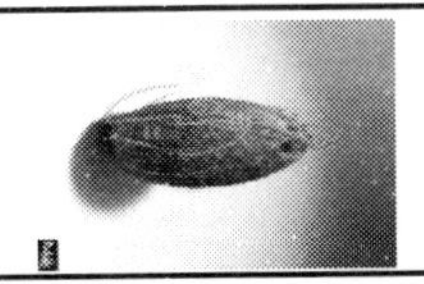	In the ripened state, the coconut fruit is still inside the shell, but not in intimate contact with the shell. In the realised soul, the contact between him and his body is much like that between the coconut fruit and the shell. The fruit is very much inside the shell, yet it has very little contact with the shell.
	In the uninitiated seeker the attachment to the body is as close as if it is in the un-ripened coconut. Very close. If one tries to separate the coconut form shell, it is very very difficult. The coconut sticks to the shell tightly. Much the same way the uninitiated identifies himself with his body closely and is unwilling even to contemplate about the possibility of him being different from his body.

क्षणप्रतियोगी परिणामापरान्तनिर्ग्राह्यः क्रमः ॥३३॥

Kshana_Pratiyogi Parināma_Aparānta_Nirgrāhyah Kramah.

In the end it becomes clear
About succession of moments
And resulting impressions that appear.

Kshana: moment
Pratiyogi: being the cause
Parināma: mutation, change, transformation
Aparānta: at the end
Nirgrāhyah: apprehended clearly
Kramah: change, order

Q. *And what in the end?*
A. Mind is still. One ceases to hold on to the perceptions of mutations during their momentary happenings.

The seeker comprehends that the uninterrupted succession of moments, much like in an animated film, gives an impression of a whole sequence. Now, he sees only the whole picture. Individual screen shots are invisible. They get merged into the whole. It is easy to understand that what belongs to the moments and is indicated by the completion of a particular mutation is sequence from that absolute stillness where nothing moves.

At last, absolute liberation reigns with all dualistic qualities gone. Realisation dawns that they do not exist individually by themselves, separate and disparate, but rather our innate true self nature shines forth as the intrinsic intelligent power of consciousness itself. Goal of yoga is fulfilled where all modifications have become eliminated and consciousness established, and where all phenomena are integrated with absolute undifferentiated consciousness. Separateness disappears as empty illusions.

The Brahma Sutra says: "When the final dissolution comes at the end of *Hiranyagarbha*, the men of knowledge, with their minds purified, enter into supreme state of liberation together with Brahma himself."

I am no misgiving of death, no chasms of race divided me,
No parent ever called me child, no bond of birth ever tied me:
I am neither disciple nor master, I have no kin, no friend -
Consciousness and joy am I, and merging in Bliss is my end.

Ādi Shankara , Ātma Shatakam

पुरुषार्थशून्यानां गुणानां प्रतिप्रसवः कैवल्यं स्वरूपप्रतिष्ठा वा चितिशक्तिरिति ॥३४॥

Purushārtha_Shunyānām_Gunānām Prati_Prasavah Kaivalyam Svarupa_ Pratishthā Vā Chiti_Shakti_Iti.

Devoid of individuality
Free from triple quality
Subsumed by nature
Liberated forever
The conscious power
Dwells in one's own nature.

Purushā: person, an individual
Gunānām: the triple qualities
Prasavah: being subsumed by nature.
Pratishthā: well established
Kaivalyam: liberation , freedom
Artha: aims of life
Prati: every
Vā: or
Shakti: power
Shunyānām: emptiness
Chiti: consciousness
Svarupa: one's own nature
Iti: in this way, thus

Q. *And in the end?*
A. Back to the beginning. Being, without becoming

Kaivalya describes the effect on the personality of being in a continuous state of *samādhi*. This is the state of inner freedom that yoga strives for. The word '*kevala*' means "to keep to oneself," and *kaivalya* is sometimes explained as isolation or aloofness

A person in the state of *kaivalya* understands the world so well that he stands apart from it in the sense that he is not influenced by it, although he may well be in a position to influence the world. People in *kaivalya* behave like normal people, but they do not carry the burden of the world on their shoulders. They live in the world, but they are not subject to it. They are not free from sensual perception or free of the body, but they are a bit different. Wherever they happen to be, they are sure of themselves. That is *kaivalya*. External forces have no power over a person like this, though he knows the external world very well.

Neither knowable, knowledge, nor knower am I, formless is my form,
I dwell within the senses but they are not my home:
Ever serenely balanced, I am neither free nor bound -
Consciousness and joy am I, and Bliss is where I am found.

Ādi Shankara, Ātma Shatakam

Buddha's Enlightenment

Here is a beautiful description of Buddha's enlightenment as told by the Vietnamese master Thich Nhat Hanh:

"Gautama felt as though a prison which had confined him for thousands of lifetimes had broken open. Ignorance had been the jail keeper. Because of ignorance, his mind had been obscured, just like the moon and stars hidden by the storm clouds. Clouded by endless waves of deluded thoughts, the mind had falsely divided reality into subject and object, self and others, existence and nonexistence, birth and death, and from these discriminations arose wrong views-the prisons of feelings, craving, grasping and becoming. The suffering of birth, old age, sickness and death only made the prison walls thicker. The only thing to do was to seize the jail keeper and see his true face. The jail keeper was ignorance….. Once the jail keeper was gone, the jail would disappear and never be built again."

I am YOU
A Sufi Story

Rabi'a is a well known Sufi Saint. Through devotion and meditation, she reaches the heavenly gates and calls for attention.

Voice inside asked: Who are you?

Rabi'a: It's me.

Voice from inside: Sorry, out you go

Disappointed Rabi'a goes back, meditates intensely once again and manages to reach the heavenly gates once more. She calls for attention.

Voice inside: Who are you?

Rabi'a: I am your servant.

Voice inside: Sorry, out you go.

Rabi'a determined as she always was, continues her meditation with devotion and dedication and manages to reach the heavenly gates the third time and as on earlier occasion, calls for attention.

Voice inside: Who are you?

Rabi'a: It is You.

Voice inside: Do come in!

Rabi'a could finally experience the Reality.

SUMMARY: *Aphorism 4.31-4.34*

What on attaining the state of detachment?

4.31
There remains nothing to be known. Questions like 'Who am I?' remain vanished. The afflications being removed, the knower, to be known and the process of knowing get merged. There are neither questions to ask, nor answers to seek.

What else on attaining the state of detachment?

4.32
The triple qualities (*Gunas*) remain detached too. The three basic qualities cease to force the individual to follow the sequence of alternating pain and pleasure.

What is a sequence?

4.33
Sequence is the uninterrupted succession of moments, much like an animated film. You see only the whole picture. Individual screen shots are invisible. They get merged into the whole. It is easy to understand that what belongs to the moments and is indicated by the completion of a particular mutation, is sequence, from that absolute stillness where nothing moves.

And, in the end?

4.34
Back to the beginning, to the source of creation. Equal with the beginning, Freedom. Free from the binding influnces of tendencies.

इति श्री पतंजलि योशास्त्रे कैवल्य निरूपानाम चतुर्थ पादः

Thus ends Patanjali Yoga Sutras Chapter 4: Liberation

Word Meaning

Abhiniveshāh	desire to cling to life--2.3
Atha	now, hereafter-- 1.1
Abhyāsa	repeated practice-- 1.12, 1.32
Anushasanam	instruction-- 1.1
Anumāna	inference, deduction--1.7
Āgamah	testimony worthy of faith, revelation-- 1.7
Ānanda	Bliss , joy -- 1.17
Asmitā	I-ness, Pure Ego-- 1.17, 2.4, 2.6, 4.4, 4.31
Aklishtāh	not producing suffering, not painful--1.5, 2.12
Anugamā	associated with-- 1.17
Avasthā	abides, dwells, resides--3.13
Anyah	that which is different from--1.18, 1.50, 2.22,. 3.49
Āsannah	about to happen, close to happening--1.21
Anavachheda	not limited by, without break--1.36
Antarāyā	obstacles--1.29, 1.30
Ālasya	sloth--1.30, 1.32
Avirati	dissipation, craving for sensory pleasures--1.30, 1.32
Alabdhabhumikatva	failure to concentrate--1.30
Angamejayattva	trembling of the body --1.31
Apunya	depressing, degrading, non meritorious--1.33
Ālambanam	to hold attention, object of meditation-- 4.11
Abhimata	per choice, desired, that which is liked--1.10,3.20
Alinga	indication--1.45, 2.15
Avidyā	ignorance--2.3, 2.4, 2.5, 2.24, 4.26
Anitya	impermanent, transient-- 2.5
Ashuchi	impure, dirty --2.5
Ātma	Inner Self --2.5, 2.21, 2.41, 4.13, 4.25
Anusayi	that which follows--2.7
Adrishta	unseen, not perceived--2.12
Āyuh	life -- 2.13
Anga	limbs, steps, parts, members, constituents--2.29
Ashuddhi	impurities--2.28
Āsana:	placing oneself in, posture--2.29, 2.46, 2.47, 2.48, 3.33
Ashta:	eight-- 2.29
Ahinsā	non violence, non injury-- 2.30,2.35
Asteya	avoidance of illegitimate/ needless --2.30, 2.37

Aparigrahāh	restraint from sense objects--2.30, 2.39
Anantaphalāh	endless results--2.34, 2.49
Artha	meaning, object of meditation--1.28, 1.32, 1.42, 1.43, 2.2, 2.18, 3.3, 3.11, 4.23
Avasthā	State--3.13
Ānupāti	experienced in succession--1.9, 3.14
Antarangam	essential, internal--3.7
Asangah	having no connection--3.39
Ākāsha	space-- 3.42
Āvarana	enveloping, veiling--3.43, 4.31
Animā	minuteness-- 3.45
Brahmacharya	celibacy, continence-- 2.30, 2.38
Bhumih	stage, level, degree--1.14, 2.27, 3.06
Bhogāh	experiences, pleasant or painful--2.13, 2.18, 3.35
Bhrāntidarshan	false vision, false perception --1.30
Bijam	seed, cause-- 1.12, 1.25, 3.50
Bhava	becoming, arising spontaneously--1.19
Bandhah	fixing--3.01, 3.38
Bahiranga	external part-- 3.08
Bala:	strength --3.24, 3.46
Bhuta	elements--3.44
Bhedah	to break, differences-- 4.03, 4.05, 4.12
Buddhi	intellect, cognition--4.21, 4.22
Chitta	mind stuff--1.2, 1.30, 1.33, 3.9, 3.19, 3.34, 4.04, 4.05, 4.15, 4.16, 4.21, 4.26
Chandra	moon--3.27
Darshan	faculty of seeing, perceiving--1.30, 2.6, 2.41, 3.32
Dvesha	hatred, aversion, repulsion--2.3, 2.8, 3.55, 4.31
Dhyāna	Meditation--1.13, 1.39, 2.11, 2.29, 3.2, 4.6
Drishta	seen-- 1.15, 2.12
Drashtuh	the seer--2.17
Dirghakāla	long time, long duration-- 1.14
Dridabhoomihi	firm foundation--1.14
Dukha	distress, grief, sorrow-- 2.16
Daurmanasya	despair--1.31, 1.32
Dhāranā	contemplation --3.53, 4.09
Desha	place--3.50
Dosha	faulty, ignorance--3.50
Devatā	deity, God --2.44
Dvandva	pairs of opposites, duality--2.48

Dirgha	long , deep--2.5
Dharma	property-- 3.13
Dharmi	substratum--3.14
Dhruva	pole star--3.28
Drishya	perception, sight-- 2.17, 2.18, 4.21, 4.23
Ekā	one--1.32, 4.5, 4.9, 4.16, 4.20
Ekāgrya	Power of concentration-- 2.41
Ekatra	in respect of one object--3.4
Ekāgratā	focused, one pointed --3.11, 3.12
Grahana	senses capture--1.41, 3.47
Gyānam	knowledge, learning--3.52, 3.54
Guna	triple qualities, attributes--1.16, 2.15, 2.19, 3.16, 3.18, 3.19, 4.13, 4.32, 4.34
Guruh	preceptor, master, teacher--1.26
Indriya	senses--2.41, 2.43, 2.54, 2.55, 3.47
Ishvara	God--1.23, 1.24, 2.1, 2.32, 2.45
Japah	repetition--1.28, 1.29
Jyotishamati	illumination, supreme light-- 1.36
Janma	birth-- 2.12, 2.39, 4.1
Jāti	class, type of birth, species-- 2.13, 2.31, 3.18, 3.53, 4.2, 4.9
Jayah	control--3.39, 3.40, 3.44, 3.47, 3.48
Hetu	reasons, causes -- 4.11
Heyah	destroyed,abolished -- 2.10, 2.11, 2.16, 2.17
Hasti	elephant--3.24
Hridaya	heart-- 3.34
Kantaka	thorn -- 3.39
Kārana	causative -- 3.38
Kshana	moment--3.52, 4.33
Kāyā	body --3.9, 3.42, 3.45
Krodha	hatred, rage, anger--2.43, 3.21
Kāla	time--4.9
Karmāshayo	based on past actions--2.12, 2.13
Kshetram	source, root cause, field--2.4
Kshina	weakened, worn out -- 1.41
Klishtā	suffering, painful-- 1.5
Kriyāyogah	yoga practice--2.1, 2.36, 2.18, 3.54
Klesha	afflictions, cause of suffering-- 1.24, 2.2, 2.3, 4.28, 4.30
Kaivalyam	liberation, absolute freedom--2.25, 3.50, 3.55, 4.26, 4.34
Karunā	compassion--1.33

Karma	action and the resulting fruit of action--2.3, 2.12, 2.16, 4.7, 4.30,
Kshaya	dissipation, weakening, declining--2.28, 3.43, 3.50
Layānām	involved, absorbed--1.19
Lobha	greed--2.34
Lakshana	character --3.13, 3.53
Lāvanya	charm, beautiful --3.46
Mahāvratam	great vow--2.31
Moola	the root cause--2.12, 2.13
Madhya	medium --1.22, 2.34
Mithyā	incorrect, false; wrong inference --1.8
Mridu	gentle -- 1.22, 2.34
Maitri	friendship, companionship--1.33, 3.23
Mudita	joy --1.33
Mānas	mind -- 1.35, 2.53, 3.48
Maner	of the flawless crystal--1.41
Mātra	alone, only-- 1.43, 3.3, 4.4
Mantra	incantation--1.13, 1.29, 4.1
Nābhi	navel region--3.29
Nādi	astral nerve--3.31
Niyamāh	observances , practices of self-training--2.29, 2.32
Nidrā	sleep-- 1.6, 1.38
Nirodhah	controlled, avoided , ceases--1.2, 1.12,1.51, 3.9
Nirantarya	uninterrupted, non stop, continuously-- 1.14
Nirbijah	without seed-- 1.51, 3.8
Nashtam	lost. ceased, dissolved, finished, destroyed--2.22
Paraih	outsiders, other bodies--2.40, 3.19, 3.35, 3.38
Phalāh	outcome, fruit--2.14, 2.36, 4.11
Parishuddhau	purification --1.43
Panchatyah	of five kinds-- 1.5
Pratyaksha	direct sensory perception-- 1.7
Pratishtham	based, established--,1.8, 4.34
Purusha	supreme among beings --1.16, 1.24, 3.35, 3.36, 3.49, 3.55, 4.18, 4.34
Pramāna	right knowledge, correct cognition--1.6
Prajnā	knowing, awareness--1.20, 1.48, 1.49, 2.27, 3.5
Purvah	previous -- 1.18, 3.18, 3.26, 3.7
Prakriti	own nature -- 3.35, 3.44, 4.2, 4.34
Pranavah	Sacred symbol AUM--1.27
Pramāda	delusion, heedlessness-- 1.30, 1.32

Pratishedha	prevention, avoidance, blocking--1.32
Punya:	elevating, meritorious -- 1.33, 2.14, 3.23
Prāna	life force, vital energy, breath--1.34, 3.29, 3.39, 3.40, 3.50
Paramānu	sub atomic, smallest of the small-- 1.40
Paramamahatva	Biggest of the big, infinitely big--1.40
Pranidhānān	dedication to God / resignation--1.23, 2.1, 2.32
Pratibandhi	obstruction--1.50
Parināma	change, transformation-- 3.9, 3.11, 3.15, 4.2, 4.14, 4.32, 4.33
Prakāsha	Illumination, brightness--2.18, 2.52, 3.21, 3.43
Pratyaya	firm conviction--1.10, 1.19, 2.2, 3.2, 3.17, 3.19, 4.27
Prānāyāma	control of vital energy --2.29, 2.45, 2.49
Pratyāhāra	withdrawal of senses from objects--2.29, 2.54
Pratipaksha	opposing, countermanding--2.33
Prasvāsa	Exhalation-- 1.31, 2.49
Prgyā	awareness-- 1.20, 1.48, 1.49, 2.27, 3.5
Prashānta	peaceful, tranquil --3.10
Pipāsā	thirst--3.30
Ratna	riches, diamonds, jewels, treasures--2.37
Rāga:	craving, attachment, attraction-- 1.37, 2.3, 2.7, 3.55, 4.31
Ritambharā	full of truth--1.48
Rupa	form, appearance--1.8, 1.17, 2.54, 2.23, 3.3, 3.46, 3.34
Rāja	Motion, activity -- 1.16, 2.18, 3.35
Saptah	seven steps ,sevenfold--2.27
Sattva	purity-- 2.36, 2.41, 3.35, 3.49, 3.55
Samāna	a manifestation of prana--3.39, 3.40
Shānta	latent -- 3.12, 3.14
Samyamah	mastery over dhyāna, dhāranā and samādhi--1.40, 3.4, 3.16, 3.17, 3.21, 3.22
Sati	associated,-- 1.49, 2.13
Sukha	happiness--1.33, 2.5, 2.7, 2.42, 2.46
Sanshaya	doubt, lack of trust in scriptures-- 1.30, 1.32
Samādhi	absorption, trance,--1.20, 1.46, 1.51, 2.2, 2.29, 2.45, 3.33, 3.11, 4.1, 4.33, 4.34
Shesho	remaining, traces, remnants-- 1.18
Samskāra	recollections, impressions1.11, 1.18, 1.50, 2.15, 3.18
Savichāra	Reflection-- 1.42, 1.46
Shunya	without any, empty 1.9, 1.43, 3.3, 4.34
Shabda	word, speech, sound1.9, 1.42
Svarupe	in Self 1.3, 1.8, 1.43, 2.23, 2.28, 2.54,3.44, 3.47, 4.12, 4.34
Smriti	Memory 1.6, 1.11, 4.9, 4.10, 4.21, 4.31

Sthitau	steadied, established1.13, 2.18
Shraddhā	faith, trust 1.20
Sarvāgnya	all knowing 3.49
Styāna	incompetence, mental laziness 1.30, 1.32
Sthiti	steadiness, state of stillness 1.13, 1.35, 2.18
Svapna	dream 1.38, 4.23
Samāpattih	transformation 4.32
Savitarka	right inference, right analysis 1.42, 1.46
Sukshma	subtle 1.44, 1.45, 2.10, 2.50, 3.25, 3.44. 4.13
Svādhyāya	Self study/ reflection -- 2.1, 2.32, 4.28
Sarvam	all-- 1.25, 1.51, 2.15, 2.31, 2.37, 3.11, 3.49, 3.54, 4.22
Samyoga	coming together, conjunction 2.17, 2.23,2.25
Shuddha	immutable 2.20
Swāmi	Lord 2.23
Satya	truthfulness, honesty 2.30, 2.36
Samaya	fixed time, situation, condition 2.31, 2.40
Shaucha	cleanliness, purity 2.32, 2.40
Saumanasya	cheerful mind 2.41
Svāsa:	inhalation 1.31, 2.49
Shakti	capability 2.6, 2.23
Stambha	retention 2.50, 3.21
Surya	sun 3.26
Sharira	body 3.38
Sthula	gross elements 3.44
Shuddhe	pure, unblemished 3.55
Vāsanā	tendencies, propensities, latent impressions 4.8, 4.24
Virya	energy, vitality 1.20, 2.38
Virāma	stoppage, cessation 1.18
Vichāra	discrimination, reflection, deliberation 1.17
Vashikāra	attraction 1.15, 1.40
Vairāgya	non attachment, dispassion, detachment1.11, 1.12, 1.15, 3.50,
Vishaya	any object or topic 1.11, 1.15, 1.44, 2.51, 2.54, 3.20, 3.44
Vastu	reality, of an object, of matter, things 1.9, 4.14, 4.15
Vikalpa	Imagination and fantasy 1.6, 1.9, 1.42
Viparyaya	wrong knowledge, misconception, illusion 1.6
Vritti	Modifications, fluctuations 1.2,1.4, 1.5, 1.10, 1.41, 2.11, 2.50, 4.18
Vaitrishnyam	without craving 1.16
Vitarka	Analysis, reasoning, inference 1.17, 2.33, 2.34

Videha	disembodied 1.19, 3.43
Visheshah	specialty, distinct1.22, 1.24, 1.49, 2.19, 4.25
Vyādhi	disease, sickness 1.30, 1.32
Vikshepah	projecting power, distraction 1.30, 1.31
Vishokā	blissful, without unhappiness, serene, 1.36
Vashikārah	with no obstruction, having no obstacle 1.15, 1.40
Vicchinna	interrupted, broken 2.4
Viveka	discriminative, discernment 1.5, 2.26, 2.28, 3.52, 3.54 ,4.29
Vishayā	objects1.11, 1.15, 1.44, 2.51, 2.54, 3.20,
Vaira	hostility, enmity, aggression 2.34
Virya	capability 2.37
Viniyogah	application, deployment 3.06
Vyavahit	veiled 3.25
Tyāgah	abandonment abandon, give up 2.34
Tanu	obscure , feeble 2.4
Tārā	stars 3.27, 3.54
Tapah	austerity/ refinement 2.1, 2.32, 2.43, 3.40,
Uttpanna	brought about, arising 1.35
Udarānām	pronounced, active, sustained 2.4
Udaya	raising 3.11
Udāna	the vital air within, a manifestation of prana 3.39
Yama	attitude to external ,codes of restraint 2.29, 2.30
Yantra	geometric symbol 4.1
Yatna	effort, 1.13
Yoga	Union, integration 1.1, 1.2, 2.1, 2.28, 3.54

॥ योगदर्शनम् समाप्तम् ॥